DETENTE
A Documentary Record

DETENTE
A Documentary Record

Charles E. Timberlake

PRAEGER PUBLISHERS
Praeger Special Studies

New York • London • Sydney • Toronto

Library of Congress Cataloging in Publication Data

Timberlake, Charles E
    Detente.

    Includes index.
    1. United States--Foreign relations--Treaties.
2. Russia--Foreign relations--Treaties.
3. Detente. I. Title.
JX236 1972.T55   341'.0266'73047   78-19465
ISBN 0-03-046666-0

PRAEGER PUBLISHERS
PRAEGER SPECIAL STUDIES
383 Madison Avenue, New York, N.Y. 10017, U.S.A.

Published in the United States of America in 1978
by Praeger Publishers,
A Division of Holt, Rinehart and Winston, CBS, Inc.

89   038   987654321

Printed in the United States of America

To Mark, Daniel, and Eric

PREFACE

This volume is intended for a broad spectrum of users, including journalists, scholars, businessmen, students, teachers, and reference librarians, who might have need to consult one or most of the agreements signed by the United States and the USSR since 1972, but who might lack access or time to search into the many government publications, which the documents are scattered throughout and from which they have been collected for this volume.

The volume contains all the bilateral agreements signed since May 1972 that are practicable to include. Because not all such documents were suited for this project, some have been omitted, or press releases that summarized well and concisely their contents have been included rather than the full text of the document. For instance, the Agreement on Chancery Construction of December 4, 1972, was not included because it contains extensive technical specifications related to building construction. A Department of State press release (Document 20) explains the main points of the agreement succinctly and well and is included instead. Many of the agreements on fisheries also contain technical information and long lists of coordinates marking fishing boundaries. They, too, have been omitted, and press releases summarizing their contents included instead where possible.

Agreements extending other agreements—usually effected by an exchange of notes—have not been included in full. An appendix contains a full list of all agreements concluded, reports the major content of each agreement, and has bibliographical data supplied to guide the user to the full text of any agreement not included in this volume. For those agreements that are included, bibliographical information is supplied after the document's entry on the contents page.

The principle of including bilateral agreements governed the compilation of the documents in all but four instances where multilateral agreements were included. The first exception is the Act of the Conference of March 2, 1973, on enforcing the agreements ending the Vietnam War in January of that year, which was signed by all parties directly involved in the Vietnamese conflict (Document 22) and is offered here to call the reader's attention to that event and form thereby a perspective against which the other agreements can be seen. The second instance related to the Middle East Crisis of October 1973 (documents grouped under Number 41), where the existence of United Nations Security Council Resolution 242, which had been passed during the Middle East Crisis of 1967, provided a basis for a jointly sponsored American-Soviet agreement that was adopted as Security Council Resolution 338 in October 1973.

The third multilateral agreement is the Helsinki agreement of August 1, 1975, signed by 35 nations (Document 60), included because of the central role the document has played as a reference point in the debate over human rights in the Soviet Union. The final multilateral agreement is the Convention on Environmental Warfare (Document 61), included because it was the result of bilateral negotiations developed stage by stage at summit meetings and in the Geneva talks (Documents 48 and 58) and became a multilateral agreement only at the conclusion of the draft when other nations expressed a desire to sign as well.

One of the tasks this volume is meant to perform is to coordinate a chronological organization of all the bilateral agreements with a bibliographical guide to their location. To the best of my knowledge, this is the only place where they are available in chronological order or in one compilation. Publication of documents in the Department of State *Bulletin* (abbreviated in this volume as DSB) is highly selective and not in chronological order. For instance, the extremely important grains agreement (commonly known as "the wheat deal") of July 1972, was not published there. The Department of State publication, *United States Treaties and Other International Acts* (abbreviated in this volume as UST), does not organize documents chronologically, although it is the most complete. It arranges documents by TIAS number; that is, by the order in which the documents were published in the Department of State's weekly *Treaties and International Acts Series* (hence TIAS).

No rhyme nor reason is apparent to the observer by which documents are scheduled for publication in the TIAS. They are greatly out of order chronologically. For instance, the American-Soviet agreement on privileges and immunities of October 17, 1967 and March 1, 1968, was not published until 1975. Furthermore, the trade agreement of October 18, 1972, still has not been published in that series and is available only in the DSB. If having the documents available in chronological order, in one compilation, with bibliographical data proves as useful to others as it has to me in teaching and research, the objective of the volume will have been fulfilled.

With the exception of Document 10, which was retyped, the documents here are photocopies of the originals. Where a choice was available, I copied the text of the document from the DSB, where the aesthetics of the printed page and utilization of space were better. Occasionally, the full text of a document was not printed in the DSB and is supplemented in this volume by the remainder of the text from UST. I have made no effort to explain in footnotes the occasions when such measures have been utilized.

I wish to express my gratitude for a wide variety of assistance in preparation of this volume. First, I salute my colleague at Missouri, David Thelen, whose initiative introduced the topics courses in the History Department, which led to my offering a course on detente and the production of this volume as a text for it. I also commend Provost Owen Koeppe and Dean of the Arts and Science College Armon Yanders for their decision to fund the topics courses, and I express my appreciation to my students at Missouri who, in using an earlier version of this volume as a text, made many valuable suggestions for adapting it to classroom and research uses.

June DeWeese and Sue McCollum of the University of Missouri Library and Meryl Atterberry of the Missouri State Library were helpful in making government documents available for photocopying.

I am particularly grateful to my wife, Pat, whose training as a reference librarian provided me with several useful suggestions for structuring the volume and with considerable aid in utilizing federal documents. I am also grateful to my departmental colleague Richard Vietor for useful suggestions about organization of the volume and for calling my attention to Congressional hearings that proved useful in supplying commentary on the documents.

Phyllis Dussel rendered meticulous service in typing the preparing the manuscript in final form. I am also grateful to Dan and Eric for the hours they spent taking care of themselves while their father ran the Xerox machine or fretted about proper numerical and chronological orders, none of which seemed to them worthy of declining their invitation to play tennis or fish in the pond. To them, and their older brother Mark, the volume is dedicated. Maybe someday they will think the enterprise was worth my, and their, while.

CONTENTS

Documents

Documents

Documents

ABBREVIATIONS

ABM   antiballistic missile

DSB   Department of State *Bulletin*. In bibliographical citations, the numbers in the example DSB 12-23-1974, 879 mean: December 23, 1974, page 879.

PNE   peaceful nuclear explosions

SALT   Strategic Arms Limitation Talks

TIAS   *Treaties and International Acts Series*. Published weekly by the United States Department of State.

TTBT   Threshold Test Ban Treaty. Short title for the Treaty and Protocol on Limitation of Underground Nuclear Weapon Tests, Signed July 3, 1974.

UST   *United States Treaties and Other International Agreements*. In bibliographical citations, the numbers in the example UST 27.2.1651 mean: Vol. 27, No. 2, page 1651.

DETENTE
A Documentary Record

I:

THE MOSCOW SUMMIT MEETING:
MAY 23 TO 29, 1972

INTRODUCTION

The term "detente" appeared rather frequently in the 1960s in the writings of American scholars and journalists as a label for the gradual transition that was occurring in U.S.-Soviet relations. A milestone in that transition was U.S. and Soviet signing in 1963 of the multilateral treaty banning nuclear weapon tests in the atmosphere, in outer space, and under water. In January 1967 the United States and the USSR signed a multilateral treaty governing activities in the exploration and use of outer space, including the moon and other celestial bodies; and in 1968 both signed the multilateral treaty on the nonproliferation of nuclear weapons. In 1969 they agreed to construct new embassies in Washington and Moscow, and in 1971 they signed three substantive agreements: the multilateral treaty prohibiting placement of nuclear and other weapons on the seabed and ocean floor; the Quadripartite agreement on Berlin; and a bilateral agreement on measures to help prevent the outbreak of nuclear war.[1]

U.S. government officials did not label any U.S. policy toward the Soviet Union as "detente," however, until a series of bilateral agreements had been signed in May of 1972 during President Richard Nixon's first Moscow summit meeting. In its initial stages, Nixon called the policy, in his State of the Union Message in January 1970, one of passing from "an era of confrontation" to "an era of negotiation."[2]

A State Department officer explained later that Nixon's policy entailed a three-step approach to an ultimate objective. Step one began in 1969 through concrete efforts at "relieving specific sources of tension" to prepare for a summit meeting. Once a summit meeting could be agreed upon, the second step was to "accelerate negotiations on a broad range of bilateral matters" of mutual interest. Improved political relations that would occur during these two stages would lead to the final stage: improved economic relations, especially removal of barriers to expanded U.S.-Soviet trade.[3] This statement, subsequently tailored by the State Department to form a pamphlet entitled "The Meaning of Detente," explained that "this complex process of adjustment" is frequently called "detente." It cautioned that the "relaxation of tensions," the literal definition of "detente," was still not "'entente' which is an understanding or alliance."[4]

After the achievements of 1969 to 1971, the Americans and Soviets began discussing the possibility of a summit meeting in Moscow. Coincidental to the political changes, one other circumstance was favorable for a Nixon visit to Moscow: no American President had repaid Nikita Khrushchev's visit to the United States in 1959. Every American president since Eisenhower had planned to repay the visit, but some event had always prevented his plans from reaching fruition.[5]

In preparing for the Moscow summit meeting of 1972, both sides sought to provide evidence that a new era in U.S.-Soviet relations was dawning. By April of that year, they had quietly negotiated several agreements that they reserved for signing at the Moscow summit, to assure the meeting some symbol of success.[6]

The Moscow summit meeting of May 23 to 29, 1972, had significance both as an event and for the substance of the agreements that emerged from it. Before the first formal talks began on May 23, both sides knew the scenario of the talks and the signing of agreements. Private talks between heads of state* and teams of specialists would occur simultaneously each morning and afternoon from Tuesday, May 23 through Friday, May 26. At approximately five o'clock each afternoon, the two sides would assemble in a room to sign agreements. On Tuesday, they were to sign agreements on environment and health; Wednesday on space and science; Thursday on trade; Friday on arms limitation.[7]

This scenario added to the drama of the Moscow summit meeting. Having a day of talks precede the signing of agreements created the image that each day's talks had produced the agreements signed that day when, in fact, all the agreements signed the first three days of the summit had been negotiated well in advance. A consequence of the talk-sign scenario was that the events of the week of May 23 to 29 appeared even more significant than they were, although they were, indeed, significant. Additionally, arranging for the agreements to be signed

---

*It is interesting to note that Leonid Brezhnev, General Secretary of the Communist Party of the Soviet Union, held no government position at the time he signed the documents. Yet he was able to commit the Soviet government formally to all the obligations contained in the agreements. He later assumed the position of chairman of the Presidium of the Supreme Soviet, constitutionally the office of the head of state in the USSR. That position was occupied by N. V. Podgorny at the time of the first Moscow summit.

in order of least to most substantive produced the impression that the talks were making daily progress toward solution of some of the more difficult problems in U.S.-Soviet relations. Of course, one cannot completely deny the summit a role in producing some of the agreements, even if they were concluded prior to it. The "imminence of the summit," as Henry Kissinger noted at the time, "gave those negotiations impetus which they would otherwise not have had."[8]

The agreements that had been negotiated before the summit meeting are Documents 1 through 5 in this collection. Document 5, the agreement on preventing incidents at sea, was not listed among those scheduled for signing on Thursday when the scenario was first revealed, however, and it came as a surprise even to those few outside government who knew of the other four agreements.

The other surprise of Thursday, May 25 was that the expected trade agreement was not signed. On the eve of departure from Washington, President Nixon had directed the attention of the press corps, which was to accompany him to Moscow, to the area of trade negotiations. "I met with congressional leaders discussing such matters as most favored nation and others, the matter of credits," he told them. "I would say that the chances for some positive results are good—not certain, but certainly good. You will be wanting to follow that very closely during the course of our visit there."[9] Despite the absence of a trade agreement on Thursday, the signing of the agreement on prevention of incidents at sea preserved the talk-sign scenario, and focused most of the journalists' attention on the "success of the day's negotiations," rather than upon the absence of a trade agreement.*

A trade agreement was signed Friday, the following day. Rather than an agreement on substantive issues, the accord created a Joint Commercial Commission (Document 6) to which it assigned the issues of substance for solution. Kissinger repeatedly asserted at two news conferences on May 29 that the negotiators never contemplated an agreement on matters of substance at the Moscow Summit and that creation of a commission was their objective. The disparity between his and the President's statement was obvious at the time as well as now.[10]

The formal talks and signing of bilateral agreements ended Friday, May 26 with the signing, in front of a Soviet national television audience, of the two agreements on arms limitation: the treaty limiting antiballistic missile systems (Document 7), and the Interim Agreement on Limitation of Strategic Offensive Arms (Document 8). On Sunday, May 28 Nixon addressed the Soviet people by national radio and television, and on Monday, May 29 the two sides issued a

---

*It would be interesting to have a broad sample of U.S. newspaper headlines and reporting on the Moscow summit generally, and on this agreement in particular. Hedrick Smith was one of the rare journalists who saw the public and private segments of the first three days of the summit. See his "The Split Level at the Summit Conference," New York *Times*, May 25, 1972, p. 4.

joint communique (not included in this collection) and a declaration of "Basic Principles of Relations Between the United States and USSR" (Document 9).

The declaration of principles had a special meaning for the Soviet and U.S. negotiators who had participated in the week of talks. At the beginning of the talks the two sides had considered including a statement of principles as a section of a final joint communique. The Americans had the Shanghai Communique in mind as a model. But by the end of the formal talks the Soviet leaders and President Nixon had decided, Kissinger explained, to issue a separate document to symbolize the progress that had been made "on a broad front" and to note "at least our intention . . . to mark the transformation from a period of rather rigid hostility to one in which, without any illusions about the differences in social systems, we would try to behave with restraint and with a maximum of creativity in bringing about a greater degree of stability and peace." The principles, therefore, should be more than "platitudes."[11]

Both sides seemed satisfied by the results of the summit meeting. Its significance was greater than the sum of its individual parts, Kissinger felt. It had brought together the negotiations of the past year "to form a pattern" of U.S.-Soviet relations that was different from "simply a series of individual actions." In the Strategic Arms Limitation Talks (SALT I) agreement the two sides had established the principle of restraint for the first time. For Kissinger, acceptance of that principle was more important than the technical aspects of the agreement, for both sides should refrain from attempting to "accumulate petty advantages" over the other. Stating his basic premise for parity of military might, he asserted: "In a nuclear age, the most dangerous thing to aim for is a qualitative edge over your major rivals."[12]

Of the documents signed in Moscow, all but one were executive agreements. Only the treaty on antiballistic missiles (ABMs) required ratification by the U.S. Senate before it could enter into force.

The tasks the two sides set for themselves in preparation for the second summit meeting, to occur in Washington in June 1973, were: resolution of the substantive issues regarding trade; negotiation of a permanent agreement on limitation of offensive weapons, which would be signed in Washington; and implementation of the agreements on cooperation in various areas. Primarily, implementation meant creation of the joint commissions that the agreements specified.

NOTES

1. The texts of the agreements mentioned in this paragraph are in UST, listed in order of TIAS numbers. Those numbers are as follows: treaty banning nuclear weapon tests in the atmosphere, signed August 5, 1963, TIAS 5433; treaty on space exploration, signed January 27, 1967, TIAS 6347; treaty on nonproliferation, signed July 1, 1968, TIAS 6839;

agreement on embassy sites, signed May 16, 1969, TIAS 6693; treaty prohibiting nuclear weapons on the seabed, signed February 11, 1971, TIAS 7337; Quadripartite agreement, signed September 3, 1971 (brought into force by a protocol of June 3, 1972), DSB 9-27-1971, 318; agreement to reduce the risk of nuclear war, signed September 30, 1971, TIAS 7186.

2. DSB 2-9-1970, 146.

3. *Detente*: Hearings before the Subcommittee on Europe of the Committee on Foreign Affairs, House of Representatives, 93d Cong., 2d sess., May 8–July 31, 1974 (Statement of Honorable Arthur A. Hartman, Assistant Secretary of State for European Affairs), p. 47.

4. Department of State Publication 8766, General Foreign Policy Series 280 (released June 1974; Office of Media Services, Bureau of Public Affairs), p. 1.

5. See Charles E. Timberlake, "The Summit Meeting as a Form of Diplomacy in American-Soviet Relations in the 1970s," in *The Soviet Union: The Seventies and Beyond*, ed. Bernard Eissenstat (Lexington, Mass.: Lexington Books, 1976), p. 93 for a list of the efforts to return the visit and of the events that prevented it.

6. See ibid., pp. 97–98 for details.

7. Various newspapers carried the UPI report from Moscow listing this schedule: for instance, Columbia *Missourian*, May 24, 1972, p. 1.

8. DSB 6-26-1972, 884.

9. DSB 6-12-1972, 804.

10. DSB 6-26-1972, 884, 890.

11. Ibid., 891–92.

12. Ibid., 892–93.

AGREEMENT ON ENVIRONMENTAL PROTECTION

AGREEMENT ON COOPERATION IN THE FIELD OF ENVIRONMENTAL PROTECTION BETWEEN THE UNITED STATES OF AMERICA AND THE UNION OF SOVIET SOCIALIST REPUBLICS

The United States of America and the Union of Soviet Socialist Republics;

Attaching great importance to the problems of environmental protection;

Proceeding on the assumption that the proper utilization of contemporary scientific, technical and managerial achievements can, with appropriate control of their undesirable consequences, make possible the improvement of the interrelationship between man and nature;

Considering that the development of mutual cooperation in the field of environmental protection, taking into account the experience of countries with different social and economic systems, will be beneficial to the United States of America and the Union of Soviet Socialist Republics, as well as to other countries;

Considering that economic and social development for the benefit of future generations requires the protection and enhancement of the human environment today;

Desiring to facilitate the establishment of closer and long-term cooperation between interested organizations of the two countries in this field;

In accordance with the Agreement between the United States of America and the Union of Soviet Socialist Republics on Exchanges and Cooperation in Scientific, Technical, Educational, Cultural, and Other Fields in 1972-1973, signed April 11, 1972, and developing further the principles of mutually beneficial cooperation between the two countries;

Have agreed as follows:

ARTICLE 1

The Parties will develop cooperation in the field of environmental protection on the basis of equality, reciprocity, and mutual benefit.

ARTICLE 2

This cooperation will be aimed at solving the most important aspects of the problems of the environment and will be devoted to working out measures to prevent pollution, to study pollution and its effect on the environment, and to develop the basis for controlling the impact of human activities on nature.

It will be implemented, in particular, in the following areas:

—air pollution;
—water pollution;
—environmental pollution associated with agricultural production;
—enhancement of the urban environment;
—preservation of nature and the organization of preserves;
—Marine pollution;
—biological and genetic consequences of environmental pollution;
—influence of environmental changes on climate;
—earthquake prediction;
—arctic and subarctic ecological systems;
—legal and administrative measures for protecting environmental quality.

In the course of this cooperation the Parties will devote special attention to joint efforts improving existing technologies and developing new technologies which do not pollute the environment, to the introduction of these new technologies into everyday use, and to the study of their economic aspects.

The Parties declare that, upon mutual agreement, they will share the results of such cooperation with other countries.

ARTICLE 3

The Parties will conduct cooperative activities in the field of environmental protection by the following means:

—exchange of scientists, experts and research scholars;
—organization of bilateral conferences, symposia and meetings of experts;
—exchange of scientific and technical information and documentation, and the results of research on environment;
—joint development and implementation of programs and projects in the field of basic and applied sciences;
—other forms of cooperation which may be agreed upon in the course of the implementation of this Agreement.

ARTICLE 4

Proceeding from the aims of this Agreement the Parties will encourage and facilitate, as appropriate, the establishment and development of direct contacts and cooperation between institutions and organizations, governmental, public and private, of the two countries, and the conclusion, where appropriate, of separate agreements and contracts.

ARTICLE 5

For the implementation of this Agreement a US-USSR Joint Committee on Cooperation in the Field of Environmental Protection shall be established. As a rule this Joint Committee shall meet once a year in Washington and Moscow, alternately. The Joint Committee shall approve concrete measures and programs of cooperation, designate the participating organizations responsible for the realization of these programs and make recommendations, as appropriate, to the two Governments.

Each Party shall designate a coordinator. These coordinators, between sessions of the Joint Committee, shall maintain contact between the United States and Soviet parts, supervise the implementation of the pertinent cooperative programs, specify the individual sections of these programs, and coordinate the activities of organizations participating in environmental cooperation in accordance with this Agreement.

ARTICLE 6

Nothing in this Agreement shall be construed to prejudice other agreements concluded between the two Parties.

ARTICLE 7

This Agreement shall enter into force upon signature and shall remain in force for five years after which it will be extended for successive five year periods unless one Party notifies the other of the termination thereof not less than six months prior to its expiration.

The termination of this Agreement shall not affect the validity of agreements and contracts between interested institutions and organizations of the two countries concluded on the basis of this Agreement.

DONE on May 23, 1972 at Moscow in duplicate, in the English and Russian languages, both texts being equally authentic.

For the United States of America:

RICHARD NIXON

President of the United States of America

For the Union of Soviet Socialist Republics:

N. V. PODGORNY

Chairman of the Presidium of the Supreme Soviet of the USSR

2 (May 23, 1972)

AGREEMENT ON MEDICAL SCIENCE AND PUBLIC HEALTH

AGREEMENT BETWEEN THE GOVERNMENT OF THE UNITED STATES OF AMERICA AND THE GOVERNMENT OF THE UNION OF SOVIET SOCIALIST REPUBLICS ON COOPERATION IN THE FIELD OF MEDICAL SCIENCE AND PUBLIC HEALTH

The Government of the United States of America and the Government of the Union of Soviet Socialist Republics;
Realizing the significance which medical science and public health have for mankind today;
Recognizing the desirability of joining in a common effort to promote their further development;
Desiring to promote the broadening of cooperation in this field, and by so doing to promote a general improvement of health;
Desiring to reaffirm the understanding reached in the Letters of Agreement between the Department of Health, Education, and Welfare of the United States of America and the Ministry of Health of the Union of Soviet Socialist Republics, signed February 11, 1972;
And in accordance with the Agreement between the United States of America and the Union of Soviet Socialist Republics on Exchanges and Cooperation in Scientific, Technical, Educational, Cultural, and Other Fields, signed April 11, 1972;
Have agreed as follows:

ARTICLE 1

The Parties undertake to develop and extend mutually beneficial cooperation in the field of medical science and public health. By mutual agreement and on the basis of reciprocity, they will determine the various directions of this cooperation, proceeding from the experience acquired by the Parties in the course of previous contacts, visits, and exchanges.
The Parties agree to direct their initial joint efforts toward combating the most widespread and serious diseases, such as cardio-vascular and oncological diseases, because of the major threat they pose to man's health, toward solving the problems associated with the effects of the environment on man's health, as well as toward the resolution of other important health problems.

ARTICLE 2

The cooperation provided for in the preceding article may be implemented specifically in the following ways:

—Coordinated scientific research programs and other activities in health fields of mutual interest;
—Exchanges of specialists and delegations;
—Organization of colloquia, scientific conferences and lectures;
—Exchange of information;
—Familiarization with technical aids and equipment.

ARTICLE 3

The Parties will encourage and facilitate the establishment of direct and regular contacts between United States and Soviet medical institutions and organizations.
The Parties will also encourage and facilitate exchanges of equipment, pharmaceutical products, and technological developments related to medicine and public health.

ARTICLE 4

The Parties will continue to provide assistance to international medical organizations, specifically the World Health Organization, and will afford these organizations the opportunity of drawing on the knowledge gained by the Parties, including knowledge gained in the course of their joint efforts.

ARTICLE 5

The Parties will delegate the practical implementation of this Agreement to the U.S.–U.S.S.R. Joint Committee for Health Cooperation. The Joint Committee shall periodically work out specific programs of cooperation, creating working subgroups whenever necessary, and shall be responsible for supervising implementation of these programs.

ARTICLE 6

Cooperation shall be financed on the basis of reciprocal agreements worked out by the Joint Committee, using the resources of the Department of Health, Education, and Welfare of the United States of America and the Ministry of Health of the Union of Soviet Socialist Republics, as well as the resources of institutions participating in direct inter-institutional cooperation.

ARTICLE 7

This Agreement shall enter into force upon signature and shall remain in force for five years, after which it will be extended for successive five-year periods unless one Party notifies the other of the termination thereof not less than six months prior to its expiration.

DONE on May 23, 1972 in Moscow in duplicate, in the English and Russian languages, both texts being equally authentic.

For the Government of the United States of America:

WILLIAM P. ROGERS

Secretary of State

For the Government of the Union of Soviet Socialist Republics:

BORIS V. PETROVSKY

Minister of Health

3 (May 24, 1972)

AGREEMENT ON COOPERATION IN SPACE

AGREEMENT BETWEEN THE UNITED STATES OF AMERICA AND THE UNION OF SOVIET SOCIALIST REPUBLICS CONCERNING COOPERATION IN THE EXPLORATION AND USE OF OUTER SPACE FOR PEACEFUL PURPOSES

The United States of America and the Union of Soviet Socialist Republics;
Considering the role which the U.S.A. and the U.S.S.R. play in the exploration and use of outer space for peaceful purposes;
Striving for a further expansion of cooperation between the U.S.A. and the U.S.S.R. in the exploration and use of outer space for peaceful purposes;
Noting the positive cooperation which the parties have already experienced in this area;
Desiring to make the results of scientific research gained from the exploration and use of outer space for peaceful purposes available for the benefit of the peoples of the two countries and of all peoples of the world;
Taking into consideration the provisions of the Treaty on Principles Governing the Activities of States in the Exploration and Use of Outer Space, including the Moon and Other Celestial Bodies, as well as the Agreement on the Rescue of Astronauts, the Return of Astronauts, and the Return of Objects Launched into Outer Space;
In accordance with the Agreement between the United States of America and the Union of Soviet Socialist Republics on Exchanges and Cooperation in Scientific, Technical, Educational, Cultural, and Other Fields, signed April 11, 1972, and in order to develop further the principles of mutually beneficial cooperation between the two countries;
Have agreed as follows:

ARTICLE 1

The Parties will develop cooperation in the fields of space meteorology; study of the natural environment; exploration of near earth space, the moon and the planets; and space biology and medicine; and, in particular, will cooperate to take all appropriate measures to encourage and achieve the fulfillment of the Summary of Results of Discussion on Space Cooperation Between the U.S. National Aeronautics and Space Administration and the Academy of Sciences of the U.S.S.R. dated January 21, 1971.

ARTICLE 2

The Parties will carry out such cooperation by means of mutual exchanges of scientific information and delegations, through meetings of scientists and specialists of both countries, and also in such other ways as may be mutually agreed. Joint working groups may be created for the development and implementation of appropriate programs of cooperation.

ARTICLE 3

The Parties have agreed to carry out projects for developing compatible rendezvous and docking systems of United States and Soviet manned spacecraft and stations in order to enhance the safety of manned flight in space and to provide the opportunity for conducting joint scientific experiments in the future. It is planned that the first experimental flight to test these systems be conducted during 1975, envisaging the docking of a United States Apollo-type spacecraft and a Soviet Soyuz-type spacecraft with visits of astronauts in each other's spacecraft. The implementation of these projects will be carried out on the basis of principles and procedures which will be developed in accordance with the Summary of Results of the Meeting Between Representatives of the U.S. National Aeronautics and Space Administration and the U.S.S.R. Academy of Sciences on the Question of Developing Compatible Systems for Rendezvous and Docking of Manned Spacecraft and Space Stations of the U.S.A. and the U.S.S.R. dated April 6, 1972.

ARTICLE 4

The Parties will encourage international efforts to resolve problems of international law in the exploration and use of outer space for peaceful purposes with the aim of strengthening the legal order in space and further developing international space law and will cooperate in this field.

ARTICLE 5

The Parties may by mutual agreement determine other areas of cooperation in the exploration and use of outer space for peaceful purposes.

ARTICLE 6

This Agreement shall enter into force upon signature and shall remain in force for five years. It may be modified or extended by mutual agreement of the Parties.

DONE at Moscow this 24th day of May 1972 in duplicate, in the English and Russian languages, both equally authentic.

For the United States of America

RICHARD NIXON

President of the United States of America

For the Union of Soviet Socialist Republics

A. N. KOSYGIN

Chairman of the Council of Ministers of the USSR

4 (May 24, 1972)

AGREEMENT ON SCIENCE AND TECHNOLOGY

AGREEMENT BETWEEN THE GOVERNMENT OF THE UNITED STATES OF AMERICA AND THE GOVERNMENT OF THE UNION OF SOVIET SOCIALIST REPUBLICS ON COOPERATION IN THE FIELDS OF SCIENCE AND TECHNOLOGY

The Government of the United States of America and the Government of the Union of Soviet Socialist Republics;

Recognizing that benefits can accrue to both countries from the development of cooperation in the fields of science and technology;

Wishing to assist in establishing closer and more regular cooperation between scientific and technical organizations of both countries;

Taking into consideration that such cooperation will serve to strengthen friendly relations between both countries;

In accordance with the Agreement between the United States of America and the Union of Soviet Socialist Republics on Exchanges and Cooperation in Scientific, Technical, Educational, Cultural, and Other Fields, signed April 11, 1972, and in order to develop further the mutually beneficial cooperation between the two countries;

Have agreed as follows:

ARTICLE 1

Both Parties pledge themselves to assist and develop scientific and technical cooperation between both countries on the basis of mutual benefit, equality and reciprocity.

ARTICLE 2

The main objective of this cooperation is to provide broad opportunities for both Parties to combine the efforts of their scientists and specialists in working on major problems, whose solution will promote the progress of science and technology for the benefit of both countries and of mankind.

ARTICLE 3

The forms of cooperation in science and technology may include the following:

a. Exchange of scientists and specialists;

b. Exchange of scientific and technical information and documentation;

c. Joint development and implementation of programs and projects in the fields of basic and applied sciences;

d. Joint research, development and testing, and exchange of research results and experience between scientific research institutions and organizations;

e. Organization of joint courses, conferences and symposia;

f. Rendering of help, as appropriate, on both sides in establishing contacts and arrangements between United States firms and Soviet enterprises where a mutual interest develops; and

g. Other forms of scientific and technical cooperation as may be mutually agreed.

ARTICLE 4

1. Pursuant to the aims of this Agreement, both Parties will, as appropriate, encourage and facilitate the establishment and development of direct contacts and cooperation between agencies, organizations and firms of both countries and the conclusion, as appropriate, of implementing agreements for particular cooperative activities engaged in under this Agreement.

2. Such agreements between agencies, organizations and enterprises will be concluded in accordance with the laws of both countries. Such agreements may cover the subjects of cooperation, organizations engaged in the implementation of projects and programs, the procedures which should be followed, and any other appropriate details.

ARTICLE 5

Unless otherwise provided in an implementing agreement, each Party or participating agency, organization or enterprise shall bear the costs of its participation and that of its personnel in cooperative activities engaged in under this Agreement, in accordance with existing laws in both countries.

ARTICLE 6

Nothing in this Agreement shall be interpreted to prejudice other agreements in the fields of science and technology concluded between the Parties.

ARTICLE 7

1. For the implementation of this Agreement there shall be established a U.S.–U.S.S.R. Joint Commission on Scientific and Technical Cooperation. Meetings will be convened not less then once a year in Washington and Moscow, alternately.

2. The Commission shall consider proposals for the development of cooperation in specific areas; prepare suggestions and recommendations, as appropriate, for the two Parties; develop and approve measures and programs for implementation of this Agreement; designate, as appropriate, the agencies, organizations or enterprises responsible for carrying out cooperative activities; and seek to assure their proper implementation.

3. The Executive Agent, which will be responsible for assuring the carrying out on its side of the Agreement, shall be, for the United States of America, the Office of Science and Technology in the Executive Office of the President and, for the Union of Soviet Socialist Republics, the State Committee of the U.S.S.R. Council of Ministers for Science and Technology. The Joint Commission will consist of United States and Soviet delegations established on an equal basis of which the chairmen and members are to be designated by the respective Executive Agents with approval by the respective parties. Regulations regarding the operation of the Commission shall be agreed by the chairmen.

4. To carry out its functions the Commission may create temporary or permanent joint subcommittees, councils or working groups.

5. During the period between meetings of the Commission additions or amendments may be made to already approved cooperative activities, as may be mutually agreed.

ARTICLE 8

1. This Agreement shall enter into force upon signature and shall remain in force for five years. It may be modified or extended by mutual agreement of the Parties.

2. The termination of this Agreement shall not affect the validity of agreements made hereunder between agencies, organizations and enterprises of both countries.

DONE at Moscow this 24 day of May, 1972, in duplicate, in the English and Russian languages, both equally authentic.

For the Government of the United States of America:

WILLIAM P. ROGERS

Secretary of State

For the Government of the Union of Soviet Socialist Republics:

V. A. KIRILLIN

Chairman of the State Committee of the Council of Ministers of the USSR on Science and Technology

5 (May 25, 1972)

AGREEMENT ON PREVENTION OF INCIDENTS AT SEA

AGREEMENT BETWEEN THE GOVERNMENT OF THE UNITED STATES OF AMERICA AND THE GOVERNMENT OF THE UNION OF SOVIET SOCIALIST REPUBLICS ON THE PREVENTION OF INCIDENTS ON AND OVER THE HIGH SEAS

The Government of the United States of America and the Government of the Union of Soviet Socialist Republics,

Desiring to assure the safety of navigation of the ships of their respective armed forces on the high seas and flight of their military aircraft over the high seas, and

Guided by the principles and rules of international law,

Have decided to conclude this Agreement and have agreed as follows:

ARTICLE I

For the purposes of this Agreement, the following definitions shall apply:

1. "Ship" means:

(a) A warship belonging to the naval forces of the Parties bearing the external marks distinguishing warships of its nationality, under the command of an officer duly commissioned by the government and whose name appears in the Navy list, and manned by a crew who are under regular naval discipline;

(b) Naval auxiliaries of the Parties, which include all naval ships authorized to fly the naval auxiliary flag where such a flag has been established by either Party.

2. "Aircraft" means all military manned heavier-than-air and lighter-than-air craft, excluding space craft.

3. "Formation" means an ordered arrangement of two or more ships proceeding together and normally maneuvered together.

ARTICLE II

The Parties shall take measures to instruct the commanding officers of their respective ships to observe strictly the letter and spirit of the International Regulations for Preventing Collisions at Sea, hereinafter referred to as the Rules of the Road. The Parties recognize that their freedom to conduct operations on the high seas is based on the principles established under recognized international law and codified in the 1958 Geneva Convention on the High Seas.

ARTICLE III

1. In all cases ships operating in proximity to each other, except when required to maintain course and speed under the Rules of the Road, shall remain well clear to avoid risk of collision.

2. Ships meeting or operating in the vicinity of a formation of the other Party shall, while conforming to the Rules of the Road, avoid maneuvering in a manner which would hinder the evolutions of the formation.

3. Formations shall not conduct maneuvers through areas of heavy traffic where internationally recognized traffic separation schemes are in effect.

4. Ships engaged in surveillance of other ships shall stay at a distance which avoids the risk of collision and also shall avoid executing maneuvers embarrassing or endangering the ships under surveillance. Except when required to maintain course and speed under the Rules of the Road, a surveillant shall take positive early action so as, in the exercise of good seamanship, not to embarrass or endanger ships under surveillance.

5. When ships of both Parties maneuver in sight

of one another, such signals (flag, sound, and light) as are prescribed by the Rules of the Road, the International Code of Signals, or other mutually agreed signals, shall be adhered to for signalling operations and intentions.

6. Ships of the Parties shall not simulate attacks by aiming guns, missile launchers, torpedo tubes, and other weapons in the direction of a passing ship of the other Party, not launch any object in the direction of passing ships of the other Party, and not use searchlights or other powerful illumination devices to illuminate the navigation bridges of passing ships of the other Party.

7. When conducting exercises with submerged submarines, exercising ships shall show the appropriate signals prescribed by the International Code of Signals to warn ships of the presence of submarines in the area.

8. Ships of one Party when approaching ships of the other Party conducting operations as set forth in Rule 4 (c) of the Rules of the Road, and particularly ships engaged in launching or landing aircraft as well as ships engaged in replenishment underway, shall take appropriate measures not to hinder maneuvers of such ships and shall remain well clear.

ARTICLE IV

Commanders of aircraft of the Parties shall use the greatest caution and prudence in approaching aircraft and ships of the other Party operating on and over the high seas, in particular, ships engaged in launching or landing aircraft, and in the interest of mutual safety shall not permit: simulated attacks by the simulated use of weapons against aircraft and ships, or performance of various aerobatics over ships, or dropping various objects near them in such a manner as to be hazardous to ships or to constitute a hazard to navigation.

ARTICLE V

1. Ships of the Parties operating in sight of one another shall raise proper signals concerning their intent to begin launching or landing aircraft.

2. Aircraft of the Parties flying over the high seas in darkness or under instrument conditions shall, whenever feasible, display navigation lights.

ARTICLE VI

Both Parties shall:

1. Provide through the established system of radio broadcasts of information and warning to mariners, not less than 3 to 5 days in advance as a rule, notification of actions on the high seas which represent a danger to navigation or to aircraft in flight.

2. Make increased use of the informative signals contained in the International Code of Signals to signify the intentions of their respective ships when maneuvering in proximity to one another. At night, or in conditions of reduced visibility, or under conditions of lighting and such distances when signal flags are not distinct, flashing light should be used to inform ships of maneuvers which may hinder the movements of others or involve a risk of collision.

3. Utilize on a trial basis signals additional to those in the International Code of Signals, submitting such signals to the Intergovernmental Maritime Consultative Organization for its consideration and for the information of other States.

ARTICLE VII

The Parties shall exchange appropriate information concerning instances of collision, incidents which result in damage, or other incidents at sea between ships and aircraft of the Parties. The United States Navy shall provide such information through the Soviet Naval Attache in Washington and the Soviet Navy shall provide such information through the United States Naval Attache in Moscow.

ARTICLE VIII

This Agreement shall enter into force on the date of its signature and shall remain in force for a period of three years. It will thereafter be renewed without further action by the Parties for successive periods of three years each.

This Agreement may be terminated by either Party upon six months written notice to the other Party.

ARTICLE IX

The Parties shall meet within one year after the date of the signing of this Agreement to review the implementation of its terms. Similar consultations shall be held thereafter annually, or more frequently as the Parties may decide.

ARTICLE X

The Parties shall designate members to form a Committee which will consider specific measures in conformity with this Agreement. The Committee will, as a particular part of its work, consider the practical workability of concrete fixed distances to be observed in encounters between ships, aircraft, and ships and aircraft. The Committee will meet within six months of the date of signature of this Agreement and submit its recommendations for decision by the Parties during the consultations prescribed in Article IX.

DONE in duplicate on the 25th day of May, 1972 in Moscow in the English and Russian languages each being equally authentic.

For the Government of the United States of America:

JOHN W. WARNER

Secretary of the Navy

For the Government of the Union of Soviet Socialist Republics:

SERGEI G. GORSHKOV

Commander-in-Chief of the Navy

COMMUNIQUE REGARDING JOINT U.S.–U.S.S.R. COMMERCIAL COMMISSION, MAY 26

Weekly Compilation of Presidential Documents dated June 5

In order to promote the development of mutually beneficial commercial relations and related economic matters between the two countries, Soviet leaders and the President of the United States Richard M. Nixon have agreed to establish a US–USSR Commercial Commission.

The US–USSR Commission is to:

Negotiate:

—an overall trade agreement including reciprocal MFN treatment;

—arrangements for the reciprocal availability of government credits;

—provisions for the reciprocal establishment of business facilities to promote trade;

—an agreement establishing an arbitration mechanism for settling commercial disputes.

Study possible US–USSR participation in the development of resources and the manufacture and sale of raw materials and other products.

Monitor the spectrum of US–USSR commercial relations, identifying and, when possible, resolving issues that may be of interest to both parties such as patents and licensing.

Sessions of the Commission will be held alternately in Moscow and Washington. The first session of the Commission is to take place in Moscow in July of this year.

1. Each Party undertakes to limit anti-ballistic missile (ABM) systems and to adopt other measures in accordance with the provisions of this Treaty.

2. Each Party undertakes not to deploy ABM systems for a defense of the territory of its country and not to provide a base for such a defense, and not to deploy ABM systems for defense of an individual region except as provided for in Article III of this Treaty.

ARTICLE II

1. For the purposes of this Treaty an ABM system is a system to counter strategic ballistic missiles or their elements in flight trajectory, currently consisting of:

(a) ABM interceptor missiles, which are interceptor missiles constructed and deployed for an ABM role, or of a type tested in an ABM mode;

(b) ABM launchers, which are launchers constructed and deployed for launching ABM interceptor missiles; and

(c) ABM radars, which are radars constructed and deployed for an ABM role, or of a type tested in an ABM mode.

2. The ABM system components listed in paragraph 1 of this Article include those which are:

(a) operational;
(b) under construction;
(c) undergoing testing;
(d) undergoing overhaul, repair or conversion; or
(e) mothballed.

ARTICLE III

Each Party undertakes not to deploy ABM systems or their components except that:

(a) within one ABM system deployment area having a radius of one hundred and fifty kilometers and centered on the Party's national capital, a Party may deploy: (1) no more than one hundred ABM launchers and no more than one hundred ABM interceptor missiles at launch sites, and (2) ABM radars within no more than six ABM radar complexes, the area of each complex being circular and having a diameter of no more than three kilometers; and

(b) within one ABM system deployment area having a radius of one hundred and fifty kilometers and

7 (May 26, 1972)

TREATY BETWEEN THE UNITED STATES OF AMERICA AND THE UNION OF SOVIET SOCIALIST REPUBLICS ON THE LIMITATION OF ANTI-BALLISTIC MISSILE SYSTEMS

The United States of America and the Union of Soviet Socialist Republics, hereinafter referred to as the Parties,

Proceeding from the premise that nuclear war would have devastating consequences for all mankind,

Considering that effective measures to limit anti-ballistic missile systems would be a substantial factor in curbing the race in strategic offensive arms and would lead to a decrease in the risk of outbreak of war involving nuclear weapons,

Proceeding from the premise that the limitation of anti-ballistic missile systems, as well as certain agreed measures with respect to the limitation of strategic offensive arms, would contribute to the creation of more favorable conditions for further negotiations on limiting strategic arms,

Mindful of their obligations under Article VI of the Treaty on the Non-Proliferation of Nuclear Weapons,

Declaring their intention to achieve at the earliest possible date the cessation of the nuclear arms race and to take effective measures toward reductions in strategic arms, nuclear disarmament, and general and complete disarmament,

Desiring to contribute to the relaxation of international tension and the strengthening of trust between States,

Have agreed as follows:

containing ICBM silo launchers, a Party may deploy: (1) no more than one hundred ABM launchers and no more than one hundred ABM interceptor missiles at launch sites, (2) two large phased-array ABM radars comparable in potential to corresponding ABM radars operational or under construction on the date of signature of the Treaty in an ABM system deployment area containing ICBM silo launchers, and (3) no more than eighteen ABM radars each having a potential less than the potential of the smaller of the above-mentioned two large phased-array ABM radars.

ARTICLE IV

The limitations provided for in Article III shall not apply to ABM systems or their components used for development or testing, and located within current or additionally agreed test ranges. Each Party may have no more than a total of fifteen ABM launchers at test ranges.

ARTICLE V

1. Each Party undertakes not to develop, test, or deploy ABM systems or components which are sea-based, air-based, space-based, or mobile land-based.

2. Each Party undertakes not to develop, test, or deploy ABM launchers for launching more than one ABM interceptor missile at a time from each launcher, nor to modify deployed launchers to provide them with such a capability, nor to develop, test, or deploy automatic or semi-automatic or other similar systems for rapid reload of ABM launchers.

ARTICLE VI

To enhance assurance of the effectiveness of the limitations on ABM systems and their components provided by this Treaty, each Party undertakes:

(a) not to give missiles, launchers, or radars, other than ABM interceptor missiles, ABM launchers, or ABM radars, capabilities to counter strategic ballistic missiles or their elements in flight trajectory, and not to test them in an ABM mode; and

(b) not to deploy in the future radars for early warning of strategic ballistic missile attack except at locations along the periphery of its national territory and oriented outward.

ARTICLE VII

Subject to the provisions of this Treaty, modernization and replacement of ABM systems or their components may be carried out.

ARTICLE VIII

ABM systems or their components in excess of the numbers or outside the areas specified in this Treaty, as well as ABM systems or their components prohibited by this Treaty, shall be destroyed or dismantled under agreed procedures within the shortest possible agreed period of time.

ARTICLE IX

To assure the viability and effectiveness of this Treaty, each Party undertakes not to transfer to other States, and not to deploy outside its national territory, ABM systems or their components limited by this Treaty.

ARTICLE X

Each Party undertakes not to assume any international obligations which would conflict with this Treaty.

ARTICLE XI

The Parties undertake to continue active negotiations for limitations on strategic offensive arms.

ARTICLE XII

1. For the purpose of providing assurance of compliance with the provisions of this Treaty, each Party shall use national technical means of verification at its disposal in a manner consistent with generally recognized principles of international law.

2. Each Party undertakes not to interfere with the national technical means of verification of the other Party operating in accordance with paragraph 1 of this Article.

3. Each Party undertakes not to use deliberate concealment measures which impede verification by national technical means of compliance with the provisions of this Treaty. This obligation shall not require changes in current construction, assembly, conversion, or overhaul practices.

ARTICLE XIII

1. To promote the objectives and implementation of the provisions of this Treaty, the Parties shall establish promptly a Standing Consultative Commission, within the framework of which they will:

(a) consider questions concerning compliance with the obligations assumed and related situations which may be considered ambiguous;

(b) provide on a voluntary basis such information as either Party considers necessary to assure confidence in compliance with the obligations assumed;

(c) consider questions involving unintended interference with national technical means of verification;

(d) consider possible changes in the strategic situation which have a bearing on the provisions of this Treaty;

(e) agree upon procedures and dates for destruction or dismantling of ABM systems or their components in cases provided for by the provisions of this Treaty;

(f) consider, as appropriate, possible proposals for further increasing the viability of this Treaty, including proposals for amendments in accordance with the provisions of this Treaty;

(g) consider, as appropriate, proposals for further measures aimed at limiting strategic arms.

2. The Parties through consultation shall establish, and may amend as appropriate, Regulations for the Standing Consultative Commission governing procedures, composition and other relevant matters.

ARTICLE XIV

1. Each Party may propose amendments to this Treaty. Agreed amendments shall enter into force in accordance with the procedures governing the entry into force of this Treaty.
2. Five years after entry into force of this Treaty, and at five year intervals thereafter, the Parties shall together conduct a review of this Treaty.

ARTICLE XV

1. This Treaty shall be of unlimited duration.
2. Each Party shall, in exercising its national sovereignty, have the right to withdraw from this Treaty if it decides that extraordinary events related to the subject matter of this Treaty have jeopardized its supreme interests. It shall give notice of its decision to the other Party six months prior to withdrawal from the Treaty. Such notice shall include a statement of the extraordinary events the notifying Party regards as having jeopardized its supreme interests.

ARTICLE XVI

1. This Treaty shall be subject to ratification in accordance with the constitutional procedures of each Party. The Treaty shall enter into force on the day of the exchange of instruments of ratification.
2. This Treaty shall be registered pursuant to Article 102 of the Charter of the United Nations.

DONE at Moscow on May 26, 1972, in two copies, each in the English and Russian languages, both texts being equally authentic.

For the United States of America:

RICHARD NIXON

President of the United States of America

For the Union of Soviet Socialist Republics:

LEONID I. BREZHNEV

General Secretary of the Central Committee of the CPSU

AGREED INTERPRETATIONS, COMMON UNDERSTAND-INGS, AND UNILATERAL STATEMENTS

1. AGREED INTERPRETATIONS

(a) *Initialed Statements.*—The document set forth below was agreed upon and initialed by the Heads of the Delegations on May 26, 1972:

AGREED STATEMENTS REGARDING THE TREATY BETWEEN THE UNITED STATES OF AMERICA AND THE UNION OF SOVIET SOCIALIST REPUBLICS ON THE LIMITATION OF ANTI-BALLISTIC MISSILE SYSTEMS

[A]

The Parties understand that, in addition to the ABM radars which may be deployed in accordance with subparagraph (a) of Article III of the Treaty, those non-phased-array ABM radars operational on the date of signature of the Treaty within the ABM system deployment area for defense of the national capital may be retained.

[B]

The Parties understand that the potential (the product of mean emitted power in watts and antenna area in square meters) of the smaller of the two large phased-array ABM radars referred to in subparagraph (b) of Article III of the Treaty is considered for purposes of the Treaty to be three million.

[C]

The Parties understand that the center of the ABM system deployment area centered on the national capital and the center of the ABM system deployment area containing ICBM silo launchers for each Party shall be separated by no less than thirteen hundred kilometers.

[D]

In order to insure fulfillment of the obligation not to deploy ABM systems and their components except as provided in Article III of the Treaty, the Parties agree that in the event ABM systems based on other physical principles and including components capable of substituting for ABM interceptor missiles, ABM launchers, or ABM radars are created in the future, specific limitations on such systems and their components would be subject to discussion in accordance with Article XIII and agreement in accordance with Article XIV of the Treaty.

[E]

The Parties understand that Article V of the Treaty includes obligations not to develop, test or deploy ABM interceptor missiles for the delivery by each ABM interceptor missile of more than one independently guided warhead.

[F]

The Parties agree not to deploy phased-array radars having a potential (the product of mean emitted power in watts and antenna area in square meters) exceeding three million, except as provided for in Articles III, IV and VI of the Treaty, or except for the purposes of tracking objects in outer space or for use as national technical means of verification.

[G]

The Parties understand that Article IX of the Treaty includes the obligation of the US and the USSR not to provide to other States technical descriptions or blue prints specially worked out for the construction of ABM systems and their components limited by the Treaty.

(b) *Common Understandings.*—Common understanding of the Parties on the following matters was reached during the negotiations:

The U.S. Delegation made the following statement on May 26, 1972:

Article III of the ABM Treaty provides for each side one ABM system deployment area centered on its national capital and one ABM system deployment area containing ICBM silo launchers. The two sides have registered agreement on the following statement: "The Parties understand that the center of the ABM system deployment area centered on the national capital and the center of the ABM system deployment area containing ICBM silo launchers for each Party shall be separated by no less than thirteen hundred kilometers." In this connection, the U.S. side notes that its ABM system deployment area for defense of ICBM silo launchers, located west of the Mississippi River, will be centered in the Grand Forks ICBM silo launcher deployment area. (See Initialed Statement [C].)

The U.S. Delegation made the following statement on April 26, 1972:

Article IV of the ABM Treaty provides that "the limitations provided for in Article III shall not apply to ABM systems or their components used for development or testing, and located within current or additionally agreed test ranges." We believe it would be useful to assure that there is no misunderstanding as to current ABM test ranges. It is our understanding that ABM test ranges encompass the area within which ABM components are located for test purposes. The current U.S. ABM test ranges are at White Sands, New Mexico, and at Kwajalein Atoll, and the current Soviet ABM test range is near Sary Shagan in Kazakhstan. We consider that non-phased array radars of types used for range safety or instrumentation purposes may be located outside of ABM test ranges. We interpret the reference in Article IV to "additionally agreed test ranges" to mean that ABM components will not be located at any other test ranges without prior agreement between our Governments that there will be such additional ABM test ranges.

On May 5, 1972, the Soviet Delegation stated that there was a common understanding on what ABM test ranges were, that the use of the types of non-ABM radars for range safety or instrumentation was not limited under the Treaty, that the reference in Article IV to "additionally agreed" test ranges was sufficiently clear, and that national means permitted identifying current test ranges.

On January 28, 1972, the U.S. Delegation made the following statement:

Article V(1) of the Joint Draft Text of the ABM Treaty includes an undertaking not to develop, test, or deploy mobile land-based ABM systems and their components. On May 5, 1971, the U.S. side indicated that, in its view, a prohibition on deployment of mobile ABM systems and components would rule out the deployment of ABM launchers and radars which were not permanent fixed types. At that time, we asked for the Soviet view of this interpretation. Does the Soviet side agree with the U.S. side's interpretation put forward on May 5, 1971?

On April 13, 1972, the Soviet Delegation said there is a general common understanding on this matter.

D. STANDING CONSULTATIVE COMMISSION

Ambassador Smith made the following statement on May 22, 1972:

The United States proposes that the sides agree that, with regard to initial implementation of the ABM Treaty's Article XIII on the Standing Consultative Commission (SCC) and of the consultation Articles to the Interim Agreement on offensive arms and the Accidents Agreement, [1] agreement establishing the SCC will be worked out early in the follow-on SALT negotiations; until that is completed, the following arrangements will prevail: when SALT is in session, any consultation desired by either side under these Articles can be carried out by the two SALT Delegations; when SALT is not in session, *ad hoc* arrangements for any desired consultations under these Articles may be made through diplomatic channels.

Minister Semenov replied that, on an *ad referendum* basis, he could agree that the U.S. statement corresponded to the Soviet understanding.

E. STANDSTILL

On May 6, 1972, Minister Semenov made the following statement:

In an effort to accommodate the wishes of the U.S. side, the Soviet Delegation is prepared to proceed on the basis that the two sides will in fact observe the obligations of both the Interim Agreement and the ABM Treaty beginning from the date of signature of these two documents.

In reply, the U.S. Delegation made the following statement on May 20, 1972:

The U.S. agrees in principle with the Soviet statement made on May 6 concerning observance of obligations beginning from date of signature but we would like to make clear our understanding that this means that, pending ratification and acceptance, neither side would take any action prohibited by the agreements after they had entered into force. This understanding would continue to apply in

---

[1] See Article 7 of Agreement to Reduce the Risk of Outbreak of Nuclear War Between the United States of America and the Union of Soviet Socialist Republics, signed Sept. 30, 1971. TIAS 7186; 22 UST 1590.

the absence of notification by either signatory of its intention not to proceed with ratification or approval.

The Soviet Delegation indicated agreement with the U.S. statement.

2. UNILATERAL STATEMENTS

(a) The following noteworthy unilateral statements were made during the negotiations by the United States Delegation:

A. WITHDRAWAL FROM THE ABM TREATY

On May 9, 1972, Ambassador Smith made the following statement:

The U.S. Delegation has stressed the importance the U.S. Government attaches to achieving agreement on more complete limitations on strategic offensive arms, following agreement on an ABM Treaty and on an Interim Agreement on certain measures with respect to the limitation of strategic offensive arms. The U.S. Delegation believes that an objective of the follow-on negotiations should be to constrain and reduce on a long-term basis threats to the survivability of our respective strategic retaliatory forces. The USSR Delegation has also indicated that the objectives of SALT would remain unfulfilled without the achievement of an agreement providing for more complete limitations on strategic offensive arms. Both sides recognize that the initial agreements would be steps toward the achievement of more complete limitations on strategic arms. If an agreement providing for more complete strategic offensive arms limitations were not achieved within five years, U.S. supreme interests could be jeopardized. Should that occur, it would constitute a basis for withdrawal from the ABM Treaty. The U.S. does not wish to see such a situation occur, nor do we believe that the USSR does. It is because we wish to prevent such a situation that we emphasize the importance the U.S. Government attaches to achievement of more complete limitations on strategic offensive arms. The U.S. Executive will inform the Congress, in connection with Congressional consideration of the ABM Treaty and the Interim Agreement, of this statement of the U.S. position.

B. TESTED IN ABM MODE

On April 7, 1972, the U.S. Delegation made the following statement:

Article II of the Joint Text Draft uses the term "tested in an ABM mode," in defining ABM components, and Article VI includes certain obligations concerning such testing. We believe that the sides should have a common understanding of this phrase. First, we would note that the testing provisions of the ABM Treaty are intended to apply to testing which occurs after the date of signature of the Treaty, and not to any testing which may have occurred in the past. Next, we would amplify the remarks we have made on this subject during the previous Helsinki phase by setting forth the objectives which govern the U.S. view on the subject, namely, while prohibiting testing of non-ABM components for ABM purposes: not to precent testing of ABM components, and not to prevent testing of non-ABM components for non-ABM purposes. To clarify our interpretation of "tested in an ABM mode," we note that we would consider a launcher, missile or radar to be "tested in an ABM mode" if, for example, any of the following events occur: (1) a launcher is used to launch an ABM interceptor missile, (2) an interceptor missile is flight tested against a target vehicle which has a flight trajectory with characteristics of a strategic ballistic missile flight trajectory, or is flight tested in conjunction with the test of an ABM interceptor missile or an ABM radar at the same test range, or is flight tested to an altitude inconsistent with interception of targets against which air defenses are deployed, (3) a radar makes measurements on a cooperative target vehicle of the kind referred to in item (2) above during the reentry portion of its trajectory or makes measurements in conjunction with the test of an ABM interceptor missile or an ABM radar at the same test range. Radars used for purposes such as range safety or instrumentation would be exempt from application of these criteria.

C. NO-TRANSFER ARTICLE OF ABM TREATY

On April 18, 1972, the U.S. Delegation made the following statement:

In regard to this Article [IX], I have a brief and I believe self-explanatory statement to make. The U.S. side wishes to make clear that the provisions of this Article do not set a precedent for whatever provision may be considered for a Treaty on Limiting Strategic Offensive Arms. The question of transfer of strategic offensive arms is a far more complex issue, which may require a different solution.

D. NO INCREASE IN DEFENSE OF EARLY WARNING RADARS

On July 28, 1970, the U.S. Delegation made the following statement:

Since Hen House radars [Soviet ballistic missile early warning radars] can detect and track ballistic missile warheads at great distances, they have a significant ABM potential. Accordingly, the U.S. would regard any increase in the defenses of such radars by surface-to-air missiles as inconsistent with an agreement.

8 (May 26, 1972)

Interim Agreement on Limitation of Strategic Offensive Arms

INTERIM AGREEMENT BETWEEN THE UNITED STATES OF AMERICA AND THE UNION OF SOVIET SOCIALIST REPUBLICS ON CERTAIN MEASURES WITH RESPECT TO THE LIMITATION OF STRATEGIC OFFENSIVE ARMS

The United States of America and the Union of Soviet Socialist Republics, hereinafter referred to as the Parties,

Convinced that the Treaty on the Limitation of Anti-Ballistic Missile Systems and this Interim Agreement on Certain Measures with Respect to the Limitation of Strategic Offensive Arms will contribute to the creation of more favorable conditions for active negotiations on limiting strategic arms as well as to the relaxation of international tension and the strengthening of trust between States,

Taking into account the relationship between strategic offensive and defensive arms,

Mindful of their obligations under Article VI of the Treaty on the Non-Proliferation of Nuclear Weapons,

Have agreed as follows:

ARTICLE I

The Parties undertake not to start construction of additional fixed land-based intercontinental ballistic missile (ICBM) launchers after July 1, 1972.

ARTICLE II

The Parties undertake not to convert land-based launchers for light ICBMs, or for ICBMs of older types deployed prior to 1964, into land-based launch-ers for heavy ICBMs of types deployed after that time.

ARTICLE III

The Parties undertake to limit submarine-launched ballistic missile (SLBM) launchers and modern ballistic missile submarines to the numbers operational and under construction on the date of signature of this Interim Agreement, and in addition to launchers and submarines constructed under procedures established by the Parties as replacements for an equal number of ICBM launchers of older types deployed prior to 1964 or for launchers on older submarines.

ARTICLE IV

Subject to the provisions of this Interim Agreement, modernization and replacement of strategic offensive ballistic missiles and launchers covered by this Interim Agreement may be undertaken.

ARTICLE V

1. For the purpose of providing assurance of compliance with the provisions of this Interim Agreement, each Party shall use national technical means of verification at its disposal in a manner consistent with generally recognized principles of international law.

2. Each Party undertakes not to interfere with the national technical means of verification of the other Party operating in accordance with paragraph 1 of this Article.

3. Each Party undertakes not to use deliberate concealment measures which impede verification by national technical means of compliance with the provisions of this Interim Agreement. This obligation shall not require changes in current construction, assembly, conversion, or overhaul practices.

ARTICLE VI

To promote the objectives and implementation of the provisions of this Interim Agreement, the Parties shall use the Standing Consultative Commission established under Article XIII of the Treaty on the Limitation of Anti-Ballistic Missile Systems in accordance with the provisions of that Article.

ARTICLE VII

The Parties undertake to continue active negotiations for limitations on strategic offensive arms. The obligations provided for in this Interim Agreement shall not prejudice the scope or terms of the limitations on strategic offensive arms which may be worked out in the course of further negotiations.

ARTICLE VIII

1. This Interim Agreement shall enter into force upon exchange of written notices of acceptance by each Party, which exchange shall take place simultaneously with the exchange of instruments of ratification of the Treaty on the Limitation of Anti-Ballistic Missile Systems.

2. This Interim Agreement shall remain in force for a period of five years unless replaced earlier by an agreement on more complete measures limiting strategic offensive arms. It is the objective of the Parties to conduct active follow-on negotiations with the aim of concluding such an agreement as soon as possible.

3. Each Party shall, in exercising its national sovereignty, have the right to withdraw from this Interim Agreement if it decides that extraordinary events related to the subject matter of this Interim Agreement have jeopardized its supreme interests. It shall give notice of its decision to the other Party six months prior to withdrawal from this Interim Agreement. Such notice shall include a statement of the extraordinary events the notifying Party regards as having jeopardized its supreme interests.

DONE at Moscow on May 26, 1972, in two copies, each in the English and Russian languages, both texts being equally authentic.

For the United States of America:

RICHARD NIXON

President of the United States of America

For the Union of Soviet Socialist Republics:

LEONID I. BREZHNEV

General Secretary of the Central Committee of the CPSU

Protocol to Interim Agreement

PROTOCOL TO THE INTERIM AGREEMENT BETWEEN THE UNITED STATES OF AMERICA AND THE UNION OF SOVIET SOCIALIST REPUBLICS ON CERTAIN MEASURES WITH RESPECT TO THE LIMITATION OF STRATEGIC OFFENSIVE ARMS

The United States of America and the Union of Soviet Socialist Republics, hereinafter referred to as the Parties,

Having agreed on certain limitations relating to submarine-launched ballistic missile launchers and modern ballistic missile submarines, and to replacement procedures, in the Interim Agreement,

Have agreed as follows:

The Parties understand that, under Article III of the Interim Agreement, for the period during which that Agreement remains in force:

The US may have no more than 710 ballistic missile launchers on submarines (SLBMs) and no more than 44 modern ballistic missile submarines. The Soviet Union may have no more than 950 ballistic missile launchers on submarines and no more than 62 modern ballistic missile submarines.

Additional ballistic missile launchers on submarines up to the above-mentioned levels, in the U.S.—over 656 ballistic missile launchers on nuclear-powered submarines, and in the U.S.S.R.—over 740 ballistic missile launchers on nuclear-powered submarines, operational and under construction, may become operational as replacements for equal numbers of ballistic missile launchers of older types deployed prior to 1964 or of ballistic missile launchers on older submarines.

The deployment of modern SLBMs on any submarine, regardless of type, will be counted against the total level of SLBMs permitted for the U.S. and the U.S.S.R.

This Protocol shall be considered an integral part of the Interim Agreement.

DONE at Moscow this 26th day of May, 1972.

For the United States of America

RICHARD NIXON

President of the United States of America

For the Union of Soviet Socialist Republics

LEONID I. BREZHNEV

General Secretary of the Central Committee of the CPSU

AGREED INTERPRETATIONS, COMMON UNDER-STANDINGS, AND UNILATERAL STATEMENTS

1. AGREED INTERPRETATIONS

(a) *Initialed Statements.*—The document set forth below was agreed upon and initialed by the Heads of the Delegations on May 26, 1972:

AGREED STATEMENTS REGARDING THE INTERIM AGREEMENT BETWEEN THE UNITED STATES OF AMERICA AND THE UNION OF SOVIET SOCIALIST REPUBLICS ON CERTAIN MEASURES WITH RESPECT TO THE LIMITATION OF STRATEGIC OFFENSIVE ARMS

[A]

The Parties understand that land-based ICBM launchers referred to in the Interim Agreement are understood to be launchers for strategic ballistic missiles capable of ranges in excess of the shortest distance between the northeastern border of the continental U.S. and the northwestern border of the continental USSR.

[B]

The Parties understand that fixed land-based ICBM launchers under active construction as of the date of signature of the Interim Agreement may be completed.

[C]

The Parties understand that in the process of modernization and replacement the dimensions of land-based ICBM silo launchers will not be significantly increased.

[D]

The Parties understand that during the period of the Interim Agreement there shall be no significant increase in the number of ICBM or SLBM test and training launchers, or in the number of such launchers for modern land-based heavy ICBMs. The Parties further understand that construction or conversion of ICBM launchers at test ranges shall be undertaken only for purposes of testing and training.

[E]

The Parties understand that dismantling or destruction of ICBM launchers of older types deployed prior to 1964 and ballistic missile launchers on older submarines being replaced by new SLBM launchers on modern submarines will be initiated at the time of the beginning of sea trials of a replacement submarine, and will be completed in the shortest possible agreed period of time. Such dismantling or destruction, and timely notification thereof, will be accomplished under procedures to be agreed in the Standing Consultative Commission.

(b) *Common Understandings.*—Common understanding of the Parties on the following matters was reached during the negotiations:

A. INCREASE IN ICBM SILO DIMENSIONS

Ambassador Smith made the following statement on May 26, 1972:

> The Parties agree that the term "significantly increased" means that an increase will not be greater than 10–15 percent of the present dimensions of land-based ICBM silo launchers.

Minister Semenov replied that this statement corresponded to the Soviet understanding.

B. STANDING CONSULTATIVE COMMISSION

Ambassador Smith made the following statement on May 22, 1972:

> The United States proposes that the sides agree that, with regard to initial implementation of the ABM Treaty's Article XIII on the Standing Consultative Commission (SCC) and of the consultation Articles to the Interim Agreement on offensive arms and the Accidents Agreement,[1] agreement establishing the SCC will be worked out early in the follow-on SALT negotiations; until that is completed, the following arrangements will prevail: when SALT is in session, any consultation desired by either side under these Articles can be carried out by the two SALT Delegations; when SALT is not in session, *ad hoc* arrangements for any desired consultations under these Articles may be made through diplomatic channels.

Minister Semenov replied that, on an *ad referendum* basis, he could agree that the U.S. statement corresponded to the Soviet understanding.

C. STANDSTILL

On May 6, 1972, Minister Semenov made the following statement:

> In an effort to accommodate the wishes of the U.S. side, the Soviet Delegation is prepared to proceed on the basis that the two sides will in fact observe the obligations of both the Interim Agreement and the ABM Treaty beginning from the date of signature of these two documents.

---

[1] See Article 7 of Agreement to Reduce the Risk of Outbreak of Nuclear War Between the United States of America and the Union of Soviet Socialist Republics, signed Sept. 30, 1971. TIAS 7186; 22 UST 1590.

In reply, the U.S. Delegation made the following statement, on May 20, 1972:

The U.S. agrees in principle with the Soviet statement made on May 6 concerning observance of obligations beginning from date of signature but we would like to make clear our understanding that this means that, pending ratification and acceptance, neither side would take any action prohibited by the agreements after they had entered into force. This understanding would continue to apply in the absence of notification by either signatory of its intention not to proceed with ratification or approval.

The Soviet Delegation indicated agreement with the U.S. statement.

2. Unilateral Statements

(a) The following noteworthy unilateral statements were made during the negotiations by the United States Delegation:

A. WITHDRAWAL FROM THE ABM TREATY

On May 9, 1972, Ambassador Smith made the following statement:

The U.S. Delegation has stressed the importance the U.S. Government attaches to achieving agreement on more complete limitations on strategic offensive arms, following agreement on an ABM Treaty and on an Interim Agreement on certain measures with respect to the limitation of strategic offensive arms. The U.S. Delegation believes that an objective of the follow-on negotiations should be to constrain and reduce on a long-term basis threats to the survivability of our respective strategic retaliatory forces. The USSR Delegation has also indicated that the objectives of SALT would remain unfulfilled without the achievement of an agreement providing for more complete limitations on strategic offensive arms. Both sides recognize that the initial agreements would be steps toward the achievement of more complete limitations on strategic arms. If an agreement providing for more complete strategic offensive arms limitations were not achieved within five years, U.S. supreme interests could be jeopardized. Should that occur, it would constitute a basis for withdrawal from the ABM Treaty. The U.S. does not wish to see such a situation occur, nor do we believe that the USSR does. It is because we wish to prevent such a situation that we emphasize the importance the U.S. Government attaches to achievement of more complete limitations on strategic offensive arms. The U.S. Executive will inform the Congress, in connection with Congressional consideration of the ABM Treaty and the Interim Agreement, of this statement of the U.S. position.

The U.S. Delegation made the following statement on May 20, 1972:

In connection with the important subject of land-mobile ICBM launchers, in the interest of concluding the Interim Agreement the U.S. Delegation now withdraws its proposal that Article I or an agreed statement explicitly prohibit the deployment of mobile land-based ICBM launchers. I have been instructed to inform you that, while agreeing to defer the question of limitation of operational land-mobile ICBM launchers to the subsequent negotiations on more complete limitations on strategic offensive arms, the U.S. would consider the deployment of operational land-mobile ICBM launchers during the period of the Interim Agreement as inconsistent with the objectives of that Agreement.

C. COVERED FACILITIES

The U.S. Delegation made the following statement on May 20, 1972:

I wish to emphasize the importance that the United States attaches to the provisions of Article V, including in particular their application to fitting out or berthing submarines.

D. "HEAVY" ICBM'S

The U.S. Delegation made the following statement on May 26, 1972:

The U.S. Delegation regrets that the Soviet Delegation has not been willing to agree on a common definition of a heavy missile. Under these circumstances, the U.S. Delegation believes it necessary to state the following: The United States would consider any ICBM having a volume significantly greater than that of the largest light ICBM now operational on either side to be a heavy ICBM. The U.S. proceeds on the premise that the Soviet side will give due account to this consideration.

(b) The following noteworthy unilateral statement was made by the Delegation of the U.S.S.R. and is shown here with the U.S. reply:
On May 17, 1972, Minister Semenov made the following unilateral "Statement of the Soviet Side":

Taking into account that modern ballistic missile submarines are presently in the possession of not only the U.S., but also of its NATO allies, the Soviet Union agrees that for the period of effectiveness of the Interim 'Freeze' Agreement the U.S. and its NATO allies have up to 50 such submarines with a total of up to 800 ballistic missile launchers thereon (including 41 U.S. submarines with 656 ballistic missile launchers). However, if during the period of effectiveness of the Agreement U.S. allies in NATO should increase the number of their modern submarines to exceed the numbers of submarines they would have operational or under construction on the

27

date of signature of the Agreement, the Soviet Union will have the right to a corresponding increase in the number of its submarines. In the opinion of the Soviet side, the solution of the question of modern ballistic missile submarines provided for in the Interim Agreement only partially compensates for the strategic imbalance in the deployment of the nuclear-powered missile submarines of the USSR and the U.S. Therefore, the Soviet side believes that this whole question, and above all the question of liquidating the American missile submarine bases outside the U.S., will be appropriately resolved in the course of follow-on negotiations.

On May 24, Ambassador Smith made the following reply to Minister Semenov:

The United States side has studied the "statement made by the Soviet side" of May 17 concerning compensation for submarine basing and SLBM submarines belonging to third countries. The United States does not accept the validity of the considerations in that statement.

On May 26 Minister Semenov repeated the unilateral statement made on May 24. Ambassador Smith also repeated the U.S. rejection on May 26.

9. BASIC PRINCIPLES OF RELATIONS BETWEEN THE UNITED STATES OF AMERICA AND THE UNION OF SOVIET SOCIALIST REPUBLICS

The United States of America and the Union of Soviet Socialist Republics,
Guided by their obligations under the Charter of the United Nations and by a desire to strengthen peaceful relations with each other and to place these relations on the firmest possible basis,
Aware of the need to make every effort to remove the threat of war and to create conditions which promote the reduction of tensions in the world and the strengthening of universal security and international cooperation,
Believing that the improvement of US-Soviet relations and their mutually advantageous development in such areas as economics, science and culture, will meet these objectives and contribute to better mutual understanding and business-like cooperation, without in any way prejudicing the interests of third countries,

Conscious that these objectives reflect the interests of the peoples of both countries,

Have agreed as follows:

First. They will proceed from the common determination that in the nuclear age there is no alternative to conducting their mutual relations on the basis of peaceful coexistence. Differences in ideology and in the social systems of the USA and the USSR are not obstacles to the bilateral development of normal relations based on the principles of sovereignty, equality, non-interference in internal affairs and mutual advantage.

Second. The USA and the USSR attach major importance to preventing the development of situations capable of causing a dangerous exacerbation of their relations. Therefore, they will do their utmost to avoid military confrontations and to prevent the outbreak of nuclear war. They will always exercise restraint in their mutual relations, and will be prepared to negotiate and settle differences by peaceful means. Discussions and negotiations on outstanding issues will be conducted in a spirit of reciprocity, mutual accommodation and mutual benefit.

Both sides recognize that efforts to obtain unilateral advantage at the expense of the other, directly or indirectly, are inconsistent with these objectives. The prerequisites for maintaining and strengthening peaceful relations between the USA and the USSR are the recognition of the security interests of the Parties based on the principle of equality and the renunciation of the use or threat of force.

Third. The USA and the USSR have a special responsibility, as do other countries which are permanent members of the United Nations Security Council, to do everything in their power so that conflicts or situations will not arise which would serve to increase international tensions. Accordingly, they will seek to promote conditions in which all countries will live in peace and security and will not be subject to outside interference in their internal affairs.

Fourth. The USA and the USSR intend to widen the juridical basis of their mutual relations and to exert the necessary efforts so that bilateral agreements which they have concluded and multilateral treaties and agreements to which they are jointly parties are faithfully implemented.

Fifth. The USA and the USSR reaffirm their readiness to continue the practice of exchanging views on problems of mutual interest and, when necessary, to conduct such exchanges at the highest level, including meetings between leaders of the two countries.

The two governments welcome and will facilitate an increase in productive contacts between representatives of the legislative bodies of the two countries.

Sixth. The Parties will continue their efforts to limit armaments on a bilateral as well as on a multilateral basis. They will continue to make special efforts to limit strategic armaments. Whenever possible, they will conclude concrete agreements aimed at achieving these purposes.

The USA and the USSR regard as the ultimate objective of their efforts the achievement of general and complete disarmament and the establishment of an effective system of international security in accordance with the purposes and principles of the United Nations.

Seventh. The USA and the USSR regard commercial and economic ties as an important and necessary element in the strengthening of their bilateral relations and thus will actively promote the growth of such ties. They will facilitate cooperation between the relevant organizations and enterprises of the two countries and the conclusion of appropriate agreements and contracts, including long-term ones.

The two countries will contribute to the improvement of maritime and air communications between them.

Eighth. The two sides consider it timely and useful to develop mutual contacts and cooperation in the fields of science and technology. Where suitable, the USA and the USSR will conclude appropriate agreements dealing with concrete cooperation in these fields.

Ninth. The two sides reaffirm their intention to deepen cultural ties with one another and to encourage fuller familiarization with each other's cultural values. They will promote improved conditions for cultural exchanges and tourism.

Tenth. The USA and the USSR will seek to ensure that their ties and cooperation in all the above-mentioned fields and in any others in their mutual interest are built on a firm and long-term basis. To give a permanent character to these efforts, they will establish in all fields where this is feasible joint commissions or other joint bodies.

Eleventh. The USA and the USSR make no claim for themselves and would not recognize the claims of anyone else to any special rights or advantages in world affairs. They recognize the sovereign equality of all states.

The development of US–Soviet relations is not directed against third countries and their interests.

Twelfth. The basic principles set forth in this document do not affect any obligations with respect to other countries earlier assumed by the USA and the USSR.

Moscow, *May 29, 1972*

For the United States of America	For the Union of Soviet Socialist Republics
RICHARD NIXON	LEONID I. BREZHNEV
President of the United States of America	General Secretary of the Central Committee, CPSU

II:

THE INTERIM BETWEEN THE MOSCOW AND WASHINGTON SUMMIT MEETINGS: MAY 1972 TO JUNE 1973

INTRODUCTION

The 16 documents of this section illustrate a flurry of activity toward accomplishing the three tasks set at the Moscow summit of 1972. Documents 11, 13, 23, and 24 implemented agreements on cooperation in science, technology, and environmental affairs, and on preventing incidents at sea. Documents 12 and 14 through 19 constitute remarkable progress toward removing trade barriers, the second task set at Moscow.

The Joint Commercial Commission that had been created during the Moscow summit met first in Moscow from July 20 to August 1, where it established five working groups to resolve the major problems related to trade: most-favored-nation status, maritime matters, credit for the USSR, Soviet repayment of lend-lease debts from World War II, and drafting of a general trade agreement.[1] After considerable progress during the first meeting, the Soviet members of the working groups came to Washington for the second meeting at the end of September,[2] where by mid-October they and their U.S. counterparts had arrived at an integrated solution to trade problems.

The interrelationship of the issues of trade is clearly illustrated in the documents. Soviet repayment of its lend-lease debt (Document 18) is clearly conditioned upon the U.S. government's granting the USSR most-favored-nation status. The maritime agreement (Document 15) provided solutions created by the grains agreement of July 8 (Document 10) and was dated to enter into force retroactively to July 1, 1972, for that reason. Disagreement about shipping rates and the portion of the total of grain that would be shipped in vessels of the respective countries had already delayed agreement on the grains sale until July 8. Other aspects of the agreement had been resolved even before Nixon went to Moscow in May.[3]

Attempting to utilize the trade agreements of mid-October to achieve the objectives of the third step of his three-step policy toward the Soviets, President Nixon wrote into Title IV of the Trade Reform Bill of 1973 a section that would have Congress authorize the president to extend most-favored-nation status to any country when the president felt that action to be in the national interest. In his message to Congress transmitting the Trade Reform Bill, on April 10, he stated specifically that he would use that new authority to grant the Soviet Union most-favored-nation (MFN) status. "This new authority," he wrote, "would enable us to carry out the trade agreement we have negotiated with the Soviet Union and thereby ensure that country's repayment of its lend-lease debt."[4] U.S.-Soviet negotiations over trade had, therefore, entered a new stage in April 1973. The major activity had been completed in the executive branch of government and rested entirely in the legislative branch in the United States. The executive branch could only cajole, placate, and otherwise try to convince the Congress to accept what the executive branch considered the best solution available to problems restraining U.S.-Soviet trade.

The two sides also made attempts to achieve the third objective set at Moscow in May 1972: negotiation of a permanent arrangement for limiting offensive weapons that would be ready for signing at the Washington summit in June 1973. Documents 21 and 25, as well as other documents listed in the Appendix, mark the creation of a mechanism for conducting the negotiations. But one year proved to be an inadequate period to achieve the final agreement.

NOTES

1. DSB 9-11-1972, 286–88.
2. DSB 10-9-1972, 389–91.
3. DSB 6-26-1972, 887.
4. DSB 4-30-1973, 518–19.

10 (July 8, 1972)

AGREEMENT BETWEEN THE GOVERNMENT OF THE UNITED STATES OF AMERICA AND THE GOVERNMENT OF THE UNION OF SOVIET SOCIALIST REPUBLICS WITH RESPECT TO PURCHASES OF GRAINS BY THE SOVIET UNION IN THE UNITED STATES AND CREDIT TO BE MADE AVAILABLE BY THE UNITED STATES

The Government of the United States of America (USA) and the Government of the Union of Soviet Socialist Republics (USSR) have agreed as follows:

Article 1

1. The Government of the USA through its Commodity Credit Corporation's Export Credit Sales Program hereby makes available a total amount of US $750 million credit for financing the payment for USA grown grains (at buyer's option—wheat, corn, barley, sorghum, rye, oats) purchased by the USSR in the USA under this Agreement. Such total amount may be increased by the USA.

2. The USSR through its foreign trade organizations shall purchase from private United States exporters not less than US $750 million port value of such grains (at buyer's option—wheat, corn, barley, sorghum, rye, oats) for delivery during the three-year period August 1, 1972, through July 31, 1975, and of such amount not less than US $200 million shall be purchased for delivery prior to August 1, 1973. In case of purchases of such grains for cash for delivery during the period of August 1, 1972, through July 31, 1975, the U.S. dollar amount of such purchases shall be counted as if they were made on credit terms under this Agreement.

3. The following provisions shall apply with respect to the credit referred to in Section I of this Article 1.

3.1 It shall continue to be available, if not previously exhausted, for deliveries made not later than July 31, 1975.

3.2 The total amount of credit outstanding at one time shall not exceed US $500 million.

3.3 Delivery for purchases shall be F.A.S. or F.O.B. port of export and interest shall run from date of delivery. The date of delivery shall be the on-board date of the ocean bill of lading.

3.4 The principal and interest for credit arising under each delivery shall be payable by the USSR as follows: one-third of the principal annually, plus accrued interest on the outstanding principal balance to the date of each principal payment.

3.5 The amount of credit for each delivery will be limited to the United States port value of the commodity, without ocean freight, insurance, or other charges or costs.

3.6 The interest rate for purchases under this Agreement for which delivery is made not later than March 31, 1973, shall be 6-1/8% per annum on that portion of the obligation confirmed by a USA bank. This rate of interest for that portion of the obligation confirmed by a USA bank shall be applicable during the whole three-year period for repayment of the credit which arises under each delivery made not later than March 31, 1973.

Article 2

This Agreement shall enter into force from the day of its signing and shall remain valid until all the obligations arising from it for both sides are fulfilled.

IN WITNESS WHEREOF, the undersigned, duly authorized thereto, have signed this Agreement.

DONE at Washington this 8th day of July 1972 in duplicate, in the English and Russian languages, each text equally authentic.

For the Government of
the United States of America:
Peter G. Peterson
Earl L. Butz
For the Government of
the Union of Soviet Socialist Republics:
M. Kuzmin

WASHINGTON, D.C., *July 8, 1972*

DEAR MR. FIRST DEPUTY MINISTER:

In connection with signing today of the Agreement between the Government of the United States of America and the Government of the Union of Soviet Socialist Republics with respect to purchases of Grains by the Soviet Union in the United States and Credit to be made available by the United States, we have the honor to confirm the understanding on interpretation reached between us that:

1. As to matters not covered in the above Agreement, the credits for grain purchases under the Export Credit Sales Program shall be governed by the "Regulations Covering Export Financing of Sales of Agricultural Commodities under the Commodity Credit Corporation Export Credit Sales Program (GSM-4)" effective in the USA on the day of signing this Agreement.

2. Grains purchased under the above Agreement shall be consumed primarily in the USSR. However the USSR shall have the right to divert some portion of the grain for consumption in European countries presently full members of the Council for Mutual Economic Assistance.

Please accept, Mr. First Deputy Minister, the assurances of our highest consideration.

PETER G. PETERSON
Peter G. Peterson

EARL L. BUTZ
Earl L. Butz

*Heads of the USA Government
Delegation*

The Honorable M. R. KUZMIN
*Head of the USSR Government Delegation
Washington, D.C.*

Translation

MINISTRY OF FOREIGN TRADE
U.S.S.R.

WASHINGTON, *July 8, 1972*

DEAR SIRS,

In connection with the signing today of the Agreement between the Government of the Union of Soviet Socialist Republics and the Government of the United States of America with respect to purchases of grains by the Soviet Union in the United States and credit to be made available by the United States, I have the honor to confirm the understanding on interpretation reached between us that:

1. As to matters not covered in the above Agreement, the credits for grain purchases under the Export Credit Sales Program will be governed by the "Regulations Covering Export Financing of Sales of Agricultural Commodities under the Commodity Credit Corporation Export Credit Sales Program (GSM–4)" effective in the USA on the day of signing this Agreement.

2. Grains purchased under the above Agreement will be consumed primarily in the USSR. However, the USSR will have the right to divert some portion of the grain for consumption in European countries presently full members of the Council for Mutual Economic Assistance.

Accept, Sirs, the assurances of my highest consideration.

M. Kuzmin

Head of the USSR Government Delegation

M. KUZMIN

The Honorable PETER G. PETERSON
The Honorable EARL L. BUTZ
   Heads of the U.S. Government Delegation
   Washington, D.C.

U.S.-U.S.S.R. Commission on Scientific and Technical Cooperation

Following is an announcement issued by the Office of Science and Technology (OST), Executive Office of the President, on July 28, together with the text of the record of discussions between U.S. and U.S.S.R. delegations drafted at Moscow July 7 and signed at Washington and Moscow July 28.

TEXT OF ANNOUNCEMENT

Office of Science and Technology press release dated July 28

American and Soviet officials outlined on July 28 six scientific and technological areas in which their nations will try to cooperate jointly in an attempt to solve common problems.

They are energy, agriculture, chemistry, water resources, microbiology, and computer usage. All will be taken up by the U.S. U.S.S.R. Joint Commission on Scientific and Technical Cooperation which was called for in the Agreement on Cooperation in the Fields of Science and Technology signed during President Nixon's Moscow summit, May 24. The Commission will hold its first meeting in Washington in the latter part of October.

The science and technology agreement marks the first time the two nations have developed an intergovernmental mechanism by which they can jointly conduct a broad range of scientific and technological efforts directed toward common goals.

A document establishing the framework for the new U.S.-U.S.S.R. Joint Commission was signed July 28. The document was a "Record of Discussions" held between U.S. and Soviet delegations in Moscow July 2–8.

In addition to setting the framework for the Joint Commission, the discussions also opened the door to possible Soviet participation in the U.S.-sponsored deep sea drilling program, a vastly successful effort to study the makeup of the earth's crust by boring into the bottoms of the world's oceans.

Dr. Edward E. David, Jr., President Nixon's Science Adviser and the leader of the eight-man delegation which worked out the details in Moscow earlier in July, signed for the United States. The ceremony took place at the White House. V. A. Kirillin, Deputy Chairman of the U.S.S.R. Council of Ministers and Dr. David's Soviet counterpart as Chairman of the State Committee for Science and Technology (SCST), signed a similar document in Moscow with U.S. Ambassador Jacob D. Beam in attendance.

Until now, interactions between American and Soviet scientists and technologists were conducted under exchange agreements dating back to 1958. Primarily, these have been exchanges of individuals or delegations.

"The new agreement does not supersede the current Exchanges Agreement," Dr. David said. "In fact, it broadens the existing arrangements as well as making possible new direct contacts between scientists, agencies within each government, and between American industrial firms and Soviet state enterprises." He emphasized that the Commission will approve and monitor the present areas proposed for cooperation and consider new possibilities. In all cases, he pointed out, the cooperation "will be on the basis of mutual benefit, equality, and reciprocity."

The Science and Technology Agreement and the Commission are designed to "combine the efforts of . . . scientists and specialists" involved in major problems. It is expected that solutions reached jointly will be achieved sooner and less expensively than if each nation attacked its problems alone.

Working groups in all six areas have already been established on both sides. Each group will develop specific proposals for cooperative work for consideration at the Commission's first meeting.

Areas being considered in the energy field include magnetohydrodynamics, fusion (thermonuclear), atomic, solar, geothermal, and other forms of power generation, as well as power transmission and increased generation efficiency.

Agricultural research efforts will be drawn from a list of proposals already exchanged.

Efforts in computer applications will be directed toward the use of computers and cybernetic techniques for management purposes.

Water resources are of interest to both governments because of common concerns in irrigation, recycling, flood control, ground water levels, and other areas.

In microbiology, the production of protein through microbial techniques will be looked at as a source of food for both human and animal consumption, along with the possible synthesis of other substances.

The Commission's initial ventures into chemistry will be in the field of chemical catalysis in both basic and applied research.

The governmental executive agencies responsible for the Commission are Dr. David's Office of Science and Technology and Minister Kirillin's State Committee for Science and Technology.

Another outcome of the negotiations in Moscow will be a joint symposium on scientific and technical information.

Named Joint Commission members on the American side were: Dr. David, Chairman; Dr. James B. Fisk, president of the Bell Telephone Laboratories; Dean Harvey Brooks, National Academy of Sciences and Harvard University; Dr. H. Guyford Stever, Director of the National Science Foundation; and Herman Pollack, Director of the State Department's Bureau of International Scientific and Technological Affairs.

Drs. David and Fisk were members of the U.S. delegation which went to Moscow July 2–8, along with Dr. Eugene Fubini of the E. G. Fubini Consultants, Ltd., of Arlington, Va., and Dr. John V. N. Granger of the State Department.

The Soviet side was represented during the July negotiations by Minister Kirillin; M. D. Millionshchikov, Vice President of the U.S.S.R. Academy of Sciences; V. A. Trapeznikov, First Deputy Chairman of the SCST; and S. M. Tikhomirov, Deputy Chairman of the SCST.

Minister Kirillin, Drs. Trapeznikov and Millionshchikov, First Deputy Minister of Higher and Secondary Specialized Education N. F. Krasnov, and D. N. Pronskiy, Director of the SCST Department of Foreign Relations, were named as the Soviet members of the Joint Commission.

TEXT OF RECORD OF DISCUSSIONS

RECORD OF DISCUSSIONS

between Dr. Edward E. David, Jr., Science Adviser to the President of the United States of America and Director of the Office of Science and Technology in the Executive Office of the President, and Academician V. A. Kirillin, Deputy Chairman of the U.S.S.R. Council of Ministers and Chairman of the State Committee of the U.S.S.R. Council of Ministers for Science and Technology (July 2–July 8, 1972).

Discussions were held between Dr. David and Academician Kirillin concerning implementation of the Agreement Between the Government of the United States of America and the Government of the Union of Soviet Socialist Republics on Cooperation in the Fields of Science and Technology, signed on May 24, 1972, at the Moscow Summit meeting.

Also taking part in the discussions were, from the U.S. side, Dr. James B. Fisk, President of Bell Telephone Laboratories; Dr. Eugene G. Fubini, President of Fubini Consultants, Ltd.; Dr. John V. N. Granger, Deputy Director, Bureau of International Scientific and Technological Affairs, Department of State; and other staff members of the Office of Science and Technology and of the Department of State.

From the Soviet side participants included Academician M. D. Millionshchikov, Vice President of the U.S.S.R. Academy of Sciences; Academician V. A. Trapeznikov, First Deputy Chairman of the State Committee of the U.S.S.R. Council of Ministers for Science and Technology; Dr. S. M. Tikhomirov, Deputy Chairman of the State Committee of the U.S.S.R. Council of Ministers for Science and Technology; and other staff members of the State Committee and the Ministry of Foreign Affairs of the U.S.S.R.

The two sides noted with satisfaction that the Agreement of May 24, 1972, provides a good basis for the long-term development and expansion of scientific and technological cooperation between the two countries. For the purpose of implementing this Agreement, they considered a number of questions concerning the structure and organization of the U.S.-U.S.S.R. Joint Commission, to be created in accordance with Article 7 of the Agreement, as well as possible areas and forms of cooperation.

The two sides reaffirmed the objectives of their

proposed scientific and technical cooperation, as set forth in the Agreement. These are to assist and develop scientific and technical cooperation between both countries on the basis of mutual benefit, equality and reciprocity, and to provide broad opportunities for both sides to combine the efforts of their scientists and specialists in working on major problems, whose solution will promote the progress of science and technology for the benefit of both countries and of mankind.

Recognizing that the achievement of common goals in the development of science and technology depends on a close working relationship between scientists and specialists, the two sides will encourage and facilitate the development of direct contacts between qualified individuals and organizations of the two countries.

The two sides discussed procedural questions concerning the work of the Joint Commission, the first meeting of which will be held in Washington, D.C., in October, 1972.

The two sides also discussed a number of specific areas of common interest which show promise for direct cooperation. U.S.-U.S.S.R. ad hoc working groups will be established as soon as possible in the following areas:

(1) Energy Research and Development, including:
    (a) magnetohydrodynamics;
    (b) fusion;
    (c) atomic energy and nuclear reactors;
    (d) solar energy;
    (e) geothermal energy;
    (f) energy transmission;
    (g) utilization of waste heat; and
    (h) increasing the efficiency of thermal power stations.
    (Working groups in the energy area will be convened only for topics not covered by the Memorandum on Cooperation Between the U.S. Atomic Energy Commission and the U.S.S.R. State Committee for the Utilization of Atomic Energy, to be renewed in July, 1972.)

(2) Application of Computers in Management;
(3) Agricultural Research;
(4) Production of substances employing microbiological means;
(5) Water Resources;
(6) Research in the Field of Chemical Catalysis.

These working groups will develop specific proposals for cooperative programs. Their reports and recommendations will be submitted to the Executive Agents in each country no later than two weeks before the date of the first meeting of the Commission for its consideration. Working groups in additional areas may be established by the Commission at its meetings or by agreement between the Executive Agents on both sides, in the period between meetings of the Commission.

The Commission will monitor the progress of joint programs established under the Agreement to assure that obstacles which may arise are promptly and effectively dealt with.

Following an exchange of views between Dr. David and Academician M. V. Keldysh, President of the U.S.S.R. Academy of Sciences, on cooperation in oceanological research, it was decided that the U.S. National Science Foundation and the U.S.S.R. Academy of Sciences would designate representatives to meet in the near future to discuss possible Soviet technical and financial participation in the program of deep ocean drilling to be carried out with the U.S. research vessel D/V GLOMAR CHALLENGER operated by Scripps Institute of Oceanography.

Desiring to achieve cooperation in the area of scientific and technical information, the two sides decided as a first step to convene in the near future a symposium on this subject between the National Science Foundation and the All-Union Scientific Research Institute for Scientific and Technical Information.

The two sides emphasized their desire to realize as quickly as possible tangible results under the Agreement. In this connection, they will render assistance in establishing closer and more regular contacts between individual scientists and specialists, and also research institutions and technical organizations of the two countries.

The subjects discussed in the course of this meeting will be reviewed by the Joint Commission in its first meeting.

EDWARD E. DAVID, JR.
Director,
Office of Science
and Technology, Executive
Office of the President,
United States of America

V. A. KIRILLIN
Chairman,
State Committee of the
U.S.S.R. Council of
Ministers for Science
and Technology

MOSCOW, July 7, 1972.

12 (August 1, 1972)

Agreement on the Establishment of the
Joint U.S.-U.S.S.R. Commercial Commission

TERMS OF REFERENCE AND RULES OF PROCEDURE

of the Joint US-USSR Commercial Commission

1. The Joint US-USSR Commercial Commission,
established by the President of the United States of
America and the Soviet leaders during their meetings in
Moscow in May, 1972, is to promote the development of
mutually beneficial commercial relations and related
economic matters, and to work out specific arrangements,
between the United States of America and the Union of
Soviet Socialist Republics.

2. The Commission is to negotiate:

-- an overall trade agreement including
reciprocal MFN treatment;

-- arrangements for the reciprocal availability of government credits;

-- provisions for the reciprocal establishment of business facilities to
promote trade;

-- an agreement establishing an arbitration
mechanism for settling commercial
disputes.

3. In addition, the Commission is to:

-- study possible US-USSR participation in
the development of natural resources and

the manufacture and sale of raw materials
and other products;

-- monitor the spectrum of US-USSR commercial and economic relations, identifying and, when possible, resolving
issues that may be of interest to both
Parties.

4. The Commission consists of an American
Section and a Soviet Section. The Parties shall
advise each other in advance of the persons designated
by them to participate at any meeting of the Commission.

5. The Commission shall hold meetings as
mutually agreed by the Parties, but not less than once
a year, alternately in Washington and Moscow. The
Chairman of the Section of the host country shall
preside over meetings of the Commission. Each Section
may invite advisers and experts to participate at any
meeting of the Commission.

6. The Parties shall, not later than one month
prior to any meeting of the Commission, agree on an
agenda for the meeting. The meeting shall consider
matters included in this agenda, as well as further
matters which may be added to the agenda by mutual agreement.

7. In order to fulfill its tasks the Commission
may establish Joint Working Groups to consider specific
matters. The Commission shall determine the assignments
of such Joint Working Groups, which shall conduct their
work in accordance with the instructions of the Commission.

8. The Commission shall work on the basis of
the principle of mutual agreement. On matters as to
which either Party advises that further approval of
its Government is required, such Party shall inform
the other Party when such approval has been obtained.

9. Any document mutually agreed upon during the work of the Commission shall be in the English and Russian languages, each language being equally authentic.

10. Each Section shall have an Executive Secretary who shall arrange the work of the respective Section of the Commission, coordinate the activities of the Joint Working Groups and perform other tasks of an organizational and administrative nature connected with the meetings of the Commission. The Executive Secretaries shall communicate with each other as necessary to perform their functions.

11. Expenses incidental to the meetings of the Commission and any Joint Working Group established by the Commission shall be borne by the host country. Travel expenses from one country to the other, as well as the living and other personal expenses, of its representatives participating in the meetings of the Commission and any Joint Working Group established by the Commission shall be borne by the Party which sends such persons to represent it at such meetings.

Moscow, August 1972

Peter G. Peterson
Chairman, American Section
Joint US-USSR Commercial
Commission

Nikolai S. Patolichev
Chairman, Soviet Section
Joint US-USSR Commercial
Commission

13 (September 21, 1972)
U.S. and U.S.S.R. Sign Memorandum of Implementation of Environmental Agreement

Press release 236 dated September 23

Following is the text of the memorandum of implementation signed at Moscow September 21 by Russell E. Train, Chairman of the U.S. Council on Environmental Quality, and E. K. Fedorov, Director of the Soviet Hydrometeorological Service.[1]

MEMORANDUM OF IMPLEMENTATION OF THE AGREEMENT BETWEEN THE UNITED STATES OF AMERICA AND THE UNION OF SOVIET SOCIALIST REPUBLICS ON COOPERATION IN THE FIELD OF ENVIRONMENTAL PROTECTION OF MAY 23, 1972

The first meeting of the U.S.-Soviet Joint Committee on Cooperation in the Field of Environmental Protection was held in Moscow September 18 to 21, 1972. The Joint Committee was established by the Agreement on Cooperation in the Field of Environmental Protection, signed in Moscow by the President of the United States Richard Nixon and Chairman of the Presidium of the Supreme Soviet N.V. Podgorny on May 23, 1972.[2] As provided for in the Agreement, the Joint Committee approved concrete measures and programs of cooperation, and designated the participating organizations responsible for the realization of the programs.

Agreement was reached upon specific projects in the eleven subject areas named in the Agreement. Work will begin on a number of high priority projects during 1972-1973. For each project, responsible organizations were named by each side, although it was understood that other organizations from each side may participate in agreed projects, in many cases by working groups established in the specific area. It was agreed that the respective coordinators would verify the initiation of the agreed projects and remain in communication regarding the development of the program as a whole.

Agreement was reached upon the following initial projects:

I. AIR POLLUTION

1. Air Pollution Modeling

The metropolitan areas of St. Louis and Lenin-grad were designated as subjects for air pollution investigations. The methods used in the USSR and the U.S. to compute dispersal of pollutants from single and multiple sources, emission limitations and forecasts of hazardous conditions of air pollution will be compared and improved with special attention to meteorological techniques and topographic factors.

2. Instrumentation and Methodology for Monitoring Major Air Pollutants

The instruments and methods used in the USSR and the U.S. for measurement, data collection and processing, and analysis are to be compared and improved.

3. Technology for Preventing Air Pollution from Industrial Enterprises

The two sides will exchange information and explore opportunities for joint research on technology for controlling pollutants, with initial work to be done on major stationary sources such as power plants. Special emphasis will be placed on the control of sulphur oxides and particulates.

4. Emissions from Transportation Sources

The two sides will explore possibilities for cooperation in reducing emissions from transportation sources, including the improvement of engine design.

Two working groups will be appointed. The first, for modeling and instrumentation, will concern itself with Projects 1 and 2 and will meet in St. Louis, Missouri, and other cities in the United States before the end of 1972. The lead agency for the U.S. is the Environmental Protection Agency, and for the USSR the Hydrometeorological Service. The second working group, for control techniques, will concern itself with Projects 3 and 4 and will meet in the USSR at the beginning of 1973. The lead agency for the U.S. is the Environmental Protection Agency and for the USSR the All-Union Association of Gas Purification and Dust Cleaning.

---

[1] For names of other members of the U.S. and Soviet delegations, see press release 236.

[2] For text of the agreement, see BULLETIN of June 26, 1972, p. 921.

II. Water Pollution

1. Studies and Modeling of River Basin Pollution

Specific river basins in each country will be selected for a joint project on water pollution river basin modeling techniques. The Delaware and other river basin models will be examined in the United States. Rivers in the Soviet Union will be designated later. Soviet specialists will visit the U.S. in early 1973.

2. Protection and Management of Lakes and Estuaries

Both sides will designate lakes and estuaries in their country for joint projects on water pollution, including eutrophication. A Soviet Union lake will be Baikal; U.S. lakes to be considered include Lake Tahoe and one of the Great Lakes. U.S. specialists will visit the Soviet Union in the summer of 1973.

3. Effects of Pollutants upon Aquatic Ecological Systems and Permissible Levels of Pollution

Experts from both sides will exchange information and visits concerning research on the effects of pollutants on water systems and the development of water quality standards.

4. Prevention or Treatment of Discharges

The two sides will exchange visits and information on specific water pollution abatement techniques, including land disposal of both untreated municipal sewage and sludge from municipal treatment systems; reduction of pollution from industrial plants, such as manufacturers of pulp and paper; and reinjection of water from oil extraction activities, including disposal of liquid wastes in permafrost conditions in arctic and subarctic regions (collection, storage, treatment and final disposal). Visits will be made to arctic sites in both countries.

A single working group will be appointed. This group will meet in the USSR in the first quarter of 1973. There will be an exchange of visits of specialists to appropriate sites in both countries including arctic and subarctic areas. The lead agency for the U.S. is the Environmental Protection Agency and for the USSR the Hydrometeorological Service and the Ministry of Amelioration and Water Management.

III. Pollution Related to Agricultural Production

1. Integrated Pest Management

The two sides will exchange visits and information relating to programs of integrated pest management. Such programs include the use of nonchemical methods such as pest predators and pathogens, along with the limited use of pesticides. Both sides agreed to develop common programs, including the exchange of useful biological agents such as parasites and predators and plant species resistant to pests.

2. Pollution Caused by Feedlots

The two sides will exchange information and visits on management of wastes from large feedlots.

3. Wind Erosion and Desiccation

Both sides will exchange information and visits on research and management practices on control of wind erosion and desiccation.

4. Effects of Pollutants on Forests and Plants

Both sides will exchange visits and information on the effects of air pollutants on forest and crop plants.

A single working group will be appointed. This group will meet in the U.S. in early 1973. Initial emphasis will be on integrated pest management and pollution caused by feedlots. A conference on integrated pest management will take place in the USSR during 1973. The lead agency for the U.S. is the Department of Agriculture and for the USSR the Ministry of Agriculture.

IV. Enhancement of Urban Environment

1. Urban Environment

Both sides will designate two metropolitan areas in its country, with others added as appropriate, to serve as a means to examine jointly methods for planning and assuring a desirable environment in urban areas, with attention to planning for appropriate land use, transportation, noise abatement, solid waste management, water purification, recreation and park development, tourist zones and resorts, preservation of historic sites, etc.

The U.S. side has designated the Atlanta and San Francisco areas and the Soviet side has designated Leningrad for the initial exchange, and will designate a second city later.

2. New Communities

Both sides will designate new communities in each country as a means of examining the environmental, physical, social, economic and other factors considered in the design and development of satellite and free standing new communities. Among those communities to be designated are Columbia, Maryland and Reston, Virginia in the United States and Togliatti and Akademgorodok in the Soviet Union.

3. Impact of Construction and Disposal of Wastes in Permafrost Areas

The two sides will exchange visits and information on methods of construction in permafrost, the impact of construction on the environment in such areas and on the collection, storage and disposal of wastes in these areas.

A single working group will be appointed. This group will meet in the U.S. in November 1972, followed by a spring or summer 1973 meeting in the

USSR. The lead agency for the U.S. is the Department of Housing and Urban Development and for the USSR the State Committee on Urban Construction and Architecture and, for noise abatement, the Ministry of the Automobile Industry.

V. NATURE AND PRESERVES

1. *Conservation of Rare and Endangered Species of Animals and Plants, and General Wildlife Conservation and Management*

Both sides will exchange visits and information and develop joint research for the purpose of improving understanding and protection of endangered species of plants and animals. A Soviet-American convention on conservation of rare species migrating between the USSR and U.S. will be prepared, and both sides agreed on the importance and desirability of concluding, as soon as possible, international agreements on conservation of wildlife in need of special protection, for example polar bears and other animals. Joint projects will also include research on preservation and management of various marine and other mammals, specifically polar bears and whales of the North Pacific, involving the bowhead, gray and fin whales. They will also carry out projects on management of free-ranging wildlife for animal production, and research on and management of predators and waterfowl, including swans and other migratory birds.

A working group will be appointed that will meet initially in Moscow in December 1972. As necessary, appropriate subgroups will be organized (for example, for whales). The lead agencies for the U.S. are the Department of the Interior and the National Oceanic and Atmospheric Administration of the Department of Commerce, and for the USSR the Soviet Academy of Sciences and the Ministry of Agriculture. Some of the indicated projects, such as these for the bowhead whale and migrating swans, may be initiated prior to the working group meetings.

2. *Tundra Ecosystems and Permafrost*

The two sides will exchange visits and information on permafrost regions and tundra ecosystems, including research on stabilization of disturbed areas and other ecological research. Visits will be made by U.S. and Soviet specialists to appropriate institutes and places in each country.

3. *Reserved Areas*

Each side will exchange information and visits and develop appropriate research projects on preserves, their classification, organization and maintenance, on arid land ecology, and on parks, including a joint project involving the Yellowstone National Park (U.S.) and the Caucasian State Preserve (USSR).

A meeting of specialists in the U.S. early in 1973 will concern itself with Projects 2 and 3. The lead

agency for the U.S. is the Department of the Interior and for the USSR the Ministry of Agriculture.

VI. MARINE POLLUTION

1. *Prevention and Clean-up of Oil Pollution in the Marine Environment*

The two sides agreed to exchange visits and information on technologies and techniques for the prevention and clean-up of oil discharges in the marine environment, including such areas as vessel design, traffic control, shore facilities and offshore oil drilling safeguards. The two sides also agreed to exchange visits and information on pipeline transport, particularly through permafrost areas.

2. *Effect of Pollutants on Marine Organisms*

The two sides will exchange visits and information on research on the chemical aspects of marine pollution and the effects of pollutants on marine organisms, including chemical and biological analyses of fish, monitoring of rare species, exchange of specimens, and rehabilitation of sea life after major pollution incidents.

A working group will be appointed to deal with the first project. It will meet in the U.S. in early 1973 with a visit of specialists to the USSR in the summer of 1973. The lead agencies for the U.S. are the Department of Transportation and the Department of the Interior and for the USSR the Ministry of Merchant Marine. A first-quarter of 1973 meeting of specialists will be held in the U.S. to discuss the second project. The lead agencies for the U.S. are the Environmental Protection Agency and the National Oceanic and Atmospheric Administration of the Department of Commerce and for the USSR the Hydrometeorological Service.

VII. BIOLOGICAL AND GENETIC CONSEQUENCES

1. *Comprehensive Analysis of the Environment*

Both sides agree to hold a symposium in the USSR in the fall of 1973 to examine scientific methods of setting standards or limits on pollution discharges into the environment from separate sources and from large territories. The symposium would focus attention on the effect of man's activity on all organisms and the biosphere as a whole to provide guidance for protection of the environment and wise use of natural resources. The two sides will communicate with each other on the design of the conference, as necessary. The lead agency for the U.S. is the Environmental Protection Agency and for the USSR the Hydrometeorological Service.

2. *Biological and Genetic Effects of Pollutants*

Both sides will exchange visits and information and conduct joint research on the health effects of mutagenic compounds, radioactivity, and heavy metals; study extrapolation of animal toxicological tests to man; and exchange visits and information on epidemiological studies. Both sides will exchange information and compare technical bases for establishing air quality standards. Specialists will meet in the U.S. during the first quarter of 1973. The lead agencies for the U.S. are the Department of Health, Education, and Welfare and the Environmental Protection Agency, and for the USSR the Ministry of Health and the Academy of Sciences.

VIII. INFLUENCE OF ENVIRONMENTAL CHANGES ON CLIMATE

1. *Effect of Changing Levels of Atmospheric Constituents on Climate*

The two sides will exchange information and participate in joint studies of the influence on climate of gaseous and particulate contaminants.

2. *Monitoring Atmospheric Constituents That Might Modify Climate*

The two sides will take steps to insure the comparability of data from their respective climate monitoring stations and cooperate in the analysis and interpretation of such data.

3. *Climate Modeling*

The two sides will exchange information and cooperate in the development and application of mathematical modeling to assess the consequences of atmospheric contamination on climate.

4. *Cooperation in Polar Research*

The two sides will explore possibilities of integrating such scientific programs as the U.S. Arctic Ice Dynamics Joint Experiment and the Soviet Polar Interaction Experiment so as to extend the fields of observation and permit more comprehensive analysis and modeling.

5. *Effects of Contamination of the Upper Atmosphere on Climate*

The two sides will exchange information and explore opportunities for cooperation in the study of the effects of perturbation of the upper atmosphere by propulsion effluents from high altitude aircraft.

A single working group will be established. It will meet in the U.S. late in 1972. A symposium will be held in the USSR in 1973. The lead agency for the U.S. is the National Oceanic and Atmospheric Administration of the Department of Commerce and for the USSR the Hydrometeorological Service.

IX. EARTHQUAKE PREDICTION

1. *Earthquake Prediction*

The San Andreas Fault area in the U.S. and the Garm-Dushanbe Region in the USSR were desig-
nated as subjects for the installation of jointly operated earthquake measurement instruments and detection equipment. Both sides will exchange visits and information with regard to earthquake prediction research, seismic risk mapping, seismicity and earthquake resistant design.

2. *Integration of U.S.-USSR Tsunami (Earthquake-Produced Tidal Waves) Warning Systems*

Both sides will exchange visits and information and will consider the possibility of the integration of the Tsunami warning systems currently being operated by the U.S. in the Hawaii area and by the USSR in the Kurile-Kamchatka area. The two systems will be integrated to provide an exchange of data produced from each one and to improve the operation of both systems.

One working group will be established. It will meet on the subject of Earthquake Prediction in the United States in early 1973 and later in 1973 in the USSR. The lead agencies for the United States will be the Department of the Interior for Earthquake Prediction Activities and the National Oceanic and Atmospheric Administration of the Department of Commerce for Integration of the Tsunami Warning Systems, and for the USSR the Academy of Sciences of the USSR.

X. ARCTIC AND SUBARCTIC ECOLOGICAL SYSTEMS

The two sides agreed to undertake a cooperative program involving arctic and subarctic areas. The specific projects agreed to will be undertaken under other areas of the agreement as follows:

1. *Prevention or Treatment of Discharges*

This project is covered under Water Pollution.

2. *Impact of Construction and Disposal of Wastes in Permafrost Environmental Areas*

This project is covered under the Urban Environment.

3. *Permafrost and Arctic Ecosystems*

This project is covered under Nature and Preserves.

4. *Prevention and Clean-up of Oil Pollution*

This project is covered under Marine Pollution.

XI. LEGAL AND ADMINISTRATIVE

Exchange of Information and Experience Regarding Legal and Administrative Measures for Protecting Environmental Quality

The two sides will exchange information and hold conferences on legal and administrative measures for protecting environmental quality, dealing with questions of government organization, procedures to analyze environmental effects of government decisions, economic aspects of pollution and enforcement techniques among others. Specialists from both countries will hold a meeting in the United States early in 1973. The lead agency for the U.S. is the Council on Environmental Quality and for the USSR the Academy of Sciences.

Both sides agreed that the present memorandum would enter into force as of thirty days from the date of signature, and that in the interim each side might propose changes of a minor character.

Both sides agreed that the next meeting of the Joint Committee would be held in Washington in 1973. At that meeting the progress of the program will be reviewed and plans made for further cooperation. The Chairman and coordinators will meet as necessary between sessions.

Signed in English and in Russian, both copies equally authentic, in Moscow, September 21, 1972.

RUSSELL E. TRAIN   E. K. FEDOROV

Chairman for the   *Chairman for the*
United States   *Soviet Union*

The U.S.-U.S.S.R. Agreement Regarding Certain Maritime Matters was signed at Washington October 14. Following are a White House fact sheet issued that day and the texts of the agreement, with annexes, and related U.S. letters.

WHITE HOUSE FACT SHEET

White House press release dated October 14

A major maritime agreement with the Soviet Union was signed on October 14 by U.S. Secretary of Commerce Peter G. Peterson and the Minister of Merchant Marine of the Union of Soviet Socialist Republics Timofey B. Guzhenko. This agreement represents another necessary link in the establishment of an expanding commercial relationship with the Soviet Union.

The negotiations which culminated in this agreement were initiated in the latter part of 1971 and have been the subject of a series of meetings in Washington and Moscow throughout 1972.

By providing a broad framework and a clear set of ground rules for maritime activities between the two countries, this agreement is an important step toward normalizing and expanding maritime relationships between the United States and the Soviet Union.

Objectives

The agreement has two basic objectives: first, to open the channels of maritime commerce between the two nations by opening major U.S. and Soviet commercial ports to calls by specified kinds of U.S.-flag and Soviet-flag vessels; and secondly, to afford to U.S.-flag vessels and Soviet-flag vessels the opportunity to participate equally and substantially in the carriage of all cargoes moving by sea between the two nations.

Salient Points of the Agreement

Port Access. The agreement provides access to specified Soviet and U.S. ports to flag vessels of both countries engaged in commercial maritime shipping and merchant marine training activities. Under the agreement, 40 ports in each nation are open to access by vessels of the other nation upon four days' advance notice to the appropriate authorities. The selection of the ports was based on commercial considerations, reasonable reciprocity, and protection of national security interests. The U.S. ports open to access by Soviet vessels on this basis are listed in annex I of the agreement.

While the four-day notice requirement is more than the normal 24-hour notice period applicable to commercial vessels, it is substantially less restrictive than the 14-day advance request requirement now applied by each government to ships bearing the other's flag. Entry of vessels to ports not specified in the agreement will continue to be permitted in accordance with existing rules and regulations; i.e., the 14-day prior request provisions will still apply. Requests for entry by Soviet vessels to U.S. ports not specified in the agreement must be made of the Department of State, Washington, D.C., and must be accompanied by an itinerary complete with ports of call and dates. Maritime training vessels and hydrographic and other research vessels may enter the ports only for purposes of resupply, rest, crew changes, minor repairs, and other services normally provided in such ports.

The agreement does not involve any concessions in the policy of the United States with respect to ships which have called on Cuban, North Vietnamese, or North Korean ports. Soviet vessels which have called or will call on Cuba, North Viet-Nam, or North Korea will not be permitted to bunker in U.S. ports, and Soviet vessels which have called on Cuba or North Viet-Nam will not be permitted to load or unload in U.S. ports government-financed cargoes such as grains sold on Commodity Credit Corporation credit terms.

In addition, the agreement contemplates the access of initially 81 U.S. and 50 Soviet vessels engaged in hydrographic, oceanographic, meteorological, or terrestrial magnetic-field research of a civilian nature. The agreement does not include vessels engaged in fishing or related activities, since these matters are covered by separate agreements; nor does it include warships or vessels carrying out state functions other than those mentioned above. It is not intended to cover any liquefied natural gas trade which may develop between the nations.

Tonnage Duties. Under the agreement, neither nation shall charge vessels of the other tonnage duties which exceed duties charged to vessels of other nations in like situations.

Equal and Substantial Sharing. The agreement sets forth the intention of both governments that the national-flag vessels of each country will each carry equal and substantial shares of the oceanborne commerce between the two nations. At the same time, the agreement recognizes the policy of both the United States and the Soviet Union with respect to participation in its trade by third-flag vessels.

The intention that a substantial share of the trade between the two nations will be carried by each national-flag merchant marine is defined as meaning that the national-flag vessels of each nation will have the opportunity to carry not less than one-third of all cargoes moving in whole or in part by sea between the two nations, whether by direct movement or by transshipment through third countries. In the case of grain shipments, the one-third requirement is to be applied retroactively to all shipments since July 1, 1972.

Equal share of the trade between the two nations is measured on the basis of U.S.-dollar freight value of cargo carryings by the national-flag vessels of each party during each calendar year accounting period. Special accounting procedures are established to determine on a uniform basis the U.S.-dollar freight value of cargo carryings and to protect against the possibility of disparities caused by the undervaluing of freight rates to increase the volume of cargo carried. These procedures are also designed to permit continuous monitoring so as to maintain parity of carriage throughout the accounting period. Cargoes carried in liner vessels and bulk cargoes carried in nonliner service are accounted for separately under the agreement due to the difference in the methods of establishing freight rates.

The opportunity for carriage of equal and substantial shares of the trade between the two nations by national-flag ships is to be assured by the routing of controlled cargoes; i.e., cargoes with respect to which entities of either government have the power to designate the carriage. On the U.S. side, this includes only those cargoes which are subject to U.S. Government control under our cargo preference laws. On the Soviet side, all exports and imports for which entities of the U.S.S.R. have or could have the power at any time to designate the carrier are included.

Recognition has been given to the practical commercial consideration that vessels of either nation may not be available to carry the amount of cargo to which they are entitled under the principles of the agreement.

Under such circumstances, a limited variance from the equal and substantial sharing rules is provided. Such variance is permitted where the cargo was offered on reasonable terms and conditions and where the unavailability of national-flag carriers is certified by a representative of the U.S. Maritime Administration or U.S.S.R. Ministry of Merchant Marine, as the case may be. Even though unavailability has been certified by the appropriate representative, there is still an obligation to continue to offer controlled cargo to restore the one-third share if possible within the same calendar year.

Freight Rates. The matter of freight rates to be paid to U.S. vessels is an important provision of the agreement. With respect to liner service, U.S.-flag carriers should face no significant problems because U.S. vessels can participate in this trade under the conference-rate system with the assistance of the U.S. operating subsidy program. Rates for shipment of bulk cargo such as grain, however, present a different situation. Bulk cargo is shipped in world trade under charter rates which are set in competition with ships of nations with far lower costs than American ships. The United States has never before had a subsidy system which permits its vessels to compete in the bulk grain trade, although such a subsidy system was legislatively authorized in 1970. In lieu of a subsidy system for bulk cargo, there were regulations which required shipments of grain to the Soviet Union to move 50 percent in U.S.-flag vessels. This, however, never resulted in significant carriage for U.S. vessels. Freight rates are a substantial part of the cost of grain, and without subsidy the rates charged by U.S.-flag carriers increased the cost of grain beyond the level buyers were willing to pay.

Under the agreement, the two governments have worked out rate provisions for two categories of bulk cargo to be carried by U.S. vessels.

For nonagricultural bulk cargoes, the agreement in essence provides that American vessels shall be paid in each year the average of the freight rate for that category of cargo on the route in question over the prior three calendar years.

The other and far more important category of charter rates is for agricultural commodities and products. With respect to these cargoes, the Soviet Union will offer to U.S. vessels the *higher of*:

1. A rate computed on the three-year-average formula described above for the years 1969, 1970, and 1971. This rate for the route most expected to be used for the current grain sales is $8.05 per ton for wheat and other heavy grains; or

2. 110 percent of the current market rates for the shipment involved.

In addition to these provisions, for agricultural cargo the Soviet Union has also agreed to terms relating to unloading ships in the Soviet Union which are more favorable to U.S. vessels than would otherwise apply in this trade. Our maritime experts estimate these special terms represent a reduction from typical rates of at least $1.75 per ton.

These special provisions for rates on agricultural cargo apply through June 30, 1973, by which time the parties will negotiate future rates. This will permit review of the actual workings of this rate system near the close of the current unusual grain shipment season.

Term of Agreement. The agreement remains in force through 1975, subject to earlier termination by either party on 90 days' notice.

U.S. Subsidy

Although not part of the agreement, a necessary part of achieving its objectives is that the United States pay a subsidy to its own vessels in the carriage of agricultural cargo. This is not a financial advantage to the Soviet Union, since it could carry all this cargo in its own vessels or third-flag vessels at lower costs than it will pay U.S. vessels. The combination of higher than market charter rates and favorable terms for unloading afforded U.S.-flag vessels reduces the subsidy costs.

The subsidy system, to be published shortly, is authorized under the Merchant Marine Act of 1970. Because the ships which will be involved in this trade—unlike U.S.-flag vessels carrying freight in the liner trade—have not received U.S. construction subsidies, the subsidy to be provided will take into account the amount by which U.S. construction costs exceed foreign construction costs. In order to keep the subsidy at a minimum, it has basically been designed to create no more than a break-even situation at $8.05 for most ships which will be likely to participate. The estimated subsidy paid to vessels carrying agricultural cargo under the agreement will be in the range of $8 to $10 a ton if market rates stay in the range of $9 to $11 a ton, which compares to the current subsidy of about $19 per ton on Public Law 480 grain shipments.

Among provisions limiting the subsidy paid for movements under the agreement will be the following:

1. Where market rates exceed the $8.05, all of the excess paid by the Soviet Union over market (i.e., 10-percent premium) is used to reduce the subsidy.

2. When the market rate is $9 or more, a substantial part of the amount over $9 will be used to reduce the subsidy.

3. Each subsidy contract will have a renegotiation clause to insure that no excess profits are made.

The exact amount of subsidy which will be involved with respect to carrying the American share of the grain cargo is difficult to predict with precision because it depends on factors such as: (1) the volume of the Soviet grain trade actually carried by U.S. ships (which will be reduced to the extent that more attractive carriage is available (such as Public Law 480 or oil)); (2) the level of market rates, since the U.S. subsidy paid will be substantially reduced as market rates go up.

TEXTS OF MARITIME AGREEMENT AND RELATED U.S. LETTERS

Text of Agreement

AGREEMENT BETWEEN THE GOVERNMENT OF THE UNITED STATES OF AMERICA AND THE GOVERNMENT OF THE UNION OF SOVIET SOCIALIST REPUBLICS REGARDING CERTAIN MARITIME MATTERS

The Government of the United States of America and the Government of the Union of Soviet Socialist Republics;

Being desirous of improving maritime relations between the United States and the Soviet Union, particularly through arrangements regarding port access and cargo carriage by sea; and

Acting in accordance with Article Seven of the Basic Principles of Relations Between the United States of America and the Union of Soviet Socialist Republics, signed in Moscow on May 29, 1972,[1]

Have agreed as follows:

ARTICLE 1

For purposes of this Agreement:

a. "Vessel" means a vessel sailing under the flag of a Party, registered in the territory of that Party, or which is an unregistered vessel belonging to the Government of such Party, and which is used for:

(i) Commercial maritime shipping, or

(ii) Merchant marine training purposes, or

(iii) Hydrographic, oceanographic, meteorological, or terrestrial magnetic field research for civil application.

b. "Vessel" does not include:

(i) Warships as defined in the 1958 Geneva Convention on the High Seas;

(ii) Vessels carrying out any form of state function except for those mentioned under paragraph a of this Article.

ARTICLE 2

This Agreement does not apply to or affect the rights of fishing vessels, fishery research vessels, or fishery support vessels. This Agreement does not affect existing arrangements with respect to such vessels.

ARTICLE 3

The ports on the attached list of ports of each Party (Annexes I and II, which are a part of this

---

[1] For text, see BULLETIN of June 26, 1972, p. 898.

Agreement) are open to access by all vessels of the other Party.

ARTICLE 4

Entry of all vessels of one Party into such ports of the other Party shall be permitted subject to four days' advance notice of the planned entry to the appropriate authority.

ARTICLE 5

Entry of all vessels referred to in subparagraphs a(ii) and a(iii) of Article 1 into the ports referred to in Article 3 will be to replenish ships' stores or fresh water, obtain bunkers, provide rest for or make changes in the personnel of such vessels, and obtain minor repairs and other services normally provided in such ports, all in accordance with applicable rules and regulations.

ARTICLE 6

Each Party undertakes to ensure that tonnage duties upon vessels of the other Party will not exceed the charges imposed in like situations with respect to vessels of any other country.

ARTICLE 7

While recognizing the policy of each Party concerning participation of third flags in its trade, each Party also recognizes the interest of the other in carrying a substantial part of its foreign trade in vessels of its own registry, and thus both Parties intend that their national flag vessels will each carry equal and substantial shares of the trade between the two nations in accordance with Annex III which is a part of this Agreement.

ARTICLE 8

Each Party agrees that, where it controls the selection of the carrier of its export and import cargoes, it will provide to vessels under the flag of the other Party participation equal to that of vessels under its own flag in accordance with the agreement in Annex III.

ARTICLE 9

The Parties shall enter into consultations within fourteen days from the date a request for consultation is received from either Party regarding any matter involving the application, interpretation, implementation, amendment, or renewal of this Agreement.

ARTICLE 10

This Agreement shall enter into force on January 1, 1973; provided that this date may be accelerated by mutual agreement of the Parties. The Agreement will remain in force for the period ending December 31, 1975, provided that the Agreement may be terminated by either Party. The termination shall be effective ninety days after the date on which written notice of termination has been received.

IN WITNESS WHEREOF, the undersigned, being duly authorized by their respective Governments, have signed this Agreement.

DONE at Washington this fourteenth day of October, 1972, in duplicate in the English and Russian languages, both equally authentic.

For the Government of the United States of America:

For the Government of the Union of Soviet Socialist Republics:

PETER G. PETERSON
Secretary of Commerce

T. GUZHENKO
*Minister
of Merchant Marine*

Texts of Annexes to Agreement

ANNEX I

PORTS OF THE UNITED STATES OF AMERICA OPEN TO
CALLS UPON NOTICE

1. Skagway, Alaska
2. Seattle, Washington
3. Longview, Washington
4. Corpus Christi, Texas
5. Port Arthur, Texas
6. Bellingham, Washington
7. Everett, Washington
8. Olympia, Washington
9. Tacoma, Washington
10. Coos Bay (including North Bend), Oregon
11. Portland (including Vancouver, Washington), Oregon
12. Astoria, Oregon
13. Sacramento, California
14. San Francisco (including Alameda, Oakland, Berkeley, Richmond), California
15. Long Beach, California
16. Los Angeles (including San Pedro, Wilmington, Terminal Island), California
17. Eureka, California
18. Honolulu, Hawaii
19. Galveston/Texas City, Texas
20. Burnside, Louisiana
21. New Orleans, Louisiana
22. Baton Rouge, Louisiana
23. Mobile, Alabama
24. Tampa, Florida
25. Houston, Texas
26. Beaumont, Texas
27. Brownsville, Texas
28. Ponce, Puerto Rico

29. New York (New York and New Jersey parts of the Port of New York Authority), New York
30. Philadelphia, Pennsylvania (including Camden, New Jersey)
31. Baltimore, Maryland
32. Savannah, Georgia
33. Erie, Pennsylvania
34. Duluth, Minnesota/Superior, Wisconsin
35. Chicago, Illinois
36. Milwaukee, Wisconsin
37. Kenosha, Wisconsin
38. Cleveland, Ohio
39. Toledo, Ohio
40. Bay City, Michigan

ANNEX II

PORTS OF THE UNION OF SOVIET SOCIALIST REPUBLICS OPEN TO CALLS UPON NOTICE

1. Murmansk
2. Onega
3. Arkhangel'sk
4. Mezen'
5. Nar'yan-Mar
6. Igarka
7. Leningrad
8. Vyborg
9. Pyarnu
10. Riga
11. Ventspils
12. Klaipeda
13. Tallinn
14. Vysotsk
15. Reni
16. Izmail
17. Kiliya
18. Belgorod-Dnestrovskiy
19. Il'ichevsk
20. Odessa
21. Kherson
22. Novorossiysk
23. Tuapse
24. Poti
25. Batumi
26. Sochi
27. Sukhumi
28. Yalta
29. Zhdanov
30. Berdyansk
31. Nakhodka
32. Aleksandrovsk-Sakhalinskiy
33. Makarevskiy Roadstead (Roadstead Doue)
34. Oktyabr'skiy
35. Shakhtersk
36. Uglesgorsk
37. Kholmsk
38. Nevel'sk
39. Makarov Roadstead
40. Poronaysk

ANNEX III

SUPPLEMENTAL AGREEMENT ON NATIONAL FLAG CARGO CARRIAGE

WHEREAS, each Party recognizes the policy of the other concerning the participation of third flags in its trade, each Party also recognizes the interest of the other in carrying a substantial part of its foreign trade in vessels of its own registry and thus both Parties intend that their national flag vessels will each carry equal and substantial shares of the trade between the two nations in accordance with this Annex, and

WHEREAS, each Party has agreed that, where it controls the selection of the carrier for its export and import cargoes, it will provide to vessels under the flag of the other Party participation equal to that of vessels under its own flag, it is agreed as follows:

1. DEFINITIONS

For the purpose of this Annex and the Agreement of which this Annex is a part:

a. "Substantial share of the trade between the two nations" means not less than one-third of bilateral cargoes.

b. "Bilateral cargo" means any cargo, the shipment of which originates in the territory of one Party and moves in whole or in part by sea to a destination in the territory of the other Party, whether by direct movement or by transshipment through third countries.

c. "Controlled cargo" means any bilateral cargo with respect to which a public authority or public entity of either Party or their agents has the power of designating the carrier or the flag of carriage at any time prior to such designation, and includes:

(i) on the Untied States side all bilateral cargo which a public authority or public entity of the United States has or could have the power at any time to designate the flag of carriage pursuant to cargo preference legislation, and

(ii) on the Soviet side all bilateral cargo imported into or exported from the territory of the USSR where a commercial body or other authority or entity of the USSR has or could have the power at any time to designate the carrier.

d. "Accountable liner share" means the U.S. dollar freight value of liner carryings of controlled cargo by vessels under the flag of each Party, computed for accounting purposes using the conference rates in effect at the time of carriage or, in the absence of such rates, using other rates to be agreed between the two Parties.

e. "Accountable charter share" means the U.S. dollar freight value of carryings under contracts or arrangements covering the carriage of controlled cargo by vessels under the flag of each Party, which are not in liner service, computed for accounting purposes at rates to be agreed between the Parties. Accountable charter share will not include movements of any bulk cargoes in shipload lots of 8,000 long tons or more from the Union of Soviet Socialist Republics to the United States that are carried by the national flag vessels of either Party provided the conditions stated in subparagraph b of paragraph 3 of this Annex have been complied with.

f. "Accounting period" means a calendar year or any portion of an incomplete calendar year during which this Agreement is in effect.

2. GENERAL OPERATING RULES

a. Each Party undertakes to ensure that its controlled cargo is directed in a manner which

(i) provides to vessels under the flag of the other Party an accountable liner share and an accountable charter share equal in each category to those of vessels under its flag, and which continually maintains parity during each accounting period, and

(ii) is consistent with the intention of the Parties that their national flag vessels will each carry not less than one-third of bilateral cargoes.

b. To the extent that bilateral cargo that is not controlled cargo is carried in a manner which does not maintain parity between national flag vessels, computed in accordance with the principles specified in subparagraphs d and e of paragraph 1 of this Annex, the excess of such carriage will be added to the accountable liner share or accountable charter share, as the case may be, of the overcarrier and will be offset to the extent possible by an entitlement of a compensating share of controlled cargo in the appropriate category to the undercarrier.

c. Whenever vessels under the flag of one Party are not available to carry controlled cargo offered for carriage between ports served by such vessels with reasonable notice and upon reasonable terms and conditions of carriage, the offering Party shall be free to direct such cargo to its national flag or to third flag vessels. Cargo so directed to the offering Party's national flag vessels will not be included in its accountable liner share or accountable charter share for purposes of subparagraph a(i) of paragraph 2 of this Annex, if the designated representative of the other Party certifies that its national flag vessels were in fact unavailable at the time of the offer.

d. Cargo not carried in the vessels of a Party because of nonavailability of a vessel shall nonetheless be included in bilateral cargo for purposes of subparagraph a(ii) of paragraph 2 of this Annex, and controlled cargo shall continue to be directed to meet the undertakings of said subparagraph. To the extent that deficiencies in meeting the undertakings in such subparagraph exist at the end of an accounting period because of unavailability of vessels of a Party which the representative of that Party has certified were unavailable as provided above in subparagraph c of paragraph 2, the other Party shall not be required to make up such deficiency in the following accounting period.

e. To the extent consistent with the foregoing provisions of this paragraph 2, each Party is free to utilize the services of third flag shipping for the carriage of controlled cargo.

3. SPECIAL BULK CARGO RULES

a. When controlled bulk cargo is carried from the United States to the Union of Soviet Socialist Republics by U.S.-flag vessels, such cargo shall be carried at a mutually acceptable rate, provided that this shall not prevent the offering and fixing of a lower rate if such lower rate is accepted by a U.S.-flag carrier at the time of offering.

b. It is recognized that movements of any bulk cargoes in shipload lots of 8,000 long tons or more from the Union of Soviet Socialist Republics to the United States shall be carried at the then current market rates. In furtherance of this objective, an equivalent quantity of such controlled cargoes as are offered to Soviet-flag vessels will be offered to U.S.-flag vessels at the current charter market rate and with reasonable notice. Any offerings of such cargoes that are not accepted by U.S.-flag vessels may be carried by Soviet-flag vessels or other vessels.

4. IMPLEMENTATION

a. Each Party shall designate a representative for implementation of the principles and rules of this Annex, the representative of the United States being the Maritime Administration, Department of Commerce, and the representative of the Union of Soviet Socialist Republics being the Ministry of Merchant Marine. Each Party shall authorize its representative to take action under its laws and procedures, and in consultation with the designated representative of the other Party, to implement this Annex as well as to remedy any departures from the agreed operating rules.

b. The Parties further agree that the designated representatives shall:

(i) meet annually for a comprehensive review of the movement of bilateral cargo and for such other purposes related to the Agreement as may be desirable;

(ii) engage in such consultations, exchange such information and take such action as may be necessary to insure effective operation of this Annex and the Agreement of which this Annex is a part;

(iii) make mutually satisfactory arrangements or adjustments, including adjustments between accounting shares and accounting periods, to carry out at all times the objectives of this Annex and the Agreement of which this Annex is a part. Any departures from such objectives shall be accommodated on a calendar quarterly basis to the extent possible and in no event shall departures be permitted to continue beyond the first three months of the next accounting period; and

(iv) resolve any other problems in the implementation of this Annex and the Agreement of which this Annex is a part.

5. COMMERCIAL ARRANGEMENTS

a. The Parties recognize that, pursuant to their respective laws or policies, carriers under their flags may enter into commercial arrangements for the service and stabilization of the trade between them which shall not unduly prejudice the rights of third-flag carriers to compete for the carriage of controlled cargo between the territories of the Parties.

b. Such commercial arrangements shall not relieve the Parties of their obligations under this Annex and the Agreement of which this Annex is a part.

Texts of Related U.S. Letters

Letter Relating to Article 1(a) and Research Vessels [2]

WASHINGTON, *October 14, 1972.*

DEAR MR. MINISTER: With reference to the Agreement between the Government of the United States of America and the Government of the Union of Soviet Socialist Republics, signed today, concerning certain maritime matters, I wish by this letter to inform the Government of the Union of Soviet Socialist Republics of the following clarifications and interpretations of statements contained in such Agreement.

The phrase in paragraph a of Article 1 "registered in the territory of that Party" shall include unregistered vessels which are numbered under the laws of a state or political subdivision of the United States.

The phrase in paragraph a of Article 1 "an unregistered vessel belonging to the Government of such Party" refers to certain vessels which belong to

---

[2] The enclosure to the U.S. letter and Minister Guzhenko's letter of confirmation enclosing a current list of major Soviet oceanographic, hydrographic, meteorological, and magnetic field research vessels are not printed here.

the Government of the United States and which are not registered vessels.

I am appending a current list of major United States oceanographic, hydrographic, meteorological and magnetic field research vessels referred to in subparagraph a(iii) of Article 1 of the Agreement mentioned above.

Very truly yours,

PETER G. PETERSON,
Secretary of Commerce.

Enclosure:

Current list of major United States oceanographic, hydrographic, meteorological and magnetic field research vessels.

His Excellency TIMOFEY B. GUZHENKO,
Minister of Merchant Marine of the Union of Soviet Socialist Republics.

Letter on Mutually Acceptable Rates

WASHINGTON, *October 14, 1972.*

DEAR MR. MINISTER: In connection with the signing today of the Agreement between the Government of the United States of America and the Government of the Union of Soviet Socialist Republics concerning certain maritime matters, I have the honor to confirm the understandings set forth in your letter of even date that: [3]

1. Under sub-paragraph a of paragraph 3 of Annex III of that Agreement, the term "mutually acceptable rate" means a rate equal to the average of the market charter rates for the three calendar years preceding the current accounting period for the relevant route and category of cargo. It is understood that such average market charter rate will apply irrespective of the current conditions of the freight market and may be higher or lower than the current market level. Market charter rates will be determined from published sources acceptable to both Parties. Where such published market charter rates do not exist for a relevant route or category of cargo, agreed adjustments will be made to published market charter rates for the most comparable route or category of cargo.

2. The provisions of the foregoing paragraph shall not apply to rates for shipments of raw or processed agricultural commodities. Under sub-paragraph a of paragraph 3 of Annex III of that Agreement the term "mutually acceptable rate" as applied to shipments of raw and processed agricultural commodities means:

a. With respect to fixtures made prior to July 1, 1973 the higher of: (i) a rate for the cargo and route involved computed upon the formula of the average of market charter rates set forth in paragraph 1 of this letter for the years 1969, 1970 and

---

[3] Not printed here.

1971; or (ii) the current market charter rate for such cargo and route plus ten percent (10%) of such rate. Current market charter rates referred to above will be determined at the time of each fixture from current sources acceptable to both Parties. Where such market charter rates do not exist for a relevant route or category of cargo, agreed adjustments will be made to current market charter rates for the most comparable route and category of cargo.

b. With respect to fixtures made after June 30, 1973, rates based upon such amounts or formulas as the Parties may hereafter agree upon, and for that purpose the United States Maritime Administration and the Ministry of Merchant Marine of the Soviet Union shall convene prior to June 30, 1973 to discuss and reach agreement upon such rates.

Very truly yours,

PETER G. PETERSON,
Secretary of Commerce.

His Excellency TIMOFEY B. GUZHENKO,
Minister of Merchant Marine of the Union of Soviet Socialist Republics.

Letter on Rates and Terms

THE ASSISTANT SECRETARY OF COMMERCE,
Washington, D.C., October 14, 1972.

Honorable N. ZUEV,
President, SOVFRACHT,
Moscow.

DEAR MR. ZUEV: This will acknowledge receipt of your letter of today transmitting a copy of the letter which you informed me SOVFRACHT proposes to transmit to its chartering agents and which sets forth the charter party terms which we have agreed upon for fixtures made for the carriage of raw and processed agricultural commodities by American flag bulk cargo vessels under the Agreement Between the Government of the United States of America and the Government of the Union of Soviet Socialist Republics Regarding Certain Maritime Matters executed today.[4]

Also enclosed with your letter was the schedule of rates we have agreed upon for practical purposes to be used under that Agreement in place of a precise calculation of the three year average rate for 1969, 1970 and 1971 for the carriage of specified categories of raw and processed agricultural commodities by American flag bulk cargo vessels on the routes specified, for fixtures made prior to July 1, 1973.

You also confirmed in your letter that with respect to Item 5 of the charter party terms, relating to cargo insurance, you will enter into discussions with officials of INGOSSTRAKH for the purpose of di-

recting the placement of a portion of the marine cargo insurance coverage for shipments of raw and processed agricultural commodities with United States underwriters.

I am pleased to confirm that your letter and the enclosures reflect our agreement and understanding.

Very truly yours,

ROBERT J. BLACKWELL,
Assistant Secretary for Maritime Affairs.

Letter on Agricultural Cargo Shares [5]

THE ASSISTANT SECRETARY OF COMMERCE,
Washington, D.C., October 14, 1972.

Mr. IGOR AVERIN,
Director of Department of Foreign Relations of the Ministry of the Merchant Marine, Union of Soviet Socialist Republics, Moscow.

DEAR MR. AVERIN: This is to confirm our mutual agreement on the understanding that the total of all agricultural cargoes fixed or shipped on and after July 1, 1972, from the United States to the Soviet Union will be included in determining the Soviet and U.S. shares under Article 7 and Annex III of the Agreement between the Government of the United States of America and the Government of the Union of Soviet Socialist Republics regarding certain maritime matters.

Sincerely,

ROBERT J. BLACKWELL,
Assistant Secretary for Maritime Affairs.

Letter on Grain Vacuvators

THE ASSISTANT SECRETARY OF COMMERCE,
Washington, D.C., October 14, 1972.

Honorable N. ZUEV,
President, SOVFRACHT,
Moscow.

DEAR MR. ZUEV: This letter will serve to confirm to you our understanding that the Maritime Administration, U.S. Department of Commerce, will use its good offices and influence with U.S. shipowners in assisting the Soviet Union in procuring vacuvators for grain discharging operations.

Additionally, we confirm our understanding that tankers can only be discharged by vacuvators and that in order to fulfill the terms agreed upon it will be necessary either for receivers to purchase vacuvators directly or for tanker owners and/or the receivers to come to some arrangement for providing a means of discharge.

Sincerely,

ROBERT J. BLACKWELL,
Assistant Secretary for Maritime Affairs.

---

[4] Mr. Zuev's letter and its enclosures are not printed here.

[5] Mr. Averin's letter of confirmation is not printed here.

Letter on Carriage of Liquefied Natural Gas [6]

WASHINGTON, *October 14, 1972.*

DEAR MR. MINISTER: With reference to the Agreement between the Government of the United States of America and the Government of the Union of Soviet Socialist Republics, signed today, concerning certain maritime matters, I have the honor to confirm the understanding reached between us that the provisions of Articles 7 and 8 of the Agreement and the provisions of Annex III thereof are not intended to apply to the carriage of liquefied natural gas (LNG) from the Union of Soviet Socialist Republics to the United States. Arrangements for such carriage will be negotiated in connection with the development of projects for the sale of LNG for use in the United States.

Very truly yours,

PETER G. PETERSON,
Secretary of Commerce.

His Excellency TIMOFEY B. GUZHENKO,
Minister of Merchant Marine of the Union of Soviet Socialist Republics.

Letter Relating to Port Procedures and Other Matters

WASHINGTON, *October 14, 1972.*

DEAR MR. MINISTER: In connection with the Agreement signed today between the Government of the United States and the Government of the Union of Soviet Socialist Republics concerning certain maritime matters, we have agreed that we would exchange information describing our port procedures and other matters. Accordingly, enclosed is a Memorandum on U.S. Port Procedures and Other Matters.[7]

This letter will also acknowledge receipt from you of your Memorandum on U.S.S.R. Port Procedures and Other Matters together with covering letter signed by you.

Very truly yours,

PETER G. PETERSON,
Secretary of Commerce.

Enclosure:

Memorandum on U.S. Port
Procedures and Other Matters.

His Excellency TIMOFEY B. GUZHENKO,
Minister of Merchant Marine of the Union of Soviet Socialist Republics.

---

[6] Minister Guzhenko's letter of confirmation is not printed here.

[7] The enclosure to the U.S. letter and Minister Guzhenko's letter enclosing a memorandum on U.S.S.R. port procedures and other matters are not printed here.

Considering that the peoples of the United States of America and of the Union of Soviet Socialist Republics seek a new era of commercial friendship, an era in which the resources of both countries will contribute to the well-being of the peoples of each and an era in which common commercial interest can point the way to better and lasting understanding,

Having agreed at the Moscow Summit that commercial and economic ties are an important and necessary element in the strengthening of their bilateral relations,

Noting that favorable conditions exist for the development of trade and economic relations between the two countries to their mutual advantage,

Desiring to make the maximum progress for the benefit of both countries in accordance with the tenets of the Basic Principles of Relations Between the United States of America and the Union of Soviet Socialist Republics signed in Moscow on May 29, 1972,

Believing that agreement on basic questions of economic trade relations between the two countries will best serve the interests of both their peoples,

Have agreed as follows:

ARTICLE 1

1. Each Government shall accord unconditionally to products originating in or exported to the other country treatment no less favorable than that accorded to like products originating in or exported to any third country in all matters relating to:

(a) customs duties and charges of any kind imposed on or in connection with importation or exportation including the method of levying such duties and charges;

(b) internal taxation, sale, distribution, storage and use;

(c) charges imposed upon the international transfer of payments for importation or exportation; and

(d) rules and formalities in connection with importation or exportation.

2. In the event either Government applies quantitative restrictions to products originating in or exported to third countries, it shall afford to like products originating in or exported to the other country equitable treatment vis-a-vis that applied in respect of such third countries.

3. Paragraphs 1 and 2 of this Article 1 shall not apply to (i) any privileges which are granted by either Government to neighboring countries with a view toward facilitating frontier traffic, or (ii) any preferences granted by either Government in recognition of Resolution 21 (II) adopted on March 26, 1968 at the Second UNCTAD [United Nations Conference on Trade and Development], or (iii)

16 (October 18, 1972)

AGREEMENT BETWEEN THE GOVERNMENT OF THE UNITED STATES OF AMERICA AND THE GOVERNMENT OF THE UNION OF SOVIET SOCIALIST REPUBLICS REGARDING TRADE

The Government of the United States of America and the Government of the Union of Soviet Socialist Republics, any action by either Government which is permitted under any multilateral trade agreement to which such Government is a party on the date of signature of this Agreement, if such agreement would permit such action in similar circumstances with respect to like products originating in or exported to a country which is a signatory thereof, or (iv) the exercise by either Government of its rights under Articles 3 or 8 of this Agreement.

ARTICLE 2

1. Both Governments will take appropriate measures, in accordance with the laws and regulations then current in each country, to encourage and facilitate the exchange of goods and services between the two countries on the basis of mutual advantage and in accordance with the provisions of this Agreement. In expectation of such joint efforts, both Governments envision that total bilateral trade in comparison with the period 1969–1971 will at least triple over the three-year period contemplated by this Agreement.

2. Commercial transactions between the United States of America and the Union of Soviet Socialist Republics shall be effected in accordance with the laws and regulations then current in each country with respect to import and export control and financing, as well as on the basis of contracts to be concluded between natural and legal persons of the United States of America and foreign trade organizations of the Union of Soviet Socialist Republics. Both Governments shall facilitate, in accordance with the laws and regulations then current in each country, the conclusion of such contracts, including those on a long-term basis, between natural and legal persons of the United States of America and foreign trade organizations of the Union of Soviet Socialist Republics. It is understood that such contracts will generally be concluded on terms customary in international commercial practice.

3. Both Governments, by mutual agreement, will examine various fields, in which the expansion of commercial and industrial cooperation is desirable, with regard for, in particular, the long-term requirements and resources of each country in raw materials, equipment and technology and, on the basis of such examination, will promote cooperation between interested organizations and enterprises of the two countries with a view toward the realization of projects for the development of natural resources and projects in the manufacturing industries.

4. The Government of the Union of Soviet Socialist Republics expects that, during the period of effectiveness of this Agreement, foreign trade organizations of the Union of Soviet Socialist Republics will place substantial orders in the United States of America for machinery, plant and equipment, agricultural products, industrial products and consumer goods produced in the United States of America.

ARTICLE 3

Each Government may take such measures as it deems appropriate to ensure that the importation of products originating in the other country does not take place in such quantities or under such conditions as to cause, threaten or contribute to disruption of its domestic market. The procedures under which both Governments shall cooperate in carrying out the objectives of this Article are set forth in Annex 1, which constitutes an integral part of this Agreement.

ARTICLE 4

All currency payments between natural and legal persons of the United States of America and foreign trade and other appropriate organizations of the Union of Soviet Socialist Republics shall be made in United States dollars or any other freely convertible currency mutually agreed upon by such persons and organizations.

ARTICLE 5

1. The Government of the United States of America may establish in Moscow a Commercial Office of the United States of America and the Government of the Union of Soviet Socialist Republics may establish in Washington a Trade Representation of the Union of Soviet Socialist Republics. The Commercial Office and the Trade Representation shall be opened simultaneously on a date and at locations to be agreed upon.

2. The status concerning the functions, privileges, immunities and organization of the Commercial Office and the Trade Representation is set forth in Annexes 2 and 3, respectively, attached to this Agreement, of which they constitute an integral part.

3. The establishment of the Commercial Office and the Trade Representation shall in no way affect the rights of natural or legal persons of the United States of America and of foreign trade organizations of the Union of Soviet Socialist Republics, either in the United States of America or in the Union of Soviet Socialist Republics, to maintain direct relations with each other with a view to the negotiation, execution and fulfillment of trade transactions. To facilitate the maintenance of such direct relations the Commercial Office may provide office facilities at its location to employees or representatives of natural and legal persons of the United States of America, and the Trade Representation may provide office facilities at its location to employees or representatives of foreign trade or-

ganizations of the Union of Soviet Socialist Republics, which employees and representatives shall not be officers or members of the administrative, technical or service staff of the Commercial Office or the Trade Representation. Accordingly, the Commercial Office and the Trade Representation, and their respective officers and staff members, shall not participate directly in the negotiation, execution or fulfillment of trade transactions or otherwise carry on trade.

ARTICLE 6

1. In accordance with the laws and regulations then current in each country, natural and legal persons of the United States of America and foreign trade organizations of the Union of Soviet Socialist Republics may open their representations in the Union of Soviet Socialist Republics and the United States of America, respectively. Information concerning the opening of such representations and provision of facilities in connection therewith shall be provided by each Government upon the request of the other Government.

2. Foreign trade organizations of the Union of Soviet Socialist Republics shall not claim or enjoy in the United States of America, and private natural and legal persons of the United States of America shall not claim or enjoy in the Union of Soviet Socialist Republics, immunities from suit or execution of judgment or other liability with respect to commercial transactions.

3. Corporations, stock companies and other industrial or financial commercial organizations, including foreign trade organizations, domiciled and regularly organized in conformity to the laws in force in one of the two countries shall be recognized as having a legal existence in the other country.

ARTICLE 7

1. Both Governments encourage the adoption of arbitration for the settlement of disputes arising out of international commercial transactions concluded between natural and legal persons of the United States of America and foreign trade organizations of the Union of Soviet Socialist Republics, such arbitration to be provided for by agreements in contracts between such persons and organizations, or, if it has not been so provided, to be provided for in separate agreements between them in writing executed in the form required for the contract itself, such agreements:

(a) to provide for arbitration under the Arbitration Rules of the Economic Commission for Europe of January 20, 1966, in which case such agreement should also designate an Appointing Authority in a country other than the United States of America or the Union of Soviet Socialist Republics for the

appointment of an arbitrator or arbitrators in accordance with those Rules; and

(b) to specify as the place of arbitration a place in a country other than the United States of America or the Union of Soviet Socialist Republics that is a party to the 1958 Convention on the Recognition and Enforcement of Foreign Arbitral Awards.

Such persons and organizations, however, may decide upon any other form of arbitration which they mutually prefer and agree best suits their particular needs.

2. Each Government shall ensure that corporations, stock companies, and other industrial or financial commercial organizations, including foreign trade organizations, domiciled and regularly organized in conformity to the laws in force in the other country shall have the right to appear before courts of the former, whether for the purpose of bringing an action or of defending themselves against one, including but not limited to, cases arising out of or relating to transactions contemplated by this Agreement. In all such cases the said corporations, companies and organizations shall enjoy in the other country the same rights which are or may be granted to similar companies of any third country.

ARTICLE 8

The provisions of this Agreement shall not limit the right of either Government to take any action for the protection of its security interests.

ARTICLE 9

1. This Agreement shall enter into force upon the exchange of written notices of acceptance. This Agreement shall remain in force for three years, unless extended by mutual agreement.

2. Both Governments will work through the Joint US-USSR Commercial Commission established in accordance with the Communique issued in Moscow on May 26, 1972, in overseeing and facilitating the implementation of this Agreement in accordance with the terms of reference and rules of procedure of the Commission.[3]

3. Prior to the expiration of this Agreement, the Joint US-USSR Commercial Commission shall begin consultations regarding extension of this Agreement or preparation of a new agreement to replace this Agreement.

IN WITNESS WHEREOF, the undersigned, duly authorized, have signed this Agreement on behalf of their respective Governments.

DONE at Washington in duplicate this 18th day of

---

[3] For text of the communique, see BULLETIN of June 26, 1972, p. 898.

October, 1972, in the English and Russian languages, each being equally authentic.

For the Government of the United States of America:

PETER G. PETERSON.

For the Government of the Union of Soviet Socialist Republics:

N. PATOLICHEV.

Texts of Annexes to Agreement

ANNEX 1 TO THE AGREEMENT BETWEEN THE GOVERNMENT OF THE UNITED STATES OF AMERICA AND THE GOVERNMENT OF THE UNION OF SOVIET SOCIALIST REPUBLICS REGARDING TRADE

PROCEDURE FOR THE IMPLEMENTATION OF ARTICLE 3

1. Both Governments agrée to consult promptly at the request of either Government whenever such Government determines that actual or prospective imports of a product originating in the other country under certain conditions or in certain quantities could cause, threaten or contribute to disruption of the market of the requesting country.

2. (a) Consultations shall include a review of the market and trade situation for the product involved and shall be concluded within sixty days of the request unless otherwise agreed during the course of such consultations. Both Governments, in carrying out these consultations, shall take due account of any contracts concluded prior to the request for consultations between natural and legal persons of the United States of America and foreign trade organizations of the Union of Soviet Socialist Republics engaged in trade between the two countries.

(b) Unless a different solution is agreed upon during the consultations, the quantitative import limitations or other conditions stated by the importing country to be necessary to prevent or remedy the market disruption situation in question shall be deemed agreed as between the two Governments.

(c) At the request of the Government of the importing country, if it determines that an emergency situation exists, the limitations or other conditions referred to in its request for consultations shall be put into effect prior to the conclusion of such consultations.

3. (a) In accordance with the laws and regulations then current in each country, each Government shall take appropriate measures to ensure that exports from its country of the products concerned do not exceed the quantities or vary from the conditions established for imports of such products into the other country pursuant to paragraphs 1 and 2 of this Annex 1.

(b) Each Government may take appropriate measures with respect to imports into its country to ensure that imports of products originating in the other country comply with such quantitative limitations or conditions as may be established in accordance with paragraphs 1 and 2 of this Annex 1.

ANNEX 2 TO THE AGREEMENT BETWEEN THE GOVERNMENT OF THE UNITED STATES OF AMERICA AND THE GOVERNMENT OF THE UNION OF SOVIET SOCIALIST REPUBLICS REGARDING TRADE

THE STATUS OF THE COMMERCIAL OFFICE OF THE UNITED STATES OF AMERICA IN THE UNION OF SOVIET SOCIALIST REPUBLICS

ARTICLE 1

The Commercial Office of the United States of America may perform the following functions:

1. Promote the development of trade and economic relations between the United States of America and the Union of Soviet Socialist Republics; and

2. Provide assistance to natural and legal persons of the United States of America in facilitating purchases, sales and other commercial transactions.

ARTICLE 2

1. The Commercial Office shall consist of one principal officer and no more than three deputy officers and a mutually agreed number of staff personnel, provided, however, that the number of officers and staff personnel permitted may be changed by mutual agreement of the two Governments.

2. The Commercial Office, wherever located, shall be an integral part of the Embassy of the United States of America in Moscow. The Government of the Union of Soviet Socialist Republics shall facilitate in accordance with its laws and regulations the acquisition or lease by the Government of the United States of America of suitable premises for the Commercial Office.

3. (a) The Commercial Office, including all of its premises and property, shall enjoy all of the privileges and immunities which are enjoyed by the Embassy of the United States of America in Moscow. The Commercial Office shall have the right to use cipher.

(b) The principal officer of the Commercial Office and his deputies shall enjoy all of the privileges and immunities which are enjoyed by members of the diplomatic staff of the Embassy of the United States of America in Moscow.

(c) Members of the administrative, technical and service staffs of the Commercial Office who are not nationals of the Union of Soviet Socialist Republics shall enjoy all of the privileges and immunities which are enjoyed by corresponding categories of personnel of the Embassy of the United States of America in Moscow.

ANNEX 3 TO THE AGREEMENT BETWEEN THE GOVERN-
MENT OF THE UNITED STATES OF AMERICA AND THE
GOVERNMENT OF THE UNION OF SOVIET SOCIALIST
REPUBLICS REGARDING TRADE

THE STATUS OF THE TRADE REPRESENTATION OF THE UNION OF SOVIET SOCIALIST REPUBLICS IN THE UNITED STATES OF AMERICA

ARTICLE 1

The Trade Representation of the Union of Soviet Socialist Republics may perform the following functions:

1. Promote the development of trade and economic relations between the Union of Soviet Socialist Republics and the United States of America; and

2. Represent the interests of the Union of Soviet Socialist Republics in all matters relating to the foreign trade of the Union of Soviet Socialist Republics with the United States of America and provide assistance to foreign trade organizations of the Union of Soviet Socialist Republics in facilitating purchases, sales and other commercial transactions.

ARTICLE 2

1. The Trade Representation shall consist of one principal officer, designated as Trade Representative, and no more than three deputy officers and a mutually agreed number of staff personnel, provided, however, that the number of officers and staff personnel permitted may be changed by mutual agreement of the two Governments.

2. The Trade Representation, wherever located, shall be an integral part of the Embassy of the Union of Soviet Socialist Republics in Washington. The Government of the United States of America shall facilitate in accordance with its laws and regulations the acquisition or lease by the Government of the Union of Soviet Socialist Republics of suitable premises for the Trade Representation.

3. (a) The Trade Representation, including all of its premises and property, shall enjoy all of the privileges and immunities which are enjoyed by the Embassy of the Union of Soviet Socialist Republics in Washington. The Trade Representation shall have the right to use cipher.

(b) The Trade Representative and his deputies shall enjoy all of the privileges and immunities which are enjoyed by members of the diplomatic staff of the Embassy of the Union of Soviet Socialist Republics in Washington.

(c) Members of the administrative, technical and service staffs of the Trade Representation who are not nationals of the United States of America shall enjoy all of the privileges and immunities which are enjoyed by corresponding categories of personnel of the Embassy of the Union of Soviet Socialist Republics in Washington.

Related U.S. Letters

U.S. Letter Relating to Article 3 [4]

OCTOBER 18, 1972.

DEAR MR. MINISTER: I have the honor to refer to our recent discussions relating to Article 3 and Annex 1 of the Agreement Between the Government of the United States of America and the Government of the Union of Soviet Socialist Republics Regarding Trade to be signed today. In accordance with those provisions and discussions, and consistent with current United States laws and regulations concerning exports, it is understood that the United States Government will meet its obligations under paragraph 3(a) of Annex 1 with respect to limitations or conditions established pursuant to a request of the Government of the Union of Soviet Socialist Republics under paragraphs 1 and 2 of Annex 1 by making available to United States exporters information regarding the quantities or conditions stated by the Government of the Union of Soviet Socialist Republics in its request, or as otherwise established following consultations provided for under Annex 1.

I further understand that the Government of the Union of Soviet Socialist Republics will limit or establish conditions on exports of any product from the Union of Soviet Socialist Republics to the United States if requested to do so in accordance with Annex 1.

I would appreciate receiving your confirmation of the foregoing understandings on behalf of the Government of the Union of Soviet Socialist Republics.

Please accept, Mr. Minister, the assurances of my highest consideration.

Sincerely yours,

PETER G. PETERSON.

MR. N. S. PATOLICHEV,
Minister of Foreign Trade of the Union of Soviet Socialist Republics.

U.S. Letter Relating to Article 5 [5]

OCTOBER 18, 1972.

DEAR MR. MINISTER: I have the honor to confirm, as was stated by my delegation in the course of the negotiations leading to the conclusion today of the Agreement Between the Government of the United States of America and the Government of the Union of Soviet Socialist Republics Regarding Trade, that while the Trade Representation of the Union of Soviet Socialist Republics in Washington estab-

---

[4] Minister Patolichev's letter of confirmation is not printed here.

[5] Minister Patolichev's reply taking note of the letter is not printed here.

lished pursuant to Article 5 of said Agreement, its officers and staff members may engage in appropriate activities to promote trade generally between the two countries for the purposes of said Agreement, as is customary in international practice, United States legislation in force, i.e., Title 22 of the United States Code, Sections 252–254, makes it inappropriate for the Trade Representation, its officers and staff to participate directly in the negotiation, execution or fulfillment of trade transactions or otherwise carry on trade.

I have the further honor to confirm that at such time as the United States of America shall have become a party to the Vienna Convention on Diplomatic Relations, dated April 18, 1961, and its domestic legislation shall have been revised to accord fully with the terms of Articles 29 through 45 of said Convention, regarding diplomatic privileges and immunities, my Government will be prepared to give favorable consideration to amending the Agreement Between the Government of the United States of America and the Government of the Union of Soviet Socialist Republics Regarding Trade by deleting the second and third sentences of paragraph 3 of Article 5, thus permitting officers and members of the administrative, technical and service staffs of the Commercial Office of the United States of America in Moscow and the Trade Representation of the Union of Soviet Socialist Republics in Washington to participate directly in the negotiation, execution and fulfillment of trade transactions and otherwise carry on trade.

Please accept, Mr. Minister, the assurances of my highest consideration.

Sincerely yours,

PETER G. PETERSON.

U.S. Reply on U.S.S.R. Accreditation and Treatment of U.S. Companies Under Article 6

OCTOBER 18, 1972.

DEAR MR. MINISTER: I have the honor to acknowledge the receipt of your letter of this date, with attachments, which reads as follows:

"Dear Mr. Secretary:

This is in response to your request for information on the procedures established by the Ministry of Foreign Trade for the accreditation of offices of foreign companies including United States companies, and on the facilities made available to such companies once accreditation has been approved.

United States companies will receive treatment no less favorable than that accorded to business entities of any third country in all matters relating to accreditation and business facilitation.

Applications by United States firms for accreditation will be handled expeditiously. Any problems arising out of these applications that cannot readily be resolved through the regular procedures shall be resolved through consultation under the Joint US-USSR Commercial Commission at the request of either side.

As you have been advised, the USSR Chamber of Commerce and Industry and the State Committee of the Council of Ministers of the USSR for Science and Technology are establishing a large trade and economic exposition center which will include display pavilions of the various participating countries. The United States has been invited to have such a pavilion. Further, to meet the growing interest of foreign firms in establishing a permanent residence in Moscow, we have decided to construct a large trade center containing offices, hotel and apartment facilities and are asking United States companies to make proposals for and cooperate in the development and building of the trade center. The trade center will be used for, among other things, housing and office facilities for accredited United States companies.

Prior to the availability of these facilities, however, office facilities of an appropriate size in buildings accessible to trade sources will be made available as soon as possible once a United States company is accredited. The facilities to which such firms shall be entitled are explained in the attached information.

It is recognized that from time to time United States businessmen may have problems regarding such facilities which they are unable to resolve through discussions with various foreign trade organizations or other organizations. In such cases officials of my Ministry, as well as those of the State Committee of the Council of Ministers of the USSR for Science and Technology, shall be available through their respective protocol sections for assistance in resolving these problems.

Please accept, Mr. Secretary, the assurances of my highest consideration.

Sincerely yours,

N. PATOLICHEV

Mr. Peter G. Peterson
Secretary of Commerce
of the United States of America"

I have the further honor to inform you that I have taken cognizance of the contents of the above letter and its attachments.

Please accept, Mr. Minister, the assurances of my highest consideration.

Sincerely yours,

PETER G. PETERSON.

SUMMARY OF BUSINESS FACILITIES
FOR FOREIGN COMPANIES

An accredited company will be authorized to employ at its office not more than five American or other non-Soviet personnel, as well as Soviet personnel if desired. If requested, such communications facilities as telephones, extensions, telex equipment will be made available promptly. The name, location and function of an accredited office will be listed in the latest issue of suitable business directories if such are published. Subject to the requirement that such equipment be exported when no longer needed by its office and subject to applicable customs regulations, accredited offices will be permitted to import, as promptly as desired, typewriters, calculators, dictation and copying equipment, one stationwagon-type automobile, as well as other equipment for the purpose of efficient and business-like operation of the office.

Subject to applicable customs regulations, each non-Soviet employee will be permitted to import a passenger car, household utilities, appliances, furniture and other necessary living items at any time within a year after the arrival of the employee in Moscow. In addition, suitable housing for such employee and family will be made available as soon as possible.

Normally, such employees and members of their families will have visas prepared for exit from and entry into the Soviet Union within three to five days. In the case of a business or personal emergency, however, a special effort is made to issue visas more promptly, and, in the case of demonstrated need, the question of granting a multiple entry and exit visa shall be examined very carefully.

INSTRUCTIONS *

on the procedure for the issuance of permits for the opening of offices of foreign firms in the USSR and for the regulation of their activity

1. Permits for the opening of offices of foreign firms in the USSR, referred to hereinafter as "Office(s)", may, in accordance with legislation in force in the USSR, be issued to foreign firms that are known on the world market and that have affirmatively presented themselves in the capacity of trade partners of Soviet foreign trade organizations with whom they have concluded especially large commercial transactions. In this connection it will also be considered that the Offices will effectively assist Soviet foreign trade organizations in the development of Soviet exports, including machinery and equipment, and also in the import of machinery and equipment that is technologically modern, and in

familiarization with the newest achievements of world technology.

2. A foreign firm interested in opening an Office shall submit to the Protocol Section of the Ministry of Foreign Trade, referred to hereinafter as the "Protocol Section", an application containing the following information:

a) the name of the firm, the date of its formation, and the place of its residence;

b) the subject matter of its activity, the organs of its administration, and the persons representing the firm according to its charter (the articles of incorporation or the articles of agreement of the firm);

c) the date and place of ratification or registration of the charter (the articles of incorporation or the articles of agreement of the firm) on the basis of which the firm operates;

d) the charter capital of the firm;

e) with which Soviet foreign trade organization the firm has concluded a transaction for the performance of which the firm requests a permit for the opening of an Office, the subject matter and amount of the transaction, and the period of operation of the transaction;

f) with which other Soviet foreign trade organizations the firm has commercial relations.

The information enumerated in subparagraphs "a", "b", "c", and "d" must be confirmed by documents (by-laws, charter, articles of incorporation or articles of agreement, an extract from a trade register, etc.) attached to the application in the form of notarized copies certified in accordance with established procedure by consular offices of the USSR abroad.

NOTE: Besides the indicated information and documents, a firm shall submit, upon inquiry by the Ministry of Foreign Trade, also other information and documents concerning the firm's activities.

3. The representative of a foreign firm presenting in its name a petition for the opening of an Office in the USSR shall give to the Protocol Section a properly prepared power of attorney.

4. In the permit for opening an Office, issued by the Protocol Section in the accompanying form, there shall be indicated:

a) the objective of opening the Office;

b) the conditions under which the firm is permitted to have the Office;

c) the period for which the permit is issued;

d) the number of personnel at the Office who are foreign citizens and employees of the firm.

5. On questions of the purchase and sale of goods the Office may communicate with Soviet organiza-

tions that do not have the right to operate in foreign trade only through the Ministry of Foreign Trade and shall conduct its activities in observance of the laws, decisions of the Government, instructions, and rules in force in the USSR.

6. Every quarter the Office shall send to the Protocol Section written information on the Office's activities, its commercial contacts with Soviet organizations, its export and import transactions concluded, and the course of their performance.

7. The person who is authorized to be the head of the Office shall give to the Protocol Section a properly prepared power of attorney from the firm, and shall inform the Protocol Section in a timely fashion of his replacement and also of the dates of arrival in the USSR and of departure from the USSR of personnel of the Office.

8. An Office opened in accordance with the procedure established by the present Instructions shall apply, on questions of the furnishing to it of day-to-day services, to the Administration for Services to the Diplomatic Corps of the Ministry of Foreign Affairs of the USSR.

9. The activity of an Office shall terminate:

a) upon expiration of the period for which its permit was issued;

b) in the event of termination of the activity abroad of the firm having the Office in the USSR;

c) upon decision of the Ministry of Foreign Trade in the event of violation by the Office of the conditions under which the firm was permitted to open the Office in the USSR, or in the event of a declaration that the Office's activity does not correspond to the interest of the USSR.

U.S. Letter Relating to Article 6 [6]

OCTOBER 18, 1972.

DEAR MR. MINISTER: This is in response to your request pursuant to Article 6 of the Agreement Between the Government of the United States of America and the Government of the Union of Soviet Socialist Republics Regarding Trade for information on policies and procedures applicable to foreign trade organizations and nationals of the Union of Soviet Socialist Republics seeking to establish business facilities in the United States for the conduct of commercial activities, and with respect to assistance that might be given by the Government of the United States of America in that regard to such organizations and persons.

From our many discussions, I am satisfied that both sides accept the principle of expansion of business facilities in each other's country as an adjunct for substantially expanded trade.

[6] Minister Patolichev's reply taking note of the letter is not printed here.

Both sides have reasons that may, in some cases, make it necessary not to honor all requests for expanded facilities and new organizations. However, we are both committed to expanding such facilities.

Where there is a clear need established for such added facilities, I will assure you that the Government of the United States will sympathetically consider such requests.

As I have told you, I believe it is important that we select examples of certain kinds of organizations and facilities that are likely to be needed in the future in order to expand trade and commerce substantially.

As one example, we recognize that certain very large projects may require from time to time purchasing organizations in the United States to coordinate such activities on those projects. We believe the Kama River Purchasing Commission is a good example of our mutual desire to improve trade between our two countries and to provide necessary facilities and organizations to achieve that objective. Thus, I am pleased to tell you the terms set out in the attachment for the Temporary Purchasing Commission for the procurement of equipment for the Kama River Truck Plant are acceptable.

As another example, the Government of the United States of America recognizes the need for the Union of Soviet Socialist Republics to stimulate more exports to the United States, and will cooperate to promote such exports where appropriate. Accordingly, if in the next few months the Soviet Government submits a request that demonstrates a clear need for a particular export facility or organization to stimulate Soviet exports to the United States, we will view such a request sympathetically.

Sincerely yours,

PETER G. PETERSON.

Attachment

With respect to the request on the part of the Government of the Union of Soviet Socialist Republics for approval of a Temporary Purchasing Commission for the Kama River Truck Complex, the Government of the United States of America understands the following:

1. The Temporary Purchasing Commission would be created with the purpose of:

a) Furnishing assistance for the placement of equipment orders for the construction of the Kama River Truck Complex in the Union of Soviet Socialist Republics.

b) Supervising on behalf of the Soviet Ministry of Foreign Trade preparation and shipment of equipment purchased from United States companies and training of Soviet experts for the Kama River Truck Complex.

c) Assisting United States companies in negotiations and fulfillment of contracts with Soviet foreign trade organizations, and assisting United States experts sent to the Union of Soviet Socialist Republics as technical consultants and coordinators of equipment assembly in connection with the Kama River Truck Complex.

2. The Temporary Purchasing Commission would be established provisionally for a period of one year, and could be renewed, by mutual agreement, for as many as three additional periods of one year each. The Temporary Purchasing Commission would be responsible to the Soviet Ministry of Foreign Trade and the Trade Representative of the Union of Soviet Socialist Republics in the United States.

3. The personnel of the Temporary Purchasing Commission would consist of a Chairman and no more than 15 additional persons, including technical assistants and staff.

4. The location of the Commission would be New York City. The specific location of the premises proposed to be occupied by the Temporary Purchasing Commission would be subject to prior agreement with the Government of the United States.

5. Permission to travel to and within the United States would be governed by existing laws and regulations.

17 (October 18, 1972)
Establishment of Temporary Purchasing Commission

The Secretary of Commerce to the Soviet Minister of Foreign Trade

THE SECRETARY OF COMMERCE
WASHINGTON, D.C. 20230

OCTOBER 18, 1972

DEAR MR. MINISTER:

This is in response to your request pursuant to Article 6 of the Agreement Between the Government of the United States of America and the Government of the Union of Soviet Socialist Republics Regarding Trade [1] for information on policies and procedures applicable to foreign trade organizations and nationals of the Union of Soviet Socialist Republics seeking to establish business facilities in the United States for the conduct of commercial activities, and with respect to assistance that might be given by the Government of the United States of America in that regard to such organizations and persons.

From our many discussions, I am satisfied that both sides accept the principle of expansion of business facilities in each other's country as an adjunct for substantially expanded trade.

Both sides have reasons that may, in some cases, make it necessary not to honor all requests for expanded facilities and new organizations. However, we are both committed to expanding such facilities.

---

[1] Signed at Washington Oct. 18, 1972. *Department of State Bulletin*, Nov. 20, 1972, p. 595.

Where there is a clear need established for such added facilities, I will assure you that the Government of the United States will sympathetically consider such requests.

As I have told you, I believe it is important that we select examples of certain kinds of organizations and facilities that are likely to be needed in the future in order to expand trade and commerce substantially.

As one example, we recognize that certain very large projects may require from time to time purchasing organizations in the United States to coordinate such activities on those projects. We believe the Kama River Purchasing Commission is a good example of our mutual desire to improve trade between our two countries and to provide necessary facilities and organizations to achieve that objective. Thus, I am pleased to tell you the terms set out in the attachment for the Temporary Purchasing Commission for the procurement of equipment for the Kama River Truck Plant are acceptable.

As another example, the Government of the United States of America recognizes the need for the Union of Soviet Socialist Republics to stimulate more exports to the United States, and will cooperate to promote such exports where appropriate. Accordingly, if in the next few months the Soviet Government submits a request that demonstrates a clear need for a particular export facility or organization to stimulate Soviet exports to the United States, we will view such a request sympathetically.

Sincerely yours,

PETER G. PETERSON

Peter G. Peterson

Attachment:
  As stated.

Mr. N. S. PATOLICHEV
Minister of Foreign Trade
of the Union of Soviet
Socialist Republics

Attachment

With respect to the request on the part of the Government of the Union of Soviet Socialist Republics for approval of a Temporary Purchasing Commission for the Kama River Truck Complex, the Government of the United States of America understands the following:

1. The Temporary Purchasing Commission would be created with the purpose of:

a) Furnishing assistance for the placement of equipment orders for the construction of the Kama River Truck Complex in the Union of Soviet Socialist Republics.

b) Supervising on behalf of the Soviet Ministry of Foreign Trade preparation and shipment of equipment purchased from United States companies and training of Soviet experts for the Kama River Truck Complex.

c) Assisting United States companies in negotiations and fulfill-ment of contracts with Soviet foreign trade organizations, and assisting United States experts sent to the Union of Soviet Socialist Republics as technical consultants and coordinators of equipment assembly in connection with the Kama River Truck Complex.

2. The Temporary Purchasing Commission would be established provisionally for a period of one year, and could be renewed, by mutual agreement, for as many as three additional periods of one year each. The Temporary Purchasing Commission would be responsible to the Soviet Ministry of Foreign Trade and the Trade Representative of the Union of Soviet Socialist Republics in the United States.

3. The personnel of the Temporary Purchasing Commission would consist of a Chairman and no more than 15 additional persons, including technical assistants and staff.

4. The location of the Commission would be New York City. The specific location of the premises proposed to be occupied by the Temporary Purchasing Commission would be subject to prior agreement with the Government of the United States.

5. Permission to travel to and within the United States would be governed by existing laws and regulations.

[AMENDING AGREEMENT]

The Secretary of the Treasury to the Soviet Minister of Foreign Trade

OCTOBER 3, 1973

DEAR MR. MINISTER:

I have the honor to refer to your letter of June 24, 1973 [1] in which you requested the continuation of the work of the temporary Kama Purchasing Commission, and to my reply of August 9, 1973. [1]

I am pleased to inform you that the United States hereby agrees to the following changes in the terms for the establishment of the Kama Purchasing Commission as set forth in the attachment [2] to the letter of Secretary Peterson to you dated October 18, 1972:

(1) The term of the Temporary Purchasing Commission is extended for the additional period of one year, that is, until October 18, 1974;

---

[1] Not printed.
[2] See above.

(2) The Temporary Purchasing Commission shall be authorized to concern itself with both the Kama River Truck Complex and the chemical production complex dealt with in the Agreement which the Occidental Petroleum Corporation signed in Moscow on April 12, 1973; and

(3) The authorized number of personnel of the Temporary Purchasing Commission is increased to 21 persons at the present time, including technical personnel. This number may be changed by mutual agreement.

I should be most grateful if you will confirm your agreement with these arrangements.

Sincerely yours,

GEORGE P. SHULTZ

George P. Shultz

His Excellency
  N. S. PATOLICHEV
    Minister of Foreign Trade
    Moscow

Translation

Moscow, *October 3, 1973*

DEAR MR. SECRETARY:
  I acknowledge the receipt of your letter of this date, reading as follows:

[For the English language text, see above.]

I have the honor to confirm agreement with the above.
Accept, Mr. Secretary, the assurances of my high consideration.

N. PATOLICHEV

Mr. GEORGE P. SHULTZ,
  Secretary of the
    Treasury of the U.S.A.

18 (October 18, 1972)

TEXT OF LEND-LEASE AGREEMENT

AGREEMENT BETWEEN THE GOVERNMENT OF THE UNITED STATES OF AMERICA AND THE GOVERNMENT OF THE UNION OF SOVIET SOCIALIST REPUBLICS REGARDING SETTLEMENT OF LEND LEASE, RECIPROCAL AID AND CLAIMS

The Government of the United States of America and the Government of the Union of Soviet Socialist Republics,

Considering the need to settle obligations arising out of prosecution of the war against aggression in order to foster mutual confidence and the development of trade and economic relations between the two countries,

Desiring to further the spirit of friendship and mutual understanding achieved by the leaders of both countries at the Moscow Summit,

Recognizing the benefits of cooperation already received by them in the defeat of their common enemies, and of the aid furnished by each Government to the other in the course of the war, and

Desiring to settle all rights and obligations of either Government from or to the other arising out of lend lease and reciprocal aid or otherwise arising out of the prosecution of the war against aggression,

Have agreed as follows:

1. This Agreement represents a full and final settlement of all rights, claims, benefits and obligations of either Government from or to the other arising out of or relating to:

(a) the Agreement of June 11, 1942, between the Governments of the United States of America and the Union of Soviet Socialist Republics on principles applying to mutual aid in the prosecution of the war against aggression, including the arrangements between the two Governments preliminary to and replaced by said Agreement,

(b) the Agreement of October 15, 1945, between the Governments of the United States of America and the Union of Soviet Socialist Republics concerning the disposition of lend-lease supplies in inventory or procurement in the United States of America, and

(c) any other matter in respect of the conduct of the war against aggression during the period June 22, 1941 through September 2, 1945.

2. In making this Agreement both Governments have taken full cognizance of the benefits and payments already received by them under the arrangements referred to in Paragraph 1 above. Accordingly, both Governments have agreed that no further benefits will be sought by either Government for any obligation to it arising out of or relating to any matter referred to in said Paragraph 1.

3. (a) The Government of the Union of Soviet Socialist Republics hereby acquires, and shall be deemed to have acquired on September 20, 1945, all such right, title and interest as the Government of the United States of America may have in all lend lease materials transferred by the Government of the United States of America to the Government of the Union of Soviet Socialist Republics, including any article (i) transferred under the Agreement of June 11, 1942, referred to above, (ii) transferred to the Government of the Union of Soviet Socialist Republics under Public Law 11 of the United States of America of March 11, 1941, or transferred under that Public Law to any other government and retransferred prior to September 20, 1945 to the Government of the Union of Soviet Socialist Republics, (iii) transferred under the Agreement of October 15, 1945, referred to above, or (iv) otherwise transferred during the period June 22, 1941 through September 20, 1945 in connection with the conduct of the war against aggression.

(b) The Government of the United States of America hereby acquires, and shall be deemed to have acquired on September 20, 1945, all such right, title and interest as the Government of the Union of Soviet Socialist Republics may have in all reciprocal aid materials transferred by the Government of the Union of Soviet Socialist Republics to the Government of the United States of America during the period June 22, 1941 through September 20, 1945.

4. (a) The total net sum due from the Government of the Union of Soviet Socialist Republics to the Government of the United States of America for the settlement of all matters set forth in Paragraph 1 of this Agreement shall be U.S. $722,000,000 payable as provided in subparagraphs (b), (c), and (d) of this Paragraph 4.

(b) (i) Three installments shall be due and payable as follows: $12,000,000 on October 18, 1972, $24,000,000 on July 1, 1973, and $12,000,000 on July 1, 1975. (ii) Subject to subparagraph (c) of this Paragraph 4, after the date ("Notice Date") on which a note from the Government of the United States of America is delivered to the Government of the Union of Soviet Socialist Republics stating that the Government of the United States of America has made available most-favored-nation treatment for the Union of Soviet Socialist Republics no less favorable than that provided in an Agreement Between the Government of the United States of America and the Union of Soviet Socialist Republics Regarding Trade signed on the date hereof, the balance of $674,000,000 in payment of lend lease accounts shall be paid in equal installments ("Regular Installments") as follows:

(1) If the Notice Date falls on or before May 31, 1974, the first Regular Installment shall be due and payable on July 1, 1974, and subsequent Regular Installments shall be due and payable annually on July 1 of each year thereafter through July 1, 2001, or

(2) If the Notice Date falls on or after June 1, 1974, and (A) If the Notice Date occurs in the period of June 1 through December 1 of any year, the first Regular Installment shall be due and payable not more than 30 days following the Notice Date and subsequent Regular Installments shall be due and payable annually on July 1 of each year thereafter through July 1, 2001; or (B) If the Notice Date occurs in the period of December 2 of any year through May 31 of the following year, the first Regular Installment shall be due and payable on the July 1 next following the Notice Date and subsequent Regular Installments shall be due and payable annually on July 1 of each year thereafter through July 1, 2001.

(c) In any year, upon written notice to the Government of the United States of America that a deferment of a Regular Installment (except the first and last Regular Installment) next due is necessary in view of its then current and prospective economic conditions, the Government of the Union of Soviet Socialist Republics shall have the right to defer payment of such Regular Installment ("Deferred Regular Installment"). Such right of deferment may be exercised on no more than four occasions. On each such occasion, without regard to whether the Government of the Union of Soviet Socialist Re-

publics defers any subsequent Regular Installments, the Deferred Regular Installment shall be due and payable in equal annual installments on July 1 of each year commencing on the July 1 next following the date the Deferred Regular Installment would have been paid if the Government of the Union of Soviet Socialist Republics had not exercised its right of deferment as to such Regular Installment, with the final payment on the Deferred Regular Installment on July 1, 2001, together with interest on the unpaid amount of the Deferred Regular Installment from time to time outstanding at three percent per annum, payable at the same time as the Deferred Regular Installment is due and payable.

(d) The Government of the Union of Soviet Socialist Republics shall have the right to prepay at any time all or any part of its total settlement obligation, provided that no such prepayment may be made at any time when any payment required to be made under this Paragraph 4 has not been paid as of the date on which it became due and payable.

5. Both Governments have agreed that this Agreement covers only rights, claims, benefits and obligations of the two Governments. Further, nothing in this Agreement shall be deemed to terminate the provisions of Article III of the Agreement of June 11, 1942, referred to above.

DONE at Washington in duplicate this eighteenth day of October, 1972, in the English and Russian languages, each text being equally authentic.

For the Government of the United States of America:

WILLIAM P. ROGERS.

For the Government of the Union of Soviet Socialist Republics:

N. PATOLICHEV.

19 (October 18, 1972)
TEXT OF PRESIDENTIAL DETERMINATION [7]

THE WHITE HOUSE,
Washington, October 18, 1972.

I hereby determine that it is in the national interest for the Export-Import Bank of the United States to guarantee, insure, extend credit and participate in the extension of credit in connection with the purchase or lease of any product or service by, for use in, or for sale or lease to the Union of Soviet Socialist Republics, in accordance with Section 2(b)(2) of the Export-Import Bank Act of 1945, as amended.

[signature: Richard Nixon]

---

[7] Presidential Determination No. 72–18100; 37 *Fed.Reg.* 22573.

71

lease the Ambassador's present residence at Spaso House, located on a 1.55-acre site. In exchange, the United States agreed to lease to the Soviet Union for 85 years free of charge the area formerly occupied by the Mount Alto Veterans Hospital (12.58 acres).

The 1969 agreement provided that the exchange of leases would take place only after both sites were cleared and acceptable as ready for construction. We expect that this exchange will take place shortly.

The tentative plans for our embassy in Moscow call for a complex of buildings to house the chancery and some of the staff. Congressional appropriations must, of course, be sought for the project. The architects of the new U.S. Embassy are the San Francisco branch of Skidmore, Owings and Merrill in collaboration with Gruzen and Partners.

The present agreement calls for the following:

—Both sides will comply with the zoning, construction, and safety regulations of the other side.

—The final design plans of both sides are subject to review by the appropriate authorities of the other side. In the U.S. case this means the National Capital Planning Commission. In the Soviet case this means the appropriate planning authorities of the Moscow City Soviet (council).

—The maximum height applicable to our Konyushkovskaya Street site in Moscow will permit buildings of approximately 12 stories. The height restrictions applicable to the Soviet Mount Alto site in Washington will permit buildings of approximately nine to 12 stories, depending upon where the Soviets build on that site.

—The parties will agree to the extent possible on target dates for the completion of the buildings. All buildings, except chanceries, may be occupied and put to their designated use upon completion. Chanceries will be occupied simultaneously at a date to to be agreed upon by the two sides.

—Each side will develop its own design project and detailed plans.

—The basic site preparation, excavation,

20 (December 4, 1972)

U.S. and U.S.S.R. Sign Agreement on Chancery Construction

The Department of State announced on December 4 (press release 298) that an agreement between the United States and the Soviet Union on the conditions of construction of complexes of embassy buildings in Washington and Moscow had been signed that day at Washington by Walter J. Stoessel, Jr., Assistant Secretary for European Affairs, and Anatoliy F. Dobrynin, Ambassador of the Soviet Union to the United States. The continuing expansion of U.S.-Soviet relations has made increasingly urgent the mutual need to obtain new embassy quarters in Moscow and Washington, a need that had already been recognized by both sides for a number of years. (For text of the agreement, see press release 298.)

The agreement was made in accordance with the agreement for the reciprocal allocation of plots of land for the construction of embassy buildings which was signed at Moscow May 16, 1969. At that time it was agreed that the United States will receive an 85-year lease free of charge for a 10.4-acre plot on Konyushkovskaya Street between our present chancery and the Moscow River and an assurance that an adjacent half-acre park would remain free of construction. It was also agreed that we will continue to

foundation, and building frame will be erected by a construction firm of the host country employing materials available in that country.

—Each side has the right to furnish its own materials and manpower to do the exterior facing of the building, final roof covering, and all the interior finishing, including electrical wiring, plumbing, and equipment.

—Under this arrangement the U.S. Government will be its own general contractor, in the sense that it will contract both with Soviet building enterprises and American firms as required. We do not know what the Soviet intentions are.

—Duty-free importation of construction materials and equipment as required for that work done by each country from its own or third-country sources will be permitted.

—Both sides will have the right to unrestricted access to the sites for the purposes of exercising technical control and supervision. However, during the final stage of interior finishing work, the side for which the buildings are being constructed will control the access to the buildings.

21 (December 21, 1972)
MEMORANDUM OF UNDERSTANDING BETWEEN
THE GOVERNMENT OF THE UNITED STATES OF AMERICA AND
THE GOVERNMENT OF THE UNION OF SOVIET SOCIALIST REPUBLICS
REGARDING THE ESTABLISHMENT OF A STANDING CONSULTATIVE COMMISSION

I.

The Government of the United States of America and the Government of the Union of Soviet Socialist Republics hereby establish a Standing Consultative Commission.

II.

The Standing Consultative Commission shall promote the objectives and implementation of the provisions of the Treaty between the USA and the USSR on the Limitation of Anti-Ballistic Missile Systems of May 26, 1972, the Interim

Agreement between the USA and the USSR on Certain Measures
with Respect to the Limitation of Strategic Offensive Arms
of May 26, 1972, and the Agreement on Measures to Reduce
the Risk of Outbreak of Nuclear War between the USA and
the USSR of September 30, 1971, [1] and shall exercise its
competence in accordance with the provisions of Article XIII
of said Treaty, Article VI of said Interim Agreement, and
Article 7 of said Agreement on Measures.

III.

Each Government shall be represented on the
Standing Consultative Commission by a Commissioner and
a Deputy Commissioner, assisted by such staff as it
deems necessary.

IV.

The Standing Consultative Commission shall hold
periodic sessions on dates mutually agreed by the
Commissioners but no less than two times per year.
Sessions shall also be convened as soon as possible,
following reasonable notice, at the request of either
Commissioner.

V.

The Standing Consultative Commission shall
establish and approve Regulations governing procedures
and other relevant matters and may amend them as it
deems appropriate.

---

[1] TIAS 7503, 7504, 7186; 23 UST 3435, 3462; 22 UST 1590.

VI

The Standing Consultative Commission will meet
in Geneva. It may also meet at such other places as
may be agreed.

Done in Geneva, on December 21, 1972, in two copies,
each in the English and Russian languages, both texts
being equally authentic.

For the Government
of the
United States of America

[1]

For the Government
of the
Union of the Soviet Socialist Republics

[2]

---

[1] Gerard C. Smith
[2] V. S. Semenov

22 (March 2, 1973)
TEXT OF ACT OF CONFERENCE, MARCH 2

Press release 55 dated March 5

ACT

OF THE INTERNATIONAL CONFERENCE ON VIET-NAM

The Government of the United States of America;
The Government of the French Republic;
The Provisional Revolutionary Government of the
Republic of South Viet-Nam;
The Government of the Hungarian People's
Republic;
The Government of the Republic of Indonesia;
The Government of the Polish People's Republic;
The Government of the Democratic Republic of Viet-
Nam;
The Government of the United Kingdom of Great
Britain and Northern Ireland;
The Government of the Republic of Viet-Nam;
The Government of the Union of Soviet Socialist
Republics;
The Government of Canada; and
The Government of the People's Republic of China;

In the presence of the Secretary-General of the
United Nations;

With a view to acknowledging the signed Agreements; guaranteeing the ending of the war, the
maintenance of peace in Viet-Nam, the respect of
the Vietnamese people's fundamental national rights,
and the South Vietnamese people's right to self-
determination; and contributing to and guaranteeing peace in Indochina;

Have agreed on the following provisions, and
undertake to respect and implement them;

ARTICLE 1

The Parties to this Act solemnly acknowledge, express their approval of, and support the Paris Agreement on Ending the War and Restoring Peace in Viet-Nam signed in Paris on January 27, 1973, and the four Protocols to the Agreement signed on the same date (hereinafter referred to respectively as the Agreement and the Protocols).

ARTICLE 2

The Agreement responds to the aspirations and fundamental national rights of the Vietnamese people, *i.e.*, the independence, sovereignty, unity, and territorial integrity of Viet-Nam, to the right of the South Vietnamese people to self-determination, and to the earnest desire for peace shared by all countries in the world. The Agreement constitutes a major contribution to peace, self-determination, national independence, and the improvement of relations among countries. The Agreement and the Protocols should be strictly respected and scrupulously implemented.

ARTICLE 3

The Parties to this Act solemnly acknowledge the commitments by the parties to the Agreement and the Protocols to strictly respect and scrupulously implement the Agreement and the Protocols.

ARTICLE 4

The Parties to this Act solemnly recognize and strictly respect the fundamental national rights of the Vietnamese people, *i.e.*, the independence, sovereignty, unity, and territorial integrity of Viet-Nam, as well as the right of the South Vietnamese people to self-determination. The Parties to this Act shall strictly respect the Agreement and the Protocols by refraining from any action at variance with their provisions.

ARTICLE 5

For the sake of a durable peace in Viet-Nam, the Parties to this Act call on all countries to strictly respect the fundamental national rights of the Vietnamese people, *i.e.*, the independence, sovereignty, unity, and territorial integrity of Viet-Nam and the right of the South Vietnamese people to self-determination and to strictly respect the Agreement and the Protocols by refraining from any action at variance with their provisions.

ARTICLE 6

(a) The four parties to the Agreement or the two South Vietnamese parties may, either individually or through joint action, inform the other Parties to this Act about the implementation of the Agreement and the Protocols. Since the reports and views submitted by the International Commission of Control and Supervision concerning the control and supervision of the implementation of those provisions of the Agreement and the Protocols which are within the tasks of the Commission will be sent to either the four parties signatory to the Agreement or to the two South Vietnamese parties, those parties shall be responsible, either individually or through joint action, for forwarding them promptly to the other Parties to this Act.

(b) The four parties to the Agreement or the two South Vietnamese parties shall also, either individually or through joint action, forward this information and these reports and views to the other participant in the International Conference on Viet-Nam for his information.

ARTICLE 7

(a) In the event of a violation of the Agreement or the Protocols which threatens the peace, the independence, sovereignty, unity, or territorial integrity of Viet-Nam, or the right of the South Vietnamese people to self-determination, the parties signatory to the Agreement and the Protocols shall, either individually or jointly, consult with the other Parties to this Act with a view to determining necessary remedial measures.

(b) The International Conference on Viet-Nam shall be reconvened upon a joint request by the Government of the United States of America and the Government of the Democratic Republic of Viet-Nam on behalf of the parties signatory to the Agreement or upon a request by six or more of the Parties to this Act.

ARTICLE 8

With a view to contributing to and guaranteeing peace in Indochina, the Parties to this Act acknowledge the commitment of the parties to the Agreement to respect the independence, sovereignty, unity, territorial integrity, and neutrality of Cambodia and Laos as stipulated in the Agreement, agree also to respect them and to refrain from any action at variance with them, and call on other countries to do the same.

ARTICLE 9

This Act shall enter into force upon signature by plenipotentiary representatives of all twelve Parties and shall be strictly implemented by all the Parties. Signature of this Act does not constitute recognition of any Party in any case in which it has not previously been accorded.

DONE in twelve copies in Paris this second day of March, One Thousand Nine Hundred and Seventy-Three, in English, French, Russian, Vietnamese, and Chinese. All texts are equally authentic.

For the Government of the United States of America

The Secretary of State   WILLIAM P. ROGERS

For the Government of the French Republic

The Minister for   MAURICE SCHUMANN
Foreign Affairs

For the Provisional Revolutionary Government of
the Republic of South Viet-Nam

The Minister for   NGUYEN THI BINH
Foreign Affairs

For the Government of the Hungarian People's
Republic

The Minister for   JANOS PETER
Foreign Affairs

For the Government of the Republic of Indonesia

The Minister for   ADAM MALIK
Foreign Affairs

For the Government of the Polish People's Republic

The Minister for   STEFAN OLSZOWSKI
Foreign Affairs

For the Government of the Democratic Republic of
Viet-Nam

The Minister for   NGUYEN DUY TRINH
Foreign Affairs

For the Government of the United Kingdom of
Great Britain and Northern Ireland

The Secretary of State   ALEC DOUGLAS-HOME
for Foreign and
Commonwealth Affairs

For the Government of the Republic of Viet-Nam

The Minister for   TRAN VAN LAM
Foreign Affairs

For the Government of the Union of Soviet Socialist
Republics

The Minister for   ANDREI A. GROMYKO
Foreign Affairs

For the Government of Canada

The Secretary of State   MITCHELL SHARP
for External Affairs

For the Government of the People's Republic of
China

The Minister for   CHI PENG-FEI
Foreign Affairs

to help strengthen relations between the two countries.

The Commission's first meeting, held in Washington, D.C., lasted three days and covered a wide range of topics in addition to the six areas which had been originally identified as showing promise for direct cooperation.[2] The six areas are energy, computer applications to management, agricultural research, microbiological synthesis, chemical catalysis, and water resources.

U.S. Chairman of the Joint Commission is Dr. H. Guyford Stever, Director of the National Science Foundation. The Soviet Chairman for this meeting was Academician V. A. Trapeznikov, First Deputy Chairman of the U.S.S.R. State Committee for Science and Technology (SCST). He replaced Academician V. A. Kirillin, Chairman of the U.S.S.R. State Committee for Science and Technology and Deputy Chairman of the Council of Ministers of the Soviet Union, who was ill and unable to attend.

The Joint Commission, which reviewed reports and recommendations of joint working groups, selected five areas for priority implementation in the field of energy research and development. The five areas are: electric power systems, transmission lines, magnetohydrodynamics, solar energy, and geothermal energy. Additional topics for cooperation will be selected after work is effectively underway in the five priority topics.

In the field of application of computers to management, the Commission decided that work should be started on all five projects recommended by the joint working group. The projects are: theory of systems analysis applied to economics and management; computer applications and software for creating system solutions for large general-purpose problems in the field of management; econometric modeling (development of forecasting models for analysis of various branches of the economy); the use of computers for

23 (March 21, 1973)
U.S.-U.S.S.R. Scientific and Technical Commission Holds First Meeting

National Science Foundation press release 73–131 dated March 21

The U.S.-U.S.S.R. Joint Commission on Scientific and Technical Cooperation on March 21 announced approval of over 25 action programs of direct cooperation in six general areas of strong mutual interest and benefit to both countries. The Joint Commission also considered six additional areas for possible cooperation which were judged to offer promise of balanced and effective programs.

The announcement came after the first meeting of the Joint Commission, established under the U.S.-U.S.S.R. Agreement on Cooperation in the Fields of Science and Technology; the agreement was signed during President Nixon's visit to Moscow in May 1972.[1] The cooperative effort also is expected

---

[1] For text of the agreement, see BULLETIN of June 26, 1972, p. 925.

[2] For text of a record of discussions signed at Washington and Moscow on July 28, 1972, see BULLETIN of Aug. 21, 1972, p. 216.

management of large cities; and theoretical foundation for the design, development, and production of software.

Three areas of agricultural research were declared ready for priority implementation by the Joint Commission. The three areas are: research in the field of breeding, growing, and protection of farm crops; research on methods to increase production of farm animals and poultry; and mechanization of agricultural production.

In the field of microbiological synthesis, it was decided that the U.S. side of the joint working group should visit the U.S.S.R. for further discussions with the Soviets before defining priority projects for cooperative work.

Four projects in the area of water resources were selected by the Commission for priority implementation. The projects include: planning, utilization, and management of water resources; cold-weather construction techniques; methods and means of automation and remote control in water resource systems; and plastics in construction.

In the field of chemical catalysis, the Commission decided that work should proceed on five projects recommended by the joint working group. A catalyst is a substance which can change the course of a chemical reaction but which can be reclaimed at the end of the reaction. The five projects are: catalysis by coordination complexes and organometallic compounds; catalytic reactor modeling; an in-depth study of selected catalytic systems; application of catalysis to life support systems for possible use in future space exploration; and catalysis in environmental control.

The Commission also considered additional specific activities which had been previously discussed between the two sides. These include the Deep Sea Drilling Project (DSDP), a symposium on scientific and technical information, and science policy. The Commission reaffirmed its approval of the proposals made in October 1972 by representatives of the U.S. National Science Foundation and the U.S.S.R. Academy of Sciences that the Soviet Union will join the Deep Sea Drilling Project. The agreement provides that the Institute of Oceanology of the U.S.S.R. Academy of Sciences will become a member of the Joint Oceanographic Institutions for Deep Earth Sampling, the advisory body for the DSDP.

In addition, the Joint Commission considered the following areas for possible cooperation: forestry, standards and standardization, oceanographic research, transportation, physics, and electrometallurgy.

The second meeting of the Joint Commission is scheduled to take place in the U.S.S.R. toward the end of 1973 at a mutually agreed date.

Under the Scientific and Technical Cooperation Agreement, forms of cooperation may include: exchange of scientists and specialists; exchange of scientific and technical information; joint research, development, and testing, and exchange of research results and experience between scientific research institutions and organizations; organization of joint courses, conferences, and symposia; rendering of help, as appropriate, on both sides in establishing contacts and arrangements between United States firms and Soviet enterprises where a mutual interest develops; and other forms of scientific and technical cooperation as may be mutually agreed.

Other American members of the Joint Commission are Dr. James B. Fisk, chairman of the board, Bell Telephone Laboratories; Dr. Harvey Brooks, National Academy of Sciences and Harvard University; Herman Pollack, Director of the State Department's Bureau of International Scientific and Technological Affairs; Dr. Eugene Fubini, E. G. Fubini Consultants, Ltd.; Dr. Clarence Larson, Commissioner, Atomic Energy Commission; and William Letson, General Counsel, Department of Commerce.

Other Soviet members of the Commission are N. M. Zhavoronkov, representing the U.S.S.R. Academy of Sciences; N. F. Krasnov, First Deputy Minister of Higher and Secondary Specialized Education; and D.N. Pronskiy, Director of the SCST Department of Foreign Relations.

PROTOCOL TO THE AGREEMENT BETWEEN THE GOVERN-MENT OF THE UNITED STATES OF AMERICA AND THE GOVERNMENT OF THE UNION OF SOVIET SOCIALIST REPUBLICS ON THE PREVENTION OF INCIDENTS ON AND OVER THE HIGH SEAS SIGNED MAY 25, 1972

The Government of the United States of America and the Government of the Union of Soviet Socialist Republics, herein referred to as the Parties;

Having agreed on measures directed to improve the safety of navigation of the ships of their respective armed forces on the high seas and flight of their military aircraft over the high seas,

Recognizing that the objectives of the Agreement may be furthered by additional understandings, in particular concerning actions of naval ships and military aircraft with respect to the non-military ships of each Party,

Further agree as follows:

ARTICLE I

The Parties shall take measures to notify the non-military ships of each Party on the provisions of the Agreement directed at securing mutual safety.

ARTICLE II

Ships and aircraft of the Parties shall not make simulated attacks by aiming guns, missile launchers, torpedo tubes and other weapons at non-military ships of the other Party, nor launch nor drop any objects near non-military ships of the other Party in such a manner as to be hazardous to these ships or to constitute a hazard to navigation.

ARTICLE III

This Protocol will enter into force on the day of its signing and will be considered as an integral part of the Agreement between the Government of the United States of America and the Government of the Union of Soviet Socialist Republics on the Prevention of Incidents On and Over the High Seas which was signed in Moscow on May 25, 1972. [1]

DONE on the 22nd day of May, 1973 in Washington, in two copies, each in the English and the Russian language, both texts having the same force.

FOR THE GOVERNMENT OF THE UNITED STATES OF AMERICA:

FOR THE GOVERNMENT OF THE UNION OF SOVIET SOCIALIST REPUBLICS

J. P. Weinel
Vice Admiral, U.S. Navy

V. Alekseyev
Admiral

---

[1] TIAS 7379; 23 UST 1168.

25 (May 30, 1973)

Standing Consultative Commission on Arms Limitation: Regulations

Protocol, with regulations, signed at Geneva May 30, 1973; Entered into force May 30, 1973.

STANDING CONSULTATIVE COMMISSION

PROTOCOL

Pursuant to the provisions of the Memorandum of Understanding between the Government of the United States of America and the Government of the Union of Soviet Socialist Republics Regarding the Establishment of a Standing Consultative Commission, dated December 21, 1972,[1] the undersigned, having been duly appointed by their respective Governments as Commissioners of said Standing Consultative Commission, hereby establish and approve, in the form attached, Regulations governing procedures and other relevant matters of the Commission, which Regulations shall enter into force upon signature of this Protocol and remain in force until and unless amended by the undersigned or their successors.

DONE in Geneva on May 30, 1973, in two copies, each in the English and Russian languages, both texts being equally authentic.

[2]

[3]

*Commissioner,
United States
of America*

*Commissioner,
Union of Soviet
Socialist Republics*

---

¹ TIAS 7545; *ante*, p. 238.
² U. Alexis Johnson
³ Ustinov

STANDING CONSULTATIVE COMMISSION
REGULATIONS

1. The Standing Consultative Commission, established by the Memorandum of Understanding between the Government of the United States of America and the Government of the Union of Soviet Socialist Republics Regarding the Establishment of a Standing Consultative Commission of December 21, 1972, shall consist of a U. S. component and Soviet component, each of which shall be headed by a Commissioner.

2. The Commissioners shall alternately preside over the meetings.

3. The Commissioners shall, when possible, inform each other in advance of the matters to be submitted for discussion, but may at a meeting submit for discussion any matter within the competence of the Commission.

4. During intervals between sessions of the Commission, each Commissioner may transmit written or oral communications to the other Commissioner concerning matters within the competence of the Commission.

5. Each component of the Commission may invite such advisers and experts as it deems necessary to participate in a meeting.

6. The Commission may establish working groups to consider and prepare specific matters.

7. The results of the discussion of questions at the meetings of the Commission may, if necessary, be entered into records which shall be in two copies, each in the English and the Russian languages, both texts being equally authentic.

8. The proceedings of the Standing Consultative Commission shall be conducted in private. The Standing Consultative Commission may not make its proceedings public except with the express consent of both Commissioners.

9. Each component of the Commission shall bear the expenses connected with its participation in the Commission.

III:

THE WASHINGTON SUMMIT MEETING:
JUNE 18 TO 25, 1973

INTRODUCTION

The Washington summit meeting produced 11 agreements and a joint communique. The thirteenth document included in this section is an announcement on fisheries agreements signed during the time period of the summit, but in Copenhagen. (See Appendix, 18A and 19A, for specific references to the fisheries agreements.)

Four of the 11 agreements built horizontally from the Moscow agreements of the previous year. That is, they established the same type of cooperative arrangements in agriculture, ocean studies, transportation, and nuclear energy (Documents 26, 27, 28, and 32) as had been done in Moscow for environment, health, and science. Agreements on trade-related topics (taxation, Chamber of Commerce, commercial facilities) tried to build vertically upon the agreements on trade signed in October 1972.

The third area in which agreements were signed, in addition to cooperative ventures and trade matters, was the area of limitation of offensive nuclear weapons. In this area the two sides attempted to build vertically upon the Interim Agreement of 1972. The permanent agreement that was to be signed at Washington to replace the Interim Agreement was not prepared, however, and the president and general secretary had to content themselves with signing a declaration of Basic Principles of Negotiations on the Further Limitation of Strategic Offensive Arms (Document 31). In that agreement, both sides committed themselves to serious negotiations during the coming year with the objective of having the final agreement ready for signature at the 1974 summit meeting that would occur in Moscow. In the agreement on preventing nuclear war, both sides promised more formally than in Moscow to restrain themselves in their bilateral relations and in their relations with third parties.

The hard issues of expanding trade relations were not visible in the documents of this meeting, for Congress was still debating the Trade Reform Bill of April 1973. General Secretary Brezhnev tried to lobby for passage of the bill. He attended a two-hour luncheon with the Senate Foreign Relations Committee and hosted an elaborate luncheon on the following day for officials from some of the nation's major corporations.[1]

In the two major areas of concern—trade and arms limitation—the Washington summit achieved considerably less than the Moscow summit had. The new agreement on arms limitation was not ready; trade issues were outside the control of the president and general secretary; and of the other agreements signed, two were merely slight revisions of existing ones (air services, cultural exchanges). Probably the document with the greatest potential significance was the agreement on prevention of nuclear wars, especially in that each side promised in its relations with third parties not to behave in such a way as to antagonize the other signatory of the agreement. The problem of implementing that promise after the Washington meeting proved great.

NOTE

1. See New York *Times*, June 20, 1973, p. 1 for some issues discussed at the luncheon with the Senate Foreign Relations Committee. See also Charles E. Timberlake, "The Summit Meeting as a Form of Diplomacy in American-Soviet Relations in the 1970s," in *The Soviet Union: The Seventies and Beyond*, ed. Bernard Eissenstat (Lexington, Mass.: Lexington Books, 1976), 107–14 for a more extensive analysis of the Washington Summit.

26 (June 19, 1973)
AGREEMENT ON COOPERATION IN AGRICULTURE

AGREEMENT BETWEEN THE GOVERNMENT OF THE UNITED STATES OF AMERICA AND THE GOVERNMENT OF THE UNION OF SOVIET SOCIALIST REPUBLICS ON COOPERATION IN THE FIELD OF AGRICULTURE

The Government of the United States of America and the Government of the Union of Soviet Socialist Republics;

Taking into account the importance which the production of food has for the peoples of both countries and for all of mankind;

Desiring to expand existing cooperation between the two countries in the field of agricultural research and development;

Wishing to apply new knowledge and technology in agricultural production and processing;

Recognizing the desirability of expanding relationships in agricultural trade and the exchange of information necessary for such trade;

Convinced that cooperation in the field of agriculture will contribute to overall improvement of relations between the two countries;

In pursuance and further development of the Agreement between the Government of the United States of America and the Government of the Union of Soviet Socialist Republics on Cooperation in the Fields of Science and Technology of May 24, 1972, and in accordance with the Agreement on Exchanges and Cooperation in Scientific, Technical, Educational, Cultural and Other Fields of April 11, 1972, and in accordance with the Agreement on Cooperation in the Field of Environmental Protection of May 23, 1972;

Have agreed as follows:

ARTICLE I

The Parties will develop and carry out cooperation in the field of agriculture on the basis of mutual benefit, equality and reciprocity.

ARTICLE II

The Parties will promote the development of mutually beneficial cooperation in the following main areas:

1. Regular exchange of relevant information, including forward estimates, on production, consumption, demand and trade of major agricultural commodities.

2. Methods of forecasting the production, demand and consumption of major agricultural products, including econometric methods.

3. Plant science, including genetics, breeding, plant protection and crop production, including production under semi-arid conditions.

4. Livestock and poultry science, including genetics, breeding, physiology, nutrition, disease protection and large-scale operations.

5. Soil science, including the theory of movement of water, gases, salts, and heat in soils.

6. Mechanization of agriculture, including development and testing of new machinery, equipment and technology, as well as repair and technical service.

7. Application, storage and transportation of mineral fertilizers and other agricultural chemicals.

8. Processing, storage and preservation of agricultural commodities, including formula feed technology.

9. Land reclamation and reclamation engineering, including development of new equipment, designs and materials.

10. Use of mathematical methods and electronic computers in agriculture, including mathematical modeling of large-scale agricultural enterprises.

Other areas of cooperation may be added by mutual agreement.

ARTICLE III

Cooperation between the Parties may take the following forms:

1. Exchange of scientists, specialists and trainees.
2. Organization of bilateral symposia and conferences.
3. Exchange of scientific, technical and relevant economic information, and methods of research.
4. Planning, development and implementation of joint projects and programs.
5. Exchange of plant germ plasm, seeds and living material.
6. Exchange of animals, biological materials, agricultural chemicals, and models of new machines, equipment and scientific instruments.
7. Direct contacts and exchanges between botanical gardens.
8. Exchange of agricultural exhibitions.

Other forms of cooperation may be added by mutual agreement.

ARTICLE IV

1. In furtherance of the aims of this Agreement, the Parties will, as appropriate, encourage, promote and monitor the development of cooperation and direct contacts between governmental and nongovernmental institutions, research and other organizations, trade associations, and firms of the two countries, including the conclusion, as appropriate, of implementing agreements for carrying out specific projects and programs under this Agreement.
2. To assure fruitful development of cooperation, the Parties will render every assistance for the travel of scientists and specialists to areas of the two countries appropriate for the conduct of activities under this Agreement.
3. Projects and exchanges under this Agreement will be carried out in accordance with the laws and regulations of the two countries.

ARTICLE V

1. For implementation of this Agreement, there shall be established a US–USSR Joint Committee on Agricultural Cooperation which shall meet, as a rule, once a year, alternately in the United States and the Soviet Union, unless otherwise mutually agreed.
2. The Joint Committee will review and approve specific projects and programs of cooperation; establish the procedures for their implementation; designate, as appropriate, institutions and organizations responsible for carrying out cooperative activities; and make recommendations, as appropriate, to the Parties.
3. Within the framework of the Joint Committee there shall be established a Joint Working Group on Agricultural Economic Research and Information and a Joint Working Group on Agricultural Research and Technological Development. Unless otherwise mutually agreed, each Joint Working Group will meet alternately in the United States and the

Soviet Union at least two times a year. The Joint Committee may establish other working groups as it deems necessary.

4. The Executive Agents for coordinating and carrying out this Agreement shall be, for the Government of the United States of America, the United States Department of Agriculture, and for the Government of the Union of Soviet Socialist Republics, the Ministry of Agriculture of the USSR. The Executive Agents will, as appropriate, assure the cooperation in their respective countries of other institutions and organizations as required for carrying out joint activities under this Agreement. During the period between meetings of the Joint Committee, the Executive Agents will maintain contact with each other and coordinate and supervise the development and implementation of cooperative activities conducted under this Agreement.

ARTICLE VI

Unless an implementing agreement contains other provisions, each Party or participating institution, organization or firm, shall bear the costs of its participation and that of its personnel in cooperative activities engaged in under this Agreement.

ARTICLE VII

1. Nothing in this Agreement shall be interpreted to prejudice or modify any existing Agreements between the Parties.
2. Projects developed by the US–USSR Joint Working Group on Agricultural Research which were approved at the first session of the US–USSR Joint Commission on Scientific and Technical Cooperation on March 21, 1973, will continue without interruption and will become the responsibility of the US–USSR Joint Committee on Agricultural Cooperation upon its formal establishment.

ARTICLE VIII

1. This Agreement shall enter into force upon signature and remain in force for five years. It will be automatically extended for successive five-year periods unless either Party notifies the other of its intent to terminate this Agreement not later than six months prior to the expiration of this Agreement.
2. This Agreement may be modified at any time by mutual agreement of the Parties.
3. The termination of this Agreement will not affect the validity of implementing agreements concluded under this Agreement between institutions, organizations and firms of the two countries.

DONE at Washington, this 19th day of June, 1973, in duplicate, in the English and Russian languages, both texts being equally authentic.

For the Government of the United States of America:

EARL L. BUTZ

For the Government of the Union of Soviet Socialist Republics:

A. GROMYKO

27 (June 19, 1973)
AGREEMENT ON COOPERATION IN STUDIES OF THE WORLD OCEAN

AGREEMENT BETWEEN THE GOVERNMENT OF THE UNITED STATES OF AMERICA AND THE GOVERNMENT OF THE UNION OF SOVIET SOCIALIST REPUBLICS ON COOPERATION IN STUDIES OF THE WORLD OCEAN

The Government of the United States of America and the Government of the Union of Soviet Socialist Republics;

Recognizing the importance of comprehensive studies of the World Ocean for peaceful purposes and for the well-being of mankind;

Striving for more complete knowledge and rational utilization of the World Ocean by all nations through broad international cooperation in oceanographic investigation and research;

Aware of the capabilities and resources of both countries for studies of the World Ocean and the extensive history and successful results of previous cooperation between them;

Desiring to combine their efforts in the further investigation of the World Ocean and to use the results for the benefit of the peoples of both countries and of all mankind; and

In pursuance and further development of the Agreement between the Government of the United States of America and the Government of the Union of Soviet Socialist Republics on Cooperation in the Fields of Science and Technology of May 24, 1972, and in accordance with the Agreement on Exchanges and Cooperation in Scientific, Technical, Educational, Cultural and Other Fields of April 11, 1972, and in accordance with the Agreement on Cooperation in the Field of Environmental Protection of May 23, 1972;

Have agreed as follows:

ARTICLE 1

The Parties will develop and carry out cooperation in studies of the World Ocean on the basis of equality, reciprocity and mutual benefit.

ARTICLE 2

In their studies of the World Ocean, the Parties will direct cooperative efforts to the investigation and solution of important basic and applied research problems. Initially, cooperation will be implemented in the following areas:

a. Large-scale ocean-atmosphere interaction, including laboratory studies, oceanic experiments, and mathematical modeling of the ocean-atmosphere system.

b. Ocean currents of planetary scale and other questions of ocean dynamics.

c. Geochemistry and marine chemistry of the World Ocean.

d. Geological and geophysical investigations of the World Ocean, including deep sea drilling for scientific purposes.

e. Biological productivity of the World Ocean and the biochemistry of the functioning of individual organisms and whole biological communities in the World Ocean.

f. Intercalibration and standardization of oceanographic instrumentation and methods.

Other areas of cooperation may be added by mutual agreement.

ARTICLE 3

Cooperation provided for in the preceding Articles may take the following forms:

a. Joint planning, development, and implementation of research projects and programs;

b. Exchange of scientists, specialists, and advanced students;

c. Exchange of scientific and technical information, documentation, and experience, including the results of national oceanographic studies;

d. Convening of joint conferences, meetings, and seminars of specialists;

e. Appropriate participation by both countries in multilateral cooperative activities sponsored by international scientific organizations;

f. Facilitation by both Parties, in accordance with laws, rules and regulations of each country and relevant bilateral agreements, of use of appropriate port facilities of the two countries for ships' services and supplies, including provision for rest and changes of ships' personnel, in connection with carrying out cooperative activities.

Other forms of cooperation may be added by mutual agreement.

ARTICLE 4

In furtherance of the aims of this Agreement, the Parties will, as appropriate, encourage, facilitate and monitor the development of cooperation and direct contacts between agencies, organizations and firms of the two countries, including the conclusion, as appropriate, of implementing agreements for carrying out specific projects and programs under this Agreement.

ARTICLE 5

1. For implementation of this Agreement, there shall be established a US–USSR Joint Committee on Cooperation in World Ocean Studies. This Joint Committee shall meet, as a rule, once a year, alternately in the United States and the Soviet Union, unless otherwise mutually agreed.

2. The Joint Committee shall take such action as is necessary for effective implementation of this Agreement including, but not limited to, approval of specific projects and programs of cooperation; designation of appropriate agencies and organizations to be

responsible for carrying out cooperative activities; and making recommendations, as appropriate, to the Parties.

3. Each Party shall designate its Executive Agent which will be responsible for carrying out this Agreement. During the period between meetings of the Joint Committee, the Executive Agents shall maintain contact with each other and coordinate and supervise the development and implementation of cooperative activities conducted under this Agreement.

ARTICLE 6

Nothing in this Agreement shall be interpreted to prejudice other agreements between the Parties or commitments of either Party to other international oceanographic programs.

ARTICLE 7

Each Party, with the consent of the other Party, may invite third countries to participate in cooperative activities engaged in under this Agreement.

ARTICLE 8

1. This Agreement shall enter into force upon signature and remain in force for five years. It may be modified or extended by mutual agreement of the Parties.

2. The termination of the Agreement shall not affect the validity of implementing agreements concluded under this Agreement between interested agencies, organizations and firms of the two countries.

DONE at Washington, this 19th day of June, 1973, in duplicate, in the English and Russian languages, both texts being equally authentic.

For the Government of the United States of America:

WILLIAM P. ROGERS

For the Government of the Union of Soviet Socialist Republics:

A. GROMYKO

28 (June 19, 1973)
AGREEMENT ON COOPERATION IN TRANSPORTATION

AGREEMENT BETWEEN THE GOVERNMENT OF THE UNITED STATES OF AMERICA AND THE GOVERNMENT OF THE UNION OF SOVIET SOCIALIST REPUBLICS ON COOPERATION IN THE FIELD OF TRANSPORTATION

The Government of the United States of America and the Government of the Union of Soviet Socialist Republics;

Recognizing the important role played by safe and efficient transportation systems in the development of all countries;

Considering that the improvement of existing transportation systems and techniques can benefit both of their peoples;

Believing that the combined efforts of the two countries in this field can contribute to more rapid and efficient solutions of transportation problems than would be possible through separate, parallel national efforts;

Desiring to promote the establishment of long-term and productive relationships between transportation specialists and institutions of both countries;

In pursuance and further development of the Agreement between the Government of the United States of America and the Government of the Union of Soviet Socialist Republics on Cooperation in the Fields of Science and Technology of May 24, 1972, and in accordance with the Agreement on Exchanges and Cooperation in Scientific, Technical, Educational, Cultural and Other Fields of April 11, 1972, and in accordance with the Agreement on Cooperation in the Field of Environmental Protection of May 23, 1972;

Have agreed as follows:

ARTICLE 1

The Parties will develop and carry out cooperation in the field of transportation on the basis of mutual benefit, equality and reciprocity.

ARTICLE 2

This cooperation will be directed to the investigation and solution of specific problems of mutual interest in the field of transportation. Initially, cooperation will be implemented in the following areas:

a. Construction of bridges and tunnels, including problems of control of structure stress and fracture, and special construction procedures under cold climatic conditions.

b. Railway transport, including problems of rolling stock, track and roadbed, high speed traffic, automation, and cold weather operation.

c. Civil aviation, including problems of increasing efficiency and safety.

d. Marine transport, including technology of maritime shipping and cargo handling in seaports.

e. Automobile transport, including problems of traffic safety.

Other areas of cooperation may be added by mutual agreement.

ARTICLE 3

Cooperation provided for in the preceding Articles may take the following forms:

a. Exchange of scientists and specialists;

b. Exchange of scientific and technical information and documentation;

c. Convening of joint conferences, meetings and seminars; and

d. Joint planning, development and implementation of research programs and projects.

Other forms of cooperation may be added by mutual agreement.

ARTICLE 4

In furtherance of the aims of this Agreement, the Parties will, as appropriate, encourage, facilitate and monitor the development of cooperation and direct contacts between agencies, organizations and firms of the two countries, including the conclusion, as appropriate, of implementing agreements for carrying out specific projects and programs under this Agreement.

ARTICLE 5

1. For the implementation of this Agreement, there shall be established a US–USSR Joint Committee on Cooperation in Transportation. This Committee shall meet, as a rule, once a year, alternately in the United States and the Soviet Union, unless otherwise mutually agreed.

2. The Joint Committee shall take such action as is necessary for effective implementation of this Agreement including, but not limited to, approval of specific projects and programs of cooperation; designation of appropriate agencies and organizations to be responsible for carrying out cooperative activities; and making recommendations, as appropriate, to the Parties.

3. Each Party shall designate its Executive Agent which will be responsible for carrying out this Agreement. During the period between meetings of the Joint Committee, the Executive Agents shall maintain contact with each other, keep each other informed of activities and progress in implementing this Agreement, and coordinate and supervise the development and implementation of cooperative activities conducted under this Agreement.

ARTICLE 6

Nothing in this Agreement shall be interpreted to prejudice other agreements between the Parties or their respective rights and obligations under such other agreements.

ARTICLE 7

1. This Agreement shall enter into force upon signature and shall remain in force for five years. It may be modified or extended by mutual agreement of the Parties.

2. The termination of this Agreement shall not affect the validity of implementing agreements concluded under this Agreement between interested agencies, organizations and firms of the two countries.

DONE at Washington, this 19th day of June, 1973, in duplicate, in the English and Russian languages, both texts being equally authentic.

For the Government of the United States of America:

WILLIAM P. ROGERS

For the Government of the Union of Soviet Socialist Republics:

A. GROMYKO

29 (June 19, 1973)
GENERAL AGREEMENT ON CONTACTS, EXCHANGES AND COOPERATION

GENERAL AGREEMENT BETWEEN THE UNITED STATES OF AMERICA AND THE UNION OF SOVIET SOCIALIST REPUBLICS ON CONTACTS, EXCHANGES AND COOPERATION

The Government of the United States of America and the Government of the Union of Soviet Socialist Republics;

Consistent with the Basic Principles of Relations Between the United States of America and the Union of Soviet Socialist Republics, signed at Moscow on May 29, 1972;

Desiring to promote better understanding between the peoples of the United States and the Soviet Union and to help improve the general state of relations between the two countries;

Believing that the further expansion of mutually beneficial contacts, exchanges and cooperation will facilitate the achievement of these aims;

Taking into account the positive experience achieved through previous agreements on exchanges in the scientific, technical, educational, cultural and other fields;

Have agreed as follows:

ARTICLE I

1. The Parties will encourage and develop contacts, exchanges and cooperation in the fields of science, technology, education and culture, and in other fields of mutual interest on the basis of equality, mutual benefit and reciprocity.

2. Such contacts, exchanges and cooperation shall be subject to the Constitution and applicable laws and regulations of the respective countries. Within this framework, the Parties will make every effort to promote favorable conditions for the fulfillment of these contacts, exchanges and cooperation.

ARTICLE II

1. The Parties take note of the following specialized agreements on cooperation in various fields and reaffirm their commitments to achieve the fulfillment of them:

a. The Agreement on Cooperation in the Field of Environmental Protection Between the United States of America and the Union of Soviet Socialist Republics, signed at Moscow on May 23, 1972;

b. The Agreement Between the Government of the United States of America and the Government of the Union of Soviet Socialist Republics on Cooperation in the Field of Medical Science and Public Health, signed at Moscow on May 23, 1972;

c. The Agreement Between the United States of America and the Union of Soviet Socialist Republics Concerning Cooperation in the Exploration and Use of Outer Space for Peaceful Purposes, signed at Moscow on May 24, 1972;

d. The Agreement Between the Government of the United States of America and the Government of the Union of Soviet Socialist Republics on Cooperation in the Fields of Science and Technology, signed at Moscow on May 24, 1972;

e. The Agreement Between the Government of the United States of America and the Government of the Union of Soviet Socialist Republics on Cooperation in the Field of Agriculture, signed at Washington on June 19, 1973;

f. The Agreement Between the Government of the United States of America and the Government of the Union of Soviet Socialist Republics on Cooperation in Studies of the World Ocean, signed at Washington on June 19, 1973; and

g. The Agreement Between the Government of the United States of America and the Government of the Union of Soviet Socialist Republics on Cooperation in the Field of Transportation, signed at Washington on June 19, 1973.

2. The Parties will support the renewal of specialized agreements, including mutually agreed upon amendments, between:

a. The National Academy of Sciences of the United States of America and the Academy of Sciences of the Union of Soviet Socialist Republics; and

b. The American Council of Learned Societies and the Academy of Sciences of the Union of Soviet Socialist Republics.

3. The Parties will encourage the conclusion, when it is considered mutually beneficial, of additional agreements in other specific fields within the framework of this Agreement.

ARTICLE III

The Parties will encourage and facilitate, as appropriate, contacts, exchanges and cooperation between organizations of the two countries in the field of science and technology and in other related fields of mutual interest which are not being carried out under specialized agreements concluded between the Parties. These activities may include:

a. the exchange of specialists, delegations, and scientific and technical information; and the organization of lectures, seminars and symposia for such specialists;

b. the participation of scientists and other specialists in scientific congresses, conferences and similar meetings being held in the two countries, and the conducting of specialized exhibits and of joint research work; and

c. other forms of contacts, exchanges and cooperation which may be mutually agreed upon.

ARTICLE IV

1. The Parties will encourage and facilitate the expansion of contacts, exchanges and cooperation in various fields of education. To this end, the Parties will:

a. provide for the exchange of students, researchers and faculty members for study and research; professors and teachers to lecture, offer instruction, and conduct research; as well as specialists and delegations in various fields of education; and

b. facilitate the exchange, by appropriate organizations, of educational and teaching materials, including textbooks, syllabi and curricula, materials on methodology, samples of teaching instruments and visual aids.

2. The Parties will also encourage the study of each other's language through the development of the exchanges and cooperation listed above and through other mutually agreed measures.

ARTICLE V

In order to promote better mutual acquaintance with the cultural achievements of each country, the Parties will encourage the development of contacts and exchanges in the field of the performing arts. To this end, the Parties will facilitate exchanges of theatrical, musical and choreographic ensembles, orchestras, other artistic and entertainment groups, and individual performers.

ARTICLE VI

1. The Parties will encourage the organizations of the film industries of both countries, as appropriate, to consider means of further expanding the purchase and distribution on a commercial basis of films produced in each country.

2. The Parties will also encourage, as appropriate, the exchange and exhibition of documentary films in the fields of science, technology, culture, education and other fields, as well as facilitate the exchange of delegations of creative and technical specialists.

3. The Parties further agree, when requested by organizations and individuals of their respective countries, to consider other proposals directed toward the expansion of exchanges in this field, including the holding of film premieres and film weeks in each country and the joint production of feature films and short and full-length educational and scientific films.

ARTICLE VII

1. The Parties will facilitate contacts and encourage exchanges between organizations of the two countries in the fields of radio and television, including the exchange of radio programs and television films and exchanges of delegations and specialists in these fields.

2. The Parties further agree, when requested by organizations and individuals of their respective countries, to consider other proposals in the fields of radio and television, including joint production of television films and the providing of assistance in the production of radio and television programs.

Article VIII

The Parties will encourage:

a. the exchange of books, magazines, newspapers and other publications devoted to scientific, technical, cultural, and general educational subjects between libraries, universities and other organizations of each country, as well as the reciprocal distribution of the magazines *Amerika* and *Soviet Life*; and

b. exchanges and visits of journalists, editors, publishers, and translators of literary works, as well as their participation in appropriate professional meetings and conferences.

Article IX

The Parties will encourage and facilitate the exchange of exhibitions on various topics of mutual interest, as well as appropriate participation by one Party in exhibitions which may take place in the other's country. The Parties will also render assistance for the exchange of exhibitions between the museums of the two countries.

Article X

The Parties will provide for reciprocal exchanges and visits of architects, art historians, artists, composers, musicologists, museum specialists, playwrights, theater directors, writers, specialists in various fields of law and those in other cultural and professional fields, to familiarize themselves with matters of interest to them in their respective fields and to participate in meetings, conferences and symposia.

Article XI

1. The Parties will render assistance to members of the Congress of the United States of America and deputies of the Supreme Soviet of the Union of Soviet Socialist Republics, as well as to officials of the national governments of both countries, making visits to the Soviet Union and the United States respectively. Arrangements for such assistance will be agreed upon in advance through diplomatic channels.

2. The Parties will encourage exchanges of representatives of municipal, local and state governments of the United States and the Soviet Union to study various functions of government at these levels.

Article XII

The Parties will encourage joint undertakings and exchanges between appropriate organizations active in civic and social life, including youth and women's organizations, recognizing that the decision to implement such joint undertakings and exchanges remains a concern of the organizations themselves.

Article XIII

The Parties will encourage exchanges of athletes and athletic teams as well as visits of specialists in the fields of physical education and sports under arrangements made between the appropriate sports organizations of the two countries.

Article XIV

The Parties will encourage the expansion of tourist travel between the two countries and the adoption of measures to satisfy the requests of tourists to acquaint themselves with the life, work and culture of the people of each country.

Article XV

The Parties note that commemorative activities may take place in their countries in connection with the celebration of anniversaries recognized by major international bodies.

Article XVI

The Parties agree to hold a meeting each year of their representatives for a general review of the implementation of contacts, exchanges and cooperation in various fields and to consider exchanges which are not being carried out under specialized agreements concluded between the Parties.

Article XVII

1. In implementation of various provisions of this Agreement, the Parties have established a Program of Exchanges for 1974–1976, which is annexed to and constitutes an integral part of this Agreement. The terms of this Program shall be in force from January 1, 1974 to December 31, 1976, and thereafter, unless and until amended by agreement of the Parties, will provide the basic guidelines for the Program of Exchanges in 1977–1979.

2. The Parties agree that their representatives will meet prior to the end of 1976 and will develop the Program of Exchanges for the succeeding three years.

Article XVIII

The Parties agree that:

a. The programs and itineraries, lengths of stay, dates of arrival, size of delegations, financial and transportation arrangements and other details of exchanges and visits, except as otherwise determined, shall be agreed upon, as a rule, not less than thirty days in advance, through diplomatic channels or between appropriate organizations requested by the Parties to carry out these exchanges;

b. Applications for visas for visitors participating in exchanges and cooperative activities shall be submitted, as a rule, at least fourteen days before the estimated time of departure;

c. Unless otherwise provided for in specialized agreements between the Parties, and except where other specific arrangements have been agreed upon, participants in exchanges and cooperative activities will pay their own expenses, including international travel, internal travel and costs of maintenance in the receiving country.

Article XIX

1. This Agreement shall enter into force on signature and shall remain in force until December 31,

1979. It may be modified or extended by mutual agreement of the Parties.

2. Nothing in this Agreement shall be construed to prejudice other agreements concluded between the two Parties.

DONE at Washington, this 19th day of June, 1973, in duplicate, in the English and Russian languages, both texts being equally authentic.

For the Government of the United States of America:

WILLIAM P. ROGERS

For the Government of the Union of Soviet Socialist Republics:

A. GROMYKO

ANNEX

Program of Exchanges for 1974–1976

In implementation of various provisions of the General Agreement between the United States of America and the Union of Soviet Socialist Republics on Contacts, Exchanges and Cooperation signed at Washington on June 19, 1973, the Parties have agreed on the following Program of Exchanges for the period January 1, 1974 to December 31, 1976:

SECTION I
Education

1. The Parties agree to provide for the exchange annually from each side of:

a. At least 40 graduate students, young researchers and instructors for study and postgraduate research in the natural sciences, technical sciences, humanities and social sciences, for periods of stay from one semester up to one academic year, including five-week courses before the beginning of the academic year to improve the participant's competence in the Russian or English language;

b. At least 30 language teachers to participate in summer courses of ten weeks to improve their competence in the Russian or English language;

c. At least 10 professors and instructors of universities and other institutions of higher learning to conduct scholarly research for periods of stay between three and six months, the total volume of these exchanges not to exceed 50 man-months for each side; and

d. At least two graduate-level students or young specialists in the fields of dance, music, theater, film and the graphic and plastic arts for the purpose of study, research and training for periods of from four to ten months in specialized schools, institutes, conservatories, theaters, museums, studios, or other institutions.

2. The Parties agree to provide for exchanges of professors and specialists from universities and other institutions of higher learning, in accordance with the desires of the receiving side, for periods of from one semester up to one academic year, to offer instruction and to lecture at universities and other institutions of higher learning in the fields of:

a. The natural sciences, technical sciences, humanities and social sciences; and

b. Language, literature and linguistics.

3. The Parties agree to provide for the exchange of at least two specialists in vocational rehabilitation or education of the handicapped from each side during the period of this Program for a period of from three to six months. The specialists will conduct research on topics to be agreed upon between the appropriate organizations of both countries.

4. The Parties agree to facilitate the conducting of bilateral seminars of United States and Soviet specialists in education: twelve participants from each side for a period of two to four weeks on subjects to be agreed upon subsequently. During the period of this Program, four seminars will be conducted in each country, two in subjects bearing on higher education, and two in subjects bearing on primary and secondary education.

5. The Parties agree to exchange during the period of this Program four delegations from each side composed of three to five specialists for a period of up to three weeks on topics to be agreed upon subsequently; two of these delegations shall be in the field of higher education, and two in primary and/or secondary education.

6. The Parties agree to explore the possibility of an exchange of primary or secondary school teachers between appropriate organizations of the two countries.

7. The United States will take measures to encourage the study of the Russian language in the United States in accordance with the Joint United States-Soviet Communique of May 29, 1972.

8. The Parties agree to explore the possibility of an exchange of information and appropriate consultation concerning equivalency of degrees.

9. The exchanges specified in this Section will be implemented in accordance with the terms of a supplemental agreement to be effected through an exchange of notes.

SECTION II
Performing Arts

1. The Parties agree to facilitate the tours of at least ten major performing arts groups from each side during the period of this Program. The detailed arrangements for tours of these groups will be provided for in contracts to be concluded between the following entities: for tours of American groups, between the Embassy of the United States of America in Moscow or authorized representatives of the groups themselves and the appropriate concert organizations of the Soviet Union; for tours of Soviet groups, between appropriate organizations or impresarios of the United States and concert organizations of the Soviet Union. The receiving Party will seek to satisfy the wishes of the sending Party concerning the timing and duration of the tours as well as the number of cities to be visited.

2. The Parties agree to facilitate the tours of at

least 35 individual performers from each side during the period of this Program. Arrangements for tours of individual performers will be made directly between appropriate organizations or impresarios of the United States and concert organizations of the Soviet Union.

SECTION III
Publications

1. The Parties agree to render practical assistance for the successful distribution of the magazines *Amerika* in the Soviet Union and *Soviet Life* in the United States on the basis of reciprocity and to consult as necessary in order to find ways to increase the distribution of these magazines. Upon reaching full distribution of the 62,000 copies of each magazine as currently provided for, the Parties will examine the possibility of expanding the reciprocal distribution of the magazines to 82,000 copies per month by December 1976. The Parties will distribute free of charge unsold copies of the magazine among visitors to mutually-arranged exhibitions.

2. The Parties agree to encourage the exchange of specialized publications and microfilms between the National Archives of the United States of America and the Main Archival Administration of the Council of Ministers of the Union of Soviet Socialist Republics.

SECTION IV
Exhibitions

1. The Parties agree to exchange exhibitions during the period of this Program, as follows:

a. From the Soviet side, either a major industrial/trade exhibition or one or two circulating exhibitions. The decision of the Soviet side on this matter will be conveyed through diplomatic channels; and

b. From the US side, one or two circulating exhibitions.

The subjects of the exhibitions will be agreed upon through diplomatic channels.

The circulating exhibitions will be shown in nine cities in each country for a period of up to 28 actual showing days in each city. The Parties will discuss in a preliminary fashion the nature and general content of each exhibition and will acquaint each other with the exhibitions before their official opening, in particular through the exchange of catalogues, prospectuses and other information pertinent to the exhibitions. Other conditions for conducting the exhibitions (dates, size and character of premises, number of personnel, financial terms, etc.) shall be subject to agreement by the Parties. Arrangements for conducting the exhibitions will be concluded no later than five months before their opening.

2. The Parties agree to render assistance for the exchange of exhibitions, including art exhibitions, between the museums of the two countries, and to encourage these museums to establish and develop direct contacts with the aim of exchanging informative materials, albums, art monographs and other publications of mutual interest. In the case of art exhibitions, their content and the conditions for conducting them would be the subject of discussion and special agreement in each case between the relevant American museums and the Ministry of Culture of the Union of Soviet Socialist Republics.

3. The Parties will agree through diplomatic channels on the arrangements for other exhibitions and on participation in national exhibitions which may take place in either country.

SECTION V
General

Each of the Parties shall have the right to include in delegations interpreters or members of its Embassy, who shall be considered as within the agreed total membership of such delegations.

30 (June 20, 1973)

CONVENTION BETWEEN THE UNITED STATES OF AMERICA AND THE UNION OF SOVIET SOCIALIST REPUBLICS ON MATTERS OF TAXATION

The President of the United States of America and the Presidium of the Supreme Soviet of the Union of Soviet Socialist Republics, desiring to avoid double taxation and to promote the development of economic, scientific, technical and cultural cooperation between both States, have appointed for this purpose as their respective plenipotentiaries:

The President of the United States of America:
George P. Shultz, Secretary of the Treasury of the USA; and

The Presidium of the Supreme Soviet of the Union of Soviet Socialist Republics:
Nikolai Semenovich Patolichev, Minister of Foreign Trade of the USSR;

Who have agreed as follows:

ARTICLE I

1. The taxes which are the subject of this Convention are:

(a) In the case of the Union of Soviet Socialist Republics, taxes and dues provided for by the All-Union legislation;

(b) In the case of the United States of America,

taxes and dues provided for by the Internal Revenue Code.

2. This Convention shall also apply to taxes and dues substantially similar to those covered by paragraph 1. which are imposed in addition to, or in place of, existing taxes and dues after the signature of this Convention.

ARTICLE II

In this Convention, the terms listed below shall have the following meaning:

1. "Soviet Union" or "USSR" means the Union of Soviet Socialist Republics and, when used in a geographical sense, means the territories of all the Union Republics. Such term also includes:

(a) The territorial sea thereof, and
(b) The seabed and subsoil of the submarine areas adjacent to the coast thereof, but beyond the territorial sea, over which the Soviet Union exercises sovereign rights, in accordance with international law, for the purpose of exploration for and exploitation of the natural resources of such areas. However, it is understood that such term includes such areas only to the extent that the person, property or activity with respect to which questions of taxation arise is connected with such exploration or exploitation.

2. "United States" or "USA" means the United States of America and, when used in a geographical sense, means the territories of all the states and of the District of Columbia. Such term also includes:

(a) The territorial sea thereof, and
(b) The seabed and subsoil of the submarine areas adjacent to the coast thereof, but beyond the territorial sea, over which the United States exercises sovereign rights, in accordance with international law, for the purpose of exploration for and exploitation of the natural resources of such areas. However, it is understood that such term includes such areas only to the extent that the person, property or activity with respect to which questions of taxation arise is connected with such exploration or exploitation.

3. "Resident of the Soviet Union" means:

(a) a legal entity or any other organization treated in the USSR as a legal entity for tax purposes which is created under the laws of the Soviet Union or any Union Republic and
(b) an individual resident in the Soviet Union for purposes of its tax.

4. "Resident of the United States" means:

(a) a corporation or any other organization treated in the United States as a corporation for tax purposes which is created or organized under the laws of the United States or any state thereof or of the District of Columbia and
(b) an individual resident in the United States for purposes of its tax.

5. "Contracting State" means the United States or the Soviet Union, as the context requires.
6. The term "competent authorities" means:

(a) in the case of the Soviet Union, the Ministry of Finance
(b) in the case of the United States, the Secretary of the Treasury or his delegate.

ARTICLE III

1. The following categories of income derived from sources within one Contracting State by a resident of the other Contracting State shall be subject to tax only in that other Contracting State:

(a) rentals, royalties, or other amounts paid as consideration for the use of or right to use literary, artistic, and scientific works, or for the use of copyrights of such works, as well as the rights to inventions (patents, author's certificates), industrial designs, processes or formulae, computer programs, trademarks, service marks, and other similar property or rights, or for industrial, commercial, or scientific equipment, or for knowledge, experience, or skill (know-how);
(b) gains derived from the sale or exchange of any such rights or property, whether or not the amounts realized on sale or exchange are contingent in whole or in part, on the extent and nature of use or disposition of such rights or property;
(c) gains from the sale or other disposition of property received as a result of inheritance or gift;
(d) income from the furnishing of engineering, architectural, designing, and other technical services in connection with an installation contract with a resident of the first Contracting State which are carried out in a period not exceeding 36 months at one location;
(e) income from the sale of goods or the supplying of services through a broker, general commission agent or other agent of independent status, where such broker, general commission agent or other agent is acting in the ordinary course of his business;
(f) reinsurance premiums; and
(g) interest on credits, loans and other forms of indebtedness connected with the financing of trade between the USA and the USSR except where received by a resident of the other Contracting State from the conduct of a general banking business in the first Contracting State.

2. A Contracting State shall not attribute taxable income to the following activities conducted within that Contracting State by a resident of the other Contracting State:

(a) the purchase of goods or merchandise;
(b) the use of facilities for the purpose of storage or delivery of goods or merchandise belonging to the resident of the other Contracting State;
(c) the display of goods or merchandise belonging to the resident of the other Contracting State, and also the sale of such items on termination of their display;

(d) advertising by a resident of the other Contracting State, the collection or dissemination of information, or the conducting of scientific research, or similar activities, which have a preparatory or auxiliary character for the resident.

ARTICLE IV

1. Income from commercial activity derived in one Contracting State by a resident of the other Contracting State, shall be taxable in the first Contracting State only if it is derived by a representation.

2. The term "representation" means:

(a) with regard to income derived within the USSR, an office or representative bureau established in the USSR by a resident of the United States in accordance with the laws and regulations in force in the Soviet Union;

(b) with regard to income derived within the USA, an office or other place of business established in the USA by a resident of the Soviet Union in accordance with the laws and regulations in force in the United States.

3. In the determination of the profits of a representation, there shall be allowed as deductions from total income the expenses that are connected with the performance of its activity, including executive and general administrative expenses.

4. This article applies to income, other than income of an individual dealt with in Article VI, from the furnishing of tour performances and other public appearances.

5. The provisions of this article shall not affect the exemptions from taxes provided for by Articles III and V.

ARTICLE V

1. Income which a resident of the Soviet Union derives from the operation in international traffic of ships or aircraft registered in the USSR and gains which a resident of the USSR derives from the sale, exchange, or other disposition of ships or aircraft operated in international traffic by such resident and registered in the USSR shall be exempt from tax in the United States.

2. Income which a resident of the United States derives from operation in international traffic of ships or aircraft registered in the USA and gains which a resident of the USA derives from the sale, exchange, or other disposition of ships or aircraft operated in international traffic by such resident and registered in the USA shall be exempt from tax in the Soviet Union.

3. Remuneration derived by an individual from the performance of labor or personal services as an employee aboard ships or aircraft operated by one of the Contracting States or a resident thereof in international traffic shall be exempt from tax in the other Contracting State if such individual is a member of the regular complement of the ship or air craft.

ARTICLE VI

1. *Special exemptions.*

Income derived by an individual who is a resident of one of the Contracting States shall be exempt from tax in the other Contracting State as provided in subparagraphs (a) through (f).

(a) *Governmental employees.*

(1) An individual receiving remuneration from government funds of the Contracting State of which the individual is a citizen for labor or personal services performed as an employee of governmental agencies or institutions of that Contracting State in the discharge of governmental functions shall not be subject to tax on such remuneration in that other Contracting State.

(2) Labor or personal services performed by a citizen of one of the Contracting States shall be treated by the other Contracting State as performed in the discharge of governmental functions if such labor or personal services would be treated under the internal laws of the first Contracting State as so performed. However, it is understood that persons engaged in commercial activity, such as employees or representatives of commercial organizations of the USA and employees or representatives of the foreign trade organizations of the USSR, shall not be considered in the USSR and USA respectively as engaged in the discharge of governmental functions.

(3) The provisions of this Convention shall not affect the fiscal privileges of diplomatic and consular officials under the general rules of international law or under special agreements.

(b) *Participants in programs of intergovernmental cooperation.*

An individual who is a resident of one of the Contracting States and who is temporarily present in the other Contracting State under an exchange program provided for by agreements between the governments of the Contracting States on cooperation in various fields of science and technology shall not be subject to tax in that other Contracting State on remuneration received from sources within either Contracting State.

(c) *Teachers and researchers.*

(1) An individual who is a resident of one of the Contracting States and who is temporarily present in the other Contracting State at the invitation of a governmental agency or institution or an educational or scientific research institution in that other Contracting State for the primary purpose of teaching, engaging in research, or participating in scientific, technical or professional conferences shall not be subject to tax in that other Contracting State on his income from teaching or research or participating in such conferences.

(2) Subparagraph (1) shall not apply to income from research if such research is undertaken primarily for the benefit of a private person or commercial enterprise of the USA or a foreign trade organization of the USSR. However, subparagraph (1) shall apply in all cases where research is conducted on the basis of intergovernmental agreements on cooperation.

(d) *Students.*

An individual who is a resident of one of the Contracting States and who is temporarily present in the other Contracting State for the primary purpose of studying at an educational or scientific research institution or for the purpose of acquiring a profession or a specialty shall be exempt from taxes in the other Contracting State on a stipend, scholarship, or other substitute type of allowance, necessary to provide for ordinary living expenses.

(e) *Trainees and specialists.*

An individual who is a resident of one of the Contracting States, who is temporarily present in the other Contracting State for the primary purpose of acquiring technical, professional, or commercial experience or performing technical services, and who is an employee of, or under contract with, a resident of the first mentioned Contracting State, shall not be subject to tax in that other Contracting State on remuneration received from abroad. Also, such individual shall not be subject to tax in that other Contracting State on amounts received from sources within that other Contracting State which are necessary to provide for ordinary living expenses.

(f) *Duration of exemptions.*

The exemptions provided for under subparagraphs (b), (c), (d), and (e) of this article shall extend only for such period of time as is required to effectuate the purpose of the visit, but in no case shall such period of time exceed:

(1) One year in the case of subparagraphs (b) (Participants in programs of intergovernmental cooperation) and (e) (Trainees and specialists);

(2) Two years in the case of subparagraph (c) (Teachers and researchers); and

(3) Five years in the case of subparagraph (d) (Students).

If an individual qualifies for exemption under more than one of subparagraphs (b), (c), (d), and (e), the provisions of that subparagraph which is most favorable to him shall apply. However, in no case shall an individual have the cumulative benefits of subparagraphs (b), (c), (d), and (e) for more than five taxable years from the date of his arrival in the other Contracting State.

2. *General exemptions.*

Income derived by an individual who is a resident of one of the Contracting States from the performance of personal services in the other Contracting State, which is not exempt from tax in accordance with paragraph 1. of this article, may be taxed in that other Contracting State, but only if the individual is present in that other Contracting State for a period aggregating more than 183 days in the taxable year.

ARTICLE VII

This Convention shall not restrict the right of a Contracting State to tax a citizen of that Contracting State.

ARTICLE VIII

This Convention shall apply only to the taxation of income from activity conducted in a Contracting State in accordance with the laws and regulations in force in such Contracting State.

ARTICLE IX

If the income of a resident of one of the Contracting States is exempt from tax in the other Contracting State, in accordance with this Convention, such resident shall also be exempt from any tax which is at present imposed or which may be imposed subsequently in that Contracting State on the transaction giving rise to such income.

ARTICLE X

1. A citizen of one of the Contracting States who is a resident of the other Contracting State shall not be subjected in that other Contracting State to more burdensome taxes than a citizen of that other Contracting State who is a resident thereof carrying on the same activities.

2. A citizen of one of the Contracting States who is a resident of the other Contracting State or a representation established by a resident of the first Contracting State in the other Contracting State shall not be subjected in that other Contracting State to more burdensome taxes than are generally imposed in that State on citizens or representations of residents of third States carrying on the same activities. However, this provision shall not require a Contracting State to grant to citizens or representations of residents of the other Contracting State tax benefits granted by special agreements to citizens or representations of a third State.

3. The provisions of paragraphs 1. and 2. of this article shall apply to taxes of any kind imposed on the Federal or All-Union level, the state or Republic level, and on the local level.

ARTICLE XI

1. If a resident of one of the Contracting States considers that the action of one or both of the Contracting States results or will result for him in taxation not in accordance with this Convention, he may, notwithstanding the remedies provided by the laws of the Contracting States, present his case to the competent authorities of the Contracting State of which he is a resident or citizen. Should the claim be considered to have merit by the competent authorities of the Contracting State to which the claim is made, they shall endeavor to come to an agreement with the competent authorities of the other Contracting State with a view to the avoidance of taxation not in accordance with the provisions of this Convention.

2. In the event that such an agreement is reached the competent authorities of the Contracting States

shall, as necessary, refund the excess amounts paid, allow tax exemptions, or levy taxes.

ARTICLE XII

The competent authorities of the Contracting States shall notify each other annually of amendments of the tax legislation referred to in paragraph 1. of Article I and of the adoption of taxes referred to in paragraph 2. of Article I by transmitting the texts of amendments or new statutes and notify each other of any material concerning the application of this Convention.

ARTICLE XIII

This Convention shall be subject to ratification and shall enter into force on the thirtieth day after the exchange of instruments of ratification. The instruments of ratification shall be exchanged at Moscow as soon as possible.

The provisions of this Convention shall, however, have effect for income derived on or after January 1 of the year following the year in which the instruments of ratification are exchanged.

ARTICLE XIV

1. This Convention shall remain in force for a period of three years after it takes effect and shall remain in force thereafter for an indefinite period. Either of the Contracting States may terminate this Convention at any time after three years from the date on which the Convention enters into force by giving notice of termination through diplomatic channels at least six months before the end of any calendar year. In such event, the Convention shall cease to have effect beginning on January 1 of the year following the year in which notice is given.

2. Notwithstanding the provisions of paragraph 1. of this article, upon prior notice to be given through diplomatic channels, the provisions of subparagraphs (e), (f), or (g) of paragraph 1. of Article III and the provisions of Article IX may be terminated separately by either Contracting State at any time after three years from the date on which this Convention enters into force. In such event such provisions shall cease to have effect ·beginning on January 1 of the year following the year in which notice is given.

IN WITNESS WHEREOF, the plenipotentiaries of the two Contracting States have signed the present Convention and have affixed their seals thereto.

DONE at Washington, this 20th day of June, 1973, in duplicate, in the English and Russian languages, both texts being equally authentic.

For the President of the United States of America	For the Presidium of the Supreme Soviet of the Union of Soviet Socialist Republics
GEORGE P. SHULTZ	N. S. PATOLICHEV

31 (June 21, 1973)

BASIC PRINCIPLES OF NEGOTIATIONS ON STRATEGIC ARMS LIMITATION

BASIC PRINCIPLES OF NEGOTIATIONS ON THE FURTHER LIMITATION OF STRATEGIC OFFENSIVE ARMS

The President of the United States of America, Richard Nixon, and the General Secretary of the Central Committee of the CPSU, L.I. Brezhnev,

Having thoroughly considered the question of the further limitation of strategic arms, and the progress already achieved in the current negotiations,

Reaffirming their conviction that the earliest adoption of further limitations of strategic arms would be a major contribution in reducing the danger of an outbreak of nuclear war and in strengthening international peace and security,

Have agreed as follows:

First. The two Sides will continue active negotiations in order to work out a permanent agreement on more complete measures on the limitation of strategic offensive arms, as well as their subsequent reduction, proceeding from the Basic Principles of Relations between the United States of America and the Union of Soviet Socialist Republics signed in Moscow on May 29, 1972, and from the Interim Agreement between the United States of America and the Union of Soviet Socialist Republics of May 26, 1972 on Certain Measures with Respect to the Limitation of Strategic Offensive Arms.

Over the course of the next year the two Sides will make serious efforts to work out the provisions of the permanent agreement on more complete measures on the limitation of strategic offensive arms with the objective of signing it in 1974.

Second. New agreements on the limitation of strategic offensive armaments will be based on the principles of the American-Soviet documents adopted in Moscow in May 1972 and the agreements reached in Washington in June 1973; and in particular, both Sides will be guided by the recognition of each other's equal security interests and by the recognition that efforts to obtain unilateral advantage, directly or indirectly, would be inconsistent with the strengthening of peaceful relations between the United States of America and the Union of Soviet Socialist Republics.

Third. The limitations placed on strategic offensive weapons can apply both to their quantitative aspects as well as to their qualitative improvement.

Fourth. Limitations on strategic offensive arms must be subject to adequate verification by national technical means.

Fifth. The modernization and replacement of strategic offensive arms would be permitted under conditions which will be formulated in the agreements to be concluded.

Sixth. Pending the completion of a permanent agreement on more complete measures of strategic offensive arms limitation, both Sides are prepared to reach agreements on separate measures to supplement the existing Interim Agreement of May 26, 1972.

Seventh. Each Side will continue to take necessary organizational and technical measures for preventing accidental or unauthorized use of nuclear weapons under its control in accordance with the Agreement of September 30, 1971 between the United States of America and the Union of Soviet Socialist Republics.

Washington, June 21, 1973

For the United States of America:

For the Union of Soviet Socialist Republics:

RICHARD NIXON

President of the United States of America

L. I. BREZHNEV

General Secretary of the Central Committee, CPSU

32 (June 21, 1973)

AGREEMENT ON SCIENTIFIC COOPERATION IN PEACEFUL USES OF ATOMIC ENERGY

AGREEMENT BETWEEN THE UNITED STATES OF AMERICA AND THE UNION OF SOVIET SOCIALIST REPUBLICS ON SCIENTIFIC AND TECHNICAL CO-OPERATION IN THE FIELD OF PEACEFUL USES OF ATOMIC ENERGY

The United States of America and the Union of Soviet Socialist Republics;

Attaching great importance to the problem of satisfying the rapidly growing energy demands in both countries as well as in other countries of the world;

Desiring to combine the efforts of both countries toward the solution of this problem through the development of highly efficient energy sources;

Recognizing that solutions to this problem may be found in more rapid development of certain nuclear technologies already under study, such as controlled thermonuclear fusion and fast breeder reactors, as well as in additional basic research on the fundamental properties of matter;

Noting with satisfaction the successful results of previous cooperation between the Parties in the field of peaceful uses of atomic energy;

Wishing to establish a more stable and long-term basis for cooperation in this field for the benefit of both their peoples and of all mankind;

In accordance with and in further development of the Agreement between the Government of the United States of America and the Government of the Union of Soviet Socialist Republics on Cooperation in the Fields of Science and Technology of May 24, 1972; the Memorandum on Cooperation in the Peaceful Uses of Atomic Energy of September 28, 1972 between the U.S. Atomic Energy Commission and the USSR State Committee for the Utilization of Atomic Energy; and the General Agreement between the United States of America and the Union of Soviet Socialist Republics on Contacts, Exchanges and Cooperation of June 19, 1973;

Have agreed as follows:

ARTICLE 1

The Parties will expand and strengthen their cooperation in research, development and utilization of nuclear energy, having as a primary objective the development of new energy sources. This cooperation will be carried out on the basis of mutual benefit, equality and reciprocity.

ARTICLE 2

1. Cooperation will be concentrated in the following three areas:

a. Controlled thermonuclear fusion.

The aim of cooperation in this area is the eventual development of prototype and demonstration-scale thermonuclear reactors. Cooperation may include theoretical, calculational, experimental and design-construction studies at all stages up to industrial-scale operations.

b. Fast breeder reactors.

Cooperation in this area will be directed toward finding solutions to mutually agreed basic and applied problems connected with the design, development, construction and operation of nuclear power plants utilizing fast breeder reactors.

c. Research on the fundamental properties of matter.

Cooperation in this area will include joint theoretical and experimental studies on mutually agreed subjects, and particularly in high, medium and low energy physics, through utilization of accelerators, data processing equipment and other facilities of the two countries. Cooperation may also be undertaken on the design, planning and construction of joint facilities to be used in this area of research.

2. Further details of cooperation in each of these three areas will be arranged through individual implementing protocols.

3. Other areas of cooperation may be added by mutual agreement.

4. Cooperation under this Agreement shall be in accordance with the laws of the respective countries.

ARTICLE 3

1. Cooperation provided for in the preceding Articles may take the following forms:

a. Establishment of working groups of scientists

and engineers for design and execution of joint projects;

b. Joint development and construction of experiments, pilot installations and equipment;

c. Joint work by theoretical and experimental scientists in appropriate research centers of the two countries;

d. Organization of joint consultations, seminars and panels;

e. Exchanges of appropriate instrumentation, equipment and construction materials;

f. Exchanges of scientists and specialists; and

g. Exchanges of scientific and technical information, documentation and results of research.

2. Other forms of cooperation may be added by mutual agreement.

ARTICLE 4

In furtherance of the aims of this Agreement, the Parties will, as appropriate, encourage, facilitate and monitor the development of cooperation and direct contacts between organizations and institutions of the two countries, including the conclusion, as appropriate, of implementing protocols and contracts for carrying out cooperative activities under this Agreement.

ARTICLE 5

1. For the implementation of this Agreement, there shall be established a US–USSR Joint Committee on Cooperation in the Peaceful Uses of Atomic Energy. Meetings will be convened once a year in the United States and the Soviet Union alternately, unless otherwise mutually agreed.

2. The Joint Committee shall take such action as is necessary for effective implementation of this Agreement including, but not limited to, approval of specific projects and programs of cooperation; designation of appropriate participating organizations and institutions responsible for carrying out cooperative activities; and making recommendations, as appropriate, to the two Governments.

3. The Executive Agents of this Agreement shall be, for the United States of America, the U.S. Atomic Energy Commission, and for the Union of Soviet Socialist Republics, the USSR State Committee for the Utilization of Atomic Energy. The Executive Agents, on their respective sides, shall be responsible for the operation of the Joint Committee and shall coordinate and supervise the development and implementation of cooperative activities conducted under this Agreement.

ARTICLE 6

Nothing in this Agreement shall be interpreted to prejudice other agreements concluded between ' the Parties.

ARTICLE 7

1. This Agreement shall enter into force upon signature and shall remain in force for ten years. It may be modified or extended by mutual agreement of the Parties.

2. The termination of this Agreement shall not affect the validity of implementing protocols and contracts concluded under this Agreement between interested organizations and institutions of the two countries.

DONE at Washington, this 21st day of June, 1973, in duplicate, in the English and Russian languages, both texts being equally authentic.

For the United States of America:

RICHARD NIXON

President of the United States of America

For the Union of Soviet Socialist Republics:

L. I. BREZHNEV

General Secretary of the Central Committee, CPSU

33 (June 21, 1973)
U.S.-U.S.S.R. Fisheries Agreement Signed at Copenhagen

Press release 224 dated June 25

Representatives of the United States and the Soviet Union signed at Copenhagen on June 21 a bilateral fisheries agreement broadening and extending through December 31, 1974, an agreement concluded December 11, 1970, concerning fishing and fishing operations in ocean areas off the Atlantic coast of the United States. Ambassador Donald L. McKernan, Special Assistant to the Secretary of State for Fisheries and Wildlife and Coordinator for Ocean Affairs in the Department of State, signed for the United States. Vladimir M. Kamentsev, Deputy Minister of Fisheries, signed for the Soviet Union. The presence of fisheries experts of both countries in Copenhagen for the 23d annual meeting of the International Commission for the Northwest Atlantic Fisheries June 5–15 facilitated final arrangements concerning the agreement.

The new agreement contains provisions to further conserve stocks of fish of mutual concern, to enhance the exchange of scientific information with respect to these stocks, to minimize fishing-gear conflicts between vessels of the two countries and to facilitate the settlement of claims arising from such conflicts, and to provide opportunities for periodic discussions of problems of mutual concern between representatives of the appropriate fisheries authorities of the two governments and fishermen's organizations. Ambassador McKernan said the new agreement has been expanded to afford new protection for bluefish, lobster, and yellowtail flounder. Protective measures are broadened for menhaden and continued for scup, flounder, hake, and river herring. The agreement also continues the seasonal closure January 1 to April 15 to fishing by all Soviet vessels in waters roughly between 50 and 100 fathoms from Rhode Island to Virginia where bottom-dwelling species concentrate early in the year.

New assurances are added to the agreement indicating that Soviet vessels shall not intentionally catch lobster north of Cape Hatteras, shall take appropriate measures to minimize incidental catches of lobster in specialized fisheries for other species, and shall return to the sea in a viable condition all lobster taken incidentally, insofar as possible.

To facilitate conservation of bottom-dwelling inshore stocks of yellowtail flounder, Soviet vessels of more than 145 feet in length will limit fishing operations to midwater trawling during the period from July 1 through December 31 in the area adjacent to the U.S. southern New England coast north of 40° 20′ N and south of 43° 17′ N and west of a line drawn between the points 68° 15′ W, 40° 20′ N, and 70° 00′ W, and 43 17′ N.

In return, the United States agreed to certain relaxation of port privileges for Soviet fisheries vessels in Baltimore, Philadelphia, New York, and Boston. In addition, Soviet fishing vessels will continue to be allowed to transfer fish and supplies in two areas within the contiguous fishing zone and to fish within a small area of the contiguous fishing zone off the United States middle Atlantic coast.

The agreement also establishes a voluntary scheme of joint inspection between the United States and the Soviet Union to help insure the enforcement of its provisions.

Both countries agreed to seek to minimize the possibility of conflicts between Soviet fisheries using mobile fishing gear and U.S. fisheries using fixed fishing gear. To facilitate settlement of claims that might arise from any such conflicts, a protocol to the agreement makes available fisheries claims boards to consider claims voluntarily submitted by either side and to attempt to conciliate the parties on the basis of factfinding.

Ambassador McKernan said, "The new agreement represents important progress in facilitating conservation of stocks of fish of importance to the United States and in providing further protection for our coastal fisheries."

Agreement on Prevention of Nuclear War Signed June 22

34 (June 22, 1973)

AGREEMENT BETWEEN THE UNITED STATES OF AMERICA AND THE UNION OF SOVIET SOCIALIST REPUBLICS ON THE PREVENTION OF NUCLEAR WAR

The United States of America and the Union of Soviet Socialist Republics, hereinafter referred to as the Parties,

Guided by the objectives of strengthening world peace and international security,

Conscious that nuclear war would have devastating consequences for mankind,

Proceeding from the desire to bring about conditions in which the danger of an outbreak of nuclear war anywhere in the world would be reduced and ultimately eliminated,

Proceeding from their obligations under the Charter of the United Nations regarding the maintenance of peace, refraining from the threat or use of force, and the avoidance of war, and in conformity with the agreements to which either Party has subscribed,

Proceeding from the Basic Principles of Relations between the United States of America and the Union of Soviet Socialist Republics signed in Moscow on May 29, 1972,

Reaffirming that the development of relations between the United States of America and the Union of Soviet Socialist Republics is not directed against other countries and their interests,

Have agreed as follows:

ARTICLE I

The United States and the Soviet Union agree that an objective of their policies is to remove the danger of nuclear war and of the use of nuclear weapons.

Accordingly, the Parties agree that they will act in such a manner as to prevent the development of situations capable of causing a dangerous exacerbation of their relations, as to avoid military confrontations, and as to exclude the outbreak of nuclear war between them and between either of the Parties and other countries.

ARTICLE II

The Parties agree, in accordance with Article I and to realize the objective stated in that Article, to proceed from the premise that each Party will refrain from the threat or use of force against the other Party, against the allies of the other Party and against other countries, in circumstances which may endanger international peace and security. The Parties agree that they will be guided by these considerations in the formulation of their foreign policies and in their actions in the field of international relations.

ARTICLE III

The Parties undertake to develop their relations with each other and with other countries in a way consistent with the purposes of this Agreement.

ARTICLE IV

If at any time relations between the Parties or between either Party and other countries appear to involve the risk of a nuclear conflict, or if relations between countries not parties to this Agreement appear to involve the risk of nuclear war between the United States of America and the Union of Soviet Socialist Republics or between either Party and other countries, the United States and the Soviet Union, acting in accordance with the provisions of this Agreement, shall immediately enter into urgent consultations with each other and make every effort to avert this risk.

ARTICLE V

Each Party shall be free to inform the Security Council of the United Nations, the Secretary General of the United Nations and the Governments of allied or other countries of the progress and outcome of consultations initiated in accordance with Article IV of this Agreement.

ARTICLE VI

Nothing in this Agreement shall affect or impair:

(a) the inherent right of individual or collective self-defense as envisaged by Article 51 of the Charter of the United Nations,

(b) the provisions of the Charter of the United Nations, including those relating to the maintenance or restoration of international peace and security, and

(c) the obligations undertaken by either Party towards its allies or other countries in treaties, agreements, and other appropriate documents.

ARTICLE VII

This Agreement shall be of unlimited duration.

ARTICLE VIII

This Agreement shall enter into force upon signature.

DONE at Washington on June 22, 1973, in two copies, each in the English and Russian languages, both texts being equally authentic.

For the United States of America:

For the Union of Soviet Socialist Republics:

RICHARD NIXON

L. I. BREZHNEV

President of the United States of America

General Secretary of the Central Committee, CPSU

35 (June 22, 1973)
PROTOCOL ON U.S.-U.S.S.R. CHAMBER OF COMMERCE

PROTOCOL

Considering the interest expressed by United States companies and Soviet foreign trade organizations in the development of organizational arrangements for increased cooperation, and

Recognizing that such increased cooperation would contribute to the promotion of contacts between businessmen of the USA and the USSR, which in turn would assist in the development of mutually beneficial trade between the two countries,

The Secretary of Commerce of the USA will meet at an early date with members of the United States business and financial community to discuss the desirability of establishing in the United States private sector a US–USSR Chamber of Commerce. The Minister of Foreign Trade of the USSR will continue similar consultations with Soviet foreign trade and other organizations.

The results of these consultations shall be reported promptly to the Joint US–USSR Commercial Commission.

DONE at Washington, this 22nd day of June, 1973, in duplicate, in the English and Russian languages, both texts being equally authentic.

For the Government of the United States of America:	For the Government of the Union of Soviet Socialist Republics:
GEORGE P. SHULTZ	N. S. PATOLICHEV
Secretary of the Treasury	*Minister of Foreign Trade*

36 (June 22, 1973)
PROTOCOL ON COMMERCIAL FACILITIES

PROTOCOL

In the interests of strengthening their commercial and economic ties, the Government of the USA and the Government of the USSR undertook in the Agreement between the Government of the USA and the Government of the USSR Regarding Trade signed in October 1972, to cooperate in the expansion and improvement of their commercial facilities in Moscow and Washington.

In accordance with that undertaking representatives of the Soviet Government and the US Embassy in Moscow have this week contracted for new facilities at a convenient location which will enable the Office of the Commercial Counselor of the USA to provide more effective services to US businessmen seeking assistance in their commercial pursuits with appropriate USSR organizations.

The US Government facilitated the acquisition by the USSR earlier this year of a building at a convenient location in Washington for use as the Office of the Commercial Counselor of the USSR.

The Government of the USSR has also informed the Government of the USA that, in connection with the Agreement Regarding Trade, it has issued accreditation to establish representations in Moscow to the following US business and financial organizations:

Pullman Incorporated
Occidental Petroleum Corporation
The Chase Manhattan Bank, N. A.
General Electric Company
International Harvester Company

Caterpillar Tractor Company
Hewlett-Packard Company
Engelhard Minerals & Chemicals Corporation
Bank of America
First National City Bank

Requests by additional US firms for accreditation in Moscow are now under consideration by Soviet authorities.

Consistent with Article 5 of the Agreement Regarding Trade, the Government of the USA and the Government of the USSR have also agreed today to undertake immediate preparations for mutually satisfactory arrangements to enlarge their commercial staffs in each other's country. A Trade Representation of the USSR in Washington and a Commercial Office of the USA in Moscow will simultaneously be opened as soon as possible and in any event not later than October 31st of this year.

DONE at Washington, this 22nd day of June, 1973, in duplicate, in the English and Russian languages, both texts being equally authentic.

For the Government of the United States of America:	For the Government of the Union of Soviet Socialist Republics:
GEORGE P. SHULTZ	N. S. PATOLICHEV
Secretary of the Treasury	*Minister of Foreign Trade*

Protocol on Expansion of Air Services Signed June 23

37 (June 23, 1973)

PROTOCOL BETWEEN THE UNITED STATES OF AMERICA AND THE UNION OF SOVIET SOCIALIST REPUBLICS ON QUESTIONS RELATING TO THE EXPANSION OF AIR SERVICES

The Government of the United States of America and the Government of the Union of Soviet Socialist Republics,

In keeping with paragraph 7 of the Basic Principles of Relations Between the United States of America and the Union of Soviet Socialist Republics signed at Moscow on May 29, 1972,

Desiring to foster expanded communications between the two countries on a mutual basis,

Recognizing the role which air transportation can play in this connection, and

Pursuant to Article 16 of the Civil Air Transport Agreement between the two Governments of November 4, 1966,

Have agreed as follows:

ARTICLE 1

The existing agreed services under the Civil Air Transport Agreement between New York and Moscow are to be expanded to include services for the designated airline of the United States from New York to Leningrad and for the designated airline of the USSR from Moscow to Washington.

ARTICLE 2

In view of the increasing traffic between the two countries, the existing arrangements under the Civil Air Transport Agreement relating to flight frequencies are to be amended to allow increases in frequency of service.

ARTICLE 3

The foregoing and other related amendments of the Civil Air Transport Agreement are incorporated in the attached Annex which supersedes the existing Annex to that Agreement.

This Protocol shall enter into force upon signature.

DONE at Washington, this 23rd day of June, 1973, in duplicate, in the English and Russian languages, both texts being equally authentic.

For the Government of the United States of America:	For the Government of the Union of Soviet Socialist Republics:
CLAUDE S. BRINEGAR	B. P. BUGAYEV

ANNEX

1. The Government of the Union of Soviet Socialist Republics entrusts the Ministry of Civil Aviation of the USSR with responsibility for the operation of the agreed services on the routes specified in Table I of this Annex, which in turn designates for this purpose the General Department of International Air Services (Aeroflot Soviet Airlines).

2. The Government of the United States of America designates Pan American World Airways, Inc., to operate the agreed services on the routes specified in Table II of this Annex.

3. Each designated airline shall have the following rights in the operation of the agreed services on the respective routes specified in Tables I and II of this Annex:

(1) The right to land for technical and commercial purposes at the terminal point of the agreed route in the territory of the other Contracting Party, as well as to use alternative airports and flight facilities in that territory for these purposes;

(2) The right to discharge passengers, baggage, cargo and mail in the territory of the other Contracting Party, but without the right to discharge

passengers, baggage, cargo and mail coming from any intermediate point in a third country on the given route, except for passengers and their accompanied baggage which have been disembarked at that intermediate point by the designated airline and subsequently reembarked during the validity of the ticket (but in no event later than one year from the date of disembarkation) and which are moving under a passenger ticket and baggage check providing for transportation on scheduled flights on each segment of the route between the two Contracting Parties; and

(3) The right to pick up passengers, baggage, cargo and mail in the territory of the other Contracting Party, but without the right to pick up passengers, baggage, cargo and mail destined for any intermediate point in a third country on the given route, except for passengers and their accompanied baggage which are to be disembarked at that intermediate point and subsequently reembarked by the designated airline during the validity of the ticket (but in no event later than one year from the date of disembarkation) and which are moving under a passenger ticket and baggage check providing for transportation on scheduled flights on each segment of the route between the two Contracting Parties.

4. In addition to the rights specified in paragraph 3 above, each designated airline shall have the right, subject to paragraph 5 below, to pick up and discharge passengers, baggage, cargo and mail in the territory of the other Contracting Party which are to be discharged or have been picked up at any intermediate point in a third country on the given route.

5. Each designated airline may operate up to two roundtrip flights per week through March 31, 1974, up to three roundtrip flights per week during the 1974 summer traffic season (April 1, 1974–October 31, 1974), up to two roundtrip flights per week during the 1974/75 winter traffic season (November 1, 1974–March 31, 1975), and thereafter such number of flights as is subsequently agreed between the Contracting Parties. The designated airline of the United States may exercise the right specified in paragraph 4 above on all its flights. The designated airline of the Soviet Union may exercise the right specified in paragraph 4 above on one of its flights.

6. The intermediate points referred to in Table I of this Annex shall be any two of the following: Amsterdam, Copenhagen, Paris, London, Frankfurt, and Brussels; and the intermediate points referred to in Table II shall be any two of the following: London, Amsterdam, Frankfurt, Copenhagen, Brussels and Paris. At the beginning of each summer and winter traffic season, each designated airline may change from one combination of two intermediate points to another combination of two intermediate points for that season. No more than one intermediate point may be served on each flight. The intermediate point or points may, at the option of each designated airline, be omitted on any or all flights.

7. Each designated airline may make a change of gauge at any intermediate point in Europe listed in paragraph 6 above provided that:

(1) carriage beyond the point of change of gauge will be performed by a single aircraft of capacity equal to or less (in the case of services outbound from the homeland) or equal to or more (in the case of services inbound to the homeland) than that of the arriving aircraft, and

(2) aircraft for such beyond carriage will be scheduled only in coincidence with the incoming aircraft (with the same flight number) to insure true and genuine continuing service.

AGREED SERVICES

TABLE I

For the Union of Soviet Socialist Republics:

Moscow to New York or Washington (Dulles) and return, via the intermediate points listed in paragraph 6 of the Annex. New York and Washington will be served on separate flights. Technical stops will be limited to those listed in Article II of the Supplementary Agreement, as amended.

TABLE II

For the United States of America:

New York to Leningrad or Moscow, and return, via the intermediate points listed in paragraph 6 of the Annex. Leningrad and Moscow will be served on separate flights. Technical stops will be limited to those listed in Article II of the Supplementary Agreement, as amended.

38 (June 25, 1973)

JOINT US–USSR COMMUNIQUE

At the invitation of the President of the United States, Richard Nixon, extended during his official visit to the USSR in May 1972, and in accordance with a subsequent agreement, General Secretary of the Central Committee of the Communist Party of the Soviet Union, Mr. Leonid I. Brezhnev, paid an official visit to the United States from June 18 to June 25. Mr. Brezhnev was accompanied by A. A. Gromyko, Minister of Foreign Affairs of the USSR, Member of the Politbureau of the Central Committee, CPSU; N. S. Patolichev, Minister of Foreign Trade; B. P. Bugayev, Minister of Civil Aviation; G. E. Tsukanov and A. M. Aleksandrov, Assistants to the General Secretary of the Central Committee, CPSU; L. I. Zamyatin, General Director of TASS; E. I. Chazov, Deputy Minister of Public Health of the USSR; G. M. Korniyenko, Member of the Collegium of the Ministry of Foreign Affairs of the USSR; G. A. Arbatov, Director of the USA Institute of the Academy of Sciences of the USSR.

President Nixon and General Secretary Brezhnev held thorough and constructive discussions on the progress achieved in the development of US-Soviet relations and on a number of major international problems of mutual interest.

Also taking part in the conversations held in Washington, Camp David, and San Clemente, were:

On the American side William P. Rogers, Secretary of State; George P. Shultz, Secretary of the Treasury; Dr. Henry A. Kissinger, Assistant to the President for National Security Affairs.

On the Soviet side A. A. Gromyko, Minister of Foreign Affairs of the USSR, Member of the Politbureau of the Central Committee, CPSU; A. F. Dobrynin, Soviet Ambassador to the USA; N. S. Patolichev, Minister of Foreign Trade; B. P. Bugayev, Minister of Civil Aviation; A. M. Aleksandrov and G. E. Tsukanov, Assistants to the General Secretary of the Central Committee, CPSU; G. M. Korniyenko, Member of the Collegium of the Ministry of Foreign Affairs of the USSR.

I. THE GENERAL STATE OF US-SOVIET RELATIONS

Both Sides expressed their mutual satisfaction with the fact that the American-Soviet summit meeting in Moscow in May 1972 and the joint decisions taken there have resulted in a substantial advance in the strengthening of peaceful relations between the USA and the USSR and have created the basis for the further development of broad and

[5] Signed at San Clemente, Calif., on June 24, released at Moscow, Washington, and San Clemente on June 25.

mutually beneficial cooperation in various fields of mutual interest to the peoples of both countries and in the interests of all mankind. They noted their satisfaction with the mutual effort to implement strictly and fully the treaties and agreements concluded between the USA and the USSR, and to expand areas of cooperation.

They agreed that the process of reshaping relations between the USA and the USSR on the basis of peaceful coexistence and equal security as set forth in the Basic Principles of Relations Between the USA and the USSR signed in Moscow on May 29, 1972 is progressing in an encouraging manner. They emphasized the great importance that each Side attaches to these Basic Principles. They reaffirmed their commitment to the continued scrupulous implementation and to the enhancement of the effectiveness of each of the provisions of that document.

Both Sides noted with satisfaction that the outcome of the US-Soviet meeting in Moscow in May 1972 was welcomed by other States and by world opinion as an important contribution to strengthening peace and international security, to curbing the arms race and to developing businesslike cooperation among States with different social systems.

Both Sides viewed the return visit to the USA of the General Secretary of the Central Committee of the CPSU, L. I. Brezhnev, and the talks held during the visit as an expression of their mutual determination to continue the course toward a major improvement in US-Soviet relations.

Both Sides are convinced that the discussions they have just held represent a further milestone in the constructive development of their relations.

Convinced that such a development of American-Soviet relations serves the interests of both of their peoples and all of mankind, it was decided to take further major steps to give these relations maximum stability and to turn the development of friendship and cooperation between their peoples into a permanent factor for worldwide peace.

II. THE PREVENTION OF NUCLEAR WAR AND THE LIMITATION OF STRATEGIC ARMAMENTS

Issues related to the maintenance and strengthening of international peace were a central point of the talks between President Nixon and General Secretary Brezhnev.

Conscious of the exceptional importance for all mankind of taking effective measures to that end, they discussed ways in which both Sides could work toward removing the danger of war, and especially nuclear war, between the USA and the USSR and between either party and other countries. Consequently, in accordance with the Charter of the United Nations and the Basic Principles of Relations of May 29, 1972, it was decided to conclude an Agreement Between the USA and the USSR on the Prevention of Nuclear War. That Agreement was signed by the President and the General Secretary on June 22, 1973. The text has been published separately.

The President and the General Secretary, in appraising this Agreement, believe that it constitutes a historical landmark in Soviet-American relations and substantially strengthens the foundations of international security as a whole. The United States and the Soviet Union state their readiness to consider additional ways of strengthening peace and removing forever the danger of war, and particularly nuclear war.

In the course of the meetings, intensive discussions were held on questions of strategic arms limitation. In this connection both Sides emphasized the fundamental importance of the Treaty on the Limitation of Anti-Ballistic Missile Systems and the Interim Agreement on Certain Measures with Respect to the Limitation of Strategic Offensive Arms signed between the USA and the USSR in May 1972 which, for the first time in history, place actual limits on the most modern and most formidable types of armaments.

Having exchanged views on the progress in the implementation of these agreements, both Sides reaffirmed their intention to carry them out and their readiness to move ahead jointly toward an agreement on the further limitation of strategic arms.

Both Sides noted that progress has been made in the negotiations that resumed in November 1972, and that the prospects for reaching a permanent agreement on more complete measures limiting strategic offensive armaments are favorable.

Both Sides agreed that the progress made in the limitation of strategic armaments is an exceedingly important contribution to the strengthening of US-Soviet relations and to world peace.

On the basis of their discussions, the President and the General Secretary signed on June 21, 1973, Basic Principles of Negotiations on the Further Limitation of Strategic Offensive Arms. The text has been published separately.

The USA and the USSR attach great importance to joining with all States in the cause of strengthening peace, reducing the burden of armaments, and reaching agreements on arms limitation and disarmament measures.

Considering the important role which an effective international agreement with respect to chemical weapons would play, the two Sides agreed to continue their efforts to conclude such an agreement in cooperation with other countries.

The two Sides agree to make every effort to facilitate the work of the Committee on Disarmament which has been meeting in Geneva. They will actively participate in negotiations aimed at working out new measures to curb and end the arms race. They reaffirm that the ultimate objective is general and complete disarmament, including nuclear disarmament, under strict international control. A world disarmament conference could play a role in this process at an appropriate time.

III. INTERNATIONAL QUESTIONS: THE REDUCTION OF TENSIONS AND STRENGTHENING OF INTERNATIONAL SECURITY

President Nixon and General Secretary Brezhnev reviewed major questions of the current international situation. They gave special attention to the developments which have occurred since the time of the US-Soviet summit meeting in Moscow. It was noted with satisfaction that positive trends are developing in international relations toward the further relaxation of tensions and the strengthening of cooperative relations in the interests of peace. In the opinion of both Sides, the current process of improvement in the international situation creates new and favorable opportunities for reducing tensions, settling outstanding international issues, and creating a permanent structure of peace.

Indochina

The two Sides expressed their deep satisfaction at the conclusion of the Agreement on Ending the War and Restoring Peace in Vietnam, and also at the results of the International Conference on Vietnam which approved and supported that Agreement.

The two Sides are convinced that the conclusion of the Agreement on Ending the War and Restoring Peace in Vietnam, and the subsequent signing of the Agreement on Restoring Peace and Achieving National Concord in Laos, meet the fundamental interests and aspirations of the people of Vietnam and Laos and open up a possibility for establishing a lasting peace in Indochina, based on respect for the independence, sovereignty, unity and territorial integrity of the countries of that area. Both Sides emphasized that these agreements must be strictly implemented.

They further stressed the need to bring an early end to the military conflict in Cambodia in order to bring peace to the entire area of Indochina. They also reaffirmed their stand that the political futures of Vietnam, Laos, and Cambodia should be left to the respective peoples to determine, free from outside interference.

Europe

In the course of the talks both Sides noted with satisfaction that in Europe the process of relaxing tensions and developing cooperation is actively continuing and thereby contributing to international stability.

The two Sides expressed satisfaction with the further normalization of relations among European countries resulting from treaties and agreements signed in recent years, particularly between the USSR and the FRG [Federal Republic of Germany]. They also welcome the coming into force of the Quadripartite Agreement of September 3, 1971.

They share the conviction that strict observance of the treaties and agreements that have been concluded will contribute to the security and well-being of all parties concerned.

They also welcome the prospect of United Nations membership this year for the FRG and the GDR [German Democratic Republic] and recall, in this connection, that the USA, USSR, UK and France have signed the Quadripartite Declaration of November 9, 1972, on this subject.

The USA and the USSR reaffirm their desire, guided by the appropriate provisions of the Joint US-USSR Communique adopted in Moscow in May 1972, to continue their separate and joint contributions to strengthening peaceful relations in Europe. Both Sides affirm that ensuring a lasting peace in Europe is a paramount goal of their policies.

In this connection satisfaction was expressed with the fact that as a result of common efforts by many States, including the USA and the USSR, the preparatory work has been successfully completed for the Conference on Security and Cooperation in Europe, which will be convened on July 3, 1973. The USA and the USSR hold the view that the Conference will enhance the possibilities for strengthening European security and developing cooperation among the participating States. The USA and the USSR will conduct their policies so as to realize the goals of the Conference and bring about a new era of good relations in this part of the world.

Reflecting their continued positive attitude toward the Conference, both Sides will make efforts to bring the Conference to a successful conclusion at the earliest possible time. Both Sides proceed from the assumption that progress in the work of the Conference will produce possibilities for completing it at the highest level.

The USA and the USSR believe that the goal of strengthening stability and security in Europe would be further advanced if the relaxation of political tensions were accompanied by a reduction of military tensions in Central Europe. In this respect they attach great importance to the negotiations on the mutual reduction of forces and armaments and associated measures in Central Europe which will begin on October 30, 1973. Both Sides state their readiness to make, along with other States, their contribution to the achievement of mutually acceptable decisions on the substance of this problem, based on the strict observance of the principle of the undiminished security of any of the parties.

Middle East

The parties expressed their deep concern with the situation in the Middle East and exchanged opinions regarding ways of reaching a Middle East settlement.

Each of the parties set forth its position on this problem.

Both parties agreed to continue to exert their efforts to promote the quickest possible settlement in the Middle East. This settlement should be in accordance with the interests of all states in the area, be consistent with their independence and sovereignty and should take into due account the legitimate interests of the Palestinian people.

IV. COMMERCIAL AND ECONOMIC RELATIONS

The President and the General Secretary thoroughly reviewed the status of and prospects for commercial and economic ties between the USA and the USSR. Both Sides noted with satisfaction the progress achieved in the past year in the normalization and development of commercial and economic relations between them.

They agreed that mutually advantageous cooperation and peaceful relations would be strengthened by the creation of a permanent foundation of economic relationships.

They recall with satisfaction the various agreements on trade and commercial relations signed in the past year. Both Sides note that American-Soviet trade has shown a substantial increase, and that there are favorable prospects for a continued rise in the exchange of goods over the coming years.

They believe that the two countries should aim at a total of 2-3 billion dollars of trade over the next three years. The Joint US-USSR Commercial Commission continues to provide a valuable mechanism to promote the broad-scale growth of economic relations. The two Sides noted with satisfaction that contacts between American firms and their Soviet counterparts are continuing to expand.

Both Sides confirmed their firm intention to proceed from their earlier understanding on measures directed at creating more favorable conditions for expanding commercial and other economic ties between the USA and the USSR.

It was noted that as a result of the Agreement Regarding Certain Maritime Matters signed in October 1972, Soviet and American commercial ships have been calling more frequently at ports of the United States and the USSR, respectively, and since late May of this year a new regular passenger line has started operating between New York and Leningrad.

In the course of the current meeting, the two Sides signed a Protocol augmenting existing civil air relations between the USA and the USSR providing for direct air services between Washington and Moscow and New York and Leningrad, increasing the frequency of flights and resolving other questions in the field of civil aviation.

In the context of reviewing prospects for further and more permanent economic cooperation, both Sides expressed themselves in favor of mutually advantageous long term projects. They discussed a number of specific projects involving the participation of American companies, including the delivery of Siberian natural gas to the United States. The President indicated that the USA encourages American firms to work out concrete proposals on these projects and will give serious and sympathetic consideration to proposals that are in the interest of both Sides.

To contribute to expanded commercial, cultural and technical relations between the USA and the USSR, the two Sides signed a tax convention to avoid double taxation on income and eliminate, as much as possible, the need for citizens of one country to become involved in the tax system of the other.

A Protocol was also signed on the opening by the end of October 1973 of a Trade Representation of the USSR in Washington and a Commercial Office of the United States in Moscow. In addition a Protocol was signed on questions related to establishing a US-Soviet Chamber of Commerce. These agreements will facilitate the further development of commercial and economic ties between the USA and the USSR.

V. FURTHER PROGRESS IN OTHER FIELDS OF BILATERAL COOPERATION

The two Sides 'reviewed the areas of bilateral cooperation in such fields as environmental protection, public health and medicine, exploration of outer space, and science and technology, established by the agreements signed in May 1972 and subsequently. They noted that those agreements are being satisfactorily carried out in practice in accordance with the programs as adopted.

In particular, a joint effort is under way to develop effective means to combat those diseases which are most widespread and dangerous for mankind: cancer, cardiovascular or infectious diseases and arthritis. The medical aspects of the environmental problems are also subjects of cooperative research.

Preparations for the joint space flight of the Apollo and Soyuz spacecraft are proceeding according to an agreed timetable. The joint flight of these spaceships for a rendezvous and docking mission, and mutual visits of American and Soviet astronauts in each other's spacecraft, are scheduled for July 1975.

Building on the foundation created in previous agreements, and recognizing the potential of both the USA and the USSR to undertake cooperative measures in current scientific and technological areas, new projects for fruitful joint efforts were identified and appropriate agreements were concluded.

Peaceful Uses of Atomic Energy

Bearing in mind the great importance of satisfying the growing energy demands in both countries and throughout the world, and recognizing that the development of highly efficient energy sources could contribute to the solution of this problem, the President and General Secretary signed an agreement to expand and strengthen cooperation in the fields of controlled nuclear fusion, fast breeder reactors, and research on the fundamental properties of matter. A Joint Committee on Cooperation in the Peaceful Uses of Atomic Energy will be established to implement this agreement, which has a duration of ten years.

Agriculture

Recognizing the importance of agriculture in meeting mankind's requirement for food products and the role of science in modern agricultural production, the two Sides concluded an agreement providing for a broad exchange of scientific experience in agricultural research and development, and of information on agricultural economics. A US-USSR Joint Committee on Agricultural Cooperation will be established to oversee joint programs to be carried out under the Agreement.

World Ocean Studies

Considering the unique capabilities and the major interest of both nations in the field of world ocean studies, and noting the extensive experience of US-USSR oceanographic cooperation, the two Sides have agreed to broaden their cooperation and have signed an agreement to this effect. In so doing, they are convinced that the benefits from further development of cooperation in the field of oceanography will accrue not only bilaterally but also to all peoples of the world. A US-USSR Joint Committee on Cooperation in World Ocean Studies will be established to coordinate the implementation of cooperative programs.

Transportation

The two Sides agreed that there are opportunities for cooperation between the USA and the USSR in the solution of problems in the field of transportation. To permit expanded, mutually beneficial cooperation in this field, the two Sides concluded an agreement on this subject. The USA and the USSR further agreed that a Joint Committee on Cooperation in Transportation would be established.

Contacts, Exchanges and Cooperation

Recognizing the general expansion of US-USSR bilateral relations and, in particular, the growing number of exchanges in the fields of science, technology, education and culture, and in other fields of mutual interest, the two Sides agreed to broaden the scope of these activities under a new General Agreement on Contacts, Exchanges, and Cooperation, with a duration of six years. The two Sides agreed to this in the mutual belief that it will further promote better understanding between the peoples of the United States and the Soviet Union and will help to improve the general state of relations between the two countries.

Both Sides believe that the talks at the highest level, which were held in a frank and constructive spirit, were very valuable and made an important contribution to developing mutually advantageous relations between the USA and the USSR. In the view of both Sides, these talks will have a favorable impact on international relations.

They noted that the success of the discussions in

the United States was facilitated by the continuing consultation and contacts as agreed in May 1972. They reaffirmed that the practice of consultation should continue. They agreed that further meetings at the highest level should be held regularly.

Having expressed his appreciation to President Nixon for the hospitality extended during the visit to the United States, General Secretary Brezhnev invited the President to visit the USSR in 1974. The invitation was accepted.

June 24, 1973

RICHARD NIXON

President of the United States of America

LEONID I. BREZHNEV

General Secretary of the Central Committee, CPSU

IV:

THE INTERIM BETWEEN THE WASHINGTON SUMMIT AND THE SECOND MOSCOW SUMMIT MEETING: JULY 1973 TO JUNE 1974

INTRODUCTION

The Yom Kippur War of October 1973 produced the first major strain on U.S.-Soviet relations since the emergence of the "new pattern" from the Moscow summit of 1972. With the two sides fighting each other through surrogates, each found the type of restraint it had promised in the agreement to prevent nuclear war just four months earlier very difficult. Once the Egyptians were clearly being defeated, the Soviets announced the possibility of sending Soviet troops to "come between the two sides." Nixon responded by placing the United States' armed forces on world-wide alert, apparently the first instance of world-wide alert associated with a Soviet action since the Cuban Missile Crisis of 1962.

One might wonder than an event such as the Yom Kippur War could occur in the new period of detente, but Nixon chose to emphasize the role detente played in ending the crisis. "Personal detente," he said, had prevented the incident from becoming a world crisis.*

In the end, the two superpowers, as cochairmen of the Geneva Convention created in 1967, introduced a joint resolution in the United Nations Security Council that was adopted as Security Council Resolution 338 (C under Docment 41). Because it built mainly upon Security Council Resolution 242 from

---

*Nixon sent personal messages through regular diplomatic channels during the early days of the war. His main efforts to credit detente for a cease-fire supported by the United States and the USSR were through national radio and television addresses. See New York *Times,* October 18, 1973, for information about the messages sent and received on Sunday.

the previous Middle East Crisis of 1967 (B under Document 41), the two sides had a convenient device for terminating the hostilities.[1] Out of conflict, some image of continuation of the new course in U.S.-Soviet relations appeared.

NOTE

1. See DSB 11-12-1973, 599–606 for statements of U.S. policy and for other Security Council Resolutions of October.

39 (July 6, 1973)
U.S. Opens Consulate General in Leningrad

Press release 236 dated July 6

DEPARTMENT ANNOUNCEMENT

At a ceremony in Leningrad July 6, Assistant Secretary of State for European Affairs Walter J. Stoessel, Jr., presided over the raising of the American flag at the office building which will house the U.S. consulate general in that city. In addition to representatives of the city of Leningrad and the Soviet Ministry of Foreign Affairs, Adolph Dubs, U.S. Chargé d'Affaires ad interim in the U.S.S.R., and Culver Gleysteen, U.S. consul general in Leningrad, were present.

The building, which is the second U.S. Foreign Service post in the Soviet Union, will house the consulate general's offices and the American Print, Film, and Music Library in addition to providing apartments for a large part of the American staff.

REMARKS BY ASSISTANT SECRETARY STOESSEL

Mr. Mayor, Mr. Popov [Georgiy I. Popov, Diplomatic Representative, Leningrad Diplomatic Agency, Ministry of Foreign Affairs], distinguished guests: We are gathered here today to open the American consulate general in Leningrad. The Soviet consulate general in San Francisco was opened two weeks ago. These two events are symbolic of a long and often difficult effort to improve U.S.-Soviet relations. The first effort to open a consulate was almost 40 years ago. Another effort was made in 1948. It is perhaps interesting to note that at that time I was to be assigned to Leningrad as a vice consul, but the office never opened. This makes it even more of a personal pleasure for me to be here today.

The current project for a consular office here was initiated by Mr. Nixon when he was Vice President. When Mr. Nixon became President, he was determined to improve relations between the United States and the Soviet Union, and I am sure it is a source of great satisfaction to him that after so many years we are now opening the American consulate general in Leningrad.

As you know, the Conference on European Security and Cooperation is now taking place in Helsinki. I can say from my personal experience there that it is working very well and the atmosphere is good. We are drawing away from confrontation and have moved toward negotiation. It is particularly fitting that the opening of this office in Leningrad is taking place at this time. General Secretary Brezhnev has just completed his visit to the United States, one year after President Nixon's visit to the U.S.S.R. These two visits have made an enormous contribution toward improving bilateral relations between our two countries and to prospects for peace everywhere. We believe that in their day-to-day operations the new consulates general in Leningrad and San Francisco will play a significant role in understanding and contacts between our two countries.

I wish on this occasion to say a special word about Leningrad. This is a city with a great history which is world famous for its culture, its beauty, and its industrial achievements. It is a hero city which has a deep meaning for all who remember the past and who are dedicated to preserving peace now and in the future. You who represent Leningrad have reason to be proud of your city, and the United States is proud to be present here.

Mr. Mayor, Mr. Popov, and other distinguished guests, let me raise a toast to your health, to the city of Leningrad, to the success of our consul general and his colleagues in their important tasks, and to the constant improvement of relations between the Soviet Union and the United States.

PROTOCOL

Recalling the undertaking of the United States of America
and the Union of Soviet Socialist Republics in the Agreement
Regarding Trade signed on October 18, 1972,[1] to cooperate in
the expansion and improvement of their commercial facilities
in Moscow and Washington, and their undertaking in the Protocol
signed on June 22, 1973,[2] to open a Trade Representation of the
U.S.S.R. in Washington and a Commercial Office of the U.S.A.
in Moscow as soon as possible,

Both Governments welcome the inauguration on October 3,
1973 of a Trade Representation of the U.S.S.R. in Washington
and a Commercial Office of the U.S.A. in Moscow and agree
that the number of authorized personnel of each of these
offices, including the principal officer and his deputies,
shall be 25 at the present time. This number may be changed
by mutual agreement.

Done at Moscow this 3rd day of October, 1973, in two
copies, in English and Russian, both texts being equally
authentic.

For the Government of the
   United States of America:

[signature: Geo. P. Shultz]

George P. Shultz
Secretary of the Treasury

[SEAL]

For the Government of the
   Union of Soviet Socialist
   Republics:

[signature: N. S. Patolichev]

N. S. Patolichev
Minister of Foreign Trade

[SEAL]

---

[1] *Department of State Bulletin*, Nov. 20, 1972, p. 595.
[2] TIAS 7657; *ante*, p. 1501.

41 THE MIDDLE EAST CRISIS OF 1973

A (October 21, 1973)

Statement of John Scali

USUN press release 96 dated October 21

The United States, together with the U.S.S.R., has called for this meeting of the Security Council with one purpose in mind: to take joint action and to present a joint proposition to the Council whose aim is to bring an immediate cease-fire-in-place and to begin promptly negotiations between the parties under appropriate auspices looking toward a just and durable peace based on the November 1967 Security Council resolution.[1]

As the members of this Council know, the tragic fighting over the past 17 days has been both furious and costly. We believe that the prolongation of the war is not in the interests of the parties or the peoples in the area and that its continuance carries grave risks for the peace of the world. Because of this, President Nixon agreed that Secretary of State Kissinger should fly to Moscow in response to an invitation of General Secretary Brezhnev. As a result of these discussions the Council has before it the resolution agreed jointly by the United States and the Soviet Governments on which both our governments request immediate action on the part of the Security Council. The resolution has already been circulated to the members of the Council.

Let me make a few brief remarks regarding the three short paragraphs of the resolution, for they all stand clearly on their own words and speak for themselves.

The first paragraph calls for an immediate cease-fire. In our view as well as that of the Soviet Union, this applies not only to the parties directly concerned but also to those who have joined in the fighting by sending units. This paragraph calls for the stopping of fighting in the positions presently occupied by the two sides. We believe that 12 hours should allow ample time to achieve the practical implementation of this paragraph.

The second paragraph calls for the implementation of the Security Council resolution in all of its parts after the cease-fire. The members of this Council, as well as the parties concerned, are fully familiar with Security Council Resolution 242, and it needs no elaboration here. The paragraph is linked to paragraph 3, which calls for the immediate beginning of negotiations between the parties concerned under appropriate auspices aimed at establishing a just and durable peace in the Middle East. We believe that from the tragic events of the past 17 days there must be a new resolve, a new attempt to remove the fundamental causes that have brought war to the Middle East so frequently and so tragically. Another respite between two wars is just not good enough. And for our part, both the United States and the Soviet Union are ready to make our joint good offices available to the parties as a means to facilitate the negotiating process.

Finally, I want to report to the Council that both the Soviet Union and the United States believe that there should be an immediate exchange of prisoners of war.

B (November 22, 1967)
TEXT OF RESOLUTION [12]

The Security Council,
Expressing its continuing concern with the grave situation in the Middle East,
Emphasizing the inadmissibility of the acquisition of territory by war and the need to work for a just and lasting peace in which every State in the area can live in security,
Emphasizing further that all Member States in their acceptance of the Charter of the United Nations have undertaken a commitment to act in accordance with Article 2 of the Charter,
1. *Affirms* that the fulfilment of Charter principles requires the establishment of a just and lasting peace in the Middle East which should include the application of both the following principles:

(i) Withdrawal of Israeli armed forces from territories occupied in the recent conflict;
(ii) Termination of all claims or states of belligerency and respect for and acknowledgement of the sovereignty, territorial integrity and political independence of every State in the area and their right to live in peace within secure and recognized boundaries free from threats or acts of force;

2. *Affirms further* the necessity

(a) For guaranteeing freedom of navigation through international waterways in the area;
(b) For achieving a just settlement of the refugee problem;

(c) For guaranteeing the territorial inviolability and political independence of every State in the area, through measures including the establishment of demilitarized zones;

3. *Requests* the Secretary-General to designate a Special Representative to proceed to the Middle East to establish and maintain contacts with the States concerned in order to promote agreement and assist efforts to achieve a peaceful and accepted settlement in accordance with the provisions and principles in this resolution;[13]
4. *Requests* the Secretary-General to report to the Security Council on the progress of the efforts of the Special Representative as soon as possible.

C (October 22, 1973)
Security Council Resolution 338 [2]

The Security Council
1. *Calls upon* all parties to the present fighting to cease all firing and terminate all military activity immediately, no later than 12 hours after the moment of the adoption of this decision, in the positions they now occupy;
2. *Calls upon* the parties concerned to start immediately after the cease-fire the implementation of Security Council resolution 242 (1967) in all of its parts;
3. *Decides* that, immediately and concurrently with the cease-fire, negotiations start between the parties concerned under appropriate auspices aimed at establishing a just and durable peace in the Middle East.

[2] Adopted on Oct. 22 at 12:50 a.m. by a vote of 14 to 0 (China did not participate in the voting).

[12] U.N. doc. S/RES/242 (1967) (S/8247); adopted unanimously on Nov. 22.

V:

THE SECOND MOSCOW
SUMMIT MEETING:
JUNE 28 TO JULY 3, 1974

INTRODUCTION

The second Moscow summit produced six agreements, a joint statement, and a joint communique. Collectively the agreements and joint statement can be grouped into three categories: additional agreements on cooperative ventures; trade matters; and control of nuclear armaments. Of the seven documents (excluding the joint communique), three (42, 43, and 44) fall into the first category and build horizontally from the earlier Moscow and Washington agreements; that is, they apply the devices the earlier cooperative ventures used (joint conferences and exchanges of specialists, information, and equipment) to three additional fields (energy, housing construction, and artificial heart research and construction). This broadened U.S.-Soviet contacts, but did not deepen them.

Only one agreement (Document 45) is related to trade. That area was still conspicuously absent from the matter under discussion, for Congress still had the Trade Reform Bill of 1973 under discussion and was in the process of attaching strong amendments to it that would restrict the President's authority in dealing with the USSR.

Three of the documents (46, 47, and 48) fall within the category of controlling nuclear arms. The protocol to the ABM treaty of 1972 reduced the number of ABM sites permitted from two to one. The statement on military use of environmental modification was the first step in a series of such statements that would eventually lead to a multilateral convention prohibiting such methods of warfare (Documents 58, 61, and 73).

The Treaty and Protocol on the Limitation of Underground Nuclear Weapon Tests, commonly called the Threshold Test Ban Treaty (TTBT), limited tests to a yield of 150 kilotons. Article III of the treaty committed the two sides to achieving an agreement regulating underground nuclear explosion for peaceful purposes (commonly abbreviated PNE, for peaceful nuclear explosions). The TTBT was to enter into force March 31, 1976, assuming, of course, that the U.S. Senate would grant its consent to the treaty in the meantime.

In spite of the substantial achievements in negotiations on nuclear arms control that these three documents reflected, the permanent agreement on strategic offensive weapons that was to have been finished in 1973, but was not, was still not ready for signature at the summit in 1974.

The drama of and media attention to the second Moscow summit were incomparably less than the first Moscow summit two years earlier. The Watergate hearings were well advanced in Washington, and Americans were so preoccupied with them that the space the press gave the scandal was equal to or greater than the space given the news from Moscow during the week of June 28 to July 3.* Whereas the three national television networks had originated much of their evening news coverage from Moscow in 1972, they ran film from Moscow during their evening news programs in 1974 and kept their anchormen at home. During the 1972 Moscow summit meeting, Walter Cronkite opened his evening news program on the south embankment of the Moscow River, with the Kremlin hill and government buildings as background. During the 1974 Moscow summit, he talked to us from his New York City newsroom. Besides the Watergate problem, the Middle East Crisis and Soviet policies on Jewish emigration and persecution of Alexander Solzhenitsyn had cast heavy shadows upon the achievements of the period from May 1972 to October 1973.

---

*For instance, the *Newsweek* issue of July 8, 1974 carried a picture of Nixon and Brezhnev on the cover, along with the words "Summit of 1974," but inside it devoted six pages of text to the summit and six to Watergate.

42 (June 28, 1974)

AGREEMENT ON COOPERATION
IN THE FIELD OF ENERGY

AGREEMENT BETWEEN THE UNITED STATES OF AMER-
ICA AND THE UNION OF SOVIET SOCIALIST REPUB-
LICS ON COOPERATION IN THE FIELD OF ENERGY

The United States of America and the Union of
Soviet Socialist Republics;

Attaching great importance to meeting the energy needs of the two countries, with proper regard to the protection of the environment;

Recognizing that the development of cooperation in the field of energy can benefit the peoples of both countries and all mankind;

Desiring to expand and to deepen the cooperation now existing between the two countries in the field of energy research and development;

Recognizing the need to create better mutual understanding of each country's national energy programs and outlook;

Convinced that cooperation in the field of energy will contribute to the overall improvement of relations between the two countries;

In accordance with and in development of the Agreement between the Government of the United States of America and the Government of the Union of Soviet Socialist Republics on Cooperation in the Fields of Science and Technology of May 24, 1972, and the Agreement on Cooperation in the Field of Environmental Protection between the United States of America and the Union of Soviet Socialist Republics of May 23, 1972, as well as in accordance with the Agreement between the United States of America and the Union of Soviet Socialist Republics on Scientific and Technical Cooperation in the Field of Peaceful Uses of Atomic Energy of June 21, 1973, and the General Agreement between the United States of America and the Union of Soviet Socialist Republics on Contacts, Exchanges and Cooperation of June 19, 1973;

Have agreed as follows:

ARTICLE I

The Parties will expand and strengthen their cooperation in the field of energy on the basis of mutual benefit, equality and reciprocity.

ARTICLE II

The main objectives of such cooperation under this Agreement are:

a. to use the scientific and technical potential of both countries to accelerate by cooperative efforts research and development in the areas of existing and alternative sources of energy as well as to increase effectiveness in the use of energy and its conservation, and

b. to achieve a better mutual understanding of each country's national energy programs and outlook.

ARTICLE III

1. Cooperation will be implemented in the following areas:

a. technologies concerning the exploration, extraction, processing and use of fossil fuels, including but not limited to oil, shale, natural gas and coal, and, in particular, new methods of drilling and of increasing the rate of extraction and degree of recovery of oil and natural gas from strata, and of mining, extracting and processing coal and shale;

b. the exchange of relevant information, views and methods of forecasting concerning the national energy programs and outlooks of the respective countries, including all questions of mutual interest related to production, demand and consumption of the major forms of fuels and energy;

c. technology for developing non-conventional sources of energy, such as solar and geothermal energy and synthetic fuels;

d. energy-related environmental technology; and

e. measures to increase the efficiency of energy use and to restrain demand.

2. Other areas of cooperation may be added by mutual agreement.

ARTICLE IV

1. Cooperation between the Parties may take the following forms:

a. exchange of scientists and specialists;

b. exchange of scientific and technical information, documentation and results of research;

c. establishment of groups of experts for the planning and execution of joint research and development programs;

d. joint work by theoretical and experimental scientists in appropriate research centers of the two countries; and

e. holding joint consultations, seminars and panels.

2. Other forms of cooperation may be added by mutual agreement.

3. Cooperation under this Agreement will be carried out in accordance with the laws and regulations of the respective countries.

ARTICLE V

1. In furtherance of this Agreement, the Parties will, as appropriate, encourage, facilitate and monitor the development of contacts and cooperation between organizations, institutions and firms of the respective countries, including the conclusion, as appropriate, of implementing agreements for carrying out cooperative activities under this Agreement.

2. To assure fruitful development of cooperation, the Parties will render every assistance for the travel of scientists and specialists to areas of the respective countries appropriate for the conduct of activities under this Agreement.

ARTICLE VI

1. For implementation of this Agreement, there shall be established a US–USSR Joint Committee on Cooperation in the Field of Energy. Meetings of the Joint Committee will be convened once a year in the United States and the Soviet Union alternately, unless otherwise mutually agreed.

2. The Joint Committee shall take such action as is necessary for effective implementation of this Agreement including, but not limited to, consultations on the energy situation and outlook of the respective countries; approval of specific projects and programs of cooperation; designation of appropriate participating organizations and institutions responsible for carrying out cooperative activities; and making recommendations, as appropriate, to the two Governments. The Joint Committee shall establish the necessary working groups to carry out the programs, projects and exchange of information contemplated by this Agreement.

3. Each Party shall designate its Executive Agent which will be responsible for carrying out this Agreement. During the period between meetings of the Joint Committee, the Executive Agents shall maintain contact with each other, keep each other informed of activities and progress in implementing this Agreement, and coordinate and supervise the development and implementation of cooperative activities conducted under this Agreement.

ARTICLE VII

Nothing in this Agreement shall be interpreted to prejudice or modify any existing agreements between the Parties, except that energy projects within the Agreement between the Government of the United States of America and the Government of the Union of Soviet Socialist Republics on Cooperation in the Fields of Science and Technology of May 24, 1972 and the Agreement between the United States of America and the Union of Soviet Socialist Republics on Cooperation in the Field of Environmental Protection of May 23, 1972 which clearly fall under this Agreement henceforward will be implemented pursuant to this Agreement.

ARTICLE VIII

Unless an implementing agreement contains other provisions, each Party or participating institution, organization or firm, shall bear the costs of its participation and that of its personnel in cooperative activities engaged in pursuant to this Agreement.

ARTICLE IX

1. This Agreement shall enter into force upon signature and remain in force for five years. It will be automatically extended for successive five-year periods unless either Party notifies the other of its intent to terminate this Agreement not later than six months prior to the expiration of this Agreement.

2. This Agreement may be modified at any time by mutual agreement of the Parties.

3. The termination of this Agreement will not affect the validity of implementing agreements concluded under this Agreement between institutions, organizations and firms of the respective countries.

DONE at Moscow on June 28, 1974, in duplicate, in the English and Russian languages, both texts being equally authentic.

For the United States of America:

RICHARD NIXON

President of the United States of America

For the Union of Soviet Socialist Republics:

N. PODGORNY

Chairman of the Presidium of the Supreme Soviet of the USSR

43 (June 28, 1974)

AGREEMENT ON COOPERATION IN HOUSING AND OTHER CONSTRUCTION

AGREEMENT BETWEEN THE UNITED STATES OF AMERICA AND THE UNION OF SOVIET SOCIALIST REPUBLICS ON COOPERATION IN THE FIELD OF HOUSING AND OTHER CONSTRUCTION

The United States of America and the Union of Soviet Socialist Republics;

Desiring to develop cooperation in the field of housing and other construction;

Realizing that more effective application of new and traditional building materials and techniques can contribute to more rational utilization of the resources available to both countries;

Desiring to exchange information and techniques in the field of housing and other construction;

Believing that cooperation in the field of housing and other construction offers benefits for both the United States of America and the Union of Soviet Socialist Republics;

Convinced that such cooperation will serve to contribute to the improvement of relations between the two countries;

Noting cooperation already being implemented in these areas under existing agreements, and in accordance with the General Agreement between the United States of America and the Union of Soviet Socialist Republics on Contacts, Exchanges, and Cooperation, signed June 19, 1973;

Have agreed as follows:

ARTICLE I

The Parties will develop and carry out cooperation in the field of housing and other construction on the basis of mutual benefit, equality and reciprocity.

ARTICLE II

This cooperation will be directed to the investigation and solution of specific problems of mutual interest in the field of housing and other construction.

Initially, cooperation will be implemented in the following areas:

a. innovative techniques for the improvement of life safety, reliability, quality, and economy of buildings and building materials including: organization and management of construction, new methods and materials, and the improved use of traditional methods and materials;

b. performance criteria for housing and other construction in seismic areas with special consideration of the impact of geophysical conditions;

c. improvement of construction methods in areas of extreme climatic conditions, such as cold and arid regions, including techniques for erection and finishing of buildings under sustained freezing, and foundation construction under unusual soil conditions;

d. services to housing and other buildings, including water supply, waste disposal, heating, lighting, and ventilation, with special reference to combined utility functions; and

e. planning, design, and construction of new towns.

Other areas of cooperation may be added by mutual agreement.

Article III

Cooperation pursuant to this Agreement may be implemented by the following means:

a. exchange of experts, advanced students and delegations;

b. exchange of scientific and technical information and documentation;

c. conducting joint conferences, meetings and seminars;

d. joint development and implementation of research programs and projects; and

e. other forms of cooperation which may be mutually agreed upon.

Such cooperation shall be conducted in accordance with the constitution and applicable laws and regulations of the respective countries.

Article IV

In furtherance of the aims of this Agreement, the Parties will, as appropriate, encourage, facilitate and monitor the development of cooperation and direct contacts between agencies, organizations and firms of the two countries, including the conclusion, as appropriate, of implementing agreements for carrying out specific projects and programs under this Agreement.

Article V

1. For the implementation of this Agreement, there shall be established a US–USSR Joint Committee on Cooperation in Housing and Other Construction. This Committee shall meet, as a rule, once a year alternately in the United States and the Soviet Union, unless otherwise mutually agreed.

2. The Joint Committee shall take such action as is necessary for the effective implementation of this Agreement, including, but not limited to, approval of specific projects and programs of cooperation, designation of appropriate agencies, organizations, and joint working groups to be responsible for carrying out cooperative activities; and making recommendations, as appropriate, to the Parties.

3. Each Party shall designate its Executive Agent which will be responsible for coordinating and carrying out this Agreement, and, as appropriate, in their respective countries, shall assure the cooperation of other participating institutions and organizations. During the period between meetings of the Joint Committee, the Executive Agents will maintain contact with each other and will coordinate and supervise the development and implementation of cooperative activities conducted under this Agreement.

4. Unless an implementing agreement contains other provisions, each Party or participating institution, organization or firm shall bear the costs of its participation and that of its personnel in cooperative activities engaged in under this Agreement.

Article VI

Nothing in this Agreement shall be interpreted to prejudice other agreements between the Parties or their respective rights and obligations under such other agreements.

Article VII

1. This Agreement shall enter into force upon signature and remain in force for five years. It will be automatically extended for successive five year periods unless either party notifies the other of its intent to terminate this Agreement not later than six months prior to the expiration of this Agreement.

2. This Agreement may be modified at any time by mutual agreement of the Parties.

3. The termination of this Agreement shall not affect the validity of implementing agreements concluded under this Agreement between interested agencies, organizations and firms of the two countries.

Done at Moscow on June 28, 1974, in duplicate, in the English and Russian languages, both texts being equally authentic.

For the United States of America:

Richard Nixon

President of the United States of America

For the Union of Soviet Socialist Republics:

A. Kosygin

Chairman of the Council of Ministers of the USSR

44 (June 28, 1974)

AGREEMENT ON COOPERATION IN ARTIFICIAL HEART RESEARCH AND DEVELOPMENT

Agreement Between the United States of America and the Union of Soviet Socialist Republics on Cooperation in Artificial Heart Research and Development

The United States of America and the Union of Soviet Socialist Republics;

Reaffirming the importance that medical science has for mankind today;

Realizing the advisability of further uniting the efforts of both countries in resolving the pressing problems of medical science;

Recognizing the great importance of scientific research and the study of heart disease, which is one of the leading causes of mortality in both their countries as well as throughout the world;

Desiring to expand and strengthen common efforts to promote the development of an artificial heart;

Realizing that the development of an effective artificial heart could eventually lead to a reduction in mortality;

In pursuance and further development of the Agreement between the Government of the United States of America and the Government of the Union of Soviet Socialist Republics on Cooperation in the Field of Medical Science and Public Health, signed May 23, 1972;

In accordance with the General Agreement between the United States of America and the Union of Soviet Socialist Republics on Contacts, Exchanges and Cooperation, signed June 19, 1973;

Have agreed as follows:

ARTICLE I

Both parties undertake to develop and extend scientific and technical cooperation in artificial heart research and development on the basis of equality, reciprocity and mutual benefit.

ARTICLE II

The cooperation will be concentrated in the areas of research on, and joint development and testing of devices, materials, instruments and control mechanisms which will provide cardiovascular support including total heart replacement.

ARTICLE III

The cooperation provided for in the preceding Articles may be implemented principally in the following ways:

a. exchange of scientific and technical information;

b. organization of joint conferences, workshops and meetings of experts;

c. exchanges of specialists and delegations;

d. preparation of joint publications and technical manuals; and

e. familiarization with and exchange of technical aids and equipment.

In the course of implementing this Agreement, other forms of cooperation may also be determined by mutual agreement.

ARTICLE IV

The parties will delegate practical implementation of this Agreement to the US–USSR Joint Committee for Health Cooperation. The Committee shall approve the programs of cooperation, designate the participating organizations responsible for the realization of these programs, and periodically review the progress of the cooperation.

ARTICLE V

Cooperation shall be financed on the basis of reciprocal agreements worked out by the Joint Committee, using the resources of the Department of Health, Education, and Welfare of the United States of America and the Ministry of Health of the Union of Soviet Socialist Republics, as well as the resources of those organizations and institutions taking part in the cooperation.

ARTICLE VI

Such cooperation will be carried out in accordance with the laws and regulations of the respective countries.

Nothing in this Agreement shall be construed to prejudice or modify other agreements concluded between the two parties.

ARTICLE VII

This Agreement shall enter into force upon signature and shall remain in force for three years after which it will be extended for successive five year periods unless one party notifies the other of its intent to terminate this agreement not less than six months prior to its expiration.

This Agreement may be modified by mutual agreement of the parties.

DONE at Moscow on June 28, 1974, in duplicate, in the English and Russian languages, both texts being equally authentic.

For the United States of America:

For the Union of Soviet Socialist Republics:

HENRY A. KISSINGER

A. GROMYKO

Secretary of State

Minister of Foreign Affairs

LONG TERM AGREEMENT ON ECONOMIC, INDUSTRIAL, AND TECHNICAL COOPERATION

LONG TERM AGREEMENT BETWEEN THE UNITED STATES OF AMERICA AND THE UNION OF SOVIET SOCIALIST REPUBLICS TO FACILITATE ECONOMIC, INDUSTRIAL, AND TECHNICAL COOPERATION

The United States of America and the Union of Soviet Socialist Republics,

Desiring to promote continuing orderly expansion of economic, industrial, and technical cooperation and the exchange of relevant information to facilitate such cooperation between the two countries and their competent organizations, enterprises, and firms on a long term and mutually beneficial basis,

Guided by the Basic Principles of Relations between the United States of America and the Union of Soviet Socialist Republics of May 29, 1972, the Joint American-Soviet Communique of June 24, 1973, and the principles set forth in the Agreement between the Government of the United States of America and the Government of the Union of Soviet Socialist Republics Regarding Trade dated October 18, 1972,

Have agreed as follows:

ARTICLE I

The Parties shall use their good offices to facilitate economic, industrial, and technical cooperation in keeping with established practices and applicable laws and regulations in the respective countries.

ARTICLE II

Cooperation which shall be facilitated as contemplated in Article I shall include:

a. purchases and sales of machinery and equipment for the construction of new enterprises and for the expansion and modernization of existing enterprises in the fields of raw materials, agriculture, machinery and equipment, finished products, consumer goods, and services;

b. purchases and sales of raw materials, agricultural products, finished products, consumer goods, and services;

c. purchases, sales and licensing of patent rights and proprietary industrial know-how, designs, and processes;

d. training of technicians and exchange of specialists; and

e. joint efforts, where appropriate, in the construction of industrial and other facilities in third countries, particularly through supply of machinery and equipment.

ARTICLE III

In order to assist relevant organizations, enterprises, and firms of both countries in determining the fields of cooperation most likely to provide a basis for mutually beneficial contracts, a working group of experts convened by the Commission mentioned in Article V shall meet not less frequently than once a year to exchange information and forecasts of basic economic, industrial, and commercial trends.

ARTICLE IV

To promote the cooperation foreseen in this Agreement the Parties undertake to facilitate, as appropriate, the acquisition or lease of suitable business and residential premises by organizations, enterprises, and firms of the other party and their employees; the importation of essential office equipment and supplies; the hiring of staffs; the issuance of visas, including multiple entry visas, to qualified officials and representatives of such organizations, enterprises, and firms and to members of their immediate families; and travel by such persons for business purposes in the territory of the receiving country.

ARTICLE V

The US–USSR Commercial Commission established pursuant to the Communique of May 26, 1972, is authorized and directed to monitor the practical implementation of this Agreement, when necessary jointly with other American-Soviet bodies created by agreement between the Governments of the two countries, with a view to facilitating the cooperation contemplated in this Agreement.

ARTICLE VI

This Agreement shall enter into force on the date of its signature, and shall remain in force for 10 years.

The Parties shall agree not later than six months prior to the expiration of the above period upon measures which may be necessary to facilitate further development of economic, industrial, and technical cooperation.

DONE at Moscow on June 29, 1974, in duplicate, in the English and Russian languages, both texts being equally authentic.

For the United States of America:

RICHARD NIXON

President of the United States of America

For the Union of Soviet Socialist Republics:

L. BREZHNEV

General Secretary of the Central Committee of the CPSU

46 (July 3, 1974)

PROTOCOL TO TREATY ON THE LIMITATION OF ANTI-BALLISTIC MISSILE SYSTEMS

Protocol to the Treaty Between the United States of America and the Union of Soviet Socialist Republics on the Limitation of Anti-Ballistic Missile Systems

The United States of America and the Union of Soviet Socialist Republics, hereinafter referred to as the Parties,

Proceeding from the Basic Principles of Relations between the United States of America and the Union of Soviet Socialist Republics signed on May 29, 1972,

Desiring to further the objectives of the Treaty between the United States of America and the Union of Soviet Socialist Republics on the Limitation of Anti-Ballistic Missile Systems signed on May 26, 1972, hereinafter referred to as the Treaty,

Reaffirming their conviction that the adoption of further measures for the limitation of strategic arms would contribute to strengthening international peace and security,

Proceeding from the premise that further limitation of anti-ballistic missile systems will create more favorable conditions for the completion of work on a permanent agreement on more complete measures for the limitation of strategic offensive arms,

Have agreed as follows:

ARTICLE I

1. Each Party shall be limited at any one time to a single area out of the two provided in Article III of the Treaty for deployment of anti-ballistic missile (ABM) systems or their components and accordingly shall not exercise its right to deploy an ABM system or its components in the second of the two ABM system deployment areas permitted by Article III of the Treaty, except as an exchange of one permitted area for the other in accordance with Article II of this Protocol.

2. Accordingly, except as permitted by Article II of this Protocol: the United States of America shall not deploy an ABM system or its components in the area centered on its capital, as permitted by Article III (a) of the Treaty, and the Soviet Union shall not deploy an ABM system or its components in the deployment area of intercontinental ballistic missile (ICBM) silo launchers as permitted by Article III (b) of the Treaty.

ARTICLE II

1. Each Party shall have the right to dismantle or destroy its ABM system and the components thereof in the area where they are presently deployed and to deploy an ABM system or its components in the alternative area permitted by Article III of the Treaty, provided that prior to initiation of construction, notification is given in accord with the procedure agreed to in the Standing Consultative Commission, during the year beginning October 3, 1977 and ending October 2, 1978, or during any year which commences at five year intervals thereafter, those being the years for periodic review of the Treaty, as provided in Article XIV of the Treaty. This right may be exercised only once.

2. Accordingly, in the event of such notice, the United States would have the right to dismantle or destroy the ABM system and its components in the deployment area of ICBM silo launchers and to deploy an ABM system or its components in an area centered on its capital, as permitted by Article III (a) of the Treaty, and the Soviet Union would have the right to dismantle or destroy the ABM system and its components in the area centered on its capital and to deploy an ABM system or its components in an area containing ICBM silo launchers, as permitted by Article III (b) of the Treaty.

3. Dismantling or destruction and deployment of ABM systems or their components and the noti-

fication thereof shall be carried out in accordance with Article VIII of the ABM Treaty and procedures agreed to in the Standing Consultative Commission.

ARTICLE III

The rights and obligations established by the Treaty remain in force and shall be complied with by the Parties except to the extent modified by this Protocol. In particular, the deployment of an ABM system or its components within the area selected shall remain limited by the levels and other requirements established by the Treaty.

ARTICLE IV

This Protocol shall be subject to ratification in accordance with the constitutional procedures of each Party. It shall enter into force on the day of the exchange of instruments of ratification and shall thereafter be considered an integral part of the Treaty.

DONE at Moscow on July 3, 1974, in duplicate, in the English and Russian languages, both texts being equally authentic.

For the United States of America:	For the Union of Soviet Socialist Republics:
RICHARD NIXON	L. BREZHNEV
President of the United States of America	*General Secretary of the Central Committee of the CPSU*

47 (July 3, 1974)

TREATY AND PROTOCOL ON THE LIMITATION OF UNDERGROUND NUCLEAR WEAPON TESTS

Text of Treaty

TREATY BETWEEN THE UNITED STATES OF AMERICA AND THE UNION OF SOVIET SOCIALIST REPUBLICS ON THE LIMITATION OF UNDERGROUND NUCLEAR WEAPON TESTS

The United States of America and the Union of Soviet Socialist Republics, hereinafter referred to as the Parties,

Declaring their intention to achieve at the earliest possible date the cessation of the nuclear arms race and to take effective measures toward reductions in strategic arms, nuclear disarmament, and general and complete disarmament under strict and effective international control,

Recalling the determination expressed by the Parties to the 1963 Treaty Banning Nuclear Weapon Tests in the Atmosphere, in Outer Space and Under Water in its Preamble to seek to achieve the discontinuance of all test explosions of nuclear weapons for all time, and to continue negotiations to this end,

Noting that the adoption of measures for the further limitation of underground nuclear weapon tests would contribute to the achievement of these objectives and would meet the interests of strengthening peace and the further relaxation of international tension,

Reaffirming their adherence to the objectives and principles of the Treaty Banning Nuclear Weapon Tests in the Atmosphere, in Outer Space and Under Water and of the Treaty on the Non-Proliferation of Nuclear Weapons,

Have agreed as follows:

ARTICLE I

1. Each Party undertakes to prohibit, to prevent, and not to carry out any underground nuclear weapon test having a yield exceeding 150 kilotons at any place under its jurisdiction or control, beginning March 31, 1976.

2. Each Party shall limit the number of its underground nuclear weapon tests to a minimum.

3. The Parties shall continue their negotiations with a view toward achieving a solution to the problem of the cessation of all underground nuclear weapon tests.

ARTICLE II

1. For the purpose of providing assurance of compliance with the provisions of this Treaty, each Party shall use national means of verification at its disposal in a manner consistent with the generally recognized principles of international law.

2. Each Party undertakes not to interfere with the national technical means of verification of the other Party operating in accordance with paragraph 1 of this Article.

3. To promote the objectives and implementation of the provisions of this Treaty the Parties shall, as necessary, consult with each other, make inquiries and furnish information in response to such inquiries.

ARTICLE III

The provisions of this Treaty do not extend to underground nuclear explosions carried out by the Parties for peaceful purposes. Underground nuclear explosions for peaceful purposes shall be governed by an agreement which is to be negotiated and concluded by the Parties at the earliest possible time.

ARTICLE IV

This Treaty shall be subject to ratification in accordance with the constitutional procedures of each Party. This Treaty shall enter into force on the day of the exchange of instruments of ratification.

ARTICLE V

1. This Treaty shall remain in force for a period of five years. Unless replaced earlier by an agreement in implementation of the objectives specified in paragraph 3 of Article I of this Treaty, it shall be extended for successive five-year periods unless either Party notifies the other of its

termination no later than six months prior to the expiration of the Treaty. Before the expiration of this period the Parties may, as necessary, hold consultations to consider the situation relevant to the substance of this Treaty and to introduce possible amendments to the text of the Treaty.

2. Each Party shall, in exercising its national sovereignty, have the right to withdraw from this Treaty if it decides that extraordinary events related to the subject matter of this Treaty have jeopardized its supreme interests. It shall give notice of its decision to the other Party six months prior to withdrawal from this Treaty. Such notice shall include a statement of the extraordinary events the notifying Party regards as having jeopardized its supreme interests.

3. This Treaty shall be registered pursuant to Article 102 of the Charter of the United Nations.

DONE at Moscow on July 3, 1974, in duplicate, in the English and Russian languages, both texts being equally authentic.

For the United States of America:

RICHARD NIXON

President of the United States of America

For the Union of Soviet Socialist Republics:

L. BREZHNEV

General Secretary of the Central Committee of the CPSU

Text of Protocol

PROTOCOL TO THE TREATY BETWEEN THE UNITED STATES OF AMERICA AND THE UNION OF SOVIET SOCIALIST REPUBLICS ON THE LIMITATION OF UNDERGROUND NUCLEAR WEAPON TESTS

The United States of America and the Union of Soviet Socialist Republics, hereinafter referred to as the Parties,

Having agreed to limit underground nuclear weapon tests,

Have agreed as follows:

1. For the purpose of ensuring verification of compliance with the obligations of the Parties under the Treaty by national technical means, the Parties shall, on the basis of reciprocity, exchange the following data:

a. The geographic coordinates of the boundaries of each test site and of the boundaries of the geophysically distinct testing areas therein.

b. Information on the geology of the testing areas of the sites (the rock characteristics of geological formations and the basic physical properties of the rock, i.e., density, seismic velocity, water saturation, porosity and depth of water table).

c. The geographic coordinates of underground nuclear weapon tests, after they have been conducted.

d. Yield, date, time, depth and coordinates for two nuclear weapon tests for calibration purposes from each geophysically distinct testing area where underground nuclear weapon tests have been and are to be conducted. In this connection the yield of such explosions for calibration purposes should be as near as possible to the limit defined in Article I of the Treaty and not less than one-tenth of that limit. In the case of testing areas where data are not available on two tests for calibration purposes, the data pertaining to one such test shall be exchanged, if available, and the data pertaining to the second test shall be exchanged as soon as possible after a second test having a yield in the above-mentioned range. The provisions of this Protocol shall not require the Parties to conduct tests solely for calibration purposes.

2. The Parties agree that the exchange of data pursuant to subparagraphs a, b, and d of paragraph 1 shall be carried out simultaneously with the exchange of instruments of ratification of the Treaty, as provided in Article IV of the Treaty, having in mind that the Parties shall, on the basis of reciprocity, afford each other the opportunity to familiarize themselves with these data before the exchange of instruments of ratification.

3. Should a Party specify a new test site or testing area after the entry into force of the Treaty, the data called for by subparagraphs a and b of paragraph 1 shall be transmitted to the other Party in advance of use of that site or area. The data called for by subparagraph d of paragraph 1 shall also be transmitted in advance of use of that site or area if they are available; if they are not available, they shall be transmitted as soon as possible after they have been obtained by the transmitting Party.

4. The Parties agree that the test sites of each Party shall be located at places under its jurisdiction or control and that all nuclear weapon tests shall be conducted solely within the testing areas specified in accordance with paragraph 1.

5. For the purposes of the Treaty, all underground nuclear explosions at the specified test sites shall be considered nuclear weapon tests and shall be subject to all the provisions of the Treaty relating to nuclear weapon tests. The provisions of Article III of the Treaty apply to all underground nuclear explosions conducted outside of the specified test sites, and only to such explosions.

This Protocol shall be considered an integral part of the Treaty.

DONE at Moscow on July 3, 1974.

For the United States of America:

RICHARD NIXON

President of the United States of America

For the Union of Soviet Socialist Republics:

L. BREZHNEV

General Secretary of the Central Committee of the CPSU

1. Advocate the most effective measures possible to overcome the dangers of the use of environmental modification techniques for military purposes.

2. Have decided to hold a meeting of United States and Soviet representatives this year for the purpose of exploring this problem.

3. Have decided to discuss also what steps might be taken to bring about the measures referred to in paragraph 1.

Moscow, July 3, 1974

For the United States of America:	For the Union of Soviet Socialist Republics:
RICHARD NIXON	L. BREZHNEV
The President of the United States of America	*General Secretary of the Central Committee of the CPSU*

49 (July 3, 1974)
TEXT OF JOINT COMMUNIQUE, JULY 3

JOINT US-SOVIET COMMUNIQUE

In accordance with the agreement to hold regular US-Soviet meetings at the highest level and at the invitation, extended during the visit of General Secretary of the Central Committee of the Communist Party of the Soviet Union L. I. Brezhnev to the USA in June 1973, the President of the United States of America and Mrs. Richard Nixon paid an official visit to the Soviet Union from June 27 to July 3, 1974.

During his stay President Nixon visited, in addition to Moscow, Minsk and the Southern Coast of the Crimea.

The President of the United States and the Soviet leaders held a thorough and useful exchange of views on major aspects of relations between the USA and the USSR and on the present international situation.

On the Soviet side the talks were conducted by L. I. Brezhnev, General Secretary of the Central Committee of the Communist Party of the Soviet Union; N. V. Podgorny, Chairman of the Presidium of the USSR Supreme Soviet; A. N. Kosygin, Chairman of the USSR Council of Ministers; and A. A. Gromyko, Minister of Foreign Affairs of the USSR.

Accompanying the President of the USA and participating in the talks was Dr. Henry A. Kissinger, US Secretary of State and Assistant to the President for National Security Affairs.

Also taking part in the talks were:

On the American Side: Walter J. Stoessel, Jr., American Ambassador to the USSR; General Alexander M. Haig, Jr., Assistant to the President; Mr. Ronald L. Ziegler, Assistant to the President and Press Secretary; Major General Brent Scowcroft, Deputy Assistant to the President for National Security Affairs; Mr. Helmut Sonnenfeldt, Counselor

48 (July 3, 1974)
STATEMENT ON DANGERS OF MILITARY USE OF ENVIRONMENTAL MODIFICATION, JULY 3

JOINT STATEMENT

The United States of America and the Union of Soviet Socialist Republics:

Desiring to limit the potential danger to mankind from possible new means of warfare;

Taking into consideration that scientific and technical advances in environmental fields, including climate modification, may open possibilities for using environmental modification techniques for military purposes;

Recognizing that such use could have widespread, longlasting, and severe effects harmful to human welfare;

Recognizing also that proper utilization of scientific and technical advances could improve the inter-relationship of man and nature;

of the Department of State; and Mr. Arthur A. Hartman, Assistant Secretary of State for European Affairs.

On the Soviet Side: A. F. Dobrynin, Soviet Ambassador to the USA; A. M. Aleksandrov, Assistant to the General Secretary of the Central Committee, CPSU; L. M. Zamyatin, Director General of TASS; and G. M. Korniyenko, Member of the Collegium of the Ministry of Foreign Affairs of the USSR.

The talks were held in a most businesslike and constructive atmosphere and were marked by a mutual desire of both Sides to continue to strengthen understanding, confidence and peaceful cooperation between them and to contribute to the strengthening of international security and world peace.

I. Progress in Improving US–Soviet Relations

Having considered in detail the development of relations between the USA and the USSR since the US-Soviet summit meeting in May 1972, both Sides noted with satisfaction that through their vigorous joint efforts they have brought about over this short period a fundamental turn toward peaceful relations and broad, mutually beneficial cooperation in the interests of the peoples of both countries and of all mankind.

They emphasized the special importance for the favorable development of relations between the USA and the USSR of meetings of their leaders at the highest level, which are becoming established practice. These meetings provide opportunities for effective and responsible discussion, for the solution of fundamental and important bilateral questions, and for mutual contributions to the settlement of international problems affecting the interests of both countries.

Both Sides welcome the establishment of official contacts between the Congress of the US and the Supreme Soviet of the USSR. They will encourage a further development of such contacts, believing that they can play an important role.

Both Sides confirmed their mutual determination to continue actively to reshape US-Soviet relations on the basis of peaceful coexistence and equal security, in strict conformity with the spirit and the letter of the agreements achieved between the two countries and their obligations under those agreements. In this connection they noted once again the fundamental importance of the joint documents adopted as a result of the summit meetings in 1972 and 1973, especially of the Basic Principles of Relations Between the USA and the USSR, the Agreement on the Prevention of Nuclear War, the Treaty on the Limitation of Anti-Ballistic Missile Systems, and the Interim Agreement on Certain Measures with Respect to the Limitation of Strategic Offensive Arms.

Both Sides are deeply convinced of the imperative necessity of making the process of improving US-Soviet relations irreversible. They believe that,

as a result of their efforts, a real possibility has been created to achieve this goal. This will open new vistas for broad mutually beneficial cooperation, and for strengthening friendship between the American and Soviet peoples, and will thus contribute to the solution of many urgent problems facing the world.

Guided by these worthy goals, both Sides decided to continue steadfastly to apply their joint efforts —in cooperation with other countries concerned, as appropriate—first of all in such important fields as:

—removing the danger of war, including particularly war involving nuclear and other mass-destruction weapons;

—limiting and eventually ending the arms race especially in strategic weapons, having in mind as the ultimate objective the achievement of general and complete disarmament under appropriate international control;

—contributing to the elimination of sources of international tension and military conflict;

—strengthening and extending the process of relaxation of tensions throughout the world;

—developing broad, mutually beneficial cooperation in commercial and economic, scientific-technical and cultural fields on the basis of the principles of sovereignty, equality and non-interference in internal affairs with a view to promoting increased understanding and confidence between the peoples of both countries.

Accordingly, in the course of this summit meeting both Sides considered it possible to take new constructive steps which, they believe, will not only advance further the development of US-Soviet relations but will also make a substantial contribution to strengthening world peace and expanding international cooperation.

II. Further Limitation of Strategic Arms and Other Disarmament Issues

Both Sides again carefully analyzed the entire range of their mutual relations connected with the prevention of nuclear war and limitation of strategic armaments. They arrived at the common view that the fundamental agreements concluded between them in this sphere continue to be effective instruments of the general improvement of US-Soviet relations and the international situation as a whole. The USA and the USSR will continue strictly to fulfill the obligations undertaken in those agreements.

In the course of the talks, the two Sides had a thorough review of all aspects of the problem of limitation of strategic arms. They concluded that the Interim Agreement on offensive strategic weapons should be followed by a new agreement between the United States and the Soviet Union on the limitation of strategic arms. They agreed that such an agreement should cover the period until 1985 and deal with both quantitative and qualitative limitations. They agreed that such an agreement should be completed at the earliest possible date, before the expiration of the Interim Agreement.

They hold the common view that such a new agreement would serve not only the interests of the United States and the Soviet Union but also those of a further relaxation of international tensions and of world peace.

Their delegations will reconvene in Geneva in the immediate future on the basis of instructions growing out of the summit.

Taking into consideration the interrelationship between the development of offensive and defensive types of strategic arms and noting the successful implementation of the Treaty on the Limitation of Anti-Ballistic Missile Systems concluded between them in May 1972, both Sides considered it desirable to adopt additional limitations on the deployment of such systems. To that end they concluded a protocol providing for the limitation of each Side to a single deployment area for ABM Systems instead of two such areas as permitted to each Side by the Treaty.

At the same time, two protocols were signed entitled "Procedures Governing Replacement, Dismantling or Destruction and Notification Thereof, for Strategic Offensive Arms" and "Procedures Governing Replacement, Dismantling or Destruction, and Notification Thereof for ABM Systems and Their Components." These protocols were worked out by the Standing Consultative Commission which was established to promote the objectives and implementation of the provisions of the Treaty and the Interim Agreement signed on May 26, 1972.

The two Sides emphasized the serious importance which the US and USSR also attach to the realization of other possible measures—both on a bilateral and on a multilateral basis—in the field of arms limitation and disarmament.

Having noted the historic significance of the Treaty Banning Nuclear Weapon Tests in the Atmosphere, in Outer Space and Under Water, concluded in Moscow in 1963, to which the United States and the Soviet Union are parties, both Sides expressed themselves in favor of making the cessation of nuclear weapon tests comprehensive. Desiring to contribute to the achievement of this goal the USA and the USSR concluded, as an important step in this direction, the Treaty on the Limitation of Underground Nuclear Weapon Tests providing for the complete cessation, starting from March 31, 1976, of the tests of such weapons above an appropriate yield threshold, and for confining other underground tests to a minimum.

The Parties emphasized the fundamental importance of the Treaty on the Non-Proliferation of Nuclear Weapons. Having reaffirmed their mutual intention to observe the obligations assumed by them under that Treaty, including Article VI thereof, they expressed themselves in favor of increasing its effectiveness.

A joint statement was also signed in which the US and USSR advocate the most effective measures possible to overcome the dangers of the use of environmental modification techniques for military purposes.

Both Sides reaffirmed their interest in an effective international agreement which would exclude from the arsenals of States such dangerous instruments of mass destruction as chemical weapons. Desiring to contribute to early progress in this direction, the USA and the USSR agreed to consider a joint initiative in the Conference of the Committee on Disarmament with respect to the conclusion, as a first step, of an international Convention dealing with the most dangerous, lethal means of chemical warfare.

Both Sides are convinced that the new important steps which they have taken and intend to take in the field of arms limitation as well as further efforts toward disarmament will facilitate the relaxation of international tensions and constitute a tangible contribution to the fulfillment of the historic task of excluding war from the life of human society and thereby of ensuring world peace. The US and the USSR reaffirmed that a world disarmament conference at an appropriate time can play a positive role in this process.

III. PROGRESS IN THE SETTLEMENT OF INTERNATIONAL PROBLEMS

In the course of the meeting detailed discussions were held on major international problems.

Both Sides expressed satisfaction that relaxation of tensions, consolidation of peace, and development of mutually beneficial cooperation are becoming increasingly distinct characteristics of the development of the international situation. They proceed from the assumption that progress in improving the international situation does not occur spontaneously but requires active and purposeful efforts to overcome obstacles and resolve difficulties that remain from the past.

The paramount objectives of all states and peoples should be to ensure, individually and collectively, lasting security in all parts of the world, the early and complete removal of existing international conflicts and sources of tension and the prevention of new ones from arising.

The United States and the Soviet Union are in favor of the broad and fruitful economic cooperation among all states, large and small, on the basis of full equality and mutual benefit.

The United States and the Soviet Union reaffirm their determination to contribute separately and jointly to the achievement of all these tasks.

Europe

Having discussed the development of the situation in Europe since the last American-Soviet summit meeting, both Sides noted with profound satisfaction the further appreciable advances toward establishing dependable relations of peace, good-neighborliness and cooperation on the European continent.

Both Sides welcome the major contribution which the Conference on Security and Cooperation in Europe is making to this beneficial process. They consider that substantial progress has already been achieved at the Conference on many significant questions. They believe that this progress indicates that the present stage of the Conference will produce agreed documents of great international significance expressing the determination of the participating states to build their mutual relations on a solid jointly elaborated basis. The US and USSR will make every effort, in cooperation with the other participants, to find solutions acceptable to all for the remaining problems.

Both Sides expressed their conviction that successful completion of the Conference on Security and Cooperation in Europe would be an outstanding event in the interests of establishing a lasting peace. Proceeding from this assumption the USA and the USSR expressed themselves in favor of the final stage of the Conference taking place at an early date. Both Sides also proceed from the assumption that the results of the negotiations will permit the Conference to be concluded at the highest level, which would correspond to the historic significance of the Conference for the future of Europe and lend greater authority to the importance of the Conference's decisions.

Both Sides reaffirmed the lasting significance for a favorable development of the situation in Europe of the treaties and agreements concluded in recent years between European states with different social systems.

They expressed satisfaction with the admission to the United Nations of the Federal Republic of Germany and the German Democratic Republic.

Both Sides also stressed that the Quadripartite Agreement of September 3, 1971, must continue to play a key role in ensuring stability and detente in Europe. The US and USSR consider that the strict and consistent implementation of this Agreement by all parties concerned is an essential condition for the maintenance and strengthening of mutual confidence and stability in the center of Europe.

The USA and the USSR believe that, in order to strengthen stability and security in Europe, the relaxation of political tension on this continent should be accompanied by measures to reduce military tensions.

They therefore attach great importance to the current negotiations on the mutual reduction of forces and armaments and associated measures in Central Europe, in which they are participating. The two Sides expressed the hope that these negotiations will result in concrete decisions ensuring the undiminished security of any of the parties and preventing unilateral military advantages.

Middle East

Both Sides believe that the removal of the danger of war and tension in the Middle East is a task of paramount importance and urgency, and therefore, the only alternative is the achievement, on the basis of UN Security Council Resolution 338, of a just and lasting peace settlement in which should be taken into account the legitimate interests of all peoples in the Middle East, including the Palestinian people, and the right to existence of all states in the area.

As Co-Chairmen of the Geneva Peace Conference on the Middle East, the USA and the USSR consider it important that the Conference resume its work as soon as possible, with the question of other participants from the Middle East area to be discussed at the Conference. Both Sides see the main purpose of the Geneva Peace Conference, the achievement of which they will promote in every way, as the establishment of just and stable peace in the Middle East.

They agreed that the USA and the USSR will continue to remain in close touch with a view to coordinating the efforts of both countries toward a peaceful settlement in the Middle East.

Indochina

Both Sides noted certain further improvements in the situation in Indochina. In the course of the exchange of views on the situation in Vietnam both Sides emphasized that peace and stability in the region can be preserved and strengthened only on the basis of strict observance by all parties concerned of the provisions of the Paris Agreement of January 27, 1973, and the Act of the International Conference on Vietnam of March 2, 1973.

As regards Laos, they noted progress in the normalization of the situation as a result of the formation there of coalition governmental bodies. Both Sides also pronounced themselves in favor of strict fulfillment of the pertinent agreements.

Both Sides also stressed the need for an early and just settlement of the problem of Cambodia based on respect for the sovereign rights of the Cambodian people to a free and independent development without any outside interference.

Strengthening the Role of the United Nations

The United States of America and the Soviet Union attach great importance to the United Nations as an instrument for maintaining peace and security and the expansion of international cooperation. They reiterate their intention to continue their efforts toward increasing the effectiveness of the United Nations in every possible way, including in regard to peacekeeping, on the basis of strict observance of the United Nations Charter.

IV. COMMERCIAL AND ECONOMIC RELATIONS

In the course of the meeting great attention was

devoted to a review of the status of and prospects for relations between the USA and the USSR in the commercial and economic field.

Both Sides reaffirmed that they regard the broadening and deepening of mutually advantageous ties in this field on the basis of equality and non-discrimination as an important part of the foundation on which the entire structure of US-Soviet relations is built. An increase in the scale of commercial and economic ties corresponding to the potentials of both countries will cement this foundation and benefit the American and Soviet peoples.

The two Sides noted with satisfaction that since the previous summit meeting US-Soviet commercial and economic relations have on the whole shown an upward trend. This was expressed, in particular, in a substantial growth of the exchange of goods between the two countries which approximated $1.5 billion in 1973. It was noted that prospects were favorable for surpassing the goal announced in the joint US–USSR communique of June 24, 1973, of achieving a total bilateral trade turnover of $2-3 billion during the three-year period 1973-1975. The Joint US–USSR Commercial Commission continues to provide an effective mechanism to promote the broad-scale growth of economic relations.

The two Sides noted certain progress in the development of long-term cooperation between American firms and Soviet organizations in carrying out large-scale projects including those on a compensation basis. They are convinced that such cooperation is an important element in the development of commercial and economic ties between the two countries. The two Sides agreed to encourage the conclusion and implementation of appropriate agreements between American and Soviet organizations and firms. Taking into account the progress made in a number of specific projects, such as those concerning truck manufacture, the trade center, and chemical fertilizers, the Sides noted the possibility of concluding appropriate contracts in other areas of mutual interest, such as pulp and paper, timber, ferrous and nonferrous metallurgy, natural gas, the engineering industry, and the extraction and processing of high energy-consuming minerals.

Both Sides noted further development of productive contacts and ties between business circles of the two countries in which a positive role was played by the decisions taken during the previous summit meeting on the opening of a United States commercial office in Moscow and a USSR trade representation in Washington as well as the establishment of a US-Soviet Commercial and Economic Council. They expressed their desire to continue to bring about favorable conditions for the successful development of commercial and economic relations between the USA and the USSR.

Both Sides confirmed their interest in bringing into force at the earliest possible time the US-Soviet trade agreement of October 1972.

Desirous of promoting the further expansion of economic relations between the two countries, the two Sides signed a Long-Term Agreement to Facilitate Economic, Industrial and Technical Cooperation between the USA and the USSR. They believe that a consistent implementation of the cooperation embodied in the Agreement over the ten-year period will be an important factor in strengthening bilateral relations in general and will benefit the peoples of both countries.

Having reviewed the progress in carrying out the Agreement Regarding Certain Maritime Matters concluded in October 1972 for a period of three years, and based on the experience accumulated thus far, the two Sides expressed themselves in favor of concluding before its expiration a new agreement in this field. Negotiations concerning such an agreement will commence this year.

V. PROGRESS IN OTHER FIELDS OF BILATERAL RELATIONS

Having reviewed the progress in the implementation of the cooperative agreements concluded in 1972-1973, both Sides noted the useful work done by joint American-Soviet committees and working groups established under those agreements in developing regular contacts and cooperation between scientific and technical organizations, scientists, specialists and cultural personnel of both countries.

The two Sides note with satisfaction that joint efforts by the USA and the USSR in such fields of cooperation as medical science and public health, protection and improvement of man's environment, science and technology, exploration of outer space and the world ocean, peaceful uses of atomic energy, agriculture and transportation create conditions for an accelerated solution of some urgent and complicated problems facing mankind.

Such cooperation makes a substantial contribution to the development of the structure of American-Soviet relations, giving it a more concrete positive content.

Both Sides will strive to broaden and deepen their cooperation in science and technology as well as cultural exchanges on the basis of agreements concluded between them.

On the basis of positive experience accumulated in their scientific and technological cooperation and guided by the desire to ensure further progress in this important sphere of their mutual relations, the two Sides decided to extend such cooperation to the following new areas.

Energy

Taking into consideration the growing energy needs of industry, transportation and other branches of the economies of both countries and the consequent need to intensify scientific and technical cooperation in the development of optimal methods of utilizing traditional and new sources of energy, and to improve the understanding of the energy programs and problems of both countries, the two Sides concluded an agreement on cooperation in the field of energy. Responsibility for the implementation of the Agreement is entrusted to a US–USSR Joint Committee on Cooperation in Energy, which will be established for that purpose.

Housing and Other Construction

The two Sides signed an agreement on cooperation in the field of housing and other construction. The aim of this Agreement is to promote the solution by joint effort of problems related to modern techniques of housing and other construction along such lines as the improvement of the reliability and quality of buildings and building materials, the planning and construction of new towns, construction in seismic areas and areas of extreme climatic conditions. For the implementation of this Agreement there will be established a Joint US–USSR Committee on Cooperation in Housing and Other Construction which will determine specific working programs.

For the purpose of enhancing the safety of their peoples living in earthquake-prone areas, the two Sides agreed to undertake on a priority basis a joint research project to increase the safety of buildings and other structures in these areas and, in particular, to study the behavior of pre-fabricated residential structures during earthquakes.

Artificial Heart Research

In the course of the implementation of joint programs in the field of medical science and public health scientists and specialists of both countries concluded that there is a need to concentrate their efforts on the solution of one of the most important and humane problems of modern medical science, development of an artificial heart. In view of the great theoretical and technical complexity of the work involved, the two Sides concluded a special agreement on the subject. The US–USSR Joint Committee for Health Cooperation will assume responsibility for this project.

Cooperation in Space

The two Sides expressed their satisfaction with the successful preparations for the first joint manned flight of the American and Soviet spacecraft, Apollo and Soyuz, which is scheduled for 1975 and envisages their docking and mutual visits of the astronauts in each other's spacecraft. In accordance with existing agreements fruitful cooperation is being carried out in a number of other fields related to the exploration of outer space.

Attaching great importance to further American-Soviet cooperation in the exploration and use of outer space for peaceful purposes, including the development of safety systems for manned flights in space, and considering the desirability of consoli-

dating experience in this field, the two Sides agreed to continue to explore possibilities for further joint space projects following the US–USSR space flight now scheduled for July 1975.

Transport of the Future

Aware of the importance of developing advanced modes of transportation, both Sides agreed that high-speed ground systems of the future, including a magnetically levitated train, which can provide economical, efficient, and reliable forms of transportation, would be a desirable and innovative area for joint activity. A working group to develop a joint research cooperation program in this area under the 1973 Agreement on Cooperation in the Field of Transportation will be established at the Fall meeting of the Joint US–USSR Transportation Committee.

Environmental Protection

Desiring to expand cooperation in the field of environmental protection, which is being successfully carried out under the US–USSR Agreement signed on May 23, 1972, and to contribute to the implementation of the "Man and the Biosphere" international program conducted on the initiative of the United Nations Educational, Scientific and Cultural Organization (UNESCO), both Sides agreed to designate in the territories of their respective countries certain natural areas as biosphere reserves for protecting valuable plant and animal genetic strains and ecosystems, and for conducting scientific research needed for more effective actions concerned with global environmental protection. Appropriate work for the implementation of this undertaking will be conducted in conformity with the goals of the UNESCO program and under the auspices of the previously established US–USSR Joint Committee on Cooperation in the Field of Environmental Protection.

Cultural Exchanges

The two Parties, aware of the importance of cultural exchanges as a means of promoting mutual understanding, express satisfaction with the agreement between the Metropolitan Museum of Art of New York City and the Ministry of Culture of the USSR leading to a major exchange of works of art. Such an exchange would be in accordance with the General Agreement on Contacts, Exchanges and Cooperation signed June 19, 1973, under which the parties agree to render assistance for the exchange of exhibitions between the museums of the two countries.

Establishment of New Consulates

Taking into consideration the intensive development of ties between the US and the USSR and the importance of further expanding consular relations on the basis of the US–USSR Consular Convention, and desiring to promote trade, tourism and cooperation between them in various areas, both Sides agreed to open additional Consulates General in two or three cities of each country.

As a first step they agreed in principle to the simultaneous establishment of a United States Consulate General in Kiev and a USSR Consulate General in New York. Negotiations for implementation of this agreement will take place at an early date.

* * * * * * * *

Both Sides highly appreciate the frank and constructive atmosphere and fruitful results of the talks held between them in the course of the present meeting. They are convinced that the results represent a new and important milestone along the road of improving relations between the USA and the USSR to the benefit of the peoples of both countries, and a significant contribution to their efforts aimed at strengthening world peace and security.

Having again noted in this connection the exceptional importance and great practical usefulness of US-Soviet summit meetings, both Sides reaffirmed their agreement to hold such meetings regularly and when considered necessary for the discussion and solution of urgent questions. Both Sides also expressed their readiness to continue their active and close contacts and consultations.

The President extended an invitation to General Secretary of the Central Committee of the CPSU, L. I. Brezhnev, to pay an official visit to the United States in 1975. This invitation was accepted with pleasure.

July 3, 1974

For the United States of America:

For the Union of Soviet Socialist Republics:

RICHARD NIXON

L. BREZHNEV

President of the United States of America

General Secretary of the Central Committee of the CPSU

VI:

FROM THE SECOND MOSCOW SUMMIT MEETING TO THE VLADIVOSTOK AGREEMENT: JULY TO NOVEMBER 1974

INTRODUCTION

Within five weeks after the second Moscow summit meeting, Richard Nixon resigned the presidency at noon on August 9, 1974, and Gerald Ford succeeded him in that office. Ford emphasized repeatedly his intentions to continue Nixon's policy of detente, and Henry Kissinger remained as Secretary of State.

On September 6, 1974, Ford announced that SALT would reconvene on September 18 of that year in Geneva, with Alexis Johnson continuing as chief of the U.S. delegation.[1] On September 19, Ford submitted the protocol to the U.S.-Soviet ABM treaty, which Nixon had signed at Moscow, to the Senate for consent.[2]

October produced a series of agreements and announcements related to the progress of SALT at Geneva. The United States extended the life of the Temporary Purchasing Commission once again and increased its size (see Appendix, 27A); the Soviets agreed to reduce the amount of grain they would purchase in 1974 to help slow the pace of inflation in the United States (Document 51); and Kissinger visited Moscow at the end of October (see Appendix, 28A) to prepare for a meeting between Ford and Brezhnev in November.

Documents 52 and 53 are the product of the Vladivostok meeting. These documents do not reveal all the understandings that were reached at Vladivostok, however. Both sides discussed specific numbers of weapons as "ceilings" and repeated those numbers in public conversations upon return to the United States.* The details that each side thought it understood at the time still have

---

*Ford told congressional leaders upon his return that he and Brezhnev agreed to restrict each side to "a rigid ceiling" of less than 2,500 strategic missiles and bombers during

not been published, however. It seems clear that some confusion existed between the two sides at the meeting in Vladivostok.

NOTES

1. DSB 9-30-1974, 461.
2. DSB 10-14-1974, 523.

---

the 10-year period for which a new agreement would be in force. See Columbia (Mo.) *Missourian*, November 27, 1974, p. 16 (UPI story from Washington). In an interview January 29, 1975, Alexis Johnson stated that "the 2,400 [sic] figure is a figure somewhat in between what we have and what the Russians have." DSB 2-17-1975, 225.

50 (October 15, 1974)
U.S.-U.S.S.R. Trade and Economic Council Meets at Moscow

Following is a statement made by Secretary of the Treasury William E. Simon before the second board meeting of the U.S.-U.S.S.R. Trade and Economic Council at Moscow on October 15.

Department of the Treasury press release dated October 15

Much has happened since the first meeting of the joint board last February in Washington. There have been unprecedented events in the political life of my country.

Many things have not changed however; high among these is the desire of the United States to further the development of peaceful, fruitful relations with the Soviet Union. As President Ford told the Congress shortly after taking office:

To the Soviet Union, I pledge continuity in our commitment to the course of the past three years. . . . there can be no alternative to a positive and peaceful relationship between our nations.

We are here today to discuss economic and trade relations between our countries. Nowhere is there more concrete evidence of the progress we are making than in this field.

Our bilateral trade is rapidly approaching the three-year goal of $2–$3 billion trade turnover which was set at the 1973 summit. In 1973 alone, U.S.-U.S.S.R. trade turnover was $1.4 billion. Although total trade is down somewhat this year after the exceptionally large agricultural shipments of 1973, U.S. sales of machinery and equipment products have risen sharply, and U.S.S.R. exports to the United States have shown a very substantial increase.

Seventeen American firms now have received permission to open accredited offices in Moscow. Export-Import Bank loans for the Soviet Union have increased to $470 million. Impressive contracts have been signed in the last nine months for the Kama River truck plant, the Moscow Trade Center, the fertilizer project, and equipment for gas pipeline development.

The U.S. commercial office opened for business in Moscow last spring. In addition to smaller exhibits staged in its display area, my government recently sponsored U.S. firms' participation in two major Soviet trade shows (health and plastics manufacturing equipment) and organized a successful solo exhibition of American machine tools in Sokolniki Park.

Our two governments are pledged to continue this momentum. In the long-term agreement signed in June, both formally agreed to facilitate economic, industrial, and technical cooperation and exchange information on economic trends.

Progress has also been made in resolving the policy problems which could inhibit further growth. Soon after entering the White House, President Ford emphasized to Congress the importance he attached to granting most-favored-nation status to the Soviet Union. I look forward to early resolution of the trade reform bill which I believe will bring about satisfactory export-import legislation. This will clear the impediments on the path of an expanding trade relationship.

The U.S. Government will continue to help clear away obstacles to improvement in our economic and commercial relations. In the final analysis, however, the action responsibility for each U.S.-Soviet commercial transaction rests with the private sector of our economy. It is for this reason that we encouraged the formation of the Trade and Economic Council, which brings together officials from your ministries and trading organizations and top management representatives from our firms—it is these people who are doing the actual work of expanding trade.

As we all know, the Council was formed as the result of a protocol entered into in June of 1973 by Minister [of Foreign Trade N.S.] Patolichev and my predecessor, Secretary [George P.] Shultz. It's important, however, to remember that while the Council is the creation of the two governments, on the U.S. side it has been adopted by the private sector—our business community. As an honorary director of the Council, I am pleased to note that the child of these two governments is healthy and growing at a rapid pace, and I am pleased with the care and upbringing it is being given by the U.S. Government. I voice our appreciation for the support and help given the Council since its inception by the Soviet Government.

While the role of the Council is to foster and promote the growth of the U.S.-Soviet trade and economic relationship, and while I am confident that the U.S. Congress will approve legislation so necessary to the normalization of this relationship, I also envisage that out of this improved relationship will emerge a larger joint economic role for our two countries.

Given the extraordinary global economic interrelationship of all countries, there is a greater-than-ever need for responsibility and cooperation between nations. It is hard to conceive of a solution fair to all countries, large and small, in any area of major interest without the full and close cooperation of the United States and the U.S.S.R.

Since February, the Council has developed into a fully functioning organization. Binational staffs are now at work on some 60 major projects in New York and Moscow. The Council has found excellent office space in Manhattan, and yesterday we dedicated the attractive offices on the Shevchenko Embankment. The Subcommittee on Science and Technology concluded a productive first meeting a few days ago in New York.

This is an excellent beginning, but is only a beginning, and I am confident that it foreshadows even greater accomplishments in the future as the Council realizes its full potential in the development of fruitful economic relations between our countries.

As an honorary director of the U.S.-U.S.S.R. Trade and Economic Council, I commend my fellow directors and the Council staff for the progress you have made so far. I wish you well in your deliberations at this meeting, and I urge you to work diligently to create an economic fabric between our two countries of so many strands so closely interwoven that not only is there no visible seam, but also that it is so strong as to be virtually unbreakable.

So while we work to intermesh and synchronize our different economic systems, we also work to prepare and strengthen ourselves for jointly addressing in harmony the problems of creating a better world for all countries and all people.

51 (October 19, 1974)

U.S.S.R. Agrees To Limit Purchases of U.S. Grain in Current Crop Year

Department of the Treasury Announcement

Department of the Treasury press release dated October 19

Secretary of the Treasury William E. Simon announced on October 19 conclusion of an agreement with the Soviet Union on purchases of U.S. grains during the current crop year.

The Soviet Union agreed to limit its total grain purchases from the United States this crop year to 2.2 million tons, including 1 million tons of corn and 1.2 million tons of wheat.

An additional 1 million tons of grain contracted for earlier in October can be delivered from other exporting countries. The Soviet purchasing agency for grains will make the necessary purchase arrangements with U.S. export firms.

The Soviet Union also agreed to make no further purchases in the U.S. market this crop year, which ends next summer. Further, the Soviet Union agreed to work with the United States toward development of a supply/demand data system for grains.

The agreement followed talks in Moscow by Secretary Simon with Minister of Foreign Trade N. S. Patolichev. Secretary Simon was in the Soviet Union October 12–15 for the opening of the Moscow office of the U.S.-U.S.S.R. Trade and Economic Council.

The grain talks were scheduled following the Soviets' buying activity in the United States earlier in October. At that time, the Soviet Union placed orders with two U.S. export firms for the purchase of 3.2 million tons of U.S. grain, including 2.3 million tons of corn and 900,000 tons of wheat for delivery during the 1974/75 crop year, which ends next summer. Following talks with President Ford on October 5, the presidents of the two export firms agreed to hold these sales in abeyance until after Secretary Simon's visit to Moscow.

This year's Soviet purchases of U.S. grain will be small compared with purchases during the past two years. The Soviet Union bought 17 million tons of U.S. grain during 1972 and 7 million tons in 1973. The smaller purchases in 1974 are in line with smaller export availabilities of U.S. grain as a result of the disappointing corn harvest this year. The United States has harvested a record wheat crop, but the corn crop is expected to be down 16 percent from last year's record harvest. Total U.S. feed grain production is expected to be down 18 percent.

In his talks with Soviet officials, Secretary Simon emphasized that the United States wants to continue developing its agricultural trade with the Soviet Union. The Soviets advised Secretary Simon that the Soviet Union will have an adequate harvest this year but that imports are needed for specialized livestock production units.

Secretary Simon reviewed with Soviet officials the type of grain data that the United States receives from other countries that purchase U.S. grain. The Soviets agreed to work toward the development of a data exchange system on grain between the two governments.

vant provisions of the Interim Agreement of May 26, 1972, which will remain in force until October 1977.

2. The new agreement will cover the period from October 1977 through December 31, 1985.

3. Based on the principle of equality and equal security, the new agreement will include the following limitations:

a. Both sides will be entitled to have a certain agreed aggregate number of strategic delivery vehicles;

b. Both sides will be entitled to have a certain agreed aggregate number of ICBMs and SLBMs [intercontinental ballistic missiles; submarine-launched ballistic missiles] equipped with multiple independently targetable warheads (MIRVs).

4. The new agreement will include a provision for further negotiations beginning no later than 1980-1981 on the question of further limitations and possible reductions of strategic arms in the period after 1985.

5. Negotiations between the delegations of the U.S. and USSR to work out the new agreement incorporating the foregoing points will resume in Geneva in January 1975.

November 24, 1974.

53 (November 24, 1974)
Joint Communique Signed at Vladisvostok November 24

JOINT US–SOVIET COMMUNIQUE

In accordance with the previously announced agreement, a working meeting between the President of the United States of America Gerald R. Ford and the General Secretary of the Central Committee of the Communist Party of the Soviet Union L. I. Brezhnev took place in the area of Vladivostok on November 23 and 24, 1974. Taking part in the talks were the Secretary of State of the United States of America and Assistant to the President for National Security Affairs, Henry A. Kissinger and Member of the Politburo of the Central Committee of the CPSU, Minister of Foreign Affairs of the USSR, A. A. Gromyko.

They discussed a broad range of questions dealing with American-Soviet relations and the current international situation.

Also taking part in the talks were:

On the American side Walter J. Stoessel, Jr., Ambassador of the USA to the USSR; Helmut Sonnenfeldt, Counselor of the Department of State; Arthur A. Hartman, Assistant Secretary of State for European Affairs; Lieutenant General Brent Scowcroft, Deputy Assistant to the President for National Security Affairs; and William Hyland, official of the Department of State.

On the Soviet side A. F. Dobrynin, Ambassador

52 (November 24, 1974)
Joint Statement on Strategic Offensive Arms Issued at Vladivostok November 24

JOINT U.S.-SOVIET STATEMENT

During their working meeting in the area of Vladivostok on November 23–24, 1974, the President of the USA Gerald R. Ford and General Secretary of the Central Committee of the CPSU L. I. Brezhnev discussed in detail the question of further limitations of strategic offensive arms.

They reaffirmed the great significance that both the United States and the USSR attach to the limitation of strategic offensive arms. They are convinced that a long-term agreement on this question would be a significant contribution to improving relations between the US and the USSR, to reducing the danger of war and to enhancing world peace. Having noted the value of previous agreements on this question, including the Interim Agreement of May 26, 1972, they reaffirm the intention to conclude a new agreement on the limitation of strategic offensive arms, to last through 1985.

As a result of the exchange of views on the substance of such a new agreement, the President of the United States of America and the General Secretary of the Central Committee of the CPSU concluded that favorable prospects exist for completing the work on this agreement in 1975.

Agreement was reached that further negotiations will be based on the following provisions.

1. The new agreement will incorporate the rele-

140

of the USSR to the USA; A. M. Aleksandrov, Assistant to the General Secretary of the Central Committee of the CPSU; and G. M. Korniyenko, Member of the Collegium of the Ministry of Foreign Affairs of the USSR.

I

The United States of America and ·the Soviet Union reaffirmed their determination to develop further their relations in the direction defined by the fundamental joint decisions and basic treaties and agreements concluded between the two States in recent years.

They are convinced that the course of American-Soviet relations, directed towards strengthening world peace, deepening the relaxation of international tensions and expanding mutually beneficial cooperation of states with different social systems meets the vital interests of the peoples of both States and other peoples.

Both Sides consider that based on the agreements reached between them important results have been achieved in fundamentally reshaping American-Soviet relations on the basis of peaceful coexistence and equal security. These results are a solid foundation for progress in reshaping Soviet-American relations.

Accordingly, they intend to continue, without a loss in momentum, to expand the scale and intensity of their cooperative efforts in all spheres as set forth in the agreements they have signed so that the process of improving relations between the US and the USSR will continue without interruption and will become irreversible.

Mutual determination was expressed to carry out strictly and fully the mutual obligations undertaken by the US and the USSR in accordance with the treaties and agreements concluded between them.

II

Special consideration was given in the course of the talks to a pivotal aspect of Soviet-American relations: measures to eliminate the threat of war and to halt the arms race.

Both sides reaffirm that the Agreements reached between the US and the USSR on the prevention of nuclear war and the limitation of strategic arms are a good beginning in the process of creating guarantees against the outbreak of nuclear conflict and war in general. They expressed their deep belief in the necessity of promoting this process and expressed their hope that other states would contribute to it as well. For their part the US and the USSR will continue to exert vigorous efforts to achieve this historic task.

A joint statement on the question of limiting strategic offensive arms is being released separately.

Both sides stressed once again the importance and necessity of a serious effort aimed at preventing the dangers connected with the spread of nuclear weapons in the world. In this connection they stressed the importance of increasing the effectiveness of the Treaty on the Non-Proliferation of Nuclear Weapons.

It was noted that, in accordance with previous agreements, initial contacts were established between representatives of the US and of the USSR on questions related to underground nuclear explosions for peaceful purposes, to measures to overcome the dangers of the use of environmental modification techniques for military purposes, as well as measures dealing with the most dangerous lethal means of chemical warfare. It was agreed to continue an active search for mutually acceptable solutions of these questions.

III

In the course of the meeting an exchange of views was held on a number of international issues: special attention was given to negotiations already in progress in which the two Sides are participants and which are designed to remove existing sources of tension and to bring about the strengthening of international security and world peace.

Having reviewed the situation at the Conference on Security and Cooperation in Europe, both Sides concluded that there is a possibility for its early successful conclusion. They proceed from the assumption that the results achieved in the course of the Conference will permit its conclusion at the highest level and thus be commensurate with its importance in ensuring the peaceful future of Europe.

The USA and the USSR also attach high importance to the negotiations on mutual reduction of forces and armaments and associated measures in Central Europe. They agree to contribute actively to the search for mutually acceptable solutions on the basis of principle of undiminished security for any of the parties and the prevention of unilateral military advantages.

Having discussed the situation existing in the Eastern Mediterranean, both Sides state their firm support for the independence, sovereignty and territorial integrity of Cyprus and will make every effort in this direction. They consider that a just settlement of the Cyprus question must be based on the strict implementation of the resolutions adopted by the Security Council and the General Assembly of the United Nations regarding Cyprus.

In the course of the exchange of views on the Middle East both Sides expressed their concern with regard to the dangerous situation in that region. They reaffirmed their intention to make every effort to promote a solution of the key issues of a just and lasting peace in that area on the basis of the United Nations resolution 338, taking into account the legitimate interests of all the peoples of the area, including the Palestinian people, and respect for the right to independent existence of all States in the area.

The Sides believe that the Geneva Conference should play an important part in the establishment of a just and lasting peace in the Middle East, and should resume its work as soon as possible.

IV

The state of relations was reviewed in the field of commercial, economic, scientific and technical ties between the USA and the USSR. Both Sides confirmed the great importance which further progress in these fields would have for Soviet-American relations, and expressed their firm intention to continue the broadening and deepening of mutually advantageous cooperation.

The two Sides emphasized the special importance accorded by them to the development on a long term basis of commercial and economic cooperation, including mutually beneficial large-scale projects. They believe that such commercial and economic cooperation will serve the cause of increasing the stability of Soviet-American relations.

Both Sides noted with satisfaction the progress in the implementation of agreements and in the development of ties and cooperation between the US and the USSR in the fields of science, technology and culture. They are convinced that the continued expansion of such cooperation will benefit the peoples of both countries and will be an important contribution to the solution of world-wide scientific and technical problems.

The talks were held in an atmosphere of frankness and mutual understanding, reflecting the constructive desire of both Sides to strengthen and develop further the peaceful cooperative relationship between the USA and the USSR, and to ensure progress in the solution of outstanding international problems in the interests of preserving and strengthening peace.

The results of the talks provided a convincing demonstration of the practical value of Soviet-American summit meetings and their exceptional importance in the shaping of a new relationship between the United . States of America and the Soviet Union.

President Ford reaffirmed the invitation to L. I. Brezhnev to pay an official visit to the United States in 1975. The exact date of the visit will be agreed upon later.

For the United States of America:	For the Union of Soviet Socialist Republics:
GERALD R. FORD	L. I. BREZHNEV
President of the United States of America	*General Secretary of the Central Committee of the CPSU*

November 24, 1974

VII:

FROM VLADIVOSTOK TO
THE END OF THE KISSENGER ERA:
1975 AND 1976

INTRODUCTION

Just after Vladivostok had shown some success toward accomplishing a permanent agreement limiting strategic offensive weapons, U.S.-Soviet relations suffered a reversal in the area of trade. After nearly two years of deliberation, Congress passed the Trade Reform Act of 1974 (originally submitted in April 1973). President Ford signed the act into law on January 3, 1975, although he disapproved of the Jackson-Vanik Amendment, on emigration (Document 54, Title IV) and the Stevenson Amendment, imposing a credit ceiling for the USSR (Document 54, Title VI). On January 14, the Soviets informed U.S. government officials that the USSR could not accept trade relations under the conditions established in the new law. Four days later, the Soviets announced that they no longer felt themselves obligated to repay the remaining $722 million of their lend-lease debt. Interpreting the new law as denying them MFN status, the Soviets asserted that the law canceled the lend-lease agreement of October 18, 1972, which conditioned repayment of the debt on the USSR's receiving MFN status.[1]

Kissinger lamented the collapse of trade negotiations at the time and ever afterward. "In 1969 we developed the theory of linkage," he said later. "The theory of linkage was that the Soviet Union would get economic concessions in return for political stabilization."[2] It was that theory he had in mind when he stated in June 1975: "The Trade Act was one of the elements we had hoped to have available . . . as an incentive for moderation" on the part of the Soviets in their relations with the United States.[3]

Very little activity occurred to expand trade relations between the United States and USSR in 1975 until September and October, when negotiations began for another grains agreement to replace the grains agreement of July 1972, which would expire in 1975.

Despite this reversal in trade relations, negotiations continued on the details left from the Vladivostok meeting. On February 4, President Ford stated that he could "see no reason why we cannot reconcile any of the relatively minor differences. The basic agreement is still in effect. . . ." He assumed that the final agreement could be concluded in time for Brezhnev to visit Washington at the traditional time established for the annual summit meetings and to sign the document on that occasion. "I am confident," he said, "that we can welcome the General Secretary to the United States in the summer of 1975, and I look forward to it."[4]

Little progress occurred in the SALT meetings during the summer, however, and Ford was hoping in June that Brezhnev's visit could occur during "the fall."[5] On July 30 and August 2, Ford met with Brezhnev in Helsinki while both attended the Conference on Security and Cooperation in Europe to participate in signing the Final Act of the Conference. There, several of the issues still dividing the two sides were discussed and some "progress" was made. On the plane homeward, Ford answered the question of whether Brezhnev could come to the United States before the end of 1975 with the word "hopefully."[6] That visit did not occur in 1975, however, nor in 1976, nor in 1977, and not as of the date of this writing in 1978.

In September and October 1975 the two sides successfully negotiated a new three-year arrangement for Soviet purchase of grain, signed October 20, 1975 (Document 62), and on December 29, a new maritime agreement (Document 63) establishing shipping rates and other terms of transfer of the grain. The previous maritime agreement, signed October 14, 1972, to govern the transfer of grain in 1972–75, was in force only until December 31, 1975. The new grains agreement had a companion document, a "letter of intent" from the Soviets, to sell to the United States Soviet oil, equal to the value of Soviet purchases of American grain in any one year (Document 62).

Of the three areas of activity—bilateral cooperative ventures, trade matters, and control of nuclear armaments—only the area of nuclear armaments had a significant agreement added in 1976. As noted in the introduction to Chapter V, on the second Moscow summit meeting, Article III of the TTBT, signed July 3, 1974, committed each side to arriving at an agreement governing underground nuclear tests for peaceful purposes (PNE). The Americans decided to withhold submitting the TTBT to the Senate for ratification until a PNE agreement had been negotiated and to submit the two treaties to the Senate as a unit.[7] By March 31, 1976, when the TTBT was to enter into force, the PNE agreement had still not been negotiated. But, on May 28, 1976, the two sides signed the Treaty and Protocol on Underground Nuclear Explosions for Peaceful Purposes (Document 65), which adopted the same limit, of 150 kiloton yield, that the TTBT had established for underground explosions for military tests. On July 29 the president submitted the two treaties to the Senate.[8]

During the latter part of 1975 the term "detente" acquired an increasingly negative connotation as U.S. policy toward the USSR underwent extensive criticism in the campaigns for the presidential elections of 1976. In response to that criticism, Ford and Kissinger found themselves constantly defining the term and explaining the U.S.-Soviet relationship for which it was a label. On June 23, 1975, Kissinger was asked to defend "detente" against the criticism that it was "a one-way street that benefits only Russia."[9] Ford even felt compelled to explain the term in his address on August 1 to the representatives of the 34 countries that, in addition to the United States, assembled at Helsinki to sign the Final Act of the Conference on Security and Cooperation in Europe.[10]

The most extensive definition Ford provided of the term was approximately two weeks later, on August 19, in an address to the fifty-seventh National Convention of the American Legion in Minneapolis. Because a "great deal" had been said about "detente" recently, Ford offered the following:

> Today, let me tell you what I personally think about detente. First of all, the word itself is confusing. Its meaning is not clear to everybody. French is a beautiful language, the classic language of diplomacy, but I wish there were one simple English word to substitute for "detente." Unfortunately, there isn't.

> Relations between the world's two strongest nuclear powers can't be summed up in a catch phrase. Detente literally means "easing" or "relaxing," but definitely not—and I emphasize not—the relaxing of diligence or easing of effort. Rather, it means movement away from the constant crisis and dangerous confrontations that have characterized relations with the Soviet Union.

> The process of detente—and it is a process—looks toward a saner and safer relationship between us and the Soviet Union. It represents our best efforts to cool the cold war, which on occasion became much too hot for comfort.[11]

Finally, during the summer of 1976, Ford forbade members of his administration to use the term to describe current United States policy toward the Soviets. As a result, on July 6, 1976, in response to a question about "detente," Kissinger jokingly stated: "Since there is press here, I want to make it clear that the word 'detente' was used by the questioner."[12]

After the election of November 1976, the United States and Soviets recessed the talks on arms limitation to await a statement from the incoming Carter administration about its desires on SALT.

NOTES

1. *Izvestiia*, January 18, 1975.
2. New York *Times*, interview of January 20, 1977, in DSB 2-7-1977, 106.
3. Interview of June 23, 1975 with *U.S. News and World Report* in DSB 7-7-1975, 253.
4. DSB 2-24-1975, 253.
5. DSB 7-7-1975, 24.
6. DSB 9-1-1975, 308.
7. DSB 4-19-1976, 507.
8. DSB 8-23-1976, 269–70.
9. DSB 7-7-1975, 17.
10. DSB 9-1-1975, 305.
11. DSB 9-15-1975, 412.
12. DSB 8-2-1976, 158.

54 (January 3, 1975)

TITLE IV—TRADE RELATIONS WITH COUNTRIES NOT CURRENTLY RECEIVING NONDISCRIMINATORY TREATMENT

SEC. 401. EXCEPTION OF THE PRODUCTS OF CERTAIN COUNTRIES OR AREAS.

Except as otherwise provided in this title, the President shall continue to deny nondiscriminatory treatment to the products of any country, the products of which were not eligible for the rates set forth in rate column numbered 1 of the Tariff Schedules of the United States on the date of the enactment of this Act.

SEC. 402. FREEDOM OF EMIGRATION IN EAST-WEST TRADE.

(a) To assure the continued dedication of the United States to fundamental human rights, and notwithstanding any other provision of law, on or after the date of the enactment of this Act products from any nonmarket economy country shall not be eligible to receive nondiscriminatory treatment (most-favored-nation treatment), such country shall not participate in any program of the Government of the United States which extends credits or credit guarantees or investment guarantees, directly or indirectly, and the President of the United States shall not conclude any commercial agreement with any such country, during the period beginning with the date on which the President determines that such country—

(1) denies its citizens the right or opportunity to emigrate;

(2) imposes more than a nominal tax on emigration or on the visas or other documents required for emigration, for any purpose or cause whatsoever; or

(3) imposes more than a nominal tax, levy, fine, fee, or other charge on any citizen as a consequence of the desire of such citizen to emigrate to the country of his choice,

and ending on the date on which the President determines that such country is no longer in violation of paragraph (1), (2), or (3).

(b) After the date of the enactment of this Act, (A) products of a nonmarket economy country may be eligible to receive nondiscriminatory treatment (most-favored-nation treatment), (B) such country may participate in any program of the Government of the United States which extends credits or credit guarantees or investment guarantees, and (C) the President may conclude a commercial agreement with such country, only after the President has submitted to the Congress a report indicating that such country is not in violation of paragraph (1), (2), or (3) of subsection (a). Such report with respect to such country shall include information as to the nature and implementation of emigration laws and policies and restrictions or discrimination applied to or against persons wishing to emigrate. The report required by this subsection shall be submitted initially as provided herein and, with current information, on or before each June 30 and December 31 thereafter so long as such treatment is received, such credits or guarantees are extended, or such agreement is in effect.

SEC. 409. FREEDOM TO EMIGRATE TO JOIN A VERY CLOSE RELATIVE IN THE UNITED STATES.

(a) To assure the continued dedication of the United States to the fundamental human rights and welfare of its own citizens, and notwithstanding any other provision of law, on or after the date of. the enactment of this Act, no nonmarket economy country shall participate in any program of the Government of the United States which extends credits or credit guarantees or investment guarantees, directly or indirectly, and the President of the United States shall not conclude any commercial agreement with any such country, during the period beginning with the date on which the President determines that such country—

(1) denies its citizens the right or opportunity to join permanently through emigration, a very close relative in the United State, such as a spouse, parent, child, brother, or sister;

(2) imposes more than a nominal tax on the visas or other documents required for emigration described in paragraph (1); or

(3) imposes more than a nominal tax, levy, fine, fee, or other charge on any citizen as a consequence of the desire of such citizen to emigrate as described in paragraph (1),

and ending on the date on which the President determines that such country is no longer in violation of paragraph (1), (2), or (3).

(b) After the date of the enactment of this Act, (A) a nonmarket economy country may participate in any program of the Government of the United States which extends credits or credit guarantees or investment guarantees, and (B) the President may conclude a commercial agreement with such country, only after the President has submitted to the Congress a report indicating that such country is not in violation of paragraph (1), (2), or (3) of subsection (a). Such report with respect to such country shall include information as to the nature and implementation of its laws and policies and restrictions or discrimination applied to or against persons wishing to emigrate to the United States to join close relatives. The report required by this subsection shall be submitted initially as provided herein and, with current information, on or before each June 30 and December 31 thereafter, so long as such credits or guarantees are extended or such agreement is in effect.

(c) This section shall not apply to any country the products of which are eligible for the rates set forth in rate column numbered 1 of the Tariff Schedules of the United States on the date of enactment of this Act.

(d) During any period that a waiver is in effect with respect to any nonmarket economy country under section 402(c), the provisions of subsections (a) and (b) shall not apply with respect to such country.

SEC. 410. EAST-WEST TRADE STATISTICS MONITORING SYSTEM.

The International Trade Commission shall establish and maintain a program to monitor imports of articles into the United States from nonmarket economy countries and exports of articles from the United States to nonmarket economy countries. To the extent feasible, the Commission shall coordinate such program with any relevant data gathering programs presently conducted by the Secretary of Commerce. The Secretary of Commerce shall provide the Commission with any information which, in the determination of the Commission, is necessary to carry out this section. The Commission shall publish a detailed summary of the data collected under the East-West Trade Statistics Monitoring System not less frequently than once each calendar quarter and shall transmit such publication to the East-West Foreign Trade Board and to Congress. Such publication shall include data on the effect of such imports, if any, on the production of like, or directly competitive, articles in the United States and on employment within the industry which produces like, or directly competitive, articles in the United States.

SEC. 411. EAST-WEST FOREIGN TRADE BOARD.

(a) The President shall establish an East-West Foreign Trade Board (hereinafter referred to as the "Board") to monitor trade between persons and agencies of the United States Government and nonmarket economy countries or instrumentalities of such countries to insure that such trade will be in the national interest of the United States.

(b)(1) Any person who exports technology vital to the national interest of the United States to a nonmarket economy country or an instrumentality of such country, and any agency of the United States which provides credits, guarantees or insurance to such country or such instrumentality in an amount in excess of $5,000,000 during any calendar year, shall file a report with the Board in such form and manner as the Board requires which describes the nature and terms of such export or such provision.

(2) For purposes of paragraph (1), if the total amount of credits, guarantees and insurance which an agency of the United States provides to all nonmarket economy countries and the instrumentalities of such countries exceeds $5,000,000 during a calendar year, then all subsequent provisions of credits, guarantees or insurance in any amount, during such year shall be reported to the Board under the provisions of paragraph (1).

(c) The Board shall submit to Congress a quarterly report on trade between the United States and nonmarket economy countries and instrumentalities of such countries. Such report shall include a review of the status of negotiations of bilateral trade agreements between the United States and such countries under this title, the activities of joint trade commissions created pursuant to such agreements, the resolution of commercial disputes between the United States and such countries, any exports from such countries which have caused disruption of United States markets, and recommendations for the promotion of east-west trade in the national interest of the United States.

TITLE VI—GENERAL PROVISIONS

SEC. 613. LIMITATION ON CREDIT TO RUSSIA.

After the date of enactment of the Trade Act of 1974, no agency of the Government of the United States, other than the Commodity Credit Corporation, shall approve any loans, guarantees, insurance, or any combination thereof, in connection with exports to the Union of Soviet Socialist Republics in an aggregate amount in excess of $300,000,000 without prior congressional approval as provided by law.

Approved January 3, 1975.

55 (January 14, 1975)

Statement by Secretary of State Henry Kissinger of Soviet Rejection of the Conditions of the Trade Act of 1974. Read at the News Conference of January 14, 1975.

Since the President signed the Trade Act on January 3, we have been in touch with the Soviet Government concerning the steps necessary to bring the 1972 U.S.-Soviet Trade Agreement into force.

Article 9 of that agreement provides for an exchange of written notices of acceptance, following which the agreement, including reciprocal extension of nondiscriminatory tariff treatment (MFN) [most-favored-nation] would enter into force. In accordance with the recently enacted Trade Act, prior to this exchange of written notices, the President would transmit to the Congress a number of documents, including the 1972 agreement, the proposed written notices, a formal proclamation extending MFN to the U.S.S.R., and a statement of reasons for the 1972 agreement. Either House of Congress would then have had 90 legislative days to veto the agreement.

In addition to these procedures, the President would also take certain steps, pursuant to the Trade Act, to waive the applicability of the Jackson-Vanik amendment. These steps would include a report to the Congress stating that the waiver will substantially promote the objectives of the amendment and that the President has received assurances that the emigration practices of the U.S.S.R. will henceforth lead substantially to the achievement of the objectives of the amendment.

It was our intention to include in the required exchange of written notices with the Soviet Government language, required by the provisions of the Trade Act, that would have made clear that the duration of three years referred to in the 1972 Trade Agreement with the U.S.S.R. was subject to continued legal authority to carry out our obligations. This caveat was necessitated by the fact that the waiver of the Jackson-Vanik amendment would be applicable only for an initial period of 18 months, with provision for renewal thereafter.

The Soviet Government has now informed us that it cannot accept a trading relationship based on the legislation recently enacted in this country. It considers this legislation as contravening both the 1972 Trade Agreement, which had called for an unconditional elimination of discriminatory trade restrictions, and the principle of noninterference in domestic affairs. The Soviet Government states that it does not intend to accept a trade status that is discriminatory and subject to political conditions and, accordingly, that it will not put into force the 1972 Trade Agreement. Finally, the Soviet Government informed us that if statements were made by the United States, in the terms required by the Trade Act, concerning assurances by the Soviet Government regarding matters it considers within its domestic jurisdiction, such statements would be repudiated by the Soviet Government.

In view of these developments, we have concluded that the 1972 Trade Agreement cannot be brought into force at this time and that the President will therefore not take the steps required for this purpose by the Trade Act. The President does not plan at this time to exercise the waiver authority.

The administration regrets this turn of events. It has regarded and continues to regard an orderly and mutually beneficial trade relationship with the Soviet Union as an important element in the overall improvement of relations. It will, of course, continue to pursue all available avenues for such an improvement, including efforts to obtain legislation that will permit normal trading relationships.

ing to improve Soviet-American relations in accordance with existing understandings and agreements of principle, which they firmly believe are in the interest of the peoples of the United States of America and the USSR and of international peace.

Both sides stressed the great significance of the agreement regarding the further limitation of strategic offensive arms reached in the course of the meeting between the President of the United States of America Gerald R. Ford and the General Secretary of the Central Committee of the Communist Party of the Soviet Union, L. I. Brezhnev in November, 1974, in Vladivostok. On the basis of this agreement, both sides intend to continue energetic efforts to work out an appropriate long-term agreement this year.

It was noted that a great deal of progress has been achieved at the Conference on Security and Cooperation in Europe. The two sides stated that they will continue to make active efforts jointly with the other participants to have the Conference successfully concluded at an early date.

They assume that the results achieved permit its conclusion at the highest level.

They also agreed that active efforts should be made to achieve positive results in the mutual reduction of forces and armaments in Central Europe on the basis of the principles referred to in the American-Soviet communique of November 24, 1974.

In the course of the conversations, particular attention was given to the Middle East. The two sides remain concerned over the dangers persisting in the situation there. They reaffirmed their intention to make every effort to promote a solution of the key issues of a just and lasting peace in the area on the basis of UN Resolution 338, taking into account the legitimate interests of all the peoples of the area, including the Palestinian people, and respect for the right to independent existence of all states in the area.

The two sides believe that the Geneva Conference should play an important part in the establishment of a just and lasting peace in the Middle East, and should resume its work at an early date.

56 (February 17, 1975)

TEXT OF U.S.-U.S.S.R. JOINT STATEMENT ISSUED AT GENEVA FEBRUARY 17

Press release 80 dated February 18

As previously agreed, a meeting between Henry A. Kissinger, Secretary of State of the United States of America and Assistant to the President for National Security Affairs, and Andrei A. Gromyko, Member of the Politburo of the Central Committee of the. CPSU [Communist Party of the Soviet Union] and Minister of Foreign Affairs of the USSR, took place on February 16 and 17 in Geneva.

They exchanged views on a number of questions of bilateral American-Soviet relations, including the various negotiations currently in progress between them, and on certain international issues of mutual interest. Both sides emphasized their determination to adhere to the course of continu-

57 (February 26, 1975)
U.S. and U.S.S.R. Hold Talks on Fisheries Issues

Press release 104 dated February 26

Discussions between the United States and the Soviet Union on Middle Atlantic and North Pacific fisheries issues which commenced February 3 were terminated on February 26. Agreement was reached between the two countries on Middle Atlantic problems, and a new agreement extending previous arrangements was signed February 26 with some modifications. The new agreement provides for stricter enforcement of U.S. regulations relating to the taking of U.S. continental shelf fishery resources and strengthens measures aimed at minimizing gear conflicts between Soviet mobile (trawl) gear and U.S. fixed gear (lobster pots).

However, the United States and the Soviet Union failed to reach agreement on issues relating to the conservation of North Pacific fishery resources and on ways of most effectively reducing conflicts between U.S. and Soviet fishermen with minimal impact on the fisheries of both countries. Deputy Assistant Secretary for Oceans and Fisheries Thomas A. Clingan, Jr., who headed the U.S. delegation, expressed concern over the continuing decline of fishery resources off the U.S. Pacific coast and the urgent need to implement measures to control overfishing. He further expressed his keen disappointment over the failure to reach an agreement that would protect and conserve resources of special interest to U.S. fishermen.

Both countries agreed to extend to July 1, 1975, the former three agreements relating to crab fishing in the eastern Bering Sea and arrangements to prevent gear conflicts in the vicinity of Kodiak Island and the fisheries of the northeastern Pacific extending from Alaska south to California and also agreed to meet again later this year. The U.S. delegation included representatives from the Departments of State and Commerce, the Coast Guard, and from state governments and industry. The Soviet delegation was led by Vladimir M. Kamentsev, Deputy Minister of Fisheries.

58 (March 7, 1975)
U.S. and U.S.S.R. Hold Second Round of Environmental Modification Talks

Joint U.S.-U.S.S.R. Release [1]

The second meeting of representatives of the United States of America and the Union of Soviet Socialist Republics on the question of measures to overcome the dangers of the use of environmental modification techniques for military purposes was held in Washington from February 24 to March 5. The American delegation was headed by Thomas D. Davies, Assistant Director, U.S. Arms Control and Disarmament Agency. Academician Y. K. Fedorov headed the Soviet delegation.

The first meeting of representatives of the U.S.A. and the U.S.S.R. was held in Moscow in November 1974.

The discussions are being conducted in accordance with the U.S.-U.S.S.R. Joint Statement signed on July 3, 1974, at the Moscow summit meeting, and also on the basis of the understanding to continue an active search for a mutually acceptable solution to this question established in the joint U.S.-U.S.S.R. communique of November 24, 1974, on the results of the Vladivostok summit meeting.

In the course of the discussions conducted in the United States, the exchange of opinions on the most effective measures possible which could be undertaken to overcome the dangers of the use of environmental modification techniques for military purposes was continued. The examination of scientific and technical questions related to environmental modification and the familiarization with laboratories working in this area, which were begun in Moscow, were also continued.

The representatives of the U.S.A. and the U.S.S.R. consider that these meetings facilitate better understanding of the points of view of the sides on the questions discussed.

The sides intend to participate actively in the discussion of this question in the Conference of the Committee on Disarmament, which reconvened in Geneva this week, with the aim of achieving positive results.

[1] Issued on Mar. 7 (text from ACDA press release 75–8).

59 (July 18, 1975)

U.S. and U.S.S.R. Sign Agreement on North Pacific Fisheries

Press release 381 dated July 18

The Governments of the United States and the Union of Soviet Socialist Republics concluded on July 18 at Washington an agreement relating to the fisheries of the North Pacific area, extending from California north to Alaska. This is the fifth such agreement concluded between the two governments on Pacific coast fisheries. The new agreement covers the period August 1, 1975, through December 31, 1976. A 30-day-notice reopening clause is provided, should the situation in the fisheries change greatly during that period.

Under the new agreement, the Soviet Union is required to place additional and extensive restrictions on its Pacific fishery off the U.S. coast. These restrictions include the closing-off of large areas to the Soviet fleets, either on a year-round basis or during periods when Soviet fishing could be harmful to stocks of fish such as halibut, rockfish, and crabs that are of particular interest to U.S. fishermen.

Limitations on Soviet catches are provided for such species as pollock, hake, and rockfish. These catch quotas, in combination with the extensive area-time closures, are expected to provide considerable protection for species of special interest to U.S. fishermen.

As has been the case in all such agreements recently concluded by the United States with foreign countries fishing off its shores, the new agreement contains measures to prevent fishing-gear conflicts, protect the species which inhabit the U.S. continental shelf, and provide for observation and enforcement of the agreement's provisions. Cooperative research and exchange of information on species of joint interest are also provided for.

The U.S. delegation, which included representatives from the Departments of State and Commerce, state agencies, and the fishing industry, was headed by Ambassador Thomas A. Clingan, Jr., Deputy Assistant Secretary of State for Oceans and Fisheries Affairs. The Soviet delegation was led by Deputy Minister of Fisheries Vladimir M. Kamentsev.

60 (August 1, 1975)
Conference on Security and Cooperation in Europe: Final Act [1]

The Conference on Security and Co-operation in Europe, which opened at Helsinki on 3 July 1973 and continued at Geneva from 18 September 1973 to 21 July 1975, was concluded at Helsinki on 1 August 1975 by the High Representatives of Austria, Belgium, Bulgaria, Canada, Cyprus, Czechoslovakia, Denmark, Finland, France, the German Democratic Republic, the Federal Republic of Germany, Greece, the Holy See, Hungary, Iceland, Ireland, Italy, Liechtenstein, Luxembourg, Malta, Monaco, the Netherlands, Norway, Poland, Portugal, Romania, San Marino, Spain, Sweden, Switzerland, Turkey, the Union of Soviet Socialist Republics, the United Kingdom, the United States of America and Yugoslavia.

During the opening and closing stages of the Conference the participants were addressed by the Secretary-General of the United Nations as their guest of honour. The Director-General of UNESCO and the Executive Secretary of the United Nations Economic Commission for Europe addressed the Conference during its second stage.

During the meetings of the second stage of the Conference, contributions were received, and statements heard, from the following non-participating Mediterranean States on various agenda items: the Democratic and Popular Republic of Algeria, the Arab Republic of Egypt, Israel, the Kingdom of

Morocco, the Syrian Arab Republic, Tunisia.

Motivated by the political will, in the interest of peoples, to improve and intensify their relations and to contribute in Europe to peace, security, justice and co-operation as well as to rapprochement among themselves and with the other States of the world,

Determined, in consequence, to give full effect to the results of the Conference and to assure, among their States and throughout Europe, the benefits deriving from those results and thus to broaden, deepen and make continuing and lasting the process of détente,

The High Representatives of the participating States have solemnly adopted the following:

QUESTIONS RELATING TO SECURITY IN EUROPE

The States participating in the Conference on Security and Co-operation in Europe,

Reaffirming their objective of promoting better relations among themselves and ensuring conditions in which their people can live in true and lasting peace free from any threat to or attempt against their security;

Convinced of the need to exert efforts to make détente both a continuing and an increasingly viable and comprehensive process, universal in scope, and

---

[1] Signed at Helsinki on Aug. 1.

154

that the implementation of the results of the Conference on Security and Co-operation in Europe will be a major contribution to this process;

Considering that solidarity among peoples, as well as the common purpose of the participating States in achieving the aims as set forth by the Conference on Security and Co-operation in Europe, should lead to the development of better and closer relations among them in all fields and thus to overcoming the confrontation stemming from the character of their past relations, and to better mutual understanding;

Mindful of their common history and recognizing that the existence of elements common to their traditions and values can assist them in developing their relations, and desiring to search, fully taking into account the individuality and diversity of their positions and views, for possibilities of joining their efforts with a view to overcoming distrust and increasing confidence, solving the problems that separate them and co-operating in the interest of mankind;

Recognizing the indivisibility of security in Europe as well as their common interest in the development of co-operation throughout Europe and among themselves and expressing their intention to pursue efforts accordingly;

Recognizing the close link between peace and security in Europe and in the world as a whole and conscious of the need for each of them to make its contribution to the strengthening of world peace and security and to the promotion of fundamental rights, economic and social progress and well-being for all peoples;

Have adopted the following:

1.

(a) Declaration on Principles Guiding Relations between Participating States

The participating States,

Reaffirming their commitment to peace, security and justice and the continuing development of friendly relations and co-operation;

Recognizing that this commitment, which reflects the interest and aspirations of peoples, constitutes for each participating State a present and future responsibility, heightened by experience of the past;

Reaffirming, in conformity with their membership in the United Nations and in accordance with the purposes and principles of the United Nations, their full and active support for the United Nations and for the enhancement of its role and effectiveness in strengthening international peace, security and justice, and in promoting the solution of international problems, as well as the development of friendly relations and co-operation among States;

Expressing their common adherence to the principles which are set forth below and are in conformity with the Charter of the United Nations, as well as their common will to act, in the application of these principles, in conformity with the purposes and principles of the Charter of the United Nations;

Declare their determination to respect and put into practice, each of them in its relations with all other participating States, irrespective of their political, economic or social systems as well as of their size, geographical location or level of economic development, the following principles, which all are of primary significance, guiding their mutual relations:

I. *Sovereign equality, respect for the rights inherent in sovereignty*

The participating States will respect each other's sovereign equality and individuality as well as all the rights inherent in and encompassed by its sovereignty, including in particular the right of every State to juridical equality, to territorial integrity and to freedom and political independence. They will also respect each other's right freely to choose and develop its political, social, economic and cultural systems as well as its right to determine its laws and regulations.

Within the framework of international law, all the participating States have equal rights and duties. They will respect each other's right to define and conduct as it wishes its relations with other States in accordance with international law and in the spirit of the present Declaration. They consider that their frontiers can be changed, in accordance with international law, by peaceful means and by agreement. They also have the right to belong or not to belong to international organizations, to be or not to be a party to bilateral or multilateral treaties including the right to be or not to be a party to treaties of alliance; they also have the right to neutrality.

II. *Refraining from the threat or use of force*

The participating States will refrain in their mutual relations, as well as in their international relations in general, from the threat or use of force against the territorial integrity or political independence of any State, or in any other manner inconsistent with the purposes of the United Nations and with the present Declaration. No consideration may be invoked to serve to warrant resort to the threat or use of force in contravention of this principle.

Accordingly, the participating States will refrain from any acts constituting a threat of force or direct or indirect use of force against another participating State. Likewise they will refrain from any manifestation of force for the purpose of inducing another participating State to renounce the full exercise of its sovereign rights. Likewise they will also refrain in their mutual relations from any act of reprisal by force.

No such threat or use of force will be employed as a means of settling disputes, or questions likely to give rise to disputes, between them.

III. *Inviolability of frontiers*

The participating States regard as inviolable all one another's frontiers as well as the frontiers of all States in Europe and therefore they will refrain now and in the future from assaulting these frontiers.

Accordingly, they will also refrain from any demand for, or act of, seizure and usurpation of part or all of the territory of any participating State.

IV. *Territorial integrity of States*

The participating States will respect the territorial integrity of each of the participating States.

Accordingly, they will refrain from any action inconsistent with the purposes and principles of the Charter of the United Nations against the territorial integrity, political independence or the unity of any participating State, and in particular from any such action constituting a threat or use of force.

The participating States will likewise refrain from making each other's territory the object of military occupation or other direct or indirect measures of force in contravention of international law, or the object of acquisition by means of such measures or the threat of them. No such occupation or acquisition will be recognized as legal.

V. *Peaceful settlement of disputes*

The participating States will settle disputes among them by peaceful means in such a manner as not to endanger international peace and security, and justice.

They will endeavour in good faith and a spirit of co-operation to reach a rapid and equitable solution on the basis of international law.

For this purpose they will use such means as negotiation, enquiry, mediation, conciliation, arbitration, judicial settlement or other peaceful means of their own choice including any settlement procedure agreed to in advance of disputes to which they are parties.

In the event of failure to reach a solution by any of the above peaceful means, the parties to a dispute will continue to seek a mutually agreed way to settle the dispute peacefully.

Participating States, parties to a dispute among them, as well as other participating States, will refrain from any action which might aggravate the situation to such a degree as to endanger the maintenance of international peace and security and thereby make a peaceful settlement of the dispute more difficult.

VI. *Non-intervention in internal affairs*

The participating States will refrain from any intervention, direct or indirect, individual or collective, in the internal or external affairs falling within the domestic jurisdiction of another participating State, regardless of their mutual relations.

They will accordingly refrain from any form of armed intervention or threat of such intervention against another participating State.

They will likewise in all circumstances refrain from any other act of military, or of political, economic or other coercion designed to subordinate to their own interest the exercise by another participating State of the rights inherent in its sovereignty and thus to secure advantages of any kind.

Accordingly, they will, inter alia, refrain from direct or indirect assistance to terrorist activities, or to subversive or other activities directed towards the violent overthrow of the regime of another participating State.

VII. *Respect for human rights and fundamental freedoms, including the freedom of thought, conscience, religion or belief*

The participating States will respect human rights and fundamental freedoms, including the freedom of thought, conscience, religion or belief, for all without distinction as to race, sex, language or religion.

They will promote and encourage the effective exercise of civil, political, economic, social, cultural and other rights and freedoms all of which derive from the inherent dignity of the human person and are essential for his free and full development.

Within this framework the participating States will recognize and respect the freedom of the individual to profess and practise, alone or in community with others, religion or belief acting in accordance with the dictates of his own conscience.

The participating States on whose territory national minorities exist will respect the right of persons belonging to such minorities to equality before the law, will afford them the full opportunity for the actual enjoyment of human rights and fundamental freedoms and will, in this manner, protect their legitimate interests in this sphere.

The participating States recognize the universal significance of human rights and fundamental freedoms, respect for which is an essential factor for the peace, justice and well-being necessary to ensure the development of friendly relations and co-operation among themselves as among all States.

They will constantly respect these rights and freedoms in their mutual relations and will endeavour jointly and separately, including in co-operation with the United Nations, to promote universal and effective respect for them.

They confirm the right of the individual to know and act upon his rights and duties in this field.

In the field of human rights and fundamental freedoms, the participating States will act in conformity with the purposes and principles of the Charter of the United Nations and with the Universal Declaration of Human Rights. They will also fulfill their obligations as set forth in the international declarations and agreements in this field, including inter alia the International Covenants on Human Rights, by which they may be bound.

VIII. *Equal rights and self-determination of peoples*

The participating States will respect the equal rights of peoples and their right to self-determination, acting at all times in conformity with the purposes and principles of the Charter of the United Nations and with the relevant norms of international law, including those relating to territorial integrity of States.

By virtue of the principle of equal rights and self-determination of peoples, all peoples always have the right, in full freedom, to determine, when and as they wish, their internal and external political status, without external interference, and to pursue as they wish their political, economic, social and cultural development.

The participating States reaffirm the universal significance of respect for and effective exercise of equal rights and self-determination of peoples for the development of friendly relations among themselves as among all States; they also recall the importance of the elimination of any form of violation of this principle.

IX. *Co-operation among States*

The participating States will develop their co-operation with one another and with all States in all fields in accordance with the purposes and principles of the Charter of the United Nations. In developing their co-operation the participating States will place special emphasis on the fields as set forth within the framework of the Conference on Security and Co-operation in Europe, with each of them making its contribution in conditions of full equality.

They will endeavour, in developing their co-operation as equals, to promote mutual understanding and confidence, friendly and good-neighbourly relations among themselves, international peace, security and justice. They will equally endeavour, in developing their co-operation, to improve the well-being of peoples and contribute to the fulfilment of their aspirations through, inter alia, the benefits resulting from increased mutual knowledge and from progress and achievement in the economic, scientific, technological, social, cultural and humanitarian fields. They will take steps to promote conditions favourable to making these benefits available to all; they will take into account the interest of all in the narrowing of differences in the levels of economic development, and in particular the interest of developing countries throughout the world.

They confirm that governments, institutions, organizations and persons have a relevant and positive role to play in contributing toward the achievement of these aims of their co-operation.

They will strive, in increasing their co-operation as set forth above, to develop closer relations among themselves on an improved and more enduring basis for the benefit of peoples.

X. *Fulfilment in good faith of obligations under international law*

The participating States will fulfil in good faith their obligations under international law, both those obligations arising from the generally recognized principles and rules of international law and those obligations arising from treaties or other agreements, in conformity with international law, to which they are parties.

In exercising their sovereign rights, including the right to determine their laws and regulations, they will conform with their legal obligations under international law; they will furthermore pay due regard to and implement the provisions in the Final Act of the Conference on Security and Co-operation in Europe.

The participating States confirm that in the event of a conflict between the obligations of the members of the United Nations under the Charter of the United Nations and their obligations under any treaty or other international agreement, their obligations under the Charter will prevail, in accordance with Article 103 of the Charter of the United Nations.

All the principles set forth above are of primary significance and, accordingly, they will be equally and unreservedly applied, each of them being interpreted taking into account the others.

The participating States express their determination fully to respect and apply these principles, as set forth in the present Declaration, in all aspects, to their mutual relations and co-operation in order to ensure to each participating State the benefits resulting from the respect and application of these principles by all.

The participating States, paying due regard to the principles above and, in particular, to the first sentence of the tenth principle, "Fulfilment in good faith of obligations under international law", note that the present Declaration does not affect their rights and obligations, nor the corresponding treaties and other agreements and arrangements.

The participating States express the conviction that respect for these principles will encourage the development of normal and friendly relations and the progress of co-operation among them in all fields. They also express the conviction that respect for these principles will encourage the development of political contacts among them which in turn would contribute to better mutual understanding of their positions and views.

The participating States declare their intention to conduct their relations with all other States in the spirit of the principles contained in the present Declaration.

(b) Matters related to giving effect to certain of the above Principles

(i) The participating States,

Reaffirming that they will respect and give effect to refraining from the threat or use of force and convinced of the necessity to make it an effective norm of international life,

Declare that they are resolved to respect and carry out, in their relations with one another, inter alia, the following provisions which are in conformity with the Declaration on Principles Guiding Relations between Participating States:

—To give effect and expression, by all the ways and forms which they consider appropriate, to the duty to refrain from the threat or use of force in their relations with one another.

—To refrain from any use of armed forces inconsistent with the purposes and principles of the Charter of the United Nations and the provisions of the Declaration on Principles Guiding Relations between Participating States, against another participating State, in particular from invasion of or attack on its territory.

—To refrain from any manifestation of force for the purpose of inducing another participating State to renounce the full exercise of its sovereign rights.

—To refrain from any act of economic coercion designed to subordinate to their own interest the exercise by another participating State of the rights inherent in its sovereignty and thus to secure advantages of any kind.

—To take effective measures which by their scope and by their nature constitute steps towards the ultimate achievement of general and complete disarmament under strict and effective international control.

—To promote, by all means which each of them considers appropriate, a climate of confidence and respect among peoples consonant with their duty to refrain from propaganda for wars of aggression or for any threat or use of force inconsistent with the purposes of the United Nations and with the Declaration on Principles Guiding Relations between Participating States, against another participating State.

—To make every effort to settle exclusively by peaceful means any dispute between them, the continuance of which is likely to endanger the maintenance of international peace and security in Europe, and to seek, first of all, a solution through the peaceful means set forth in Article 33 of the United Nations Charter.

To refrain from any action which could hinder the peaceful settlement of disputes between the participating States.

(ii) The participating States,

Reaffirming their determination to settle their disputes as set forth in the Principle of Peaceful Settlement of Disputes;

Convinced that the peaceful settlement of disputes is a complement to refraining from the threat or use of force, both being essential though not exclusive factors for the maintenance and consolidation of peace and security;

Desiring to reinforce and to improve the methods at their disposal for the peaceful settlement of disputes;

1. Are resolved to pursue the examination and elaboration of a generally acceptable method for the peaceful settlement of disputes aimed at complementing existing methods, and to continue to this end to work upon the "Draft Convention on a European System for the Peaceful Settlement of Disputes" submitted by Switzerland during the second stage of the Conference on Security and Co-operation in Europe, as well as other proposals relating to it and directed towards the elaboration of such a method.

2. Decide that, on the invitation of Switzerland, a meeting of experts of all the participating States will be convoked in order to fulfil the mandate described in paragraph 1 above within the framework and under the procedures of the follow-up to the Conference laid down in the chapter "Follow-up to the Conference".

3. This meeting of experts will take place after the meeting of the representatives appointed by the Ministers of Foreign Affairs of the participating States, scheduled according to the chapter "Follow-up to the Conference" for 1977; the results of the work of this meeting of experts will be submitted to Governments.

2.

Document on confidence-building measures and certain aspects of security and disarmament

The participating States,

Desirous of eliminating the causes of tension that may exist among them and thus of contributing to the strengthening of peace and security in the world;

Determined to strengthen confidence among them and thus to contribute to increasing stability and security in Europe;

Determined further to refrain in their mutual relations, as well as in their international relations in general, from the threat or use of force against the territorial integrity or political independence of any State, or in any other manner inconsistent with the purposes of the United Nations and with the Declaration on Principles Guiding Relations between Participating States as adopted in this Final Act;

Recognizing the need to contribute to reducing the dangers of armed conflict and of misunderstanding or miscalculation of military activities which could give rise to apprehension, particularly in a situation where the participating States lack clear and timely information about the nature of such activities;

Taking into account considerations relevant to efforts aimed at lessening tension and promoting disarmament;

Recognizing that the exchange of observers by invitation at military manoeuvres will help to promote contacts and mutual understanding;

Having studied the question of prior notification of major military movements in the context of confidence-building;

Recognizing that there are other ways in which individual States can contribute further to their common objectives;

Convinced of the political importance of prior notification of major military manoeuvres for the promotion of mutual understanding and the strengthening of confidence, stability and security;

Accepting the responsibility of each of them to promote these objectives and to implement this measure, in accordance with the accepted criteria and modalities, as essentials for the realization of these objectives;

Recognizing that this measure deriving from political decision rests upon a voluntary basis;

Have adopted the following:

I

Prior notification of major military manoeuvres

They will notify their major military manoeuvres to all other participating States through usual diplomatic channels in accordance with the following provisions:

Notification will be given of major military manoeuvres exceeding a total of 25,000 troops, independently or combined with any possible air or naval components (in this context the word "troops" includes amphibious and airborne troops). In the case of independent manoeuvres of amphibious or airborne troops, or of combined manoeuvres involving them, these troops will be included in this total. Furthermore, in the case of combined manoeuvres which do not reach the above total but which involve land forces together with significant numbers of either amphibious or airborne troops, or both, notification can also be given.

Notification will be given of major military manoeuvres which take place on the territory, in Europe, of any participating State as well as, if applicable, in the adjoining sea area and air space.

In the case of a participating State whose territory extends beyond Europe, prior notification need be given only of manoeuvres which take place in an area within 250 kilometres from its frontier facing or shared with any other European participating State, the participating State need not, however, give notification in cases in which that area is also contiguous to the participating State's frontier facing or shared with a non-European non-participating State.

Notification will be given 21 days or more in advance of the start of the manoeuvre or in the case of a manoeuvre arranged at shorter notice at the earliest possible opportunity prior to its starting date.

Notification will contain information of the designation, if any, the general purpose of and the States involved in the manoeuvre, the type or types and numerical strength of the forces engaged, the area and estimated time-frame of its conduct. The participating States will also, if possible, provide additional relevant information, particularly that related to the components of the forces engaged and the period of involvement of these forces.

Prior notification of other military manoeuvres

The participating States recognize that they can contribute further to strengthening confidence and increasing security and stability, and to this end may also notify smaller-scale military manoeuvres to other participating States, with special regard for those near the area of such manoeuvres.

To the same end, the participating States also recognize that they may notify other military manoeuvres conducted by them.

Exchange of observers

The participating States will invite other participating States, voluntarily and on a bilateral basis, in a spirit of reciprocity and goodwill towards all participating States, to send observers to attend military manoeuvres.

The inviting State will determine in each case the number of observers, the procedures and conditions of their participation, and give other information which it may consider useful. It will provide appropriate facilities and hospitality.

The invitation will be given as far ahead as is conveniently possible through usual diplomatic channels.

Prior notification of major military movements

In accordance with the Final Recommendations of the Helsinki Consultations the participating States studied the question of prior notification of major military movements as a measure to strengthen confidence.

Accordingly, the participating States recognize that they may, at their own discretion and with a view to contributing to confidence-building, notify their major military movements.

In the same spirit, further consideration will be given by the States participating in the Conference on Security and Co-operation in Europe to the question of prior notification of major military movements, bearing in mind, in particular, the experience gained by the implementation of the measures which are set forth in this document.

Other confidence-building measures

The participating States recognize that there are other means by which their common objectives can be promoted.

In particular, they will, with due regard to reciprocity and with a view to better mutual understanding, promote exchanges by invitation among their military personnel, including visits by military delegations.

* * *

In order to make a fuller contribution to their common objective of confidence-building, the participating States, when conducting their military activities in the area covered by the provisions for the prior notification of major military manoeuvres, will duly take into account and respect this objective.

They also recognize that the experience gained by the implementation of the provisions set forth above, together with further efforts, could lead to developing and enlarging measures aimed at strengthening confidence.

II

Questions relating to disarmament

The participating States recognize the interest of all of them in efforts aimed at lessening military confrontation and promoting disarmament which are designed to complement political détente in Europe and to strengthen their security. They are convinced of the necessity to take effective measures in these fields which by their scope and by their nature constitute steps towards the ultimate achievement of general and complete disarmament under strict and effective international control, and which should result in strengthening peace and security throughout the world.

III

General considerations

Having considered the views expressed on various subjects related to the strengthening of security in Europe through joint efforts aimed at promoting détente and disarmament, the participating States, when engaged in such efforts, will, in this context, proceed, in particular, from the following essential considerations:

—The complementary nature of the political and military aspects of security;

—The interrelation between the security of each participating State and security in Europe as a whole and the relationship which exists, in the broader context of world security, between security in Europe and security in the Mediterranean area;

—Respect for the security interests of all States participating in the Conference on Security and Co-operation in Europe inherent in their sovereign equality;

—The importance that participants in negotiating fora see to it that information about relevant developments, progress and results is provided on an appropriate basis to other States participating in the Conference on Security and Co-operation in Europe and, in return, the justified interest of any of those States in having their views considered.

CO-OPERATION IN THE FIELD OF ECONOMICS, OF SCIENCE AND TECHNOLOGY AND OF THE ENVIRONMENT

The participating States,
Convinced that their efforts to develop co-operation in the fields of trade, industry, science and technology, the environment and other areas of economic activity contribute to the reinforcement of peace and security in Europe and in the world as a whole,
Recognizing that co-operation in these fields would promote economic and social progress and the improvement of the conditions of life,
Aware of the diversity of their economic and social systems,
Reaffirming their will to intensify such co-operation between one another, irrespective of their systems,
Recognizing that such co-operation, with due regard for the different levels of economic development, can be developed, on the basis of equality and mutual satisfaction of the partners, and of reciprocity permitting, as a whole, an equitable distribution of advantages and obligations of comparable scale, with respect for bilateral and multilateral agreements,
Taking into account the interests of the develop-

ing countries throughout the world, including those among the participating countries as long as they are developing from the economic point of view; reaffirming their will to co-operate for the achievement of the aims and objectives established by the appropriate bodies of the United Nations in the pertinent documents concerning development, it being understood that each participating State maintains the positions it has taken on them; giving special attention to the least developed countries,
Convinced that the growing world-wide economic interdependence calls for increasing common and effective efforts towards the solution of major world economic problems such as food, energy, commodities, monetary and financial problems, and therefore emphasizes the need for promoting stable and equitable international economic relations, thus contributing to the continuous and diversified economic development of all countries,
Having taken into account the work already undertaken by relevant international organizations and wishing to take advantage of the possibilities offered by these organizations, in particular by the United Nations Economic Commission for Europe, for giving effect to the provisions of the final documents of the Conference,
Considering that the guidelines and concrete recommendations contained in the following texts are aimed at promoting further development of their mutual economic relations, and convinced that their co-operation in this field should take place in full respect for the principles guiding relations among participating States as set forth in the relevant document,
Have adopted the following:

1. Commercial Exchanges

General provisions

The participating States,
Conscious of the growing role of international trade as one of the most important factors in economic growth and social progress,
Recognizing that trade represents an essential sector of their co-operation, and bearing in mind that the provisions contained in the above preamble apply in particular to this sector,
Considering that the volume and structure of trade among the participating States do not in all cases correspond to the possibilities created by the current level of their economic, scientific and technological development,

are resolved to promote, on the basis of the modalities of their economic co-operation, the expansion of their mutual trade in goods and services, and to ensure conditions favourable to such development;

recognize the beneficial effects which can result for the development of trade from the application of most favoured nation treatment;

will encourage the expansion of trade on as broad a multilateral basis as possible, thereby endeavouring to utilize the various economic and commercial possibilities;

recognize the importance of bilateral and multilateral intergovernmental and other agreements for the long-term development of trade;

note the importance of monetary and financial questions for the development of international trade, and will endeavour to deal with them with a view to contributing to the continuous expansion of trade;

will endeavour to reduce or progressively eliminate all kinds of obstacles to the development of trade;

will foster a steady growth of trade while avoiding as far as possible abrupt fluctuations in their trade;

consider that their trade in various products should be conducted in such a way as not to cause or threaten to cause serious injury—and should the situation arise, market disruption—in domestic markets for these products and in particular to the detriment of domestic producers of like or directly competitive products; as regards the concept of market disruption, it is understood that it should not be invoked in a way inconsistent with the relevant provisions of their international agreements; if they resort to safeguard measures, they will do so in conformity with their commitments in this field arising from international agreements to which they are parties and will take account of the interests of the parties directly concerned;

will give due attention to measures for the promotion of trade and the diversification of its structure;

note that the growth and diversification of trade would contribute to widening the possibilities of choice of products;

consider it appropriate to create favourable conditions for the participation of firms, organizations and enterprises in the development of trade.

Business contacts and facilities

The participating States,
Conscious of the importance of the contribution which an improvement of business contacts, and the accompanying growth of confidence in business relationships, could make to the development of commercial and economic relations,

will take measures further to improve conditions for the expansion of contacts between representatives of official bodies, of the different organizations, enterprises, firms and banks concerned with foreign trade, in particular, where useful, between sellers and users of products and services, for the purpose of studying commercial possibilities, concluding contracts, ensuring their implementation and providing after-sales services;

will encourage organizations, enterprises and firms concerned with foreign trade to take measures to accelerate the conduct of business negotiations;

will further take measures aimed at improving working conditions of representatives of foreign organizations, enterprises, firms and banks concerned with external trade, particularly as follows:

—by providing the necessary information, including information on legislation and procedures relating to the establishment and operation of permanent representation by the above mentioned bodies;

—by examining as favourably as possible requests

for the establishment of permanent representation and of offices for this purpose, including, where appropriate, the opening of joint offices by two or more firms;

—by encouraging the provision, on conditions as favourable as possible and equal for all representatives of the above-mentioned bodies, of hotel accommodation, means of communication, and of other facilities normally required by them, as well as of suitable business and residential premises for purposes of permanent representation;

recognize the importance of such measures to encourage greater participation by small and medium sized firms in trade between participating States.

Economic and commercial information

The participating States,
Conscious of the growing role of economic and commercial information in the development of international trade,
Considering that economic information should be of such a nature as to allow adequate market analysis and to permit the preparation of medium and long term forecasts, thus contributing to the establishment of a continuing flow of trade and a better utilization of commercial possibilities,
Expressing their readiness to improve the quality and increase the quantity and supply of economic and relevant administrative information,
Considering that the value of statistical information on the international level depends to a considerable extent on the possibility of its comparability,

will promote the publication and dissemination of economic and commercial information at regular intervals and as quickly as possible, in particular:

—statistics concerning production, national income, budget, consumption and productivity;

—foreign trade statistics drawn up on the basis of comparable classification including breakdown by product with indication of volume and value, as well as country of origin or destination;

—laws and regulations concerning foreign trade;

—information allowing forecasts of development of the economy to assist in trade promotion, for example, information on the general orientation of national economic plans and programmes;

—other information to help businessmen in commercial contacts, for example, periodic directories, lists, and where possible, organizational charts of firms and organizations concerned with foreign trade;

will in addition to the above encourage the development of the exchange of economic and commercial information through, where appropriate, joint commissions for economic, scientific and technical cooperation, national and joint chambers of commerce, and other suitable bodies;

will support a study, in the framework of the United Nations Economic Commission for Europe, of the possibilities of creating a multilateral system of notification of laws and regulations concerning foreign trade and changes therein;

will encourage international work on the harmonization of statistical nomenclatures, notably in the United Nations Economic Commission for Europe.

Marketing

The participating States,

Recognizing the importance of adapting production to the requirements of foreign markets in order to ensure the expansion of international trade,

Conscious of the need of exporters to be as fully familiar as possible with and take account of the requirements of potential users,

will encourage organizations, enterprises and firms concerned with foreign trade to develop further the knowledge and techniques required for effective marketing;

will encourage the improvement of conditions for the implementation of measures to promote trade and to satisfy the needs of users in respect of imported products, in particular through market research and advertising measures as well as, where useful, the establishment of supply facilities, the furnishing of spare parts, the functioning of after sales services, and the training of the necessary local technical personnel;

will encourage international co-operation in the field of trade promotion, including marketing, and the work undertaken on these subjects within the international bodies, in particular the United Nations Economic Commission for Europe.

2. Industrial co-operation and projects of common interest

Industrial co-operation

The participating States,

Considering that industrial co-operation, being motivated by economic considerations, can

—create lasting ties thus strengthening long-term overall economic co-operation,

—contribute to economic growth as well as to the expansion and diversification of international trade and to a wider utilization of modern technology,

—lead to the mutually advantageous utilization of economic complementarities through better use of all factors of production, and

—accelerate the industrial development of all those who take part in such co-operation,

propose to encourage the development of industrial co-operation between the competent organizations, enterprises and firms of their countries;

consider that industrial co-operation may be facilitated by means of intergovernmental and other bilateral and multilateral agreements between the interested parties;

note that in promoting industrial co-operation they should bear in mind the economic structures and the development levels of their countries;

note that industrial co-operation is implemented by means of contracts concluded between competent organizations, enterprises and firms on the basis of economic considerations;

express their willingness to promote measures designed to create favourable conditions for industrial co-operation;

recognize that industrial co-operation covers a number of forms of economic relations going beyond the framework of conventional trade, and that in concluding contracts on industrial co-operation the partners will determine jointly the appropriate forms and conditions of co-operation, taking into account their mutual interests and capabilities;

recognize further that, if it is in their mutual interest, concrete forms such as the following may be useful for the development of industrial co-operation: joint production and sale, specialization in production and sale, construction, adaptation and modernization of industrial plants, co-operation for the setting up of complete industrial installations with a view to thus obtaining part of the resultant products, mixed companies, exchanges of "know-how", of technical information, of patents and of licences, and joint industrial research within the framework of specific co-operation projects;

recognize that new forms of industrial co-operation can be applied with a view to meeting specific needs;

note the importance of economic, commercial, technical and administrative information such as to ensure the development of industrial co-operation;

Consider it desirable:

—to improve the quality and the quantity of information relevant to industrial co-operation, in particular the laws and regulations, including those relating to foreign exchange, general orientation of national economic plans and programmes as well as programme priorities and economic conditions of the market; and

—to disseminate as quickly as possible published documentation thereon;

will encourage all forms of exchange of information and communication of experience relevant to industrial co-operation, including through contacts between potential partners and, where appropriate, through joint commissions for economic, industrial, scientific and technical co-operation, national and joint chambers of commerce, and other suitable bodies;

consider it desirable, with a view to expanding industrial co-operation, to encourage the exploration of co-operation possibilities and the implementation of co-operation projects and will take measures to this end, *inter alia*, by facilitating and increasing all forms of business contacts between competent organizations, enterprises and firms and between their respective qualified personnel;

note that the provisions adopted by the Conference relating to business contacts in the economic and commercial fields also apply to foreign organizations, enterprises and firms engaged in industrial co-operation, taking into account the specific conditions of this co-operation, and will endeavour to ensure, in particular, the existence of appropriate working conditions for personnel engaged in the implementation of co-operation projects;

consider it desirable that proposals for industrial co-operation projects should be sufficiently specific and should contain the necessary economic and technical data, in particular preliminary estimates of the cost of the project, information on the form of co-operation envisaged, and market possibilities, to enable potential partners to proceed with initial studies and to arrive at decisions in the shortest possible time;

will encourage the parties concerned with industrial co-operation to take measures to accelerate the conduct of negotiations for the conclusion of co-operation contracts;

recommend further the continued examination—for example within the framework of the United Nations Economic Commission for Europe—of means of improving the provision of information to those concerned on general conditions of industrial co-operation and guidance on the preparation of contracts in this field;

consider it desirable to further improve conditions for the implementation of industrial co-operation projects, in particular with respect to:

—the protection of the interests of the partners in industrial co-operation projects, including the legal protection of the various kinds of property involved;

—the consideration, in ways that are compatible with their economic systems, of the needs and possibilities of industrial co-operation within the framework of economic policy and particularly in national economic plans and programmes;

consider it desirable that the partners, when concluding industrial co-operation contracts, should devote due attention to provisions concerning the extension of the necessary mutual assistance and the provision of the necessary information during the implementation of these contracts, in particular with a view to attaining the required technical level and quality of the products resulting from such co-operation;

recognize the usefulness of an increased participation of small and medium sized firms in industrial co-operation projects.

Projects of common interest

The participating States,

Considering that their economic potential and their natural resources permit, through common efforts, long-term co-operation in the implementation, including at the regional or sub-regional level, of major projects of common interest, and that these may contribute to the speeding-up of the economic development of the countries participating therein,

Considering it desirable that the competent organizations, enterprises and firms of all countries should be given the possibility of indicating their interest in participating in such projects, and, in case of agreement, of taking part in their implementation,

Noting that the provisions adopted by the Conference relating to industrial cooperation are also applicable to projects of common interest,

regard it as necessary to encourage, where appropriate, the investigation by competent and interested organizations, enterprises and firms of the possibilities for the carrying out of projects of common interest in the fields of energy resources and of the exploitation of raw materials, as well as of transport and communications;

regard it as desirable that organizations, enterprises and firms exploring the possibilities of taking part in projects of common interest exchange with their potential partners, through the appropriate channels, the requisite economic, legal, financial and technical information pertaining to these projects;

consider that the fields of energy resources, in particular, petroleum, natural gas and coal, and the extraction and processing of mineral raw materials, in particular, iron ore and bauxite, are suitable ones for strengthening long-term economic co-operation and for the development of trade which could result;

consider that possibilities for projects of common interest with a view to long-term economic co-operation also exist in the following fields:

—exchanges of electrical energy within Europe with a view to utilizing the capacity of the electrical power stations as rationally as possible;

—co-operation in research for new sources of energy and, in particular, in the field of nuclear energy;

—development of road networks and co-operation aimed at establishing a coherent navigable network in Europe;

—co-operation in research and the perfecting of equipment for multimodal transport operations and for the handling of containers;

recommend that the States interested in projects of common interest should consider under what conditions it would be possible to establish them, and if they so desire, create the necessary conditions for their actual implementation.

3. Provisions concerning trade and industrial co-operation

Harmonization of standards

The participating States,

Recognizing the development of international harmonization of standards and technical regulations and of international co-operation in the field of certification as an important means of eliminating technical obstacles to international trade and industrial co-operation, thereby facilitating their development and increasing productivity,

reaffirm their interest to achieve the widest possible international harmonization of standards and technical regulations;

express their readiness to promote international agreements and other appropriate arrangements on acceptance of certificates of conformity with standards and technical regulations;

consider it desirable to increase international co-operation on standardization, in particular by supporting the activities of intergovernmental and other appropriate organizations in this field.

Arbitration

The participating States,

Considering that the prompt and equitable settlement of disputes which may arise from commercial transactions relating to goods and services and contracts for industrial co-operation would contribute to expanding and facilitating trade and co-operation,

Considering that arbitration is an appropriate means of settling such disputes,

recommend, where appropriate, to organizations, enterprises and firms in their countries, to include arbitration clauses in commercial contracts and industrial co-operation contracts, or in special agreements;

recommend that the provisions on arbitration should provide for arbitration under a mutually acceptable set of arbitration rules, and permit arbitration in a third country, taking into account existing intergovernmental and other agreements in this field.

Specific bilateral arrangements

The participating States,

Conscious of the need to facilitate trade and to promote the application of new forms of industrial co-operation,

will consider favourably the conclusion, in appropriate cases, of specific bilateral agreements concerning various problems of mutual interest in the fields of commercial exchanges and industrial co-operation, in particular with a view to avoiding double taxation and to facilitating the transfer of profits and the return of the value of the assets invested.

4. Science and technology

The participating States,

Convinced that scientific and technological co-operation constitutes an important contribution to the strengthening of security and co-operation among them, in that it assists the effective solution of problems of common interest and the improvement of the conditions of human life,

Considering that in developing such co-operation, it is important to promote the sharing of information and experience, facilitating the study and transfer of scientific and technological achievements, as well as the access to such achievements on a mutually advantageous basis and in fields of co-operation agreed between interested parties,

Considering that it is for the potential partners, i.e. the competent organizations, institutions, enterprises, scientists and technologists of the participating States to determine the opportunities for mutually beneficial co-operation and to develop its details,

Affirming that such co-operation can be developed and implemented bilaterally and multilaterally at the governmental and non-governmental levels, for example, through intergovernmental and other agreements, international programmes, co-operative projects and commercial channels, while utilizing also various forms of contacts, including direct and individual contacts,

Aware of the need to take measures further to improve scientific and technological co-operation between them,

Possibilities for improving co-operation

Recognize that possibilities exist for further improving scientific and technological co-operation, and to this end, express their intention to remove obstacles to such co-operation, in particular through:

—the improvement of opportunities for the exchange and dissemination of scientific and technological information among the parties interested in scientific and technological research and co-operation including information related to the organization and implementation of such co-operation;

—the expeditious implementation and improvement in organization, including programmes, of international visits of scientists and specialists in connexion with exchanges, conferences and co-operation;

—the wider use of commercial channels and activities for applied scientific and technological research and for the transfer of achievements obtained in this field while providing information on and protection of intellectual and industrial property rights;

Fields of co-operation

Consider that possibilities to expand co-operation exist within the areas given below as examples, noting that it is for potential partners in the participating countries to identify and develop projects and arrangements of mutual interest and benefit:

Agriculture

Research into new methods and technologies for increasing the productivity of crop cultivation and animal husbandry; the application of chemistry to agriculture; the design, construction and utilization of agricultural machinery; technologies of irrigation and other agricultural land improvement works;

Energy

New technologies of production, transport and distribution of energy aimed at improving the use of existing fuels and sources of hydroenergy, as well as research in the field of new energy sources, including nuclear, solar and geothermal energy;

New technologies, rational use of resources

Research on new technologies and equipment designed in particular to reduce energy consumption and to minimize or eliminate waste;

Transport technology

Research on the means of transport and the technology applied to the development and operation of international, national and urban transport networks including container transport as well as transport safety;

Physics

Study of problems in high energy physics and plasma physics; research in the field of theoretical and experimental nuclear physics;

Chemistry

Research on problems in electrochemistry and the chemistry of polymers, of natural products, and of metals and alloys, as well as the development of improved chemical technology, especially materials processing; practical application of the latest achievements of chemistry to industry, construction and other sectors of the economy;

Meteorology and hydrology

Meteorological and hydrological research, including methods of collection, evaluation and transmission of data and their utilization for weather forecasting and hydrology forecasting;

Oceanography

Oceanographic research, including the study of air/sea interactions;

Seismological research

Study and forecasting of earthquakes and associated geological changes; development and research of technology of seism-resisting constructions;

Research on glaciology, permafrost and problems of life under conditions of cold

Research on glaciology and permafrost; transportation and construction technologies; human adaptation to climatic extremes and changes in the living conditions of indigenous populations;

Computer, communication and information technologies

Development of computers as well as of telecommunications and information systems; technology associated with computers and telecommunications, including their use for management systems, for production processes, for automation, for the study of economic problems, in scientific research and for the collection, processing and dissemination of information;

Space research

Space exploration and the study of the earth's natural resources and. the natural environment by remote sensing in particular with the assistance of satellites and rocket-probes;

Medicine and public health

Research on cardiovascular, tumour and virus diseases, molecular biology, neurophysiology; development and testing of new drugs; study of contemporary problems of pediatrics, gerontology and the organization and techniques of medical services;

Environmental research

Research on specific scientific and technological problems related to human environment.

Forms and methods of co-operation

Express their view that scientific and technological co-operation should, in particular, employ the following forms and methods:

—exchange and circulation of books, periodicals and other scientific and technological publications and papers among interested organizations, scientific and technological institutions, enterprises and scientists and technologists, as well as participation in international programmes for the abstracting and indexing of publications;

—exchanges and visits as well as other direct contacts and communications among scientists and technologists, on the basis of mutual agreement and other arrangements, for such purposes as consultations, lecturing and conducting research, including the use of laboratories, scientific libraries, and other documentation centres in connexion therewith;

—holding of international and national conferences, symposia, seminars, courses and other meetings of a scientific and technological character, which would include the participation of foreign scientists and technologists;

—joint preparation and implementation of programmes and projects of mutual interest on the basis of consultation and agreement among all parties concerned, including, where possible and appropriate, exchanges of experience and research results, and correlation of research programmes, between scientific and technological research institutions and organizations;

—use of commercial channels and methods for identifying and transferring technological and scientific developments, including the conclusion of mutually beneficial co-operation arrangements between firms and enterprises in fields agreed upon between them and for carrying out, where appropriate, joint research and development programmes and projects;

consider it desirable that periodic exchanges of views and information take place on scientific policy, in particular on general problems of orientation and administration of research and the question of a better use of large-scale scientific and experimental equipment on a co-operative basis;

recommend that, in developing co-operation in the field of science and technology, full use be made of existing practices of bilateral and multilateral co-operation, including that of a regional or sub-regional character, together with the forms and methods of co-operation described in this document;

recommend further that more effective utilization be made of the possibilities and capabilities of existing international organizations, intergovernmental and non-governmental, concerned with science and technology, for improving exchanges of information and experience, as well as for developing other forms of co-operation in fields of common interest, for example:

—in the United Nations Economic Commission for Europe, study of possibilities for expanding multilateral co-operation, taking into account models for projects and research used in various international organizations; and for sponsoring conferences, symposia, and study and working groups such as those which would bring together younger scientists and technologists with eminent specialists in their field;

—through their participation in particular international scientific and technological co-operation programmes, including those of UNESCO and other international organizations, pursuit of continuing progress towards the objectives of such programmes, notably those of UNISIST [World Science Information System] with particular respect to information policy guidance, technical advice, information contributions and data processing.

5. Environment

The participating States,

Affirming that the protection and improvement of the environment, as well as the protection of nature and the rational utilization of its resources in the interests of present and future generations, is one of the tasks of major importance to the well-being of peoples and the economic development of all countries and that many environmental problems, particularly in Europe, can be solved effectively only through close international co-operation,

Acknowledging that each of the participating States, in accordance with the principles of international law, ought to ensure, in a spirit of co-operation, that activities carried out on its territory do not cause degradation of the environment in another State or in areas lying beyond the limits of national jurisdiction,

Considering that the success of any environmental policy presupposes that all population groups and social forces, aware of their responsibilities, help to protect and improve the environment, which necessitates continued and thorough educative action, particularly with regard to youth,

Affirming that experience has shown that economic development and technological progress must be compatible with the protection of the environment and the preservation of historical and cultural values; that damage to the environment is best avoided by preventive measures; and that the ecological balance must be preserved in the exploitation and management of natural resources,

Aims of co-operation

Agree to the following aims of co-operation, in particular:

—to study, with a view to their solution, those environmental problems which, by their nature, are of a multilateral, bilateral, regional or sub-regional dimension; as well as to encourage the development of an interdisciplinary approach to environmental problems;

—to increase the effectiveness of national and international measures for the protection of the environment, by the comparison and, if appropriate, the harmonization of methods of gathering and analyzing facts, by improving the knowledge of pollution phenomena and rational utilization of natural resources, by the exchange of information, by the harmonization of definitions and the adoption, as far as possible, of a common terminology in the field of the environment;

—to take the necessary measures to bring environmental policies closer together and, where appropriate and possible, to harmonize them;

—to encourage, where possible and appropriate, national and international efforts by their interested organizations, enterprises and firms in the development, production and improvement of equipment designed for monitoring, protecting and enhancing the environment.

Fields of co-operation

To attain these aims, the participating States will make use of every suitable opportunity to co-operate in the field of environment and, in particular, within the areas described below as examples:

Control of air pollution

Desulphurization of fossil fuels and exhaust gases; pollution control of heavy metals, particles, aerosols, nitrogen oxides, in particular those emitted by transport, power stations, and other industrial plants; systems and methods of observation and control of air pollution and its effects, including long-range transport of air pollutants;

Water pollution control and fresh water utilization

Prevention and control of water pollution, in particular of transboundary rivers and international lakes; techniques for the improvement of the quality of water and further development of ways and means for industrial and municipal sewage effluent purification; methods of assessment of fresh water resources and the improvement of their utilization, in particular by developing methods of production which are less polluting and lead to less consumption of fresh water;

Protection of the marine environment

Protection of the marine environment of participating States, and especially the Mediterranean Sea, from pollutants emanating from land-based sources and those from ships and other vessels, notably the harmful substances listed in Annexes I and II to the London Convention on the Prevention of Marine Pollution by the Dumping of Wastes and Other Matters; problems of maintaining marine ecological balances and food chains, in particular such problems as may arise from the exploration and exploitation of biological and mineral resources of the seas and the sea-bed;

Land utilization and soils

Problems associated with more effective use of lands, including land amelioration, reclamation and recultivation; control of soil pollution, water and air erosion, as well as other forms of soil degradation; maintaining and increasing the productivity of soils with due regard for the possible negative effects of the application of chemical fertilizers and pesticides;

Nature conservation and nature reserves

Protection of nature and nature reserves; conservation and maintenance of existing genetic resources, especially rare animal and plant species; conservation of natural ecological systems; establishment of nature reserves and other protected landscapes and areas, including their use for research, tourism, recreation and other purposes;

Improvement of environmental conditions in areas of human settlement

Environmental conditions associated with transport, housing, working areas, urban development and planning, water supply and sewage disposal systems; assessment of harmful effects of noise, and noise control methods; collection, treatment and utilization of wastes, including the recovery and recycling of materials; research on substitutes for non-biodegradable substances;

Fundamental research, monitoring, forecasting and assessment of environmental changes

Study of changes in climate, landscapes and ecological balances under the impact of both natural factors and human activities; forecasting of possible genetic changes in flora and fauna as a result of environmental pollution; harmonization of statistical data, development of scientific concepts and systems of monitoring networks, standardized methods of observation, measurement and assessment of changes in the biosphere; assessment of the effects of environmental pollution levels and degradation of the environment upon human health; study and development of criteria and standards for various environmental pollutants and regulation regarding production and use of various products;

Legal and administrative measures

Legal and administrative measures for the protection of the environment including procedures for establishing environmental impact assessments.

Forms and methods of co-operation

The participating States declare that problems relating to the protection and improvement of the environment will be solved on both a bilateral and a multilateral, including regional and sub-regional, basis, making full use of existing patterns and forms of co-operation. They will develop co-operation in the field of the environment in particular by taking into consideration the Stockholm Declaration on the Human Environment, relevant resolutions of the United Nations General Assembly and the United Nations Economic Commission for Europe Prague symposium on environmental problems.

The participating States are resolved that co-operation in the field of the environment will be implemented in particular through:

—exchanges of scientific and technical information, documentation and research results, including information on the means of determining the possible effects on the environment of technical and economic activities;
—organization of conferences, symposia and meetings of experts;
—exchanges of scientists, specialists and trainees;
—joint preparation and implementation of programmes and projects for the study and solution of various problems of environmental protection;
—harmonization, where appropriate and necessary, of environmental protection standards and norms, in particular with the object of avoiding possible difficulties in trade which may arise from efforts to resolve ecological problems of production processes and which relate to the achievement of certain environmental qualities in manufactured products;

—consultations on various aspects of environmental protection, as agreed upon among countries concerned, especially in connexion with problems which could have international consequences.

The participating States will further develop such co-operation by:

—promoting the progressive development, codification and implementation of international law as one means of preserving and enhancing the human environment, including principles and practices, as accepted by them, relating to pollution and other environmental damage caused by activities within the jurisdiction or control of their States affecting other countries and regions;
—supporting and promoting the implementation of relevant international Conventions to which they are parties, in particular those designed to prevent and combat marine and fresh water pollution, recommending States to ratify Conventions which have already been signed, as well as considering possibilities of accepting other appropriate Conventions to which they are not parties at present;
—advocating the inclusion, where appropriate and possible, of the various areas of co-operation into the programmes of work of the United Nations Economic Commission for Europe, supporting such co-operation within the framework of the Commission and of the United Nations Environment Programme, and taking into account the work of other competent international organizations of which they are members;
—making wider use, in all types of co-operation, of information already available from national and international sources, including internationally agreed criteria, and utilizing the possibilities and capabilities of various competent international organizations.

The participating States agree on the following recommendations on specific measures:

—to develop through international co-operation an extensive programme for the monitoring and evaluation of the long-range transport of air pollutants, starting with sulphur dioxide and with possible extension to other pollutants, and to this end to take into account basic elements of a co-operation programme which were identified by the experts who met in Oslo in December 1974 at the invitation of the Norwegian Institute of Air Research;
—to advocate that within the framework of the United Nations Economic Commission for Europe a study be carried out of procedures and relevant experience relating to the activities of Governments in developing the capabilities of their countries to predict adequately environmental consequences of economic activities and technological development.

6. Co-operation in other areas

Development of transport

The participating States,
Considering that the improvement of the conditions of transport constitutes one of the factors essential to the development of co-operation among them,

167

Considering that it is necessary to encourage the development of transport and the solution of existing problems by employing appropriate national and international means,

Taking into account the work being carried out on these subjects by existing international organizations, especially by the Inland Transport Committee of the United Nations Economic Commission for Europe,

note that the speed of technical progress in the various fields of transport makes desirable a development of co-operation and an increase in exchanges of information among them;

declare themselves in favour of a simplification and a harmonization of administrative formalities in the field of international transport, in particular at frontiers;

consider it desirable to promote, while allowing for their particular national circumstances in this sector, the harmonization of administrative and technical provisions concerning safety in road, rail, river, air and sea transport;

express their intention to encourage the development of international inland transport of passengers and goods as well as the possibilities of adequate participation in such transport on the basis of reciprocal advantage;

declare themselves in favour, with due respect for their rights and international commitments, of the elimination of disparities arising from the legal provisions applied to traffic on inland waterways which are subject to international conventions and, in particular, of the disparity in the application of those provisions; and to this end invite the member States of the Central Commission for the Navigation of the Rhine, of the Danube Commission and of other bodies to develop the work and studies now being carried out, in particular within the United Nations Economic Commission for Europe;

express their willingness, with a view to improving international rail transport and with due respect for their rights and international commitments, to work towards the elimination of difficulties arising from disparities in existing international legal provisions governing the reciprocal railway transport of passengers and goods between their territories;

express the desire for intensification of the work being carried out by existing international organizations in the field of transport, especially that of the Inland Transport Committee of the United Nations Economic Commission for Europe, and express their intention to contribute thereto by their efforts;

consider that examination by the participating States of the possibility of their accession to the different conventions or to membership of international organizations specializing in transport matters, as well as their efforts to implement conventions when ratified, could contribute to the strengthening of their co-operation in this field.

Promotion of tourism

The participating States,

Aware of the contribution made by international tourism to the development of mutual understanding among peoples, to increased knowledge of other countries' achievements in various fields, as well as to economic, social and cultural progress,

Recognizing the interrelationship between the development of tourism and measures taken in other areas of economic activity,

express their intention to encourage increased tourism on both an individual and group basis in particular by:

—encouraging the improvement of the tourist infrastructure and co-operation in this field;

—encouraging the carrying out of joint tourist projects including technical co-operation, particularly where this is suggested by territorial proximity and the convergence of tourist interests;

—encouraging the exchange of information, including relevant laws and regulations, studies, data and documentation relating to tourism, and by improving statistics with a view to facilitating their comparability;

—dealing in a positive spirit with questions connected with the allocation of financial means for tourist travel abroad, having regard to their economic possibilities, as well as with those connected with the formalities required for such travel, taking into account other provisions on tourism adopted by the Conference;

—facilitating the activities of foreign travel agencies and passenger transport companies in the promotion of international tourism;

—encouraging tourism outside the high season;

—examining the possibilities of exchanging specialists and students in the field of tourism, with a view to improving their qualifications;

—promoting conferences and symposia on the planning and development of tourism;

consider it desirable to carry out in the appropriate international framework, and with the co-operation of the relevant national bodies, detailed studies on tourism, in particular:

—a comparative study on the status and activities of travel agencies as well as on ways and means of achieving better co-operation among them;

—a study of the problems raised by the seasonal concentration of vacations, with the ultimate objective of encouraging tourism outside peak periods;

—studies of the problems arising in areas where tourism has injured the environment;

consider also that interested parties might wish to study the following questions:

—uniformity of hotel classification; and

—tourist routes comprising two or more countries;

will endeavour, where possible, to ensure that the development of tourism does not injure the environment and the artistic, historic and cultural heritage in their respective countries;

will pursue their co-operation in the field of tourism bilaterally and multilaterally with a view to attaining the above objectives.

Economic and social aspects of migrant labour

The participating States,

Considering that the movements of migrant

workers in Europe have reached substantial proportions, and that they constitute an important economic, social and human factor for host countries as well as for countries of origin,

Recognizing that workers' migrations have also given rise to a number of economic, social, human and other problems in both the receiving countries and the countries of origin,

Taking due account of the activities of the competent international organizations, more particularly the International Labour Organisation, in this area,

are of the opinion that the problems arising bilaterally from the migration of workers in Europe as well as between the participating States should be dealt with by the parties directly concerned, in order to resolve these problems in their mutual interest, in the light of the concern of each State involved to take due account of the requirements resulting from its socio-economic situation, having regard to the obligation of each State to comply with the bilateral and multilateral agreements to which it is party, and with the following aims in view:

to encourage the efforts of the countries of origin directed towards increasing the possibilities of employment for their nationals in their own territories, in particular by developing economic co-operation appropriate for this purpose and suitable for the host countries and the countries of origin concerned;

to ensure, through collaboration between the host country and the country of origin, the conditions under which the orderly movement of workers might take place, while at the same time protecting their personal and social welfare and, if appropriate, to organize the recruitment of migrant workers and the provision of elementary language and vocational training;

to ensure equality of rights between migrant workers and nationals of the host countries with regard to conditions of employment and work and to social security, and to endeavour to ensure that migrant workers may enjoy satisfactory living conditions, especially housing conditions;

to endeavour to ensure, as far as possible, that migrant workers may enjoy the same opportunities as nationals of the host countries of finding other suitable employment in the event of unemployment;

to regard with favour the provision of vocational training to migrant workers and, as far as possible, free instruction in the language of the host country, in the framework of their employment;

to confirm the right of migrant workers to receive, as far as possible, regular information in their own language, covering both their country of origin and the host country;

to ensure that the children of migrant workers established in the host country have access to the education usually given there, under the same conditions as the children of that country and, furthermore, to permit them to receive supplementary education in their own language, national culture, history and geography;

to bear in mind that migrant workers, particularly those who have acquired qualifications, can by re-turning to their countries after a certain period of time help to remedy any deficiency of skilled labour in their country of origin;

to facilitate, as far as possible, the reuniting of migrant workers with their families;

to regard with favour the efforts of the countries of origin to attract the savings of migrant workers, with a view to increasing, within the framework of their economic development, appropriate opportunities for employment, thereby facilitating the reintegration of these workers on their return home.

Training of personnel

The participating States,

Conscious of the importance of the training and advanced training of professional staff and technicians for the economic development of every country,

declare themselves willing to encourage co-operation in this field notably by promoting exchange of information on the subject of institutions, programmes and methods of training and advanced training open to professional staff and technicians in the various sectors of economic activity and especially in those of management, public planning, agriculture and commercial and banking techniques;

consider that it is desirable to develop, under mutually acceptable conditions, exchanges of professional staff and technicians, particularly through training activities, of which it would be left to the competent and interested bodies in the participating States to discuss the modalities—duration, financing, education and qualification levels of potential participants;

declare themselves in favour of examining, through appropriate channels, the possibilities of co-operating on the organization and carrying out of vocational training on the job, more particularly in professions involving modern techniques.

QUESTIONS RELATING TO SECURITY AND CO-OPERATION IN THE MEDITERRANEAN

The participating States,

Conscious of the geographical, historical, cultural, economic and political aspects of their relationship with the non-participating Mediterranean States,

Convinced that security in Europe is to be considered in the broader context of world security and is closely linked with security in the Mediterranean area as a whole, and that accordingly the process of improving security should not be confined to Europe but should extend to other parts of the world, and in particular to the Mediterranean area,

Believing that the strengthening of security and the intensification of co-operation in Europe would stimulate positive processes in the Mediterranean region, and expressing their intention to contribute towards peace, security and justice in the region, in which ends the participating States and the non-participating Mediterranean States have a common interest,

Recognizing the importance of their mutual economic relations with the non-participating Mediterranean States, and conscious of their common interest in the further development of co-operation,

Noting with appreciation the interest expressed by the non-participating Mediterranean States in the Conference since its inception, and having duly taken their contributions into account,

Declare their intention:

—to promote the development of good-neighbourly relations with the non-participating Mediterranean States in conformity with the purposes and principles of the Charter of the United Nations, on which their relations are based, and with the United Nations Declaration on Principles of International Law concerning Friendly Relations and Co-operation among States and accordingly, in this context, to conduct their relations with the non-participating Mediterranean States in the spirit of the principles set forth in the Declaration on Principles Guiding Relations between Participating States;

—to seek, by further improving their relations with the non-participating Mediterranean States, to increase mutual confidence, so as to promote security and stability in the Mediterranean area as a whole;

—to encourage with the non-participating Mediterranean States the development of mutually beneficial co-operation in the various fields of economic activity, especially by expanding commercial exchanges, on the basis of a common awareness of the necessity for stability and progress in trade relations, of their mutual economic interests, and of differences in the levels of economic development, thereby promoting their economic advancement and well-being;

—to contribute to a diversified development of the economies of the non-participating Mediterranean countries, whilst taking due account of their national development objectives, and to co-operate with them, especially in the sectors of industry, science and technology, in their efforts to achieve a better utilization of their resources, thus promoting a more harmonious development of economic relations;

—to intensify their efforts and their co-operation on a bilateral and multilateral basis with the non-participating Mediterranean States directed towards the improvement of the environment of the Mediterranean, especially the safeguarding of the biological resources and ecological balance of the sea, by appropriate measures including the prevention and control of pollution; to this end, and in view of the present situation, to co-operate through competent international organizations and in particular within the United Nations Environment Programme (UNEP);

—to promote further contacts and co-operation with the non-participating Mediterranean States in other relevant fields.

In order to advance the objectives set forth above, the participating States also declare their intention of maintaining and amplifying the contacts and dialogue as initiated by the CSCE with the non-participating Mediterranean States to include all the States of the Mediterranean, with the purpose of contributing to peace, reducing armed forces in the region, strengthening security, lessening tensions in the region, and widening the scope of co-operation, ends in which all share a common interest, as well as with the purpose of defining further common objectives.

The participating States would seek, in the framework of their multilateral efforts, to encourage progress and appropriate initiatives and to proceed to an exchange of views on the attainment of the above purposes.

CO-OPERATION IN HUMANITARIAN AND OTHER FIELDS

The participating States,

Desiring to contribute to the strengthening of peace and understanding among peoples and to the spiritual enrichment of the human personality without distinction as to race, sex, language or religion,

Conscious that increased cultural and educational exchanges, broader dissemination of information, contacts between people, and the solution of humanitarian problems will contribute to the attainment of these aims,

Determined therefore to co-operate among themselves, irrespective of their political, economic and social systems, in order to create better conditions in the above fields, to develop and strengthen existing forms of co-operation and to work out new ways and means appropriate to these aims,

Convinced that this co-operation should take place in full respect for the principles guiding relations among participating States as set forth in the relevant document,

Have adopted the following:

1. Human Contacts

The participating States,

Considering the development of contacts to be an important element in the strengthening of friendly relations and trust among peoples,

Affirming, in relation to their present effort to improve conditions in this area, the importance they attach to humanitarian considerations,

Desiring in this spirit to develop, with the continuance of détente, further efforts to achieve continuing progress in this field

And conscious that the questions relevant hereto must be settled by the States concerned under mutually acceptable conditions,

Make it their aim to facilitate freer movement and contacts, individually and collectively, whether privately or officially, among persons, institutions and organizations of the participating States, and to contribute to the solution of the humanitarian problems that arise in that connexion,

Declare their readiness to these ends to take measures which they consider appropriate and to conclude agreements or arrangements among themselves, as may be needed, and

Express their intention now to proceed to the implementation of the following:

(a) Contacts and Regular Meetings on the Basis of Family Ties

In order to promote further development of contacts on the basis of family ties the participating States will favourably consider applications for travel with the purpose of allowing persons to enter or leave their territory temporarily, and on a regular basis if desired, in order to visit members of their families.

Applications for temporary visits to meet members of their families will be dealt with without distinction as to the country of origin or destination: existing requirements for travel documents and visas will be applied in this spirit. The preparation and issue of such documents and visas will be effected within reasonable time limits; cases of urgent necessity—such as serious illness or death—will be given priority treatment. They will take such steps as may be necessary to ensure that the fees for official travel documents and visas are acceptable.

They confirm that the presentation of an application concerning contacts on the basis of family ties will not modify the rights and obligations of the applicant or of members of his family.

(b) Reunification of Families

The participating States will deal in a positive and humanitarian spirit with the applications of persons who wish to be reunited with members of their family, with special attention being given to requests of an urgent character—such as requests submitted by persons who are ill or old.

They will deal with applications in this field as expeditiously as possible.

They will lower where necessary the fees charged in connexion with these applications to ensure that they are at a moderate level.

Applications for the purpose of family reunification which are not granted may be renewed at the appropriate level and will be reconsidered at reasonably short intervals by the authorities of the country of residence or destination, whichever is concerned; under such circumstances fees will be charged only when applications are granted.

Persons whose applications for family reunification are granted may bring with them or ship their household and personal effects; to this end the participating States will use all possibilities provided by existing regulations.

Until members of the same family are reunited meetings and contacts between them may take place in accordance with the modalities for contacts on the basis of family ties.

The participating States will support the efforts of Red Cross and Red Crescent Societies concerned with the problems of family reunification.

They confirm that the presentation of an application concerning family reunification will not modify the rights and obligations of the applicant or of members of his family.

The receiving participating State will take appropriate care with regard to employment for persons from other participating States who take up permanent residence in that State in connexion with family reunification with its citizens and see that they are afforded opportunities equal to those enjoyed by its own citizens for education, medical assistance and social security.

(c) Marriage between Citizens of Different States

The participating States will examine favourably and on the basis of humanitarian considerations requests for exit or entry permits from persons who have decided to marry a citizen from another participating State.

The processing and issuing of the documents required for the above purposes and for the marriage will be in accordance with the provisions accepted for family reunification.

In dealing with requests from couples from different participating States, once married, to enable them and the minor children of their marriage to transfer their permanent residence to a State in which either one is normally a resident, the participating States will also apply the provisions accepted for family reunification.

(d) Travel for Personal or Professional Reasons

The participating States intend to facilitate wider travel by their citizens for personal or professional reasons and to this end they intend in particular:

—gradually to simplify and to administer flexibly the procedures for exit and entry;

—to ease regulations concerning movement of citizens from the other participating States in their territory, with due regard to security requirements.

They will endeavour gradually to lower, where necessary, the fees for visas and official travel documents.

They intend to consider, as necessary, means—including, in so far as appropriate, the conclusion of multilateral or bilateral consular conventions or other relevant agreements or understandings—for the improvement of arrangements to provide consular assistance.

* * *

They confirm that religious faiths, institutions and organizations, practising within the constitutional framework of the participating States, and their representatives can, in the field of their activities, have contacts and meetings among themselves and exchange information.

(e) Improvement of Conditions for Tourism on an Individual or Collective Basis

The participating States consider that tourism contributes to a fuller knowledge of the life, culture and history of other countries, to the growth of understanding among peoples, to the improvement of contacts and to the broader use of leisure. They intend to promote the development of tourism, on an individual or collective basis, and, in particular, they intend:

—to promote visits to their respective countries by encouraging the provision of appropriate facilities and the simplification and expediting of necessary formalities relating to such visits;
—to increase, on the basis of appropriate agreements or arrangements where necessary, co-operation in the development of tourism, in particular by considering bilaterally possible ways to increase information relating to travel to other countries and to the reception and service of tourists, and other related questions of mutual interest.

(f) Meetings among Young People

The participating States intend to further the development of contacts and exchanges among young people by encouraging:

—increased exchanges and contacts on a short or long term basis among young people working, training or undergoing education through bilateral or multilateral agreements or regular programmes in all cases where it is possible;
—study by their youth organizations of the question of possible agreements relating to frameworks of multilateral youth co-operation;
—agreements or regular programmes relating to the organization of exchanges of students, of international youth seminars, of courses of professional training and foreign language study;
—the further development of youth tourism and the provision to this end of appropriate facilities;
—the development, where possible, of exchanges, contacts and co-operation on a bilateral or multilateral basis between their organizations which represent wide circles of young people working, training or undergoing education;
—awareness among youth of the importance of developing mutual understanding and of strengthening friendly relations and confidence among peoples.

(g) Sport

In order to expand existing links and co-operation in the field of sport the participating States will encourage contacts and exchanges of this kind, including sports meetings and competitions of all sorts, on the basis of the established international rules, regulations and practice.

(h) Expansion of Contacts

By way of further developing contacts among governmental institutions and non-governmental organizations and associations, including women's organizations, the participating States will facilitate the convening of meetings as well as travel by delegations, groups and individuals.

2. Information

The participating States,
Conscious of the need for an ever wider knowledge and understanding of the various aspects of life in other participating States,
Acknowledging the contribution of this process to the growth of confidence between peoples,
Desiring, with the development of mutual understanding between the participating States and with the further improvement of their relations, to continue further efforts towards progress in this field,
Recognizing the importance of the dissemination of information from the other participating States and of a better acquaintance with such information,
Emphasizing therefore the essential and influential role of the press, radio, television, cinema and news agencies and of the journalists working in these fields,
Make it their aim to facilitate the freer and wider dissemination of information of all kinds, to encourage co-operation in the field of information and the exchange of information with other countries, and to improve the conditions under which journalists from one participating State exercise their profession in another participating State, and
Express their intention in particular:

(a) Improvement of the Circulation of, Access to, and Exchange of Information

(i) Oral Information

—To facilitate the dissemination of oral information through the encouragement of lectures and lecture tours by personalities and specialists from the other participating States, as well as exchanges of opinions at round table meetings, seminars, symposia, summer schools, congresses and other bilateral and multilateral meetings.

(ii) Printed Information

—To facilitate the improvement of the dissemination, on their territory, of newspapers and printed publications, periodical and non-periodical, from the other participating States. For this purpose:

they will encourage their competent firms and organizations to conclude agreements and contracts designed gradually to increase the quantities and the number of titles of newspapers and publications imported from the other participating States. These agreements and contracts should in particular mention the speediest conditions of delivery and the use of the normal channels existing in each country for the distribution of its own publications and newspapers, as well as forms and means of payment agreed between the parties making it possible to achieve the objectives aimed at by these agreements and contracts;
where necessary, they will take appropriate measures to achieve the above objectives and to implement the provisions contained in the agreements and contracts.

—To contribute to the improvement of access by the public to periodical and non-periodical printed publications imported on the bases indicated above. In particular:

they will encourage an increase in the number of places where these publications are on sale;
they will facilitate the availability of these periodical publications during congresses, conferences,

official visits and other international events and to tourists during the season;

they will develop the possibilities for taking out subscriptions according to the modalities particular to each country;

they will improve the opportunities for reading and borrowing these publications in large public libraries and their reading rooms as well as in university libraries.

They intend to improve the possibilities for acquaintance with bulletins of official information issued by diplomatic missions and distributed by those missions on the basis of arrangements acceptable to the interested parties.

(iii) *Filmed and Broadcast Information*

—To promote the improvement of the dissemination of filmed and broadcast information. To this end:

they will encourage the wider showing and broadcasting of a greater variety of recorded and filmed information from the other participating States, illustrating the various aspects of life in their countries and received on the basis of such agreements or arrangements as may be necessary between the organizations and firms directly concerned;

they will facilitate the import by competent organizations and firms of recorded audio-visual material from the other participating States.

The participating States note the expansion in the dissemination of information broadcast by radio, and express the hope for the continuation of this process, so as to meet the interest of mutual understanding among peoples and the aims set forth by this Conference.

(b) Co-operation in the Field of Information

—To encourage co-operation in the field of information on the basis of short or long term agreements or arrangements. In particular:

they will favour increased co-operation among mass media organizations, including press agencies, as well as among publishing houses and organizations;

they will favour co-operation among public or private, national or international radio and television organizations, in particular through the exchange of both live and recorded radio and television programmes, and through the joint production and the broadcasting and distribution of such programmes;

they will encourage meetings and contacts both between journalists' organizations and between journalists from the participating States;

they will view favourably the possibilities of arrangements between periodical publications as well as between newspapers from the participating States, for the purpose of exchanging and publishing articles;

they will encourage the exchange of technical information as well as the organization of joint research and meetings devoted to the exchange of experience and views between experts in the field of the press, radio and television.

(c) Improvement of Working Conditions for Journalists

The participating States, desiring to improve the conditions under which journalists from one participating State exercise their profession in another participating State, intend in particular to:

—examine in a favourable spirit and within a suitable and reasonable time scale requests from journalists for visas;

—grant to permanently accredited journalists of the participating States, on the basis of arrangements, multiple entry and exit visas for specified periods;

—facilitate the issue to accredited journalists of the participating States of permits for stay in their country of temporary residence and, if and when these are necessary, of other official papers which it is appropriate for them to have;

—ease, on a basis of reciprocity, procedures for arranging travel by journalists of the participating States in the country where they are exercising their profession, and to provide progressively greater opportunities for such travel, subject to the observance of regulations relating to the existence of areas closed for security reasons;

—ensure that requests by such journalists for such travel receive, in so far as possible, an expeditious response, taking into account the time scale of the request;

—increase the opportunities for journalists of the participating States to communicate personally with their sources, including organizations and official institutions;

—grant to journalists of the participating States the right to import, subject only to its being taken out again, the technical equipment (photographic, cinematographic, tape recorder, radio and television) necessary for the exercise of their profession;*

—enable journalists of the other participating States, whether permanently or temporarily accredited, to transmit completely, normally and rapidly by means recognized by the participating States to the information organs which they represent, the results of their professional activity, including tape recordings and undeveloped film, for the purpose of

---

*While recognizing that appropriate local personnel are employed by foreign journalists in many instances, the participating States note that the above provisions would be applied, subject to the observance of the appropriate rules, to persons from the other participating States, who are regularly and professionally engaged as technicians, photographers or cameramen of the press, radio, television or cinema. [Footnote in original.]

publication or of broadcasting on the radio or television.

The participating States reaffirm that the legitimate pursuit of their professional activity will neither render journalists liable to expulsion nor otherwise penalize them. If an accredited journalist is expelled, he will be informed of the reasons for this act and may submit an application for re-examination of his case.

3. Co-operation and Exchanges in the Field of Culture

The participating States,

Considering that cultural exchanges and co-operation contribute to a better comprehension among people and among peoples, and thus promote a lasting understanding among States,

Confirming the conclusions already formulated in this field at the multilateral level, particularly at the Intergovernmental Conference on Cultural Policies in Europe, organized by UNESCO in Helsinki in June 1972, where interest was manifested in the active participation of the broadest possible social groups in an increasingly diversified cultural life,

Desiring, with the development of mutual confidence and the further improvement of relations between the participating States, to continue further efforts toward progress in this field,

Disposed in this spirit to increase substantially their cultural exchanges, with regard both to persons and to cultural works, and to develop among them an active co-operation, both at the bilateral and the multilateral level, in all the fields of culture,

Convinced that such a development of their mutual relations will contribute to the enrichment of the respective cultures, while respecting the originality of each, as well as to the reinforcement among them of a consciousness of common values, while continuing to develop cultural co-operation with other countries of the world,

Declare that they jointly set themselves the following objectives:

(a) to develop the mutual exchange of information with a view to a better knowledge of respective cultural achievements,

(b) to improve the facilities for the exchange and for the dissemination of cultural property,

(c) to promote access by all to respective cultural achievements,

(d) to develop contacts and co-operation among persons active in the field of culture,

(e) to seek new fields and forms of cultural co-operation,

Thus *give expression to* their common will to take progressive, coherent and long-term action in order to achieve the objectives of the present declaration; and

Express their intention now to proceed to the implementation of the following:

Extension of Relations

To expand and improve at the various levels co-operation and links in the field of culture, in particular by:

—concluding, where appropriate, agreements on a bilateral or multilateral basis, providing for the extension of relations among competent State institutions and non-governmental organizations in the field of culture, as well as among people engaged in cultural activities, taking into account the need both for flexibility and the fullest possible use of existing agreements, and bearing in mind that agreements and also other arrangements constitute important means of developing cultural co-operation and exchanges;

—contributing to the development of direct communication and co-operation among relevant State institutions and non-governmental organizations, including, where necessary, such communication and co-operation carried out on the basis of special agreements and arrangements;

—encouraging direct contacts and communications among persons engaged in cultural activities, including, where necessary, such contacts and communications carried out on the basis of special agreements and arrangements.

Mutual Knowledge

Within their competence to adopt, on a bilateral and multilateral level, appropriate measures which would give their peoples a more comprehensive and complete mutual knowledge of their achievements in the various fields of culture, and among them:

—to examine jointly, if necessary with the assistance of appropriate international organizations, the possible creation in Europe and the structure of a bank of cultural data, which would collect information from the participating countries and make it available to its correspondents on their request, and to convene for this purpose a meeting of experts from interested States;

—to consider, if necessary in conjunction with appropriate international organizations, ways of compiling in Europe an inventory of documentary films of a cultural or scientific nature from the participating States;

—to encourage more frequent book exhibitions and to examine the possibility of organizing periodically in Europe a large-scale exhibition of books from the participating States;

—to promote the systematic exchange, between the institutions concerned and publishing houses, of catalogues of available books as well as of pre-publication material which will include, as far as possible, all forthcoming publications; and also to promote the exchange of material between firms publishing encyclopaedias, with a view to improving the presentation of each country;

—to examine jointly questions of expanding and improving exchanges of information in the various fields of culture, such as theatre, music, library work as well as the conservation and restoration of cultural property.

Exchanges and Dissemination

To contribute to the improvement of facilities for exchanges and the dissemination of cultural property, by appropriate means, in particular by:

—studying the possibilities for harmonizing and reducing the charges relating to international commercial exchanges of books and other cultural materials, and also for new means of insuring works of art in foreign exhibitions and for reducing the risks of damage or loss to which these works are exposed by their movement;

—facilitating the formalities of customs clearance, in good time for programmes of artistic events, of the works of art, materials and accessories appearing on lists agreed upon by the organizers of these events;

—encouraging meetings among representatives of competent organizations and relevant firms to examine measures within their field of activity—such as the simplification of orders, time limits for sending supplies and modalities of payment—which might facilitate international commercial exchanges of books;

—promoting the loan and exchange of films among their film institutes and film libraries;

—encouraging the exchange of information among interested parties concerning events of a cultural character foreseen in the participating States, in fields where this is most appropriate, such as music, theatre and the plastic and graphic arts, with a view to contributing to the compilation and publication of a calendar of such events, with the assistance, where necessary, of the appropriate international organizations;

—encouraging a study of the impact which the foreseeable development, and a possible harmonization among interested parties, of the technical means used for the dissemination of culture might have on the development of cultural co-operation and exchanges, while keeping in view the preservation of the diversity and originality of their respective cultures;

—encouraging, in the way they deem appropriate, within their cultural policies, the further development of interest in the cultural heritage of the other participating States, conscious of the merits and the value of each culture;

—endeavouring to ensure the full and effective application of the international agreements and conventions on copyrights and on circulation of cultural property to which they are party or to which they may decide in the future to become party.

Access

To promote fuller mutual access by all to the achievements—works, experiences and performing arts—in the various fields of culture of their countries, and to that end to make the best possible efforts, in accordance with their competence, more particularly:

—to promote wider dissemination of books and artistic works, in particular by such means as:

facilitating, while taking full account of the international copyright conventions to which they are party, international contacts and communications between authors and publishing houses as well as other cultural institutions, with a view to a more complete mutual access to cultural achievements;

recommending that, in determining the size of editions, publishing houses take into account also the demand from the other participating States, and that rights of sale in other participating States be granted, where possible, to several sales organizations of the importing countries, by agreement between interested partners;

encouraging competent organizations and relevant firms to conclude agreements and contracts and contributing, by this means, to a gradual increase in the number and diversity of works by authors from the other participating States available in the original and in translation in their libraries and bookshops;

promoting, where deemed appropriate, an increase in the number of sales outlets where books by authors from the other participating States, imported in the original on the basis of agreements and contracts, and in translation, are for sale;

promoting, on a wider scale, the translation of works in the sphere of literature and other fields of cultural activity, produced in the languages of the other participating States, especially from the less widely-spoken languages, and the publication and dissemination of the translated works by such measures as:

encouraging more regular contacts between interested publishing houses;

developing their efforts in the basic and advanced training of translators;

encouraging, by appropriate means, the publishing houses of their countries to publish translations;

facilitating the exchange between publishers and interested institutions of lists of books which might be translated;

promoting between their countries the professional activity and co-operation of translators;

carrying out joint studies on ways of further promoting translations and their dissemination;

improving and expanding exchanges of books, bibliographies and catalogue cards between libraries;

—to envisage other appropriate measures which would permit, where necessary by mutual agreement among interested parties, the facilitation of access to their respective cultural achievements, in particular in the field of books;

—to contribute by appropriate means to the wider use of the mass media in order to improve mutual acquaintance with the cultural life of each;

—to seek to develop the necessary conditions for migrant workers and their families to preserve their links with their national culture, and also to adapt themselves to their new cultural environment;

—to encourage the competent bodies and enterprises to make a wider choice and effect wider distribution of full-length and documentary films from the other participating States, and to promote more frequent non-commercial showings, such as premières, film weeks and festivals, giving due consideration to films from countries whose cinematographic works are less well known;

—to promote, by appropriate means, the extension of opportunities for specialists from the other participating States to work with materials of a cultural character from film and audio-visual archives, within the framework of the existing rules for work on such archival materials;

—to encourage a joint study by interested bodies, where appropriate with the assistance of the competent international organizations, of the expediency and the conditions for the establishment of a repertory of their recorded television programmes of a cultural nature, as well as of the means of viewing them rapidly in order to facilitate their selection and possible acquisition.

Contacts and Co-operation

To contribute, by appropriate means, to the development of contacts and co-operation in the various fields of culture, especially among creative artists and people engaged in cultural activities, in particular by making efforts to:

—promote for persons active in the field of culture, travel and meetings including, where necessary, those carried out on the basis of agreements, contracts or other special arrangements and which are relevant to their cultural co-operation;

—encourage in this way contacts among creative and performing artists and artistic groups with a view to their working together, making known their works in other participating States or exchanging views on topics relevant to their common activity;

—encourage, where necessary through appropriate arrangements, exchanges of trainees and specialists and the granting of scholarships for basic and advanced training in various fields of culture such as the arts and architecture, museums and libraries, literary studies and translation, and contribute to the creation of favourable conditions of reception in their respective institutions;

—encourage the exchange of experience in the training of organizers of cultural activities as well as of teachers and specialists in fields such as theatre, opera, ballet, music and fine arts;

—continue to encourage the organization of international meetings among creative artists, especially young creative artists, on current questions of artistic and literary creation which are of interest for joint study;

—study other possibilities for developing exchanges and co-operation among persons active in the field of culture, with a view to a better mutual knowledge of the cultural life of the participating States.

Fields and Forms of Co-operation

To encourage the search for new fields and forms of cultural co-operation, to these ends contributing to the conclusion among interested parties, where necessary, of appropriate agreements and arrange-

ments, and in this context to promote:

—joint studies regarding cultural policies, in particular in their social aspects, and as they relate to planning, town-planning, educational and environmental policies, and the cultural aspects of tourism;

—the exchange of knowledge in the realm of cultural diversity, with a view to contributing thus to a better understanding by interested parties of such diversity where it occurs;

—the exchange of information, and as may be appropriate, meetings of experts, the elaboration and the execution of research programmes and projects, as well as their joint evaluation, and the dissemination of the results, on the subjects indicated above;

—such forms of cultural co-operation and the development of such joint projects as:

international events in the fields of the plastic and graphic arts, cinema, theatre, ballet, music, folklore, etc.; book fairs and exhibitions, joint performances of operatic and dramatic works, as well as performances given by soloists, instrumental ensembles, orchestras, choirs and other artistic groups, including those composed of amateurs, paying due attention to the organization of international cultural youth events and the exchange of young artists;

the inclusion of works by writers and composers from the other participating States in the repertoires of soloists and artistic ensembles;

the preparation, translation and publication of articles, studies and monographs, as well as of low-cost books and of artistic and literary collections, suited to making better known respective cultural achievements, envisaging for this purpose meetings among experts and representatives of publishing houses;

the co-production and the exchange of films and of radio and television programmes, by promoting, in particular, meetings among producers, technicians and representatives of the public authorities with a view to working out favourable conditions for the execution of specific joint projects and by encouraging, in the field of co-production, the establishment of international filming teams;

the organization of competitions for architects and town-planners, bearing in mind the possible implementation of the best projects and the formation, where possible, of international teams;

the implementation of joint projects for conserving, restoring and showing to advantage works of art, historical and archaeological monuments and sites of cultural interest, with the help, in appropriate cases, of international organizations of a governmental or non-governmental character as well as of private institutions—competent and active in these fields—envisaging for this purpose:

periodic meetings of experts of the interested parties to elaborate the necessary proposals, while bearing in mind the need to consider these questions in a wider social and economic context;

the publication in appropriate periodicals of articles designed to make known and to compare, among the participating States, the most significant achievements and innovations;

a joint study with a view to the improvement and possible harmonization of the different systems used to inventory and catalogue the historical monuments and places of cultural interest in their countries;

the study of the possibilities for organizing international courses for the training of specialists in different disciplines relating to restoration.

* * *

National minorities or regional cultures. The participating States, recognizing the contribution that national minorities or regional cultures can make to co-operation among them in various fields of culture, intend, when such minorities or cultures exist within their territory, to facilitate this contribution, taking into account the legitimate interests of their members.

4. Co-operation and Exchanges in the Field of Education

The participating States,

Conscious that the development of relations of an international character in the fields of education and science contributes to a better mutual understanding and is to the advantage of all peoples as well as to the benefit of future generations,

Prepared to facilitate, between organizations, institutions and persons engaged in education and science, the further development of exchanges of knowledge and experience as well as of contacts, on the basis of special arrangements where these are necessary,

Desiring to strengthen the links among educational and scientific establishments and also to encourage their co-operation in sectors of common interest, particularly where the levels of knowledge and resources require efforts to be concerted internationally, and

Convinced that progress in these fields should be accompanied and supported by a wider knowledge of foreign languages,

Express to these ends their intention in particular:

(a) Extension of Relations

To expand and improve at the various levels co-operation and links in the fields of education and science, in particular by:

—concluding, where appropriate, bilateral or multilateral agreements providing for co-operation and exchanges among State institutions, non-governmental bodies and persons engaged in activities in education and science, bearing in mind the need both for flexibility and the fuller use of existing agreements and arrangements;

—promoting the conclusion of direct arrangements between universities and other institutions of higher education and research, in the framework of agreements between governments where appropriate;

—encouraging among persons engaged in education and science direct contacts and communications, including those based on special agreements or arrangements where these are appropriate.

(b) Access and Exchanges

To improve access, under mutually acceptable conditions, for students, teachers and scholars of the participating States to each other's educational, cultural and scientific institutions, and to intensify exchanges among these institutions in all areas of common interest, in particular by:

—increasing the exchange of information on facilities for study and courses open to foreign participants, as well as on the conditions under which they will be admitted and received;

—facilitating travel between the participating States by scholars, teachers and students for purposes of study, teaching and research as well as for improving knowledge of each other's educational, cultural and scientific achievements;

—encouraging the award of scholarships for study, teaching and research in their countries to scholars, teachers and students of other participating States;

—establishing, developing or encouraging programmes providing for the broader exchange of scholars, teachers and students, including the organization of symposia, seminars and collaborative projects, and the exchanges of educational and scholarly information such as university publications and materials from libraries;

—promoting the efficient implementation of such arrangements and programmes by providing scholars, teachers and students in good time with more detailed information about their placing in universities and institutes and the programmes envisaged for them; by granting them the opportunity to use relevant scholarly, scientific and open archival materials; and by facilitating their travel within the receiving State for the purpose of study or research as well as in the form of vacation tours on the basis of the usual procedures;

—promoting a more exact assessment of the problems of comparison and equivalence of academic degrees and diplomas by fostering the exchange of information on the organization, duration and content of studies, the comparison of methods of assessing levels of knowledge and academic qualifications, and, where feasible, arriving at the mutual recognition of academic degrees and diplomas either through governmental agreements, where necessary, or direct arrangements between universities and other institutions of higher learning and research;

—recommending, moreover, to the appropriate international organizations that they should intensify their efforts to reach a generally acceptable solution to the problems of comparison and equivalence between academic degrees and diplomas.

(c) Science

Within their competence to broaden and improve co-operation and exchanges in the field of science, in particular:

To increase, on a bilateral or multilateral basis, the exchange and dissemination of scientific information and documentation by such means as:

—making this information more widely available to scientists and research workers of the other participating States through, for instance, participation in international information-sharing programmes or through other appropriate arrangements;

—broadening and facilitating the exchange of samples and other scientific materials used particularly for fundamental research in the fields of natural sciences and medicine;

—inviting scientific institutions and universities to keep each other more fully and regularly informed about their current and contemplated research work in fields of common interest.

To facilitate the extension of communications and direct contacts between universities, scientific institutions and associations as well as among scientists and research workers, including those based where necessary on special agreements or arrangements, by such means as:

—further developing exchanges of scientists and research workers and encouraging the organization of preparatory meetings or working groups on research topics of common interest;

—encouraging the creation of joint teams of scientists to pursue research projects under arrangements made by the scientific institutions of several countries;

—assisting the organization and successful functioning of international conferences and seminars and participation in them by their scientists and research workers;

—furthermore envisaging, in the near future, a "Scientific Forum" in the form of a meeting of leading personalities in science from the participating States to discuss interrelated problems of common interest concerning current and future developments in science, and to promote the expansion of contacts, communications and the exchange of information between scientific institutions and among scientists;

—foreseeing, at an early date, a meeting of experts representing the participating States and their national scientific institutions, in order to prepare such a "Scientific Forum" in consultation with appropriate international organizations, such as UNESCO and the ECE;

—considering in due course what further steps might be taken with respect to the "Scientific Forum".

To develop in the field of scientific research, on a bilateral or multilateral basis, the co-ordination of programmes carried out in the participating States and the organization of joint programmes, especially in the areas mentioned below, which may involve the combined efforts of scientists and in certain cases the use of costly or unique equipment. The list of subjects in these areas is illustrative; and specific projects would have to be determined subsequently by the potential partners in the participating States, taking account of the contribution which could be made by appropriate international organizations and scientific institutions:

—*exact and natural sciences*, in particular fundamental research in such fields as mathematics, physics, theoretical physics, geophysics, chemistry, biology, ecology and astronomy;

—*medicine*, in particular basic research into cancer and cardiovascular diseases, studies on the diseases endemic in the developing countries, as well as medico-social research with special emphasis on occupational diseases, the rehabilitation of the handicapped and the care of mothers, children and the elderly;

—*the humanities and social sciences*, such as history, geography, philosophy, psychology, pedagogical research, linguistics, sociology, the legal, political and economic sciences; comparative studies on social, socio-economic and cultural phenomena which are of common interest to the participating States, especially the problems of human environment and urban development; and scientific studies on the methods of conserving and restoring monuments and works of art.

(d) Foreign Languages and Civilizations

To encourage the study of foreign languages and civilizations as an important means of expanding communication among peoples for their better acquaintance with the culture of each country, as well as for the strengthening of international co-operation; to this end to stimulate, within their competence, the further development and improvement of foreign language teaching and the diversification of choice of languages taught at various levels, paying due attention to less widely-spread or studied languages, and in particular:

—to intensify co-operation aimed at improving the teaching of foreign languages through exchanges of information and experience concerning the development and application of effective modern teaching methods and technical aids, adapted to the needs of different categories of students, including methods of accelerated teaching; and to consider the possibility of conducting, on a bilateral or multilateral basis, studies of new methods of foreign language teaching;

—to encourage co-operation between institutions concerned, on a bilateral or multilateral basis, aimed at exploiting more fully the resources of modern educational technology in language teaching, for example through comparative studies by their specialists and, where agreed, through exchanges or transfers of audio-visual materials, of materials used for preparing textbooks, as well as of information about new types of technical equipment used for teaching languages;

—to promote the exchange of information on the experience acquired in the training of language teachers and to intensify exchanges on a bilateral basis of language teachers and students as well as to facilitate their participation in summer courses in languages and civilizations, wherever these are organized;

—to encourage co-operation among experts in the field of lexicography with the aim of defining the necessary terminological equivalents, particularly in the scientific and technical disciplines, in order to facilitate relations among scientific institutions and specialists;

—to promote the wider spread of foreign language study among the different types of secondary education establishments and greater possibilities of choice between an increased number of European languages; and in this context to consider, wherever appropriate, the possibilities for developing the recruitment and training of teachers as well as the organization of the student groups required;

—to favour, in higher education, a wider choice in the languages offered to language students and greater opportunities for other students to study various foreign languages; also to facilitate, where desirable, the organization of courses in languages and civilizations, on the basis of special arrangements as necessary, to be given by foreign lecturers, particularly from European countries having less widely-spread or studied languages;

—to promote, within the framework of adult education, the further development of specialized programmes, adapted to various needs and interests, for teaching foreign languages to their own inhabitants and the languages of host countries to interested adults from other countries; in this context to encourage interested institutions to co-operate, for example, in the elaboration of programmes for teaching by radio and television and by accelerated methods, and also, where desirable, in the definition of study objectives for such programmes, with a view to arriving at comparable levels of language proficiency;

—to encourage the association, where appropriate, of the teaching of foreign languages with the study of the corresponding civilizations and also to make further efforts to stimulate interest in the study of foreign languages, including relevant out-of-class activities.

(e) Teaching Methods

To promote the exchange of experience, on a bilateral or multilateral basis, in teaching methods at all levels of education, including those used in permanent and adult education, as well as the exchange of teaching materials, in particular by:

—further developing various forms of contacts and co-operation in the different fields of pedagogical science, for example through comparative or joint studies carried out by interested institutions or through exchanges of information on the results of teaching experiments;

—intensifying exchanges of information on teaching methods used in various educational systems and on results of research into the processes by which pupils and students acquire knowledge, taking account of relevant experience in different types of specialized education;

—facilitating exchanges of experience concerning the organization and functioning of education intended for adults and recurrent education, the relationships between these and other forms and levels of education, as well as concerning the means of adapting education, including vocational and technical training, to the needs of economic and social development in their countries;

—encouraging exchanges of experience in the education of youth and adults in international understanding, with particular reference to those major problems of mankind whose solution calls for a common approach and wider international co-operation;

—encouraging exchanges of teaching materials—including school textbooks, having in mind the possibility of promoting mutual knowledge and facilitating the presentation of each country in such books—as well as exchanges of information on technical innovations in the field of education.

* * *

National minorities or regional cultures. The participating States, recognizing the contribution that national minorities or regional cultures can make to co-operation among them in various fields of education, intend, when such minorities or cultures exist within their territory, to facilitate this contribution, taking into account the legitimate interests of their members.

FOLLOW-UP TO THE CONFERENCE

The participating States,

Having considered and evaluated the progress made at the Conference on Security and Co-operation in Europe,

Considering further that, within the broader context of the world, the Conference is an important part of the process of improving security and developing co-operation in Europe and that its results will contribute significantly to this process,

Intending to implement the provisions of the Final Act of the Conference in order to give full effect to its results and thus to further the process of improving security and developing co-operation in Europe,

Convinced that, in order to achieve the aims sought by the Conference, they should make further unilateral, bilateral and multilateral efforts and continue, in the appropriate forms set forth below, the multilateral process initiated by the Conference,

1. *Declare their resolve*, in the period following the Conference, to pay due regard to and implement the provisions of the Final Act of the Conference:

(a) unilaterally, in all cases which lend themselves to such action;

(b) bilaterally, by negotiations with other participating States;

(c) multilaterally, by meetings of experts of the participating States, and also within the framework of existing international organizations, such as the United Nations Economic Commission for Europe and UNESCO, with regard to educational, scientific and cultural co-operation;

2. *Declare furthermore their resolve* to continue the multilateral process initiated by the Conference:

(a) by proceeding to a thorough exchange of views both on the implementation of the provisions of the Final Act and of the tasks defined by the Conference, as well as, in the context of the questions dealt with by the latter, on the deepening of their mutual relations, the improvement of security and the development of co-operation in Europe, and the development of the process of détente in the future;

(b) by organizing to these ends meetings among their representatives, beginning with a meeting at the level of representatives appointed by the Ministers of Foreign Affairs. This meeting will define the appropriate modalities for the holding of other meetings which could include further similar meetings and the possibility of a new Conference;

3. The first of the meetings indicated above will be held at Belgrade in 1977. A preparatory meeting to organize this meeting will be held at Belgrade on 15 June 1977. The preparatory meeting will decide on the date, duration, agenda and other modalities of the meeting of representatives appointed by the Ministers of Foreign Affairs;

4. The rules of procedure, the working methods and the scale of distribution for the expenses of the Conference will, *mutatis mutandis*, be applied to the meetings envisaged in paragraphs 1 (c), 2 and 3 above. All the above-mentioned meetings will be held in the participating States in rotation. The services of a technical secretariat will be provided by the host country.

The original of this Final Act, drawn up in English, French, German, Italian, Russian and Spanish, will be transmitted to the Government of the Republic of Finland, which will retain it in its archives. Each of the participating States will receive from the Government of the Republic of Finland a true copy of this Final Act.

The text of this Final Act will be published in each participating State, which will disseminate it and make it known as widely as possible.

The Government of the Republic of Finland is requested to transmit to the Secretary-General of the United Nations the text of this Final Act, which is not eligible for registration under Article 102 of the Charter of the United Nations, with a view to its circulation to all the members of the Organization as an official document of the United Nations.[2]

The Government of the Republic of Finland is also requested to transmit the text of this Final Act to the Director-General of UNESCO and to the Executive Secretary of the United Nations Economic Commission for Europe.

Wherefore, the undersigned High Representatives of the participating States, mindful of the high political significance which they attach to the results of the Conference, and declaring their determination to act in accordance with the provisions contained in the above texts, have subscribed their signatures below:[3]

The Federal Republic of Germany:
HELMUT SCHMIDT, *Federal Chancellor*

The German Democratic Republic:
ERICH HONECKER, *First Secretary of the Central Committee of the Socialist Unity Party of Germany*

The United States of America:
GERALD R. FORD, *President of the United States of America*

The Republic of Austria:
BRUNO KREISKY, *Federal Chancellor*

The Kingdom of Belgium:
LEO TINDEMANS, *Prime Minister*

The People's Republic of Bulgaria:
TODOR JIVKOV, *First Secretary, Central Committee of the Communist Party of Bulgaria and President of the Council of State of the People's Republic of Bulgaria*

Canada:
PIERRE ELLIOTT TRUDEAU, *Prime Minister*

The Republic of Cyprus:
His Beatitude Archbishop MAKARIOS III, *President of the Republic of Cyprus*

Denmark:
ANKER JORGENSEN, *Prime Minister*

Spain:
CARLOS ARIAS NAVARRO, *Head of the Government*

The Republic of Finland:
URHO KEKKONEN, *President of the Republic*

The French Republic:
VALERY GISCARD D'ESTAING

The United Kingdom of Great Britain and Northern Ireland:
The Rt. Hon. HAROLD WILSON, O.B.E., M.P., F.R.S., *First Lord of the Treasury and Prime Minister of the United Kingdom of Great Britain and Northern Ireland*

The Hellenic Republic:
CONSTANTIN CARAMANLIS, *Prime Minister*

---

[2] Journal no. 80/*bis* of the Co-ordinating Committee of the Conference on Security and Cooperation in Europe, July 18, 1975, reported that the delegate of Finland had on that day informed the committee of the intention of his government to send the following letter to the Secretary General of the United Nations:

"SIR, I have the honour to inform you that the High Representatives of the States participating in the Conference on Security and Co-operation in Europe have requested the Government of the Republic of Finland to transmit to you the text of the Final Act of the Conference signed at Helsinki on [1 August 1975].

"I have also been asked to request you, Mr. Secretary General, to arrange for the circulation of this Final Act to Member States of the Organization as an official document of the United Nations, and to draw your attention to the fact that this Final Act is not eligible, in whole or in part, for registration with the Secretariat under Article 102 of the Charter of the United Nations, as would be the case were it a matter of a treaty or international agreement, under the aforesaid Article.

"Accept, Sir, the assurance of my highest consideration."

[3] The final act was signed in alphabetical order according to the French spelling of the names of the countries.

The Hungarian People's Republic:
JANOS KADAR, *First Secretary of the Central Committee of the Hungarian Socialist Workers' Party, Member of the Presidential Council of the Hungarian People's Republic*

Ireland:
LIAM COSGRAVE, *Prime Minister*

Iceland:
GEIR HALLGRIMSSON, *Prime Minister*

The Italian Republic:
ALDO MORO, *Prime Minister of the Italian Republic and in his capacity as President in office of the Council of the European Communities*

The Principality of Liechtenstein:
WALTER KIEBER, *Head of Government*

The Grand Duchy of Luxembourg:
GASTON THORN, *Prime Minister, Minister for Foreign Affairs*

The Republic of Malta:
DOM MINTOFF, *Prime Minister, Minister for Commonwealth and Foreign Affairs*

The Principality of Monaco:
ANDRE SAINT-MLEUX, *Minister of State, President of the Government Council, Representing H.S.H. the Prince of Monaco*

Norway:
TRYGVE BRATTELI, *Prime Minister*

The Kingdom of the Netherlands:
J.M. DEN UYL, *Prime Minister*

Polish People's Republic:
EDWARD GIEREK, *First Secretary of the Central Committee of the Polish United Worker's Party*

Portugal:
FRANCISCO DA COSTA GOMES, *President of the Republic*

The Socialist Republic of Romania:
NICOLAE CEAUSESCU, *President of the Socialist Republic of Romania*

San Marino:
GIAN LUIGI BERTI, *Secretary of State for Foreign and Political Affairs*

The Holy See:
Son Excellence Monseigneur AGOSTINO CASAROLI, *Secretary of the Council for Church Public Affairs, Special Delegate of His Holiness Pope Paul VI*

Sweden:
OLOF PALME, *Prime Minister*

The Swiss Confederation:
PIERRE GRABER, *President of the Confederation, Head of the Federal Political Department*

The Czechoslovak Socialist Republic:
GUSTAV HUSAK, *Secretary-General of the Communist Party of Czechoslovakia and President of the Czechoslovak Socialist Republic*

The Republic of Turkey:
SULEYMAN DEMIREL, *Prime Minister*

The Union of Soviet Socialist Republics:
L. BREJNEV, *General Secretary of the CC of the CPSU*

The Socialist Federal Republic of Jugoslavia:
JOSIP BROZ TITO, *President of the Socialist Federal Republic of Jugoslavia*

61 (August 21, 1975)
Draft Convention on Environmental Warfare Tabled in Geneva Disarmament Committee

On August 21 the U.S. and U.S.S.R. Representatives to the Conference of the Committee on Disarmament (CCD) at Geneva tabled, in parallel, identical draft texts of a Convention on the Prohibition of Military or Any Other·Hostile Use of Environmental Modification Techniques.[1] Following is a statement made before the conference that day by U.S. Representative Joseph Martin, Jr., together with the text of the draft convention.

U.S. delegation press release (Geneva) dated August 21

STATEMENT BY AMBASSADOR MARTIN

The United States today is tabling a draft Convention on the Prohibition of Military or Any Other Hostile Use of Environmental Modification Techniques. A parallel draft is being tabled by the delegation of the Soviet Union. We are presenting the draft convention as a basis for consideration by all governments and for negotiation in the CCD.

Previous discussions in the U.N. General Assembly, in the series of bilateral meetings between representatives of the Soviet Union and my government, and here in this committee, have indicated clearly the serious concern felt by many states, including my own, over the potential catastrophic dangers to mankind if environmental modification techniques were to be developed as weapons

of war. Comments made by the experts at our recent informal meetings on this subject underline the need to develop effective measures to control military or any other hostile use of those techniques having major adverse effects before such techniques can be developed and perfected.

In the past few weeks, various delegations have provided data on the existing state of the art in environmental modification and have hypothesized about the nature of possible future techniques. From these data we can see that, while environmental warfare is not practical on a militarily significant scale at present, understanding and technology in the field are increasing. Significant advances may be possible in the course of time. Some scientists believe, for example, that methods might be developed for intentionally and selectively effecting harmful changes in the composition of the earth's atmosphere or in its climate, or for causing floods or drought. An ambitious, incautious, or desperate state might then resort to the use of such techniques. At present there is an opportunity to prohibit such use. We should seize that opportunity.

The U.S. delegation believes that development of a generally accepted convention along the lines of the draft we are tabling today would best allow us to accomplish the objectives of the General Assembly, the CCD, and of the U.S.-U.S.S.R. joint statement of July 3, 1974. At the same time it would not discourage the development of peaceful and beneficial environmental modification techniques.

The formulation of a convention imposing

---

[1] The draft text is the result of bilateral talks held at Moscow Nov. 1–5, 1974, at Washington Feb. 24–Mar. 5, 1975, and at Geneva June 16–20, 1975, pursuant to the U.S.-U.S.S.R. joint statement of July 3, 1974.

restraints on environmental warfare presented difficult and complex problems of definition. This is the case because the development of environmental modification techniques is still at an early stage and a treaty will necessarily have to deal with future discoveries. This draft seeks to resolve such definitional problems.

The draft convention would prohibit military or any other hostile use, as a means of destruction, damage, or injury, of environmental modification techniques having widespread, long-lasting, or severe effects. The prohibition against "military or any other hostile use" covers two types of environmental warfare. First, it covers the hostile use of environmental modification techniques in armed conflict or to initiate such conflict. Second, it covers the use of such techniques for the specific purpose of causing destruction, damage, or injury, even when no other weapons are used or there is no other military operation taking place. We believe this draft provides a basis for distinguishing between the use of environmental modification techniques as weapons, which is covered by the prohibition, and the environmental impact of other weapons, which is not covered.

The draft deals with environmental modification techniques whose use would have widespread, long-lasting, or severe effects. This is in order to focus on the most important aspects of the problem—potential applications of such techniques as weapons which could cause the gravest harm to man and his environment.

An important consideration in this regard is that in any limitation on the hostile uses of environmental modification techniques, the attainable degree of verification of compliance with treaty constraints obviously is related to the scale of activity. Accordingly, the possibilities for verification decrease as the size, duration, or severity of the activity diminishes.

CONVENTION ON THE PROHIBITION OF MILITARY OR ANY OTHER HOSTILE USE OF ENVIRONMENTAL MODIFICATION TECHNIQUES

The States Party to this Convention,

Guided by the interest of consolidating peace, and wishing to contribute to the cause of limiting the arms race, and of bringing about disarmament, and of saving mankind from the danger of using new means of warfare;

Recognizing that scientific and technical advances may open new possibilities with respect to modification of the environment;

Realizing that military use of environmental modification techniques could have widespread, long-lasting or severe effects harmful to human welfare, but that the use of environmental modification techniques for peaceful purposes could improve the interrelationship of man and nature and contribute to the preservation and improvement of the environment for the benefit of present and future generations;

Desiring to limit the potential danger to mankind from means of warfare involving the use of environmental modification techniques;

Desiring also to contribute to the strengthening of trust among nations and to the further improvement of the international situation in accordance with the purposes and principles of the Charter of the United Nations,

Have agreed as follows:

ARTICLE I

1. Each State Party to this Convention undertakes not to engage in military or any other hostile use of environmental modification techniques having widespread, long-lasting or severe effects as the means of destruction, damage or injury to another State Party.

2. Each State Party to this Convention undertakes not to assist, encourage or induce any State, group of States or international organization to engage in activities contrary to the provision of paragraph 1 of this article.

ARTICLE II

As used in Article I, the term "environmental modification techniques" refers to any technique for changing—through the deliberate manipulation of natural processes—the dynamics, composition or structure of the Earth, including its biota, lithosphere, hydrosphere, and atmosphere, or of outer space, so as to cause such effects as earthquakes and tsunamis, an upset in the ecological balance of a region, or changes in weather patterns (clouds, precipitation, cyclones of various types and tornadic storms), in the state of the ozone layer or ionosphere, in climate patterns, or in ocean currents.

ARTICLE III

The provisions of this Convention shall not hinder the use of environmental modification techniques for peaceful purposes by States Party, or international economic and scientific cooperation in the utilization, preservation and improvement of the environment for peaceful purposes.

ARTICLE IV

Each State Party to this Convention undertakes, in accordance with its constitutional processes, to take any necessary measures to prohibit and prevent any activity in violation of the provisions of the Convention anywhere under its jurisdiction or control.

ARTICLE V

1. The States Party to this Convention undertake to consult one another and to cooperate in solving any problems which may arise in relation to the objectives of, or in the application of the provisions of this Convention. Consultation and cooperation pursuant to this article may also be undertaken through appropriate international procedures within the framework of the United Nations and in accordance with its Charter.

2. Any State Party to this Convention which finds that any other State Party is acting in breach of obligations deriving from the provisions of the Convention may lodge a complaint with the Security Council of the United Nations. Such a complaint should include all possible evidence confirming its validity, as well as a request for its consideration by the Security Council.

3. Each State Party to this Convention undertakes to cooperate in carrying out any investigation which the Security Council may initiate, in accordance with the provisions of the Charter of the United Nations, on the basis of the complaint received by the Council. The Security Council shall inform the States Party to the Convention of the results of the investigation.

4. Each State Party to this Convention undertakes to provide or support assistance, in accordance with the United Nations Charter, to any Party to the Convention which so requests, if the Security Council decides that such Party has been harmed or is likely to be harmed as a result of violation of the Convention.

ARTICLE VI

1. Any State Party may propose amendments to this Convention. The text of any proposed amendment shall be submitted to ——————— which shall circulate it to all States Party.

2. An amendment shall enter into force for all States Party which have accepted it, upon the deposit with ——————— of instruments of acceptance by ———————. Thereafter it shall enter into force for any remaining State Party on the date of deposit of its instruments of acceptance.·

ARTICLE VII

This Convention shall be of unlimited duration.

ARTICLE VIII

1. This Convention shall be open to all States for signature. Any State which does not sign the Convention before its entry into force in accordance with paragraph 3 of this article may accede to it at any time.

2. This Convention shall be subject to ratification by signatory States. Instruments of ratification and instruments of accession shall be deposited with ———————.

3. This Convention shall enter into force after the deposit of instruments of ratification by ——————— in accordance with paragraph 2 of this article.

4. For those States whose instruments of ratification or accession are deposited after the entry into force of this Convention, it shall enter into force on the date of the deposit of their instruments of ratification or accession.

5. The ——————— shall promptly inform all signatory and acceding States of the date of each signature, the date of deposit of each instrument of ratification or of accession and the date of the entry into force of this Convention, and of the receipt of other notices.

6. This Convention shall be registered by ——————— in accordance with Article 102 of the Charter of the United Nations.

ARTICLE IX

This Convention, the Chinese, English, French, Russian, and Spanish texts of which are equally authentic, shall be deposited with ——————— who shall send certified copies thereof to the Governments of the signatory and acceding States.

In witness whereof, the undersigned, duly authorized thereto, have signed this Convention.

Done in ——————— on ———————.

Agreement is in force, except as otherwise agreed by the Parties, (i) the foreign trade organizations of the USSR shall purchase from private commercial sources, for shipment in each twelve month period beginning October 1, 1976, six million metric tons of wheat and corn, in approximately equal proportions, grown in the USA; and (ii) the Government of the USA shall employ its good offices to facilitate and encourage such sales by private commercial sources.

The foreign trade organizations of the USSR may increase this quantity without consultations by up to two million metric tons in any twelve month period, beginning October 1, 1976 unless the Government of the USA determines that the USA has a grain supply of less than 225 million metric tons as defined in Article V.

Purchases/sales of wheat and corn under this Agreement will be made at the market price prevailing for these products at the time of purchase/sale and in accordance with normal commercial terms.

ARTICLE II

During the term of this Agreement, except as otherwise agreed by the Parties, the Government of the USA shall not exercise any discretionary authority available to it under United States law to control exports of wheat and corn purchased for supply to the USSR in accordance with Article I.

ARTICLE III

In carrying out their obligations under this Agreement, the foreign trade organizations of the USSR shall endeavor to space their purchases in the USA and shipments to the USSR as evenly as possible over each 12-month period.

ARTICLE IV

The Government of the USSR shall assure that, except as the Parties may otherwise agree, all wheat and corn grown in the USA and purchased by foreign trade organizations of the USSR shall be supplied for consumption in the USSR.

ARTICLE V

In any year this Agreement is in force when the total grain supply in the USA, defined as the official United States Department of Agriculture estimates of the carry-in stocks of grain plus the official United States Department of Agriculture forward crop estimates for the coming crop year, falls below 225 million metric tons of all grains, the Government of the USA may reduce the quantity of wheat and corn available for purchase by foreign trade organizations of the USSR under Article I(i).

ARTICLE VI

Whenever the Government of the USSR wishes the foreign trade organizations of the USSR to be able

62 (October 20, 1975)

AGREEMENT BETWEEN THE GOVERNMENT OF THE UNITED STATES OF AMERICA AND THE GOVERNMENT OF THE UNION OF SOVIET SOCIALIST REPUBLICS ON THE SUPPLY OF GRAIN

The Government of the United States of America ("USA") and the Government of the Union of Soviet Socialist Republics ("USSR");

Recalling the "Basic Principles of Relations Between the United States of America and the Union of Soviet Socialist Republics" of May 29, 1972;

Desiring to strengthen long-term cooperation between the two countries on the basis of mutual benefit and equality;

Mindful of the importance which the production of food, particularly grain, has for the peoples of both countries;

Recognizing the need to stabilize trade in grain between the two countries;

Affirming their conviction that cooperation in the field of trade will contribute to overall improvement of relations between the two countries;

Have agreed as follows:

ARTICLE I

The Government of the USA and the Government of the USSR hereby enter into an Agreement for the purchase and sale of wheat and corn for supply to the USSR. To this end, during the period that this

to purchase more wheat or corn grown in the USA than the amounts specified in Article I, it shall immediately notify the Government of the USA.

Whenever the Government of the USA wishes private commercial sources to be able to sell more wheat or corn grown in the USA than the amounts specified in Article I, it shall immediately notify the Government of the USSR.

In both instances, the Parties will consult as soon as possible in order to reach agreement on possible quantities of grain to be supplied to the USSR prior to purchase/sale or conclusion of contracts for the purchase/sale of grain in amounts above those specified in Article I.

ARTICLE VII

It is understood that the shipment of wheat and corn from the USA to the USSR under this Agreement shall be in accord with the provisions of the American-Soviet Agreement on Maritime Matters which is in force during the period of shipments hereunder.

ARTICLE VIII

The Parties shall hold consultations concerning the implementation of this Agreement and related matters at intervals of six months beginning six months after the date of entry into force of this Agreement, and at any other time at the request of either Party.

ARTICLE IX

This Agreement shall enter into force on execution and shall remain in force until September 30, 1981 unless extended for a mutually agreed period.

DONE at Moscow, this 20th day of October, 1975, in duplicate, in the English and Russian languages, both texts being equally authentic.

For the Government of the United States of America:

CHARLES W. ROBINSON

For the Government of the Union of Soviet Socialist Republics:

N. S. PATOLICHEV

U.S. and U.S.S.R. Negotiating on Purchase of Soviet Oil

Following is a letter of intent dated October 20 signed by Charles W. Robinson, Under Secretary for Economic Affairs.

HIS EXCELLENCY
N. S. PATOLICHEV
Minister of Foreign Trade
Moscow, U.S.S.R.

DEAR MR. MINISTER: This is to confirm the understanding arising out of our discussions that our two Governments intend to commence negotiation promptly to conclude an Agreement concerning the purchase and shipment of Soviet oil. This Agreement will provide for the following:

(1) The Government of the Union of Soviet Socialist Republics will, for a period of five years, offer for sale annually ten million metric tons of crude oil and petroleum products.

The Government of the United States may purchase the crude oil and petroleum products for its own use or, by the agreement of the Parties, the purchase of crude oil and petroleum products may be made by United States' firms.

(3) About 70 percent of the total quantity offered for sale will be crude oil. The remainder may be petroleum products, in particular diesel oil and naphtha.

(4) Some portion of the crude oil or petroleum products will be shipped to the United States, partly in tankers used to transport grain from the United States to the Soviet Union.

(5) Some portion of the crude oil or petroleum products may be delivered to Europe or other agreed marketing areas.

(6) Prices for crude oil and petroleum products will be mutually agreed at a level which will assure the interests of both the Government of the United States and the Government of the Union of Soviet Socialist Republics.

In addition it is further understood that both Governments will work for the extension and expansion of the cooperative efforts already underway in the field of energy. Such efforts will be particularly directed toward the fuller application of the technological capability of both countries in increasing energy output from existing sources and in developing new sources of energy.

Sincerely yours,

CHARLES W. ROBINSON
Under Secretary of State
for Economic Affairs

63 (December 29, 1975)

AGREEMENT BETWEEN THE GOVERNMENT OF THE UNITED
STATES OF AMERICA AND THE GOVERNMENT OF THE UNION
OF SOVIET SOCIALIST REPUBLICS REGARDING CERTAIN
MARITIME MATTERS

The Government of the United States of America and the Government of the Union of Soviet Socialist Republics;

Recognizing the importance of maritime relations for both countries; and

Desiring to improve these relations between the United States and the Soviet Union, particularly through arrangements regarding port access and cargo carriage by sea; and

Acting in accordance with the Basic Principles of Relations Between the United States of America and the Union of Soviet Socialist Republics signed in Moscow on May 29, 1972, [1] and in particular with Article Seven thereof,

Have agreed as follows:

Article 1

For purposes of this Agreement:

a. "Vessel" means a vessel under the flag of either Party, carrying the papers required by its law in proof of nationality, and which is used for:

   (i) Commercial maritime shipping, or

   (ii) Merchant Marine training purposes, or

   (iii) Hydrographic, oceanographic, meterological, or terrestrial magnetic field research for civil application.

---

[1] *Department of State Bulletin,* June 26, 1972, p. 898.

b. "Vessel" does not include:

    (i)   Warships as defined in the 1958 Geneva Convention on the High Seas;[1]

    (ii)   Vessels carrying out any form of state function except for those mentioned under paragraph a of this Article;

    (iii) Fishing vessels, fishery research vessels, or fishery support vessels.

Article 2

The ports on the attached list of ports of each Party (Annexes I and II, which are a part of this Agreement) are open to access by all vessels of the other Party.

Article 3

Entry of all vessels of one Party into such ports of the other Party shall be permitted subject to four days' advance notice of the planned entry to the appropriate authority.

Article 4

Entry of vessels referred to in subparagraphs a(ii) and a(iii) of Article 1 into the ports referred to in Article 2 will be to replenish ships' stores or fresh water, obtain bunkers, provide rest for or make changes in the personnel of such vessels, and obtain minor repairs and other services normally provided in such ports, in accordance with applicable rules and regulations.

Article 5

Each Party undertakes to ensure that tonnage duties upon vessels of the other Party will not exceed the charges imposed in like situations with respect to vessels of any other country.

Article 6

Each Party recognizes the interest of the other Party in carrying a substantial part of its foreign trade in vessels of its own flag and both Parties intend that their national flag vessels will each carry equal and substantial shares of the trade between the two nations in accordance with the provisions of Annex III, which is a part of this Agreement. Each Party also recognizes the policy of the other Party concerning participation of third flags in its trade.

Article 7

Each Party, where it controls the selection of the carrier of its export or import cargoes, will provide to vessels under the flag of the other Party participation equal to that of vessels under its own flag in accordance with the provisions of Annex III, which is a part of this Agreement.

Article 8

The Parties shall enter into consultations within fourteen days from the date a request for consultation is received from either Party regarding any matter involving the application, interpretation, implementation or amendment of this Agreement.

Article 9

This Agreement shall be in force from January 1, 1976 through December 31, 1981.

This Agreement may be terminated by either Party prior to December 31, 1981. Such termination shall be effective ninety days after the date on which written notice of termination has been received by the other Party.

---

[1] TIAS 5200; 13 UST 2312.

IN WITNESS WHEREOF, the undersigned, duly authorized by their respective Governments, have signed this Agreement.

DONE at Washington and Moscow this 29th day of December , 1975 in duplicate in English and Russian languages, both equally authentic.

FOR THE GOVERNMENT OF THE
UNITED STATES OF AMERICA:

FOR THE GOVERNMENT OF THE UNION
OF SOVIET SOCIALIST REPUBLICS.

[1]

[2]

[1] Rogers C. B. Morton
[2] T. Guzhenko

<table>
<tr><td colspan="2">ANNEX I
PORTS OF THE UNITED STATES OF AMERICA
OPEN TO CALLS UPON NOTICE</td><td colspan="2">ANNEX II
PORTS OF THE UNION OF SOVIET SOCIALIST REPUBLICS
OPEN TO CALLS UPON NOTICE</td></tr>
<tr><td>1.</td><td>Skagway, Alaska</td><td></td><td></td></tr>
<tr><td>2.</td><td>Seattle, Washington</td><td>1.</td><td>Murmansk</td></tr>
<tr><td>3.</td><td>Longview, Washington</td><td>2.</td><td>Onega</td></tr>
<tr><td>4.</td><td>Corpus Christi, Texas</td><td>3.</td><td>Arkhangel'sk</td></tr>
<tr><td>5.</td><td>Port Arthur, Texas</td><td>4.</td><td>Mezen'</td></tr>
<tr><td>6.</td><td>Bellingham, Washington</td><td>5.</td><td>Nar'yan-Mar</td></tr>
<tr><td>7.</td><td>Everett, Washington</td><td>6.</td><td>Igarka</td></tr>
<tr><td>8.</td><td>Olympia, Washington</td><td>7.</td><td>Leningrad</td></tr>
<tr><td>9.</td><td>Tacoma, Washington</td><td>8.</td><td>Vyborg</td></tr>
<tr><td>10.</td><td>Coos Bay (including North Bend), Oregon</td><td>9.</td><td>Pyarnu</td></tr>
<tr><td>11.</td><td>Portland (including Vancouver, Washington), Oregon</td><td>10.</td><td>Riga</td></tr>
<tr><td>12.</td><td>Astoria, Oregon</td><td>11.</td><td>Ventspils</td></tr>
<tr><td>13.</td><td>Sacramento, California</td><td>12.</td><td>Klaipeda</td></tr>
<tr><td>14.</td><td>San Francisco (including Alameda, Oakland, Berkeley, Richmond), California</td><td>13.</td><td>Tallinn</td></tr>
<tr><td></td><td></td><td>14.</td><td>Vysotsk</td></tr>
<tr><td>15.</td><td>Long Beach, California</td><td>15.</td><td>Reni</td></tr>
<tr><td>16.</td><td>Los Angeles (including San Pedro, Wilmington, Terminal Island), California</td><td>16.</td><td>Izmail</td></tr>
<tr><td></td><td></td><td>17.</td><td>Kiliya</td></tr>
<tr><td>17.</td><td>Eureka, California</td><td>18.</td><td>Belgorod-Dnestrovskiy</td></tr>
<tr><td>18.</td><td>Honolulu, Hawaii</td><td>19.</td><td>Il'ichevsk</td></tr>
<tr><td>19.</td><td>Galveston/Texas City, Texas</td><td>20.</td><td>Odessa</td></tr>
<tr><td>20.</td><td>Burnside, Louisiana</td><td>21.</td><td>Kherson</td></tr>
<tr><td>21.</td><td>New Orleans, Louisiana</td><td>22.</td><td>Novorossiysk</td></tr>
<tr><td>22.</td><td>Baton Rouge, Louisiana</td><td>23.</td><td>Tuapse</td></tr>
<tr><td>23.</td><td>Mobile, Alabama</td><td>24.</td><td>Poti</td></tr>
<tr><td>24.</td><td>Tampa, Florida</td><td>25.</td><td>Batumi</td></tr>
<tr><td>25.</td><td>Houston, Texas</td><td>26.</td><td>Sochi</td></tr>
<tr><td>26.</td><td>Beaumont, Texas</td><td>27.</td><td>Sukhumi</td></tr>
<tr><td>27.</td><td>Brownsville, Texas</td><td>28.</td><td>Yalta</td></tr>
<tr><td>28.</td><td>Ponce, Puerto Rico</td><td>29.</td><td>Zhdanov</td></tr>
<tr><td>29.</td><td>New York (New York and New Jersey parts of the Port of New York Authority), New York</td><td>30.</td><td>Berdyansk</td></tr>
<tr><td></td><td></td><td>31.</td><td>Nakhodka</td></tr>
<tr><td>30.</td><td>Philadelphia, Pennsylvania (including Camden, New Jersey)</td><td>32.</td><td>Aleksandrovsk-Sakhalinskiy</td></tr>
<tr><td>31.</td><td>Baltimore, Maryland</td><td>33.</td><td>Makarevskiy Roadstead (Roadstead Doue)</td></tr>
<tr><td>32.</td><td>Savannah, Georgia</td><td>34.</td><td>Oktyabr'skiy</td></tr>
<tr><td>33.</td><td>Erie, Pennsylvania</td><td>35.</td><td>Shakhtersk</td></tr>
<tr><td>34.</td><td>Duluth, Minnesota/Superior, Wisconsin</td><td>36.</td><td>Uglegorsk</td></tr>
<tr><td>35.</td><td>Chicago, Illinois</td><td>37.</td><td>Kholmsk</td></tr>
<tr><td>36.</td><td>Milwaukee, Wisconsin</td><td>38.</td><td>Nevel'sk</td></tr>
<tr><td>37.</td><td>Kenosha, Wisconsin</td><td>39.</td><td>Makarov Roadstead</td></tr>
<tr><td>38.</td><td>Cleveland, Ohio</td><td>40.</td><td>Poronaysk</td></tr>
<tr><td>39.</td><td>Toledo, Ohio</td><td></td><td></td></tr>
<tr><td>40.</td><td>Bay City, Michigan</td><td></td><td></td></tr>
</table>

64 (March 1, 1976)
U.S. and U.S.S.R. Sign New Agreement on Middle Atlantic Fisheries

Joint Communique [1]

Representatives of the United States of America and the Union of Soviet Socialist Republics met in Washington February 17 to March 1, 1976, to renegotiate the agreement between their two governments concerning fisheries in the Middle Atlantic Ocean off the coast of the United States and discuss related matters. The United States was represented by Ambassador Rozanne L. Ridgway, Deputy Assistant Secretary of State for Oceans and Fisheries Affairs. The Soviet Union was represented by Vladimir M. Kamentsev, First Deputy Minister of Fisheries of the U.S.S.R.

The two representatives succeeded in completing negotiations on a new agreement that will provide improved protection to stocks of fish in the Middle Atlantic region in the interests of sound conservation and management and based on the best available scientific evidence. The new agreement was signed on March 1, 1976.

The new agreement also provides for an expanded joint research program on the principal fish stocks of the region. Progress on these studies will be reviewed later in the year at a special meeting of American and Soviet scientists and statistical specialists.

Taking into account anticipated legal and jurisdictional changes in the field of fisheries off the coasts of the United States, and the need to provide for an orderly transition to the future regime, both sides agreed to meet at a convenient time for the purpose of discussing questions of mutual interest regarding the principles that will apply to their future fisheries relations.

Both sides expressed their satisfaction with the new agreement and their interest in continued mutually beneficial cooperation in the field of fisheries.

---

[1] Issued on Mar. 1 (text from press release 110).

65 (May 28, 1976)

TEXTS OF TREATY AND PROTOCOL AND AGREED STATEMENT

Text of Treaty

TREATY BETWEEN THE UNITED STATES OF AMERICA AND THE UNION OF SOVIET SOCIALIST REPUBLICS ON UNDERGROUND NUCLEAR EXPLOSIONS FOR PEACEFUL PURPOSES

The United States of America and the Union of Soviet Socialist Republics, hereinafter referred to as the Parties,

Proceeding from a desire to implement Article III of the Treaty between the United States of America and the Union of Soviet Socialist Republics on the Limitation of Underground Nuclear Weapon Tests, which calls for the earliest possible conclusion of an agreement on underground nuclear explosions for peaceful purposes,

Reaffirming their adherence to the objectives and principles of the Treaty Banning Nuclear Weapon Tests in the Atmosphere, in Outer Space and Under Water, the Treaty on Non-Proliferation of Nuclear Weapons, and the Treaty on the Limitation of Underground Nuclear Weapon Tests, and their determination to observe strictly the provisions of these international agreements,

Desiring to assure that underground nuclear explosions for peaceful purposes shall not be used for purposes related to nuclear weapons,

Desiring that utilization of nuclear energy be directed only toward peaceful purposes,

Desiring to develop appropriately cooperation in the field of underground nuclear explosions for peaceful purposes,

Have agreed as follows:

ARTICLE I

1. The Parties enter into this Treaty to satisfy the obligations in Article III of the Treaty on the Limitation of Underground Nuclear Weapon Tests, and assume additional obligations in accordance with the provisions of this Treaty.

2. This Treaty shall govern all underground nuclear explosions for peaceful purposes conducted by the Parties after March 31, 1976.

ARTICLE II

For the purposes of this Treaty:

(a) "explosion" means any individual or group underground nuclear explosion for peaceful purposes;

(b) "explosive" means any device, mechanism or system for producing an individual explosion;

(c) "group explosion" means two or more individual explosions for which the time interval between successive individual explosions does not exceed five seconds and for which the emplacement points of all explosives can be interconnected by straight line segments, each of which joins two emplacement points and each of which does not exceed 40 kilometers.

ARTICLE III

1. Each Party, subject to the obligations assumed under this Treaty and other international agreements, reserves the right to:

(a) carry out explosions at any place under its jurisdiction or control outside the geographical boundaries of test sites specified under the provisions of the Treaty on the Limitation of Underground Nuclear Weapon Tests; and

(b) carry out, participate or assist in carrying out explosions in the territory of another State at the request of such other State.

2. Each Party undertakes to prohibit, to prevent and not to carry out at any place under its jurisdiction or control, and further undertakes not to carry out, participate or assist in carrying out anywhere:

(a) any individual explosion having a yield exceeding 150 kilotons;

(b) any group explosion:

(1) having an aggregate yield exceeding 150 kilotons except in ways that will permit identification of each individual explosion and determination of the yield of each individual explosion in the group in accordance with the provisions of Article IV of and the Protocol to this Treaty;

(2) having an aggregate yield exceeding one and one-half megatons;

(c) any explosion which does not carry out a peaceful application;

(d) any explosion except in compliance with the provisions of the Treaty Banning Nuclear Weapon Tests in the Atmosphere, in Outer Space and Under Water, the Treaty on the Non-Proliferation of Nuclear Weapons, and other international agreements entered into by that Party.

3. The question of carrying out any individual explosion having a yield exceeding the yield specified in paragraph 2(a) of this article will be considered

by the Parties at an appropriate time to be agreed.

ARTICLE IV

1. For the purpose of providing assurance of compliance with the provisions of this Treaty, each Party shall:

(a) use national technical means of verification at its disposal in a manner consistent with generally recognized principles of international law; and

(b) provide to the other Party information and access to sites of explosions and furnish assistance in accordance with the provisions set forth in the Protocol to this Treaty.

2. Each Party undertakes not to interfere with the national technical means of verification of the other Party operating in accordance with paragraph 1(a) of this article, or with the implementation of the provisions of paragraph 1(b) of this article.

ARTICLE V

1. To promote the objectives and implementation of the provisions of this Treaty, the Parties shall establish promptly a Joint Consultative Commission within the framework of which they will:

(a) consult with each other, make inquiries and furnish information in response to such inquiries, to assure confidence in compliance with the obligations assumed;

(b) consider questions concerning compliance with the obligations assumed and related situations which may be considered ambiguous;

(c) consider questions involving unintended interference with the means for assuring compliance with the provisions of this Treaty;

(d) consider changes in technology or other new circumstances which have a bearing on the provisions of this Treaty; and

(e) consider possible amendments to provisions governing underground nuclear explosions for peaceful purposes.

2. The Parties through consultation shall establish, and may amend as appropriate, Regulations for the Joint Consultative Commission governing procedures, composition and other relevant matters.

ARTICLE VI

1. The Parties will develop cooperation on the basis of mutual benefit, equality, and reciprocity in various areas related to carrying out underground nuclear explosions for peaceful purposes.

2. The Joint Consultative Commission will facilitate this cooperation by considering specific areas and forms of cooperation which shall be determined by agreement between the Parties in accordance with their constitutional procedures.

3. The Parties will appropriately inform the International Atomic Energy Agency of results of their cooperation in the field of underground nuclear explosions for peaceful purposes.

ARTICLE VII

1. Each Party shall continue to promote the development of the international agreement or agreements and procedures provided for in Article V of the Treaty on the Non-Proliferation of Nuclear Weapons, and shall provide appropriate assistance to the International Atomic Energy Agency in this regard.

2. Each Party undertakes not to carry out, participate or assist in the carrying out of any explosion in the territory of another State unless that State agrees to the implementation in its territory of the international observation and procedures contemplated by Article V of the Treaty on the Non-Proliferation of Nuclear Weapons and the provisions of Article IV of and the Protocol to this Treaty, including the provision by that State of the assistance necessary for such implementation and of the privileges and immunities specified in the Protocol.

ARTICLE VIII

1. This Treaty shall remain in force for a period of five years, and it shall be extended for successive five-year periods unless either Party notifies the other of its termination no later than six months prior to its expiration. Before the expiration of this period the Parties may, as necessary, hold consultations to consider the situation relevant to the substance of this Treaty. However, under no circumstances shall either Party be entitled to terminate this Treaty while the Treaty on the Limitation of Underground Nuclear Weapon Tests remains in force.

2. Termination of the Treaty on the Limitation of Underground Nuclear Weapon Tests shall entitle either Party to withdraw from this Treaty at any time.

3. Each Party may propose amendments to this Treaty. Amendments shall enter into force on the day of the exchange of instruments of ratification of such amendments.

ARTICLE IX

1. This Treaty including the Protocol which forms an integral part hereof, shall be subject to ratification in accordance with the constitutional procedures of each Party. This Treaty shall enter into force on the day of the exchange of instruments of ratification which exchange shall take place simultaneously with the exchange of instruments of ratification of the Treaty on the Limitation of Underground Nuclear Weapon Tests.

2. This Treaty shall be registered pursuant to Article 102 of the Charter of the United Nations.

Done at Washington and Moscow, on May 28,

1976, in duplicate, in the English and Russian languages, both texts being equally authentic.

For the United States of America:

GERALD R. FORD
The President of the United States of America

For the Union of Soviet Socialist Republics:

L. I. BREZHNEV
General Secretary of the Central Committee of the CPSU

Text of Protocol

PROTOCOL TO THE TREATY BETWEEN THE UNITED STATES OF AMERICA AND THE UNION OF SOVIET SOCIALIST REPUBLICS ON UNDERGROUND NUCLEAR EXPLOSIONS FOR PEACEFUL PURPOSES

The United States of America and the Union of Soviet Socialist Republics, hereinafter referred to as the Parties,
Having agreed to the provisions in the Treaty on Underground Nuclear Explosions for Peaceful Purposes, hereinafter referred to as the Treaty,
Have agreed as follows:

ARTICLE I

1. No individual explosion shall take place at a distance, in meters, from the ground surface which is less than 30 times the 3.4 root of its planned yield in kilotons.
2. Any group explosion with a planned aggregate yield exceeding 500 kilotons shall not include more than five individual explosions, each of which has a planned yield not exceeding 50 kilotons.

ARTICLE II

1. For each explosion, the Party carrying out the explosion shall provide the other Party:

(a) not later than 90 days before the beginning of emplacement of the explosives when the planned aggregate yield of the explosion does not exceed 100 kilotons, or not later than 180 days before the beginning of emplacement of the explosives when the planned aggregate yield of the explosion exceeds 100 kilotons, with the following information to the extent and degree of precision available when it is conveyed:

(1) the purpose of the planned explosion;
(2) the location of the explosion expressed in geographical coordinates with a precision of four or less kilometers, planned date and aggregate yield of the explosion;
(3) the type or types of rock in which the explosion will be carried out, including the degree of liquid saturation of the rock at the point of emplacement of each explosive; and
(4) a description of specific technological features of the project, of which the explosion is a part,

that could influence the determination of its yield and confirmation of purpose; and

(b) not later than 60 days before the beginning of emplacement of the explosives the information specified in subparagraph 1(a) of this article to the full extent and with the precision indicated in that subparagraph.

2. For each explosion with a planned aggregate yield exceeding 50 kilotons, the Party carrying out the explosion shall provide the other Party, not later than 60 days before the beginning of emplacement of the explosives, with the following information:

(a) the number of explosives, the planned yield of each explosive, the location of each explosive to be used in a group explosion relative to all other explosives in the group with a precision of 100 or less meters, the depth of emplacement of each explosive with a precision of one meter and the time intervals between individual explosions in any group explosion with a precision of one-tenth second; and
(b) a description of specific features of geological structure or other local conditions that could influence the determination of the yield.

3. For each explosion with a planned aggregate yield exceeding 75 kilotons, the Party carrying out the explosion shall provide the other Party, not later than 60 days before the beginning of emplacement of the explosives, with a description of the geological and geophysical characteristics of the site of each explosion which could influence determination of the yield, which shall include: the depth of the water table; a stratigraphic column above each emplacement point; the position of each emplacement point relative to nearby geological and other features which influenced the design of the project of which the explosion is a part; and the physical parameters of the rock, including density, seismic velocity, porosity, degree of liquid saturation, and rock strength, within the sphere centered on each emplacement point and having a radius, in meters, equal to 30 times the cube root of the planned yield in kilotons of the explosive emplaced at that point.

4. For each explosion with a planned aggregate yield exceeding 100 kilotons, the Party carrying out the explosion shall provide the other Party, not later than 60 days before the beginning of emplacement of the explosives, with:

(a) information on locations and purposes of facilities and installations which are associated with the conduct of the explosion;
(b) information regarding the planned date of the beginning of emplacement of each explosive; and
(c) a topographic plan in local coordinates of the areas specified in paragraph 7 of Article IV, at a scale of 1:24,000 or 1:25,000 with a contour interval of 10 meters or less.

5. For application of an explosion to alleviate the

consequences of an emergency situation involving an unforeseen combination of circumstances which calls for immediate action for which it would not be practicable to observe the timing requirements of paragraphs 1, 2 and 3 of this article, the following conditions shall be met:

(a) the Party carrying out an explosion for such purposes shall inform the other Party of that decision immediately after it has been made and describe such circumstances;

(b) the planned aggregate yield of an explosion for such purpose shall not exceed 100 kilotons; and

(c) the Party carrying out an explosion for such purpose shall provide to the other Party the information specified in paragraph 1 of this article, and the information specified in paragraphs 2 and 3 of this article if applicable, after the decision to conduct the explosion is taken, but not later than 30 days before the beginning of emplacement of the explosives.

6. For each explosion, the Party carrying out the explosion shall inform the other Party, not later than two days before the explosion, of the planned time of detonation of each explosive with a precision of one second.

7. Prior to the explosion, the Party carrying out the explosion shall provide the other Party with timely notification of changes in the information provided in accordance with this article.

8. The explosion shall not be carried out earlier than 90 days after notification of any change in the information provided in accordance with this article which requires more extensive verification procedures than those required on the basis of the original information, unless an earlier time for carrying out the explosion is agreed between the Parties.

9. Not later than 90 days after each explosion the Party carrying out the explosion shall provide the other Party with the following information:

(a) the actual time of the explosion with a precision of one-tenth second and its aggregate yield;

(b) when the planned aggregate yield of a group explosion exceeds 50 kilotons, the actual time of the first individual explosion with a precision of one-tenth second, the time interval between individual explosions with a precision of one millisecond and the yield of each individual explosion; and

(c) confirmation of other information provided in accordance with paragraphs 1, 2, 3 and 4 of this article and explanation of any changes or corrections based on the results of the explosion.

10. At any time, but not later than one year after the explosion, the other Party may request the Party carrying out the explosion to clarify any item

of the information provided in accordance with this article. Such clarification shall be provided as soon as practicable, but not later than 30 days after the request is made.

ARTICLE III

1. For the purposes of this Protocol:

(a) "designated personnel" means those nationals of the other Party identified to the Party carrying out an explosion as the persons who will exercise the rights and functions provided for in the Treaty and this Protocol; and

(b) "emplacement hole" means the entire interior of any drill-hole, shaft, adit or tunnel in which an explosive and associated cables and other equipment are to be installed.

2. For any explosion with a planned aggregate yield exceeding 100 kilotons but not exceeding 150 kilotons if the Parties, in consultation based on information provided in accordance with Article II and other information that may be introduced by either Party, deem it appropriate for the confirmation of the yield of the explosion, and for any explosion with a planned aggregate yield exceeding 150 kilotons, the Party carrying out the explosion shall allow designated personnel within the areas and at the locations described in Article V to exercise the following rights and functions:

(a) confirmation that the local circumstances, including facilities and installations associated with the project, are consistent with the stated peaceful purposes;

(b) confirmation of the validity of the geological and geophysical information provided in accordance with Article II through the following procedures:

(1) examination by designated personnel of research and measurement data of the Party carrying out the explosion and of rock core or rock fragments removed from each emplacement hole, and of any logs and drill core from existing exploratory holes which shall be provided to designated personnel upon their arrival at the site of the explosion;

(2) examination by designated personnel of rock core or rock fragments as they become available in accordance with the procedures specified in subparagraph 2(b)(3) of this article; and

(3) observation by designated personnel of implementation by the Party carrying out the explosion of one of the following four procedures, unless this right is waived by the other Party:

(i) construction of that portion of each emplacement hole starting from a point nearest the entrance of the emplacement hole which is at a distance, in meters, from the nearest emplacement point equal to 30 times the cube root of the planned yield in kilotons of the explosive to be emplaced at that point and continuing to the completion of the emplacement hole; or

(ii) construction of that portion of each emplacement hole starting from a point nearest the entrance of the emplacement hole which is at a distance, in meters, from the nearest emplacement point equal to six times the cube root of the planned yield in kilotons of the explosive to be emplaced at that point and continuing to the completion of the emplacement hole as well as the removal of rock core or rock fragments from the wall of an existing exploratory hole, which is substantially parallel with and at no point more than 100 meters from the emplacement hole, at locations specified by designated personnel which lie within a distance, in meters, from the same horizon as each emplacement point of 30 times the cube root of the planned yield in kilotons of the explosive to be emplaced at that point; or

(iii) removal of rock core or rock fragments from the wall of each emplacement hole at locations specified by designated personnel which lie within a distance, in meters, from each emplacement point of 30 times the cube root of the planned yield in kilotons of the explosive to be emplaced at each such point; or

(iv) construction of one or more new exploratory holes so that for each emplacement hole there will be a new exploratory hole to the same depth as that of the emplacement of the explosive, substantially parallel with and at no point more than 100 meters from each emplacement hole, from which rock cores would be removed at locations specified by designated personnel which lie within a distance, in meters, from the same horizon as each emplacement point of 30 times the cube root of the planned yield in kilotons of the explosive to be emplaced at each such point;

(c) observation of the emplacement of each explosive, confirmation of the depth of its emplacement and observation of the stemming of each emplacement hole;

(d) unobstructed visual observation of the area of the entrance to each emplacement hole at any time from the time of emplacement of each explosive until all personnel have been withdrawn from the site for the detonation of the explosion; and

(e) observation of each explosion.

3. Designated personnel, using equipment provided in accordance with paragraph 1 of Article IV, shall have the right, for any explosion with a planned aggregate yield exceeding 150 kilotons, to determine the yield of each individual explosion in a group explosion in accordance with the provisions of Article VI.

4. Designated personnel, when using their equipment in accordance with paragraph 1 of Article IV, shall have the right, for any explosion with a planned aggregate yield exceeding 500 kilotons, to emplace, install and operate under the observation and with the assistance of personnel of the Party carrying out the explosion, if such assistance is requested by designated personnel, a local seismic network in accordance with the provisions of paragraph 7 of Article IV. Radio links may be used for the transmission of data and control signals between the seismic stations and the control center. Frequencies, maximum power output of radio transmitters, directivity of antennas and times of operation of the local seismic network radio transmitters before the explosion shall be agreed between the Parties in accordance with Article X and time of operation after the explosion shall conform to the time specified in paragraph 7 of Article IV.

5. Designated personnel shall have the right to:

(a) acquire photographs under the following conditions:

(1) the Party carrying out the explosion shall identify to the other Party those personnel of the Party carrying out the explosion who shall take photographs as requested by designated personnel;

(2) photographs shall be taken by personnel of the Party carrying out the explosion in the presence of designated personnel and at the time requested by designated personnel for taking such photographs. Designated personnel shall determine whether these photographs are in conformity with their requests and, if not, additional photographs shall be taken immediately;

(3) photographs shall be taken with cameras provided by the other Party having built-in, rapid developing capability and a copy of each photograph shall be provided at the completion of the development process to both Parties;

(4) cameras provided by designated personnel shall be kept in agreed secure storage when not in use; and

(5) the requests for photographs can be made, at any time, of the following:

(i) exterior views of facilities and installations associated with the conduct of the explosion as described in subparagraph 4(a) of Article II;

(ii) geological samples used for confirmation of geological and geophysical information, as provided for in subparagraph 2(b) of this article and the equipment utilized in the acquisition of such samples;

(iii) emplacement and installation of equipment and associated cables used by designated personnel for yield determination;

(iv) emplacement and installation of the local seismic network used by designated personnel;

(v) emplacement of the explosives and the stemming of the emplacement hole; and

(vi) containers, facilities and installations for storage and operation of equipment used by designated personnel;

(b) photographs of visual displays and records produced by the equipment used by designated personnel and photographs within the control centers taken by cameras which are component parts of such equipment; and

(c) receive at the request of designated personnel and with the agreement of the Party carrying out the explosion supplementary photographs taken by the Party carrying out the explosion.

ARTICLE IV

1. Designated personnel in exercising their rights and functions may choose to use the following equipment of either Party, of which choice the Party carrying out the explosion shall be informed not later than 150 days before the beginning of emplacement of the explosives:

(a) electrical equipment for yield determination and equipment for a local seismic network as described in paragraphs 3, 4 and 7 of this article; and

(b) geologist's field tools and kits and equipment for recording of field notes.

2. Designated personnel shall have the right in exercising their rights and functions to utilize the following additional equipment which shall be provided by the Party carrying out the explosion, under procedures to be established in accordance with Article X to ensure that the equipment meets the specifications of the other Party: portable short-range communication equipment, field glasses, optical equipment for surveying and other items which may be specified by the other Party. A description of such equipment and operating instructions shall be provided to the other Party not later than 90 days before the beginning of emplacement of the explosives in connection with which such equipment is to be used.

3. A complete set of electrical equipment for yield determination shall consist of:

(a) sensing elements and associated cables for transmission of electrical power, control signals and data;

(b) equipment of the control center, electrical power supplies and cables for transmission of electrical power, control signals and data; and

(c) measuring and calibration instruments, maintenance equipment and spare parts necessary for ensuring the functioning of sensing elements, cables and equipment of the control center.

4. A complete set of equipment for the local seismic network shall consist of:

(a) seismic stations each of which contains a seismic instrument, electrical power supply and associated cables and radio equipment for receiving and transmission of control signals and data or equipment for recording control signals and data;

(b) equipment of the control center and electrical power supplies; and

(c) measuring and calibration instruments, maintenance equipment and spare parts necessary

for ensuring the functioning of the complete network.

5. In case designated personnel, in accordance with paragraph 1 of this article, choose to use equipment of the Party carrying out the explosion for yield determination or for a local seismic network, a description of such equipment and installation and operating instructions shall be provided to the other Party not later than 90 days before the beginning of emplacement of the explosives in connection with which such equipment is to be used. Personnel of the Party carrying out the explosion shall emplace, install and operate the equipment in the presence of designated personnel. After the explosion, designated personnel shall receive duplicate copies of the recorded data. Equipment for yield determination shall be emplaced in accordance with Article VI. Equipment for a local seismic network shall be emplaced in accordance with paragraph 7 of this article.

6. In case designated personnel, in accordance with paragraph 1 of this article, choose to use their own equipment for yield determination and their own equipment for a local seismic network, the following procedures shall apply:

(a) the Party carrying out the explosion shall be provided by the other Party with the equipment and information specified in subparagraphs (a)(1) and (a)(2) of this paragraph not later than 150 days prior to the beginning of emplacement of the explosives in connection with which such equipment is to be used in order to permit the Party carrying out the explosion to familiarize itself with such equipment, if such equipment and information has not been previously provided, which equipment shall be returned to the other Party not later than 90 days before the beginning of emplacement of the explosives. The equipment and information to be provided are:

(1) one complete set of electrical equipment for yield determination as described in paragraph 3 of this article, electrical and mechanical design information, specifications and installation and operating instructions concerning this equipment; and

(2) one complete set of equipment for the local seismic network described in paragraph 4 of this article, including one seismic station, electrical and mechanical design information, specifications and installation and operating instructions concerning this equipment;

(b) not later than 35 days prior to the beginning of emplacement of the explosives in connection with which the following equipment is to be used, two complete sets of electrical equipment for yield determination as described in paragraph 3 of this article and specific installation instructions for the emplacement of the sensing elements based on information provided in accordance with subparagraph

2(a) of Article VI and two complete sets of equipment for the local seismic network as described in paragraph 4 of this article, which sets of equipment shall have the same components and technical characteristics as the corresponding equipment specified in subparagraph 6(a) of this article, shall be delivered in sealed containers to the port of entry;

(c) the Party carrying out the explosion shall choose one of each of the two sets of equipment described above which shall be used by designated personnel in connection with the explosion;

(d) the set or sets of equipment not chosen for use in connection with the explosion shall be at the disposal of the Party carrying out the explosion for a period that may be as long as 30 days after the explosion at which time such equipment shall be returned to the other Party;

(e) the set or sets of equipment chosen for use shall be transported by the Party carrying out the explosion in the sealed containers in which this equipment arrived, after seals of the Party carrying out the explosion have been affixed to them, to the site of the explosion, so that this equipment is delivered to designated personnel for emplacement, installation and operation not later than 20 days before the beginning of emplacement of the explosives. This equipment shall remain in the custody of designated personnel in accordance with paragraph 7 of Article V or in agreed secure storage. Personnel of the Party carrying out the explosion shall have the right to observe the use of this equipment by designated personnel during the time the equipment is at the site of the explosion. Before the beginning of emplacement of the explosives, designated personnel shall demonstrate to personnel of the Party carrying out the explosion that this equipment is in working order;

(f) each set of equipment shall include two sets of components for recording data and associated calibration equipment. Both of these sets of components in the equipment chosen for use shall simultaneously record data. After the explosion, and after duplicate copies of all data have been obtained by designated personnel and the Party carrying out the explosion, one of each of the two sets of components for recording data and associated calibration equipment shall be selected, by an agreed process of chance, to be retained by designated personnel. Designated personnel shall pack and seal such components for recording data and associated calibration equipment which shall accompany them from the site of the explosion to the port of exit; and

(g) all remaining equipment may be retained by the Party carrying out the explosion for a period that may be as long as 30 days, after which time this equipment shall be returned to the other Party.

7. For any explosion with a planned aggregate yield exceeding 500 kilotons, a local seismic network, the number of stations of which shall be determined by designated personnel but shall not exceed the number of explosives in the group plus five, shall be emplaced, installed and operated at agreed sites of emplacement within an area circumscribed by circles of 15 kilometers in radius centered on points on the surface of the earth above the points of emplacement of the explosives during a period beginning not later than 20 days before the beginning of emplacement of the explosives and continuing after the explosion not later than three days unless otherwise agreed between the Parties.

8. The Party carrying out the explosion shall have the right to examine in the presence of designated personnel all equipment, instruments and tools of designated personnel specified in subparagraph 1(b) of this article.

9. The Joint Consultative Commission will consider proposals that either Party may put forward for the joint development of standardized equipment for verification purposes.

ARTICLE V

1. Except as limited by the provisions of paragraph 5 of this article, designated personnel in the exercise of their rights and functions shall have access along agreed routes:

(a) for an explosion with a planned aggregate yield exceeding 100 kilotons in accordance with paragraph 2 of Article III:

(1) to the locations of facilities and installations associated with the conduct of the explosion provided in accordance with subparagraph 4(a) of Article II; and

(2) to the locations of activities described in paragraph 2 of Article III; and

(b) for any explosion with a planned aggregate yield exceeding 150 kilotons, in addition to the access described in subparagraph 1(a) of this article:

(1) to other locations within the area circumscribed by circles of 10 kilometers in radius centered on points on the surface of the earth above the points of emplacement of the explosives in order to confirm that the local circumstances are consistent with the stated peaceful purposes;

(2) to the locations of the components of the electrical equipment for yield determination to be used for recording data when, by agreement between the Parties, such equipment is located outside the area described in subparagraph 1(b)(1) of this article; and

(3) to the sites of emplacement of the equipment of the local seismic network provided for in paragraph 7 of Article IV.

2. The Party carrying out the explosion shall notify the other Party of the procedure it has chosen

from among those specified in subparagraph 2(b)(3) of Article III not later than 30 days before beginning the implementation of such procedure. Designated personnel shall have the right to be present at the site of the explosion to exercise their rights and functions in the areas and at the locations described in paragraph 1 of this article for a period of time beginning two days before the beginning of the implementation of the procedure and continuing for a period of three days after the completion of this procedure.

3. Except as specified in paragraph 4 of this article, designated personnel shall have the right to be present in the areas and at the locations described in paragraph 1 of this article:

(a) for an explosion with a planned aggregate yield exceeding 100 kilotons but not exceeding 150 kilotons, in accordance with paragraph 2 of Article III, at any time beginning five days before the beginning of emplacement of the explosives and continuing after the explosion and after safe access to evacuated areas has been established according to standards determined by the Party carrying out the explosion for a period of two days; and

(b) for any explosion with a planned aggregate yield exceeding 150 kilotons, at any time beginning 20 days before the beginning of emplacement of the explosives and continuing after the explosion and after safe access to evacuated areas has been established according to standards determined by the Party carrying out the explosion for a period of:

(1) five days in the case of an explosion with a planned aggregate yield exceeding 150 kilotons but not exceeding 500 kilotons; or

(2) eight days in the case of an explosion with a planned aggregate yield exceeding 500 kilotons.

4. Designated personnel shall not have the right to be present in those areas from which all personnel have been evacuated in connection with carrying out an explosion, but shall have the right to re-enter those areas at the same time as personnel of the Party carrying out the explosion.

5. Designated personnel shall not have or seek access by physical, visual or technical means to the interior of the canister containing an explosive, to documentary or other information descriptive of the design of an explosive nor to equipment for control and firing of explosives. The Party carrying out the explosion shall not locate documentary or other information descriptive of the design of an explosive in such ways as to impede the designated personnel in the exercise of their rights and functions.

6. The number of designated personnel present at the site of an explosion shall not exceed:

(a) for the exercise of their rights and functions in connection with the confirmation of the geological and geophysical information in accordance with the provisions of subparagraph 2(b) and applicable provisions of paragraph 5 of Article III—the number of emplacement holes plus three;

(b) for the exercise of their rights and functions in connection with confirming that the local circumstances are consistent with the information provided and with the stated peaceful purposes in accordance with the provisions in subparagraphs 2(a), 2(c), 2(d) and 2(e) and applicable provisions of paragraph 5 of Article III—the number of explosives plus two;

(c) for the exercise of their rights and functions in connection with confirming that the local circumstances are consistent with the information provided and with the stated peaceful purposes in accordance with the provisions in subparagraphs 2(a), 2(c), 2(d) and 2(e) and applicable provisions of paragraph 5 of Article III and in connection with the use of electrical equipment for determination of the yield in accordance with paragraph 3 of Article III—the number of explosives plus seven; and

(d) for the exercise of their rights and functions in connection with confirming that the local circumstances are consistent with the information provided and with the stated peaceful purposes in accordance with the provisions in subparagraph 2(a), 2(c), 2(d) and 2(e) and applicable provisions of paragraph 5 of Article III and in connection with the use of electrical equipment for determination of the yield in accordance with paragraph 3 of Article III and with the use of the local seismic network in accordance with paragraph 4 of Article III—the number of explosives plus 10.

7. The Party carrying out the explosion shall have the right to assign its personnel to accompany designated personnel while the latter exercise their rights and functions.

8. The Party carrying out an explosion shall assure for designated personnel telecommunications with their authorities, transportation and other services appropriate to their presence and to the exercise of their rights and functions at the site of the explosion.

9. The expenses incurred for the transportation of designated personnel and their equipment to and from the site of the explosion, telecommunications provided for in paragraph 8 of this article, their living and working quarters, subsistence and all other personal expenses shall be the responsibility of the Party other than the Party carrying out the explosion.

10. Designated personnel shall consult with the Party carrying out the explosion in order to coordinate the planned program and schedule of activities of designated personnel with the program of the Party carrying out the explosion for the conduct of the project so as to ensure that designated personnel are able to conduct their activities in an orderly and timely way that is compatible with the

implementation of the project. Procedures for such consultations shall be established in accordance with Article X.

ARTICLE VI

For any explosion with a planned aggregate yield exceeding 150 kilotons, determination of the yield of each explosive used shall be carried out in accordance with the following provisions:

1. Determination of the yield of each individual explosion in the group shall be based on measurements of the velocity of propagation, as a function of time, of the hydrodynamic shock wave generated by the explosion, taken by means of electrical equipment described in paragraph 3 of Article IV.

2. The Party carrying out the explosion shall provide the other Party with the following information:

(a) not later than 60 days before the beginning of emplacement of the explosives, the length of each canister in which the explosive will be contained in the corresponding emplacement hole, the dimensions of the tube or other device used to emplace the canister and the cross-sectional dimensions of the emplacement hole to a distance, in meters, from the emplacement point of 10 times the cube root of its yield in kilotons;

(b) not later than 60 days before the beginning of emplacement of the explosives, a description of materials, including their densities, to be used to stem each emplacement hole; and

(c) not later than 30 days before the beginning of emplacement of the explosives, for each emplacement hole of a group explosion, the local coordinates of the point of emplacement of the explosive, the entrance of the emplacement hole, the point of the emplacement hole most distant from the entrance, the location of the emplacement hole at each 200 meters distance from the entrance and the configuration of any known voids larger than one cubic meter located within the distance, in meters, of 10 times the cube root of the planned yield in kilotons measured from the bottom of the canister containing the explosive. The error in these coordinates shall not exceed one percent of the distance between the emplacement hole and the nearest other emplacement hole or one percent of the distance between the point of measurement and the entrance of the emplacement hole, whichever is smaller, but in no case shall the error be required to be less than one meter.

3. The Party carrying out the explosion shall emplace for each explosive that portion of the electrical equipment for yield determination described in subparagraph 3(a) of Article IV, supplied in accordance with paragraph 1 of Article IV, in the same emplacement hole as the explosive in accordance with the installation instructions supplied under the provisions of paragraph 5 or 6 of Article

IV. Such emplacement shall be carried out under the observation of designated personnel. Other equipment specified in subparagraph 3(b) of Article IV shall be emplaced and installed:

(a) by designated personnel under the observation and with the assistance of personnel of the Party carrying out the explosion, if such assistance is requested by designated personnel; or

(b) in accordance with paragraph 5 of Article IV.

4. That portion of the electrical equipment for yield determination described in subparagraph 3(a) of Article IV that is to be emplaced in each emplacement hole shall be located so that the end of the electrical equipment which is farthest from the entrance to the emplacement hole is at a distance, in meters, from the bottom of the canister containing the explosive equal to 3.5 times the cube root of the planned yield in kilotons of the explosive when the planned yield is less than 20 kilotons and three times the cube root of the planned yield in kilotons of the explosive when the planned yield is 20 kilotons or more. Canisters longer than 10 meters containing the explosive shall only be utilized if there is prior agreement between the Parties establishing provisions for their use. The Party carrying out the explosion shall provide the other Party with data on the distribution of density inside any other canister in the emplacement hole with a transverse cross-sectional area exceeding 10 square centimeters located within a distance, in meters, of 10 times the cube root of the planned yield in kilotons of the explosion from the bottom of the canister containing the explosive. The Party carrying out the explosion shall provide the other Party with access to confirm such data on density distribution within any such canister.

5. The Party carrying out an explosion shall fill each emplacement hole, including all pipes and tubes contained therein which have at any transverse section an aggregate cross-sectional area exceeding 10 square centimeters in the region containing the electrical equipment for yield determination and to a distance, in meters, of six times the cube root of the planned yield in kilotons of the explosive from the explosive emplacement point, with material having a density not less than seven-tenths of the average density of the surrounding rock, and from that point to a distance of not less than 60 meters from the explosive emplacement point with material having a density greater than one gram per cubic centimeter.

6. Designated personnel shall have the right to:

(a) confirm information provided in accordance with subparagraph 2(a) of this article;

(b) confirm information provided in accordance with subparagraph 2(b) of this article and be provided, upon request, with a sample of each batch of stemming material as that material is put into the emplacement hole; and

(c) confirm the information provided in accordance with subparagraph 2(c) of this article by having access to the data acquired and by observing, upon their request, the making· of measurements.

7. For those explosives which are emplaced in separate emplacement holes, the emplacement shall be such that the distance D, in meters, between any explosive and any portion of the electrical equipment for determination of the yield of any other explosive in the group shall be not less than 10 times the cube root of the planned yield in kilotons of the larger explosive of such a pair of explosives. Individual explosions shall be separated by time intervals, in milliseconds, not greater than one-sixth the amount by which the distance D, in meters, exceeds 10 times the cube root of the planned yield in kilotons of the larger explosive of such a pair of explosives.

8. For those explosives in a group which are emplaced in a common emplacement hole, the distance, in meters, between each explosive and any other explosive in that emplacement hole shall be not less than 10 times the cube root of the planned yield in kilotons of the larger explosive of such a pair of explosives, and the explosives shall be detonated in sequential order, beginning with the explosive farthest from the entrance to the emplacement hole, with the individual detonations separated by time intervals, in milliseconds, of not less than one times the cube root of the planned yield in kilotons of the largest explosive in this emplacement hole.

ARTICLE VII

1. Designated personnel with their personal baggage and their equipment as provided in Article IV shall be permitted to enter the territory of the Party carrying out the explosion at an entry port to be agreed upon by the Parties, to remain in the territory of the Party carrying out the explosion for the purpose of fulfilling their rights and functions provided for in the Treaty and this Protocol, and to depart from an exit port to be agreed upon by the Parties.

2. At all times while designated personnel are in the territory of the Party carrying out the explosion, their persons, property, personal baggage, archives and documents as well their temporary official and living quarters shall be accorded the same privileges and immunities as provided in Articles 22, 23, 24, 29, 30, 31, 34 and 36 of the Vienna Convention on Diplomatic Relations of 1961 to the persons, property, personal baggage, archives and documents of diplomatic agents as well as to the premises of diplomatic missions and private residences of diplomatic agents.

3. Without prejudice to their privileges and immunities it shall be the duty of designated personnel to respect the laws and regulations of the State in whose territory the explosion is to be carried out insofar as they do not impede in any way whatsoever the proper exercising of their rights and functions provided for by the Treaty and this Protocol.

ARTICLE VIII

The Party carrying out an explosion shall have sole and exclusive control over and full responsibility for the conduct of the explosion.

ARTICLE IX

1. Nothing in the Treaty and this Protocol shall affect proprietary rights in information made available under the Treaty and this Protocol and in information which may be disclosed in preparation for and carrying out of explosions; however, claims to such proprietary rights shall not impede implementation of the provisions of the Treaty and this Protocol.

2. Public release of the information provided in accordance with Article II or publication of material using such information, as well as public release of the results of observation and measurements obtained by designated personnel, may take place only by agreement with the Party carrying out an explosion; however, the other Party shall have the right to issue statements after the explosion that do not divulge information in which the Party carrying out the explosion has rights which are referred to in paragraph 1 of this article.

ARTICLE X

The Joint Consultative Commission shall establish procedures through which the Parties will, as appropriate, consult with each other for the purpose of ensuring efficient implementation of this Protocol.

Done at Washington and Moscow, on May 28, 1976.

For the United States of America:

GERALD R. FORD
The President of the United States of America

For the Union of Soviet Socialist Republics:

L. I. BREZHNEV
General Secretary of the Central Committee of the CPSU

Text of Agreed Statement

The Parties to the Treaty Between the United States of America and the Union of Soviet Socialist Republics on Underground Nuclear Explosions for Peaceful Purposes, hereinafter referred to as the Treaty, agree that under subparagraph 2(c) of Article III of the Treaty:

(a) Development testing of nuclear explosives

does not constitute a "peaceful application" and any such development tests shall be carried out only within the boundaries of nuclear weapon test sites specified in accordance with the Treaty between the United States of America and the Union of Soviet Socialist Republics on the Limitation of Underground Nuclear Weapon Tests;

(b) Associating test facilities, instrumentation or procedures related only to testing of nuclear weapons or their effects with any explosion carried out in accordance with the Treaty does not constitute a "peaceful application."

MAY 13, 1976.

66 (July 29, 1976)

Senate Asked To Approve Treaties With U.S.S.R. on Nuclear Explosions

Message From President Ford [1]

To the Senate of the United States:

With a view to receiving the advice and consent of the Senate to ratification, I transmit herewith the Treaty between the United States of America and the Union of Soviet Socialist Republics on the Limitation of Underground Nuclear Weapon Tests, and the Protocol thereto, referred to as the Threshold Test Ban Treaty (TTB Treaty), and the Treaty between the United States of America and the Union of Soviet Social-

---

[1] Transmitted on July 29 (text from White House press release); also printed as S. Ex. N, 94th Cong., 2d sess., which includes the texts of the treaties and protocols and the report of the Department of State. For texts of the Threshold Test Ban Treaty and Protocol, see BULLETIN of July 29, 1974, p. 217; for texts of the Peaceful Nuclear Explosion Treaty and Protocol, see BULLETIN of June 28, 1976, p. 801.

ist Republics on Underground Nuclear Explosions for Peaceful Purposes, and the Protocol thereto (PNE Treaty). The TTBT was signed in Moscow on July 3, 1974 and the PNE Treaty was signed in Washington and Moscow on May 28, 1976. For the information of the Senate, I transmit also the detailed report of the Department of State on these Treaties.

These Treaties together establish procedures for the conduct of all underground nuclear explosions by the United States and the Soviet Union. All nuclear explosions other than underground nuclear explosions are prohibited by the Treaty Banning Nuclear Weapon Tests in the Atmosphere, in Outer Space and Under Water (the Limited Test Ban Treaty) of 1963. The TTB Treaty and PNE Treaty are the first agreements since the Limited Test Ban Treaty to impose direct restraints on nuclear explosions by the Parties and, as such, contribute to limiting nuclear arms competition.

These two Treaties represent approximately two years of intensive effort. Negotiation of the TTB Treaty began in the Spring of 1974 and was completed in July of that year. However, the question of the relationship of underground nuclear explosions for peaceful purposes to limitations on nuclear weapon testing was not then resolved. As a result, Article III of the TTB Treaty provided that the Parties would negotiate and conclude an agreement governing underground nuclear explosions for peaceful purposes. Work on the PNE Treaty began in the Fall of 1974 and after six lengthy negotiating sessions was completed in April of 1976.

The TTB Treaty and the PNE Treaty are closely interrelated and complement one another. The TTB Treaty places a limitation of 150 kilotons on all underground nuclear weapon tests carried out by the Parties. The PNE Treaty similarly provides for a limitation of 150 kilotons on all individual underground nuclear explosions for peaceful purposes.

During the negotiation of the PNE Treaty, the Parties investigated whether individual explosions with yields above 150 kilotons could be accommodated consistent with the agreed aim of not providing weapon-related benefits otherwise precluded by the TTB Treaty. The Parties did not develop a basis for such an accommodation, largely because it has not been possible to distinguish between nuclear explosive device technology as applied for weapon-related purposes and as applied for peaceful purposes. The Parties therefore agreed that the yield limitations on individual explosions in the two Treaties would be the same.

The TTB Treaty and the PNE Treaty contain numerous provisions to ensure adequate verification, including some concepts, more far-reaching than those found in previous arms control agreements, which are not only important in themselves but which will have significant precedential value as well. For example, the Limited Test Ban Treaty is verified only by national technical means. The TTB and PNE Treaties add requirements for exchange of specific information in advance to assist verification by national technical means, and the PNE Treaty establishes procedures for on-site observation under certain conditions on the territory of the Party conducting the explosion.

The TTB Treaty provides for an exchange of data on the geography and geology of nuclear weapon test sites as well as the yields of some actual weapons tests conducted at each site. The PNE Treaty requires that the Party conducting any underground nuclear explosion for peaceful purposes provide the other Party in advance with data on the geography and geology of the place where the explosion is to be carried out, its purpose, and specific information on each explosion itself. These requirements are related to the yield of the explosion and become more detailed as the magnitude of the explosions increase.

In addition to the limitation on individual nuclear explosions of 150 kilotons, the PNE Treaty provides for an aggregate yield limitation of 1.5 megatons on group underground nuclear explosions for peaceful purposes. A group explosion consists of substantially simultaneous individual explosions located within a specific geometrical relationship to one another. The Treaty provides for mandatory on-site observer rights for group explosions with an aggregate yield in excess of 150 kilotons in order to determine that the yield of each individual explosion in the group does not exceed 150 kilotons and that the explosions serve the stated peaceful purposes. The Treaty also provides for on-site observers for explosions with an aggregate yield between 100 and 150 kilotons if both Parties agree, on the basis of information provided, that such observers would be appropriate for the confirmation of the yield of the explosion.

The TTB Treaty and the PNE Treaty, taken together as integrated and complementary components of this important limitation on nuclear explosions, provide that very large yield nuclear explosions will no longer be carried out by the Parties. This is one more useful step in our continuing efforts to develop comprehensive and balanced limitations on nuclear weapons. We will continue our efforts to reach an adequately verifiable agreement banning all nuclear weapon testing, but in so doing we must ensure that controls on peaceful nuclear explosions are consistent with such a ban. These Treaties are in the national interest, and I respectfully recommend that the Senate give its advice and consent to ratification.

GERALD R. FORD.

THE WHITE HOUSE, *July 29, 1976.*

67 (November 26, 1976)
United States and U.S.S.R. Sign New Fisheries Agreement

Joint Statement

Press release 572 dated November 26

Representatives of the Union of Soviet Socialist Republics and the United States of America on November 26, 1976, signed [at Washington] a new agreement relating to fishing activities of the Soviet Union off the coasts of the United States. The agreement sets out the arrangements between the countries which will govern fishing by the Soviet Union within the fishery conservation zone of the United States beginning March 1, 1977. The agreement will come into force after the completion of internal procedures by both governments.

Vladimir M. Kamentsev, First Deputy Minister of Fisheries, U.S.S.R., signed for the Union of Soviet Socialist Republics. Ambassador Thomas A. Clingan, Jr., Chairman of the U.S. Delegation, signed for the United States.

Both delegations expressed their satisfaction with the new accord and the hope that it will contribute to mutual understanding and cooperation between the two governments.

VIII:

THE FIRST YEAR OF THE CARTER ADMINISTRATION: 1977

INTRODUCTION

The rhetoric of U.S.-Soviet relations has changed with the advent of the Carter administration, but the content of the relationship remains the same as in 1976. No new agreements have been signed to expand U.S.-Soviet trade, but an active trade continues under the auspices of the Temporary Purchasing Commission and the Trade Representation.

In the area of bilateral cooperative ventures, the Carter administration has created nothing new, but it renewed the agreement on scientific and technological cooperation when it was due to expire in May (Document 75).

Documents 70 through 74 reveal that the Carter administration is continuing the previous policy of working for an agreement to replace the Interim Agreement of 1972 on strategic offensive arms. When the Interim Agreement expired in May, the Carter administration announced its intention to abide by the terms of the 1972 agreement if the Soviets would do likewise (Document 76), and it renewed the ABM treaty when that agreement, too, was ready to expire (Documents 77 and 78).

Once the election was over, the term "detente" made a reappearance, and is now with us regularly to describe the policy of the past and present administrations.

Copyright License

AGREEMENT

WASHINGTON, D.C.

made this 14 day of February 1977 between the Copyright Agency of the USSR (hereinafter VAAP) and the National Technical Information Service, United States Department of Commerce, USA (hereinafter NTIS), concerning the translation and publication in English of Soviet journals and articles from Soviet journals.

1

VAAP hereby grants to NTIS the non-exclusive right to translate into English, to publish (subject to section 3 of this Agreement) n the form of journals in English, and sell throughout the world:

a) Soviet journals listed in Appendix A; and

b) Articles from Soviet journals listed in Appendix B. These articles will be selected by NTIS at its own choice and published by NTIS in topical journals such as those listed in Appendix B.

VAAP reserves the right to grant to other publishers the non-exclusive right to publish in English cover-to-cover translations of the journals listed in Appendix A and to publish in English separate articles selected from the journals listed in Appendix B.

3

NTIS agrees to publish translations of journals listed in Appendix A and translations of articles from Soviet journals listed in Appendix B within the period indicated in the Appendices A and B for each journal (beginning from the date of publication of Soviet original). NTIS will continue to sell these journals and articles from journals as long as a reasonable buyer demand for such publications exists.

NTIS agrees that it shall not include in its compilations any Soviet fiction materials whatsoever.

4

The names of Soviet Publishing Houses (in Russian, written in Latin letters) and the titles of the journals listed in Appendix A (in Russian, written in Latin letters) shall appear beneath the English title or on the back of the title page of every copy of the journals issued by NTIS, together with full copyright notice of the Soviet publishers.

The name of the author of the article; the original title of the article (in English); the page numbers of the article in the original Soviet journal; the number of the issue; the year of publication; and the title and full copyright notice of the original Soviet journal (in Russian, written in Latin letters) from which the article was selected by NTIS as per Appendix B shall appear above or beneath each article published in NTIS's topical compilations.

5

If the author (authors) of any article published in any Soviet journal as per Appendix A and Appendix B expresses unwillingness to have an English language translation of the article published and to be sold or being sold by NTIS, VAAP shall notify NTIS which shall refrain from publishing the work or discontinue its public sale of the work.

6

Soviet copyright holders of the works from the journals listed in Appendix A and Appendix B have the right to reprint English translations of their works made by NTIS, in a few copies for non-commercial use.

7

In consideration of the copyright license granted herein, NTIS shall pay to VAAP a royalty of six percent (6%) of the sale price of each cover-to-cover translation listed in Appendix A and each topical compilation such as those listed in Appendix B which is sold by NTIS. Royalty payments shall be made annually by NTIS, not later than three (3) months after the end of each calendar year. All sums due VAAP will be remitted by NTIS to the account of VAAP at the Bank for Foreign Trade of the USSR, Moscow.

NTIS shall immediately notify VAAP that the payments have been made.

Simultaneously with payments NTIS will render to VAAP annual accounts of the payments made containing the following data:

a) as per Appendix A:

    1) Numbers of issues of each separate Soviet journal (in Soviet edition) which were published by NTIS during the calendar year;

    2) Number of subscriptions sold and subscription price of each NTIS journal separately and the sum of royalty to be paid to VAAP for the numbers of issues of each separate Soviet journal (in Soviet edition) published during the calendar year; and

b) as per Appendix B, the number of subscriptions sold, subscription price, and the sum of royalty paid to VAAP for each NTIS's journal separately.

9

NTIS agrees:

a) to send two free copies of each journal published cover-to-cover in the translated edition to VAAP and two free copies to the address of the Soviet publishers; and

b) to send four free copies of NTIS's topical journals to VAAP.

10

All expenses in connection with the translation, publication, advertising and distribution of the journals in accordance with the present Agreement are to be borne by NTIS.

11

NTIS will act on its own behalf in all operations with third parties in connection with the fulfillment of the present Agreement and VAAP will bear no responsibility for NTIS's transactions with third parties.

12

All differences and disputes which may arise from the present Agreement or in connection therewith are to be settled by direct discussion between the parties.

13

NTIS agrees to pay to VAAP the sum of four thousand dollars ($4000) as royalty for sales of copyrighted Soviet works covered by this Agreement occurring between May 27, 1973 and prior to the date of execution of this Agreement.

The present Agreement shall enter into force upon the date of its signing and shall continue in full force and effect for a period of five (5) calendar years. At the expiration of this initial five-year period, the Agreement may be renewed indefinitely for additional one (1) year periods.

Either party may terminate this Agreement at any time upon ninety (90) days prior written notice to the opposite party. In case of termination of the Agreement, however, NTIS shall have the right to publish the remaining copies of the journals of current year, to sell the remaining copies of the journals, and shall be liable to make payments to VAAP in accordance with the conditions of the present Agreement.

14

All amendments and supplements to the present Agreement are valid provided they are made in writing and duly signed by authorized representatives of both parties.

After the signing of the present Agreement all previous negotiations and correspondence on the questions settled by the Agreement shall become null and void.

This Agreement shall be binding and have full force and effect upon the parties and their successors.

The Agreement is signed in two copies in English.

Legal addresses of the parties:

VAAP – Copyright Agency of the USSR
6a Bolshaya Bronnaya,
Moscow 103104, USSR

NTIS – National Technical Information Service
425 13th Street N.W. Washington, D.C. 20004

IN WITNESS THEREOF this Agreement has been signed by the parties hereto:

Signatures:

VAAP:	Yu GRADOV	NTIS:	W T KNOX
	Y VHAROV		PETER F URBACH
Date:	February, 14, 1977	Date:	14 February 1977

Appendix A

to the Agreement between Copyright Agency of the USSR and National Technical Information Service, USA dated February 14th 1977

Cover-to-cover Translations

	Period for first publication of English translation counted from date of Soviet publication:
1. Kommunist Communist	One Year
2. SSha: Ekonomika, Politika, Ideologiya USA: Economics, Politics, Ideology	One Year
3. Sotsiologicheskiye Issledo-vaniya Sociological Studies	One Year
4. Ksomicheskaya Biologiya i Aviakosmicheskaya Medit-sina Space Biology and Aerospace Medicine	One Year

5. Radiobiologiya   One Year
   Radio Biology
6. Problemy Dal'nego Vostoka One Year
   Problems of the Far East

<table>
<tr><td>THE COPYRIGHT AGENCY
OF THE USSR</td><td>NATIONAL TECHNICAL
INFORMATION SERVICE</td></tr>
<tr><td>Yu Gradov</td><td>W T Knox</td></tr>
<tr><td>Y Vharov</td><td>Peter F Urbach</td></tr>
</table>

Appendix B

to the Agreement between the Copyright Agency of the USSR and
the National Technical Information Service, USA dated February
14th, 1977

The NTIS topical compilations shall be composed of articles selected
from a list of copyrighted Soviet journals attached to this Appendix
and made a part of this Agreement. The list of journals shall be made
final through an exchange of special letters between VAAP and NTIS.
A representative list of NTIS topical compilations is as follows:

1. Translations on USSR
   Economic Affairs

2. Translations on USSR
   Agriculture

3. Translations on USSR
   Industrial Affairs

4. Translations on USSR
   Resources

5. Translations on USSR
   Trade and Services

6. Translations on USSR
   Political & Sociological
   Affairs

7. Translations on USSR
   Military Affairs

English language translations of articles appearing in the journals
on the list described above shall be initially offered for sale by NTIS
within eighteen (18) months of the date of publication in the Soviet
Union of the journals from which the articles were taken.

<table>
<tr><td>THE COPYRIGHT AGENCY
OF THE USSR</td><td>NATIONAL TECHNICAL
INFORMATION SERVICE</td></tr>
<tr><td>Yu Gradov</td><td>W T Knox</td></tr>
<tr><td>Y Vharov</td><td>Peter F Urbach</td></tr>
</table>

69 (March 30, 1977)
Embassy Sites

The American Embassy to the Soviet Ministry of Foreign Affairs

Note No. 409

The Embassy of the United States of America presents its compliments to the Ministry of Foreign Affairs of the Union of Soviet Socialist Republics and, referring to the Agreement between the Government of the United States of America and the Government of the Union of Soviet Socialist Republics on the Reciprocal Allocation for Use Free of Charge of Plots of Land in Moscow and Washington, of May 16, 1969,[1] and the Agreement between the Government of the United States of America and the Government of the Union of Soviet Socialist Republics on the Conditions of Construction of Complexes of Buildings of the Embassy of the United States of America in Moscow and of the Embassy of the Union of Soviet Socialist Republics in Washington, of December 4, 1972,[2] has the honor to inform the Ministry of the following:

The plot of land known as Mount Alto in Washington, D.C., designated for construction of a complex of buildings of the Embassy of the Union of Soviet Socialist Republics and which is described in attachment III of the Agreement of May 16, 1969, is hereby allocated for use free of charge to the Soviet side. The plot of land located on Konyushkovskaya Ulitsa in the Krasnopresnenskiy region in Moscow designated for construction of a complex of buildings of the Embassy of the United States of America and which is described in attachment I of the Agreement of May 16, 1969, is hereby accepted for use free of charge by the U.S. side.

In accordance with Article III, 2 of the Agreement of May 16, 1969, the date of beginning of the period of use of the plots is March 30, 1977.

In accordance with Article IV, 4 of the Agreement of December 4, 1972, the date of beginning of construction on the plot known as Mount Alto in Washington will be March 30, 1977, and the date of beginning of construction on the plot on Konyushkovskaya Ulitsa in Moscow will be May 15, 1978.

The preparation for construction on the Moscow plot designated for the complex of buildings of the Embassy of the United States of America will begin not later than October 1, 1977. The scope of this work will be determined later.

In accordance with Article I, 6 of the Agreement of December 4, 1972, both sides agree that the target date for completion of construction of Embassy complexes in Washington and Moscow, respectively, will be July 1, 1982. Residential, school and club buildings of the respective embassies in Washington and Moscow can be occupied at any time after completion and acceptance for their designated use.

The present Note of the Embassy of the United States of America and the corresponding Note of the Ministry of Foreign Affairs of the Union of Soviet Socialist Republics constitute an agreement between the sides on this question, this agreement coming into force on the date of the exchange of notes.

EMBASSY OF THE UNITED STATES OF AMERICA,
Moscow, *March 30, 1977.*

---

1 TIAS 6693, 6763, 6796, 6872, 6956, 7066; 20 UST 789, 2871, 4067; 21 UST 1159, 2093; 22 UST 366.
2 TIAS 7512; 23 UST 3544.

MINISTRY OF FOREIGN AFFAIRS
OF THE USSR

No. 16/dusa

The Ministry of Foreign Affairs of the Union of Soviet Socialist
Republics presents its compliments to the Embassy of the United States
of America and, referring to the Agreement between the Government of
the Union of Soviet Socialist Republics and the Government of the
United States of America on the Reciprocal Allocation for Use Free of
Charge of Plots of Land in Moscow and Washington of May 16, 1969, and
to the Agreement between the Government of the Union of Soviet Socialist
Republics and the Government of the United States of America on the
Conditions of Construction of Complexes of Buildings of the Embassy of
the United States of America in Moscow of December 4, 1972, has the
honor to inform the Embassy of the following.

A plot of land is herewith allocated for use free of charge to the
American side, located at Konyushkovskaya Ulitsa in the Krasnopresnenskiy
District of the city of Moscow, which is set aside for the construction
of the complex of buildings of the Embassy of the United States of
America, and the description of which is given in Attachment I to the
Agreement of May 16, 1969, and a plot of land known as Mount Alto in
the city of Washington, District of Columbia, is herewith taken over
for use free of charge by the Soviet side, which is set aside for
the construction of the complex of buildings of the Embassy of the
Union of Soviet Socialist Republics, and a description of which is
given in Attachment III of the Agreement of May 16, 1969.

In accordance with Article III, paragraph 2, of the Agreement of
May 16, 1969, the date of the beginning of the period of use of the
plots of land is March 30, 1977.

In accordance with Article IV, paragraph 4, of the Agreement of
December 4, 1972, the date of the beginning of construction on the
plot of land known as Mount Alto in Washington is March 30, 1977, and
the date of the beginning of construction on the plot of land on
Konyushkovskaya Ulitsa in Moscow will be May 15, 1978.

Preparation for construction on the plot of land in Moscow, set
aside for the complex of buildings of the Embassy of the United States
of America, is to begin no later than October 1, 1977. The volume of
this work will be determined later.

In accordance with Article I, paragraph 6, of the Agreement of
December 4, 1972, both parties agree that the planned date for completion
of the construction of the complexes of buildings of the Embassies in
Washington and Moscow respectively, will be July 1, 1982. Residential
home, school and club buildings of the Embassies in Washington and
Moscow respectively can be occupied any time after their construction
and acceptance for their designated use.

This note of the Ministry of Foreign Affairs of the Union of Soviet
Socialist Republics and the corresponding note of the Embassy of the
United States of America constitute an agreement between the parties
on this question, which enters into force on the day of the exchange
of notes.

Moscow, March 30, 1977

[SEAL]

Embassy of the United States of America,
Moscow

70 (March 30, 1977)
JOINT U.S.–U.S.S.R. COMMUNIQUE, MARCH 30

Press release 144 dated March 30

On March 28–30, 1977, General Secretary of the
Central Committee of the Communist Party of the
Soviet Union, L.I. Brezhnev and member of the Polit-
buro of the Central Committee of the Communist
Party of the Soviet Union, Minister of Foreign Affairs
of the U.S.S.R., A.A. Gromyko, held talks with the
Secretary of State of the United States of America,
Cyrus R. Vance, who was in Moscow on an official
visit.

In the course of the talks there was a general
discussion of American-Soviet relations, as well as certain international problems of mutual interest for the
U.S. and the U.S.S.R.

Consideration of questions relevant to the completion of the new agreement on the limitation of
strategic offensive arms occupied the central place in
the talks. The sides have agreed to continue the consideration of these issues.

An exchange of views also took place on a number of
other questions concerning the limitation of armaments
and disarmament. It was agreed that bilateral contacts, including meetings of experts, would be held to
discuss these matters.

The discussion of international issues included the
Belgrade preparatory conference, and the situation in
Cyprus and southern Africa. They reaffirmed the importance of the Quadripartite Agreement of September
1971. Special attention was given to the situation in
the Middle East. The sides have agreed that cooperation between the U.S. and the U.S.S.R. as co-
chairmen of the Geneva conference is essential in
bringing about a just and lasting peace in the area. An
understanding was reached to hold, in the first half of
May, 1977 in Geneva, a meeting between the Secretary
of State of the U.S. and the Minister of Foreign Affairs of the U.S.S.R. for a thorough exchange of views
on the Middle East problem, including the question of
resuming the work of the Geneva conference. Some of
the other issues discussed in the talks in Moscow will
be reviewed at that time.

The consideration of practical questions of bilateral
relations produced several specific understandings.

71 (April 26, 1977)
Strategic Arms Limitation Talks To Resume at Geneva

Joint U.S.-U.S.S.R. Statement [1]

The United States and the U.S.S.R. have agreed that their delegations will resume negotiations on strategic arms limitations in Geneva beginning May 11, 1977. The discussions will consider questions related to the text of a SALT agreement which were considered but not settled in previous Geneva negotiations.

In addition to the Geneva negotiations, the two sides have agreed to continue to exchange views at other levels in an effort to conclude a SALT agreement.

---

[1] Read to news correspondents on Apr. 26 by Department spokesman Hodding Carter III; also released that day at Moscow.

72 (May 17, 1977)
U.S.-U.S.S.R. Working Groups Meet on Arms Limitation Questions

Joint U.S.-U.S.S.R. Communique [1]

Pursuant to agreement reached in the course of the talks during the visit of United States Secretary of State Cyrus Vance to Moscow in March 1977, bilateral consultations on some questions of arms limitation and disarmament were held in Geneva from 9 to 13 May between delegations of the USA and the USSR.

In the course of the consultations, questions of the prohibition of the development and production of new types and new systems of weapons of mass destruction were considered. In particular, the question of the prohibition of radiological weapons was examined. The sides discussed certain aspects and identified areas of agreement on questions under discussion.

The sides continued the consideration of questions related to a possible joint initiative in the CCD with respect to the conclusion of an international convention dealing with the most dangerous, lethal means of chemical warfare as a first step toward complete and effective prohibition of chemical weapons. The negotiations on this issue were held on the basis of the summit agreement between the USA and the USSR of July 3, 1974, and were a continuation of the US-Soviet consultations on lethal and other highly toxic means of chemical warfare conducted in Geneva in August 1976 and in April 1977. The discussion of these matters provided a useful basis for the continuation of the work with a view to preparing the text of an appropriate document which would be a practical implementation of the joint initiative.

The two sides agreed to meet in the near future to continue consideration of all the matters which had been under discussion.

---

[1] Issued at Washington, Geneva, and Moscow on May 17 following meetings of the working groups on the prohibition of chemical weapons and on weapons of mass destruction (text from U.S. Arms Control and Disarmament Agency press release 77-6 dated May 17).

73 (May 18, 1977)
United States Signs Convention Banning Environmental Warfare

Statement by Secretary Vance [1]

On behalf of the United States of America, I am pleased to sign the Convention on the Prohibition of Military or Any Other Hostile Use of Environmental Modification Techniques. It is especially significant that this ceremony is taking place here in Geneva where, for a decade and a half, dedicated officials have labored to bring the goal of disarmament closer to reality. This convention was negotiated in this city by the Conference of the Committee on Disarmament and is an achievement to be added to other significant arms control agreements, such as the nonproliferation treaty, seabed arms control treaty, and the biological weapons convention.

While the intentional modification of the environment at present can be done only on a local and small scale at best, we scarcely need remind ourselves that in our era technology can advance to make possible actions which would cause hitherto inconceivable environmental consequences. So we believe it wise to outlaw what is commonly called "environmental warfare" before it has a real chance to be developed significantly for military purposes, with potentially disastrous consequences.

The convention does not prohibit research on and development of, or the use of, environmental modification techniques for peaceful purposes. The United States earnestly desires that all research and development, as well as use of environmental modification techniques, be dedicated solely to peaceful ends. To this end, as we have made clear in the past, we have no secrets in this area: All of our activities in the area of environmental modification are carried out on an open basis and the information is shared with others.

In the view of the United States, the effect of the convention should be to eliminate the danger of environmental warfare because it prohibits all significant hostile use of environmental modification techniques. According to the present terms, the convention limits the prohibition to those uses having "widespread, long-lasting or severe effects." The United States will be prepared to reexamine this limitation on the scope of the convention at the review conference or possibly before.

74 (May 21, 1977)
JOINT COMMUNIQUE

Press release 224 dated May 21

In the course of the discussions between Cyrus R. Vance, Secretary of State of the USA, and L. I. Brezhnev, General Secretary of the Central Committee of the CPSU, and A. A. Gromyko, Member of the Politburo of the CPSU, Minister of Foreign Affairs of the USSR, held in Moscow at the end of March, 1977, Cyrus R. Vance and A. A. Gromyko met in Geneva on May 18–20.

They examined in detail the situation regarding the preparation of a new agreement on the limitation of strategic offensive arms based on the Vladivostok Accord and taking into account the results of subsequent discussions. Both sides agreed that the discussions in Geneva were necessary and useful and that progress had been made in developing a common framework for further negotiations. As a result of the exchange of views, the differences between the two sides on several of the previously unresolved questions have been narrowed. It is agreed that the discussions of all unresolved questions will be continued with the aim of an early conclusion of a new agreement that will replace the interim agreement on certain measures with respect to the limitation of strategic offensive armaments.

Cyrus R. Vance and A. A. Gromyko also had a thorough exchange of views on the problem of the settlement in the Middle East.

Both sides proceed on the premise that elimination of the continuing source of tension in the Middle East constitutes one of the primary tasks in ensuring peace and international security. They are convinced that in achieving this goal an important role belongs to the Geneva Peace Conference on the Middle East, an international forum specifically set up to negotiate a settlement of the Middle East problem in the interests of all the parties concerned.

Having confirmed that mutual efforts of the US and the USSR, who are co-chairmen of the Geneva Conference, are of substantial importance for achieving a just, durable and stable peace in the Middle East, the sides agreed to direct their joint efforts toward resuming the work of the Conference during the fall of 1977, while recognizing the importance of careful preparation before the Conference meets. For these purposes, the US and the USSR will be conducting monthly consultations at the level of ambassadors in Washington or Moscow.

75 (July 8, 1977)
Scientific and Technical Cooperation

AGREEMENT BETWEEN
THE GOVERNMENT OF THE UNITED STATES OF AMERICA AND
THE GOVERNMENT OF THE UNION OF SOVIET SOCIALIST REPUBLICS
ON COOPERATION IN THE FIELDS OF SCIENCE AND TECHNOLOGY

The Government of the United States of America and the Government of the Union of Soviet Socialist Republics,

Noting that the Agreement between the Government of the United States of America and the Government of the Union of Soviet Socialist Republics on Cooperation in the fields of Science and Technology, signed in Moscow on May 24, 1972, had a validity of five years and was extended on an interim basis by an exchange of notes in Washington on May 24, 1977; [1]

Recognizing that cooperation carried out in various fields between scientific and technical organizations of the two countries brings mutual benefits and useful practical results;

Noting with satisfaction the progress made in the course of mutually agreed activities carried out in accordance with the aforementioned Agreement;

Desiring to continue in the future cooperation in various fields of science and technology;

Taking into consideration that such cooperation will serve to strengthen friendly relations between the two countries;

And in accordance with the general agreement between the United States of America and the Union of Soviet Socialist Republics on contacts, exchanges, and cooperation signed June 19, 1973; [2]

Have agreed as follows:

ARTICLE 1

Both Parties pledge themselves to assist and develop scientific and technical cooperation between both countries on the basis of mutual benefit, equality and reciprocity.

ARTICLE 2

The main objective of this cooperation is to provide broad opportunities for both Parties to combine the efforts of their scientists and specialists in working on major problems, whose solution will promote the progress of science and technology for the benefit of both countries and of mankind.

---

[1] TIAS 7346, 8619
[2] TIAS 7649

ARTICLE 3

The forms of cooperation in science and technology may include the following:

a.   Exchange of scientists and specialists;

b.   Exchange of scientific and technical information and documentation;

c.   Joint development and implementation of programs and projects in the fields of basic and applied sciences;

d.   Joint research, development and testing, and exchange of research results and experience between scientific research institutions and organizations;

e.   Organization of joint courses, conferences and symposia;

f.   Rendering of help, as appropriate, on both sides in establishing contacts and arrangements between United States firms and Soviet enterprises where a mutual interest develops; and

g.   Other forms of scientific and technical cooperation as may be mutally agreed.

ARTICLE 4

1.   Pursuant to the aims of this Agreement, both Parties will, as appropriate, encourage and facilitate the establishment and development of direct contacts and cooperation between agencies, organizations and firms of both countries and the conclusion, as appropriate, of implementing agreements for particular cooperative activities engaged in under this Agreement.

2.   Such agreements between agencies, organizations and enterprises will be concluded in accordance with the laws of both countries. Such agreements may cover the subjects of cooperation, organizations engaged in the implementation of projects and programs, the procedures which should be followed, and any other appropriate details.

ARTICLE 5

Unless otherwise provided in an implementing agreement, each Party or participating agency, organization or enterprise shall bear the costs of its participation and that of its personnel in cooperative activities engaged in under this Agreement, in accordance with existing laws in both countries.

217

ARTICLE 6

Nothing in this Agreement shall be interpreted to prejudice other agreements in the fields of science and technology concluded between the Parties.

ARTICLE 7

1. For the implementation of this Agreement there shall be established a U.S.-U.S.S.R. Joint Commission on Scientific and Technical Cooperation. The Commission shall consist of United States and Soviet parts, of which the chairmen and members shall be designated by the respective Parties. The Commission shall meet, as a rule, once a year in the United States and the Soviet Union alternately. The Commission shall adopt regulations for its operation.

2. The Commission shall consider proposals for the development of cooperation in specific areas; prepare suggestions and recommendations, as appropriate, for the two Parties; develop and approve measures and programs for implementation of this Agreement; designate, as appropriate, the agencies, organizations or enterprises responsible for carrying out cooperative activities; and seek to assure their proper implementation.

3. To carry out its functions, the Commission may create temporary or permanent joint subcommittees, councils or working groups.

4. During the period between meetings of the Commission additions or amendments may be made to already approved cooperative activities, as may be mutually agreed.

5. The Executive Agent for this Agreement shall be for the United States of America the Office of Science and Technology Policy and for the Union of Soviet Socialist Republics the State Committee of the U.S.S.R. Council of Ministers for Science and Technology. The Executive Agents will encourage and facilitate cooperation in the fields of science and technology carried out under other U.S.-U.S.S.R. intergovernmental agreements.

ARTICLE 8

1.   This Agreement shall enter into force upon signature and shall remain in force for five years. It may be modified or extended by mutual agreement of the Parties.

2.   The termination of this Agreement shall not affect the validity of agreements made hereunder between agencies, organizations and enterprises of both countries.

DONE at Washington this 8th day of July, 1977, in duplicate, in the English and Russian languages, both equally authentic.

FOR THE GOVERNMENT OF THE
UNITED STATES OF AMERICA:

Frank Press [1]

Science Adviser
to the President

FOR THE GOVERNMENT OF THE UNION
OF SOVIET SOCIALIST REPUBLICS:

[2]

Chairman of the State
Committee of the U.S.S.R.
Council of Ministers for
Science and Technology

---

[1] Frank Press
[2] V. A. Kirillin

United States intends not to take any action inconsistent with the Interim Agreement or the goals of the ongoing negotiations, provided that the Soviet Union exercises similar restraint. The Soviets have now issued a policy statement along the lines of our statement.

STATEMENT BY SECRETARY VANCE, SEPTEMBER 23

In order to maintain the status quo while SALT II negotiations are being completed, the United States declares its intention not to take any action inconsistent with the provisions of the Interim Agreement on Certain Measures With Respect to the Limitation of Strategic Offensive Arms which expires October 3, 1977, and with the goals of these ongoing negotiations provided that the Soviet Union exercises similar restraint.

---

76 (September 23 & 26, 1977)
U.S. Intent With Regard to SALT I Interim Agreement

Following is a statement by Paul C. Warnke, Director of the Arms Control and Disarmament Agency and Chairman of the U.S. delegation to the Strategic Arms Limitation Talks (SALT), made before the Senate Foreign Relations Committee on September 26.[1]

I appreciate the opportunity to appear before the committee today to discuss the expiration of the SALT I Interim Agreement on Certain Measures With Respect to the Limitation of Strategic Offensive Arms. The 1972 Interim Agreement expires on October 3, and it is clear that a SALT II agreement to replace it cannot be concluded by that date.

In recent days, there has been much discussion in the press about the Administration's plans with respect to this matter. On September 23, Secretary Vance issued a statement to the effect that, in order to maintain a stable situation while the SALT II negotiations are being completed, the

---

[1] The complete transcript of the hearings will be published by the committee and will be available from the Superintendent of Documents, U.S. Government Printing Office, Washington, D.C. 20402.

It should be noted that U.S. defense plans would not cause us to exceed any of the Interim Agreement limits in the near future, while the Soviets are in a position to do so because of their active ongoing SLBM [submarine-launched ballistic missiles] construction program.

We carefully considered what action should be taken in view of the fact that the October 3 date would pass before the completion of negotiations on a new agreement. In our deliberations, we concluded, after consultation with a number of Members of both the Senate and House, that an extension of the Interim Agreement would be inappropriate for two reasons:

—First, it would have reduced the pressure on the Soviets and on us to pursue a SALT II agreement based on equal aggregates of strategic offensive arms and

—Second, it would formally reaffirm acceptance of the disparity in numbers of strategic weapons established in the Interim Agreement.

Our policy statement is exactly what it says—a declaration of present intent. It is

nonbinding and nonobligatory. The Interim Agreement will expire on October 3 and will not be extended; no agreement limiting strategic offensive arms will be in force after next Monday. The United States will be free to change the policy announced in its statement of September 23 at any time.

Because our nonbinding statement is not part of an international agreement and does not impose any obligation on the United States, we have not requested congressional approval for it. We will carefully and continually monitor Soviet activities.

If these activities or any other circumstances warrant, we will be free to take whatever actions are appropriate, irrespective of the provisions set forth in the Interim Agreement.

We will, of course, continue to consult closely with members of this committee and other Members of Congress on the progress of SALT. We hope you will support our efforts in this regard.

JOINT STATEMENT

In discussions between Secretary Vance and Minister Gromyko on the questions related to strategic arms, both sides—the Soviet Union and the United States of America—have reaffirmed their determination to conclude a new agreement limiting strategic offensive arms and have declared their intention to continue active negotiations with a view to completing within the near future the work on that agreement.

The United States and the Soviet Union agree that the Treaty on the Limitation of Anti-Ballistic Missile Systems, signed in Moscow in 1972 and amended in 1974, serves the security interests of both countries. They share the view that this treaty decreases the risk of nuclear war and facilitates progress in the further limitation and reduction of strategic offensive arms. Both sides also agree that the ABM treaty has operated effectively, thus demonstrating the mutual commitment of the U.S.S.R. and the U.S.A. to the goal of nuclear arms limitations and to the principle of equal security.

Accordingly, in connection with the 5-year review of the ABM treaty, the two sides reaffirm their commitment to the treaty. It is agreed that this review will be conducted in the Standing Consultative Committee after its regular fall meeting.

78 (November 21, 1977)

U.S.-U.S.S.R. Communique on Antiballistic Missile Systems

Following is the text of the communique of the U.S.-U.S.S.R. Standing Consultative Commission (SCC) on the Review of the Treaty on the Limitation of Anti-Ballistic Missile Systems (ABM Treaty) issued at Geneva on November 21.[1]

Press Release 520 dated November 21

In accordance with the provisions of Article XIV of the Treaty Between the United States of America and the Union of Soviet Socialist Republics on the Limitation of Anti-Ballistic Missile Systems of May 26, 1972, which entered into force on October 3, 1972, and was amended by the protocol thereto of July 3, 1974, the parties to the treaty together conducted a review of the treaty after 5 years of its operation. By agreement between the parties, the review was conducted from November 4 to November 21, 1977, in a special session of the Standing Consultative Commission which was convened for that purpose.

---

[1] The Standing Consultative Commission was established in 1972 by the ABM Treaty (Article XIII) as a forum for discussion of questions of compliance and other issues related to that treaty. Article VI of the SALT I Interim Agreement on Certain Measures With Respect to the Limitation of Strategic Offensive Arms provided that the SCC would also address questions related to the Interim Agreement. Before the Interim Agreement expired on October 3, Secretary Vance announced that: "In order to maintain the status quo while SALT II negotiations are being completed, the United States declares its intention not to take any action inconsistent with the provisions of the Interim Agreement. . . ." (For full text, see BULLETIN of Nov. 7, 1977, p. 642.) Since October 3, the SCC has continued to address questions related to the Interim Agreement.

The parties agree that the treaty is operating effectively, thus demonstrating the mutual commitment of the United States and the Soviet Union to the goal of limiting nuclear arms and to the principle of equal security, serves the security interests of both parties, decreases the risk of outbreak of nuclear war, facilitates progress in the further limitation and reduction of strategic offensive arms, and requires no amendment at this time.

The parties note, in connection with the conduct of the review, that during the aforementioned period of operation of the treaty consultations and discussions have been held in the Standing Consultative Commission on matters pertaining to promoting the implementation of the objectives and provisions of the treaty. These consultations and discussions have been productive and useful in clarifying the mutual understanding of the parties concerning certain provisions of the treaty, in working out appropriate procedures for implementation of its provisions, and in resolving a number of questions related to complete and precise implementation of the provisions of the treaty.

Mindful of their obligation to conduct together a review of the treaty at 5-year intervals, the parties will continue the process of consultation concerning the implementation, as well as the enhancement of the viability and effectiveness, of the provisions of the treaty.

The parties reaffirm their mutual commitment to the objectives and provisions of the treaty and their resolve to maintain and further increase the viability and effectiveness of the treaty.

APPENDIX: DOCUMENTS AND AGREEMENTS
NOT INCLUDED

Chapter I (May 23 to 29, 1972)

1A. President Nixon's Radio-Television Address to the People of the Soviet Union. May 28, 1972. DSB 6-26-1972, 880–83.

2A. Joint U.S.-USSR Communique. May 29, 1972. DSB 6-26-1972, 899–902.

Chapter II (May 1972 to June 1973)

3A. Final Protocol to the Quadripartite Agreement on Berlin. June 3, 1972. DSB 9-27-1971, 318 contains a copy of the draft of this protocol. Announcement of U.S. signing of the protocol is in DSB 7-3-1972, 15. The Final Protocol brought the Quadripartite agreement of September 3, 1971 into force.

4A. Agreement on Exchange of Experimental Drugs for Cancer Treatment. June 30, 1972. Text not available.

5A. U.S.-USSR Joint Statement. September 14, 1972. DSB 10-9-1972, 398. A report on understandings and arrangements made during Kissinger's discussions in Moscow from September 10 to 14, 1972.

6A. Joint U.S.-USSR Announcement that arms limitation talks would resume in Geneva, November 21, 1972. DSB 11-13-1972, 565.

7A. Agreement on the Conditions of Construction of Complexes of Buildings of the U.S. Embassy in Moscow and the Soviet Embassy in Washington, with attachment. December 4, 1972. TIAS 7512; UST 23.4. 3544. A press release on the contents of this agreement is included as Document 20 of this volume.

8A. Agreement Extending the Agreement of December 11, 1970, Agreement of February 2, 1971, Agreements of February 12, 1971, and December 31, 1972. TIAS 7541; UST 23.4.4337. These agreements relate to fisheries.

9A.   Agreement on Air Transport Services Extending the Amendment of March 17, 1972, to the Agreement of November 4, 1966. Signed January 11, 1973. TIAS 7609; UST 24.1.986. Extended the effective date of the amendment to March 31, 1974.

10A.   Agreement on Pilot Project to Collect Heart Attack Information. February 9, 1973. Text not available.

11A.   Agreement on Fisheries (king and tanner crab). February 21, 1973. TIAS 7571; UST 24.1.603.

12A.   Agreement on Fishing Operations (Northeastern Pacific Ocean). February 21, 1973. TIAS 7572; UST 24.1.617.

13A.   Agreement on Fisheries (Northeastern part of the Pacific Ocean off the United States Coast). February 21, 1973. TIAS 7573; UST 24.1.631.

14A.   Agreement on Fisheries (Certain Fishery Problems on the High Seas in the Western Areas of the Middle Atlantic Ocean). February 21, 1973. TIAS 7574; UST 24.1.663.

15A.   Agreement on Fisheries (Consideration of Claims Resulting from Damage to Fishing Vessels or Gear and Measures to Prevent Fishing Conflicts), with annex and protocol. February 21, 1973. TIAS 7575; UST 24.1.669.

       These five agreements contain long, extensive accounts of technical matters and are, therefore, not included.

16A.   Status, Privileges and Immunities of the Delegations of the U.S.-USSR Standing Consultative Commission on Arms Limitation. Signed between the United States, the USSR, and Switzerland, March 5, 1973. TIAS 7582; UST 24.1.772.

17A.   President Nixon's "Message to Congress" regarding the Trade Reform Act of 1973, which would authorize him to extend most-favored-nation status to the USSR and thereby fulfill the commitments of the Trade Agreement of October 18, 1972. DSB 4-30-1973, 518–19.

Chapter III (June 18 to 25, 1973)

18A.   Protocol adding Annex II to the Agreement on Fisheries (Consideration of Claims Resulting from Damage to Fishing Vessels or Gear and Measures to Prevent Fishing Conflicts) of February 21, 1973 (TIAS ˙7575). Signed June 21, 1973. TIAS 7663; UST 24.2.1588.

19A. Agreement on Fisheries (Certain Fisheries Problems on the High Seas in the Western Areas of the Middle Atlantic Ocean). Signed June 21, 1973. TIAS 7664; UST 24.2.1603.

The contents of these two fisheries agreements (18A and 19A) are summarized in a press release that is Document 33 in this volume.

20A. Address by General Secretary Brezhnev on Television and Radio. June 24, 1973. DSB 7-23-1973, 124–29.

Chapter IV (July 1973 to June 1974)

21A. Protocol on Exchange of Scientists and Engineers. Signed November 30, 1973. Text not available.

22A. Joint U.S.-Soviet Communique on Andrei Gromyko's Visit to Washington, February 3 to 5, 1974. Issued February 5, 1974. DSB 2-25-1974, 185.

23A. Memorandum of Understanding on Soviet Participation in Deep Sea Drilling Project. Signed February 27, 1974. Text not available.

24A. Joint U.S.-Soviet Communique on the Visit in the USSR of U.S. Secretary of State Henry A. Kissinger, March 24 to 28, 1974. Issued March 28, 1974. DSB 4-22-1974, 417–18.

25A. Joint U.S.-USSR Statement at Geneva. April 29, 1974. DSB 6-24-1974, 677.

Chapter V (June 28 to July 3, 1974)

26A. President Nixon's Address to the People of the Soviet Union by Radio and Television. July 2, 1974. DSB 7-29-1974, 179–82.

Chapter VI (July to November 1974)

27A. Agreement Extending and Amending the Agreement Establishing a Temporary Purchasing Commission for the Kama River Truck Complex of October 18, 1972, as amended and extended, and amending the protocol of October 3, 1973. Effected by exchange of letters May 21, June 21, and October 7, 1974. TIAS 8356.

This agreement extended the life of the Temporary Purchasing Commission for two additional years (to October 18, 1976) and increased the number of personnel from a limit of 21 to a limit of 31. It also increased the limit of personnel of the USSR Trade Representation in Washington from 25 to 30.

28A.   Joint U.S.-Soviet Communique on Henry Kissinger's Visit to the USSR, October 27, 1974. DSB 11-25-1974, 703–4.

Chapter VII (1975 and 1976)

29A.   Amendment to June 1973 Expansion of Air Services Agreement. Signed December 9, 1974. (See below, Document 33A, April 16, 1975, for TIAS number.)

30A.   Agreement on Fisheries. February 26, 1975. TIAS 8020; UST 26.1. 133.

31A.   Agreement on Fisheries (Certain Fisheries Problems on the High Seas in the Western Areas of the Middle Atlantic Ocean). Signed February 26, 1975, with related letters. TIAS 8021; UST 26.1.138.

32A.   Agreement on Fisheries (Consideration of Claims Resulting from Damage to Fishing Vessels or Gear and Measures to Prevent Fishing Conflicts). Signed February 26, 1975. TIAS 8022; UST 26.1.167.

The contents of these three fisheries agreements of February 26, 1975 were summarized in Document 57 in this volume.

33A.   Agreement amending the protocol of June 23, 1973, on questions relating to the Expansion of Air Services under the Civil Air Transport Agreement of November 4, 1966. Effected by exchange of letters December 9, 1974 and April 16, 1975. TIAS 8058; UST 26.1.560.

34A.   Agreement amending the agreement of September 30, 1971, on Measures to Improve the Direct Communications Link. Effected by exchange of notes March 20 and April 29, 1975. TIAS 8059; UST 26.1. 564.

35A.   Joint U.S.-USSR Statement at Vienna. May 20, 1975. DSB 6-16-1975, 810–11.

36A.   Agreement on Fisheries. Signed June 30, 1975. TIAS 8150; UST 26.2.1999.

37A.   Agreement Regarding Fisheries in the Northeastern Pacific Ocean off the U.S. Coast, with related letters. Signed July 18, 1975. TIAS 8207; UST 26.3.2979.

38A. Agreement Relating to Fishing for King and Tanner Crab, with related letters and statement. Signed July 18, 1975. TIAS 8160; UST 26.2. 2348.

The contents of these three fisheries agreements were summarized in Document 59 in this volume.

39A. Agreement Relating to the Reciprocal Issuance of Multiple Entry and Exit Visas for Correspondents. Effected by exchange of notes September 29, 1975. TIAS 8448.

40A. Agreement on Expanded Joint Studies in Environmental Health. October 24, 1975. Text not available.

41A. Agreement Amending the Agreement on Civil Air Transport Services of November 4, 1966, as Amended and Extended. Effected by exchange of notes December 4 and 22, 1975. TIAS 8217; UST 26.3.3852.

42A. Agreement extending the agreement of February 26, 1975 (TIAS 8021) on Certain Fisheries Problems on the High Seas in the Western Areas of the Middle Atlantic Ocean. Effected by exchange of notes December 18 and 30, 1975. TIAS 8221; UST 26.3.3874.

43A. Agreement on Certain Fishery Problems on the High Seas in the Western Areas of the Middle Atlantic Ocean, with annex and related letters. Signed March 1, 1976. TIAS 8349.

The Joint Communique that is Document 64 of this volume summarized the contents of this fisheries agreement.

44A. Agreement Amending and Extending the Agreement on Establishment of a Temporary Purchasing Commission for the Kama River Truck Complex of October 18, 1972. Effected by exchange of letters June 7 and September 13, 1976. TIAS 8375.

This agreement extended the life of the commission for three more years, until October 18, 1979, and broadened the commission's activities to allow it to make purchases for a large number of other industrial projects being undertaken by arrangements with foreign companies.

45A. Convention on the Conservation of Migratory Birds and Their Environment. Signed November 19, 1976. Text not available.

Chapter VIII (1977)

46A. President Jimmy Carter's Letter to Andrei Sakharov. February 18, 1977. Text not available.

47A. Agreement Amending and Extending the Agreement of October 18, 1972, on the Establishment of a Temporary Purchasing Commission for the Kama River Truck Complex. Effected by exchange of letters July 14 and September 27, 1977. Text not available.

48A. Agreement on Measures to Improve the Direct Communications Link. January 1978. Text not available.

INDEX

agriculture, 85–86. *See also* grains.
air services: agreement of Jan. 11,
1973, 224 (9A); protocol of
June 23, 1973, 103–04; amendment of Dec. 9, 1974, April 15,
1975, 225, 226 (29A and 33A);
amendment of Dec. 4 and 22,
1975, 226 (41A)
antiballistic missiles (ABM), treaty of
May 26, 1972, 3, 14–21; protocol of July 3, 1974, 117, 125–
26; communique of Nov. 21,
1977, 222.
artificial heart. *See* medicine.
atomic energy, agreement of June 21,
1973, 98–99. *See also* nuclear
weapons.

Basic Principles of Negotiations on
Further Limitation of Strategic
Offensive Arms (Signed June 21,
1973), 97–98. *See also* Strategic
Arms Limitation Talks.
Basic Principles of Relations between
the United States and the USSR
(Signed May 29, 1972), 1–4,
28–29.

chamber of commerce (U.S.-USSR),
protocol of June 22, 1973,
102.
chancèries. *See* embassy sites.
Commercial Commission (Joint U.S.-
USSR), created May 26, 1972,
3, 13–31; terms of reference and
rules of procedure (August 1,
1972), 40–42; monitors agreement of June 29, 1974, 124.
commercial facilities, protocol of June
22, 1973, 102–3; protocol of
Oct. 3, 1973, 114.
Commercial Office of the U.S.A. (in
the USSR), 61–62.

Commission on Scientific and Technical Cooperation, 10, 37–39, 78–
79. *See also* science.
Committee for Health Cooperation, 8.
Committee on Cooperation in the
Field of Environmental Protection, 7. *See also* environmental protection.
Conference on Security and Cooperation in Europe ("The Helsinki
Conference"), 144, 154–81.
consulate general (of the U.S.A.) in
Leningrad, 113.
copyright license, agreement of Feb.
14, 1977, 206–10.
correspondents, visas for. Agreement
of Sept. 29, 1975, 226 (39A).
cultural exchanges. Agreement of June
19, 1973, 89–93, 133.

Deep Sea Drilling Project, 225 (23A).
"detente," defined, 1–2, 145.
Direct Communication Link ("hot-
line"). Agreement of March 20
and April 29, 1975, 226 (34A);
agreement of Jan. 1978, 227
(48A).

embassy sites, agreement of 1969, 1;
agreement of Dec. 4, 1972,
72–73, 223 (7A); agreement of
March 30, 1977, 211–13.
energy agreement of June 28, 1974,
119–21; *See also* atomic energy,
oil.
environmental modification, statement
of July 3, 1974, 117–18, 128;
talks of February to March
1975, 152; draft convention on,
tabled, 182–84; U.S.A. signs
convention on, 215.
environmental protection, agreement
of May 23, 1972, 6–8; memoran-

dum of Sept. 21, 1972, 43–47; agreement of Oct. 24, 1975, 226 (40A).
Export-Import Bank, 71.

fisheries, agreement of Dec. 31, 1972, 223 (8A); agreements of Feb. 21, 1973, 224 (11A–15A); agreements of June 21, 1973, 100, 224 (18A–19A); agreements of Feb. 26, 1975, 152, 226 (30-A–32A), 224 (42A); agreement of June 30, 1975, 153, 226 (36A); agreements of July 18, 1975, 153, 226 (37A–38A); agreement of March 1, 1976, 190, 227 (43A); agreement of Nov. 26, 1976, 203.

grains, agreement of July 8, 1972, 19, 33–36; Soviets limit purchases, 1974, 139; agreement of Oct. 20, 1975, 185–86.

health, 6–8. *See also* environmental protection.
Helsinki Agreement (Helsinki Conference). *See* Conference on Security and Cooperation in Europe.
housing, agreement of June 28, 1974, 121–22.

Interim Agreement of May 26, 1972. *See* Strategic Arms Limitation Talks.

Jackson Amendment (or Jackson-Vanik Amendment), 143, 147–49.

Kama River Truck Complex. *See* Temporary Purchasing Commission.

lend-lease, 31–32, 143; agreement of

Oct. 18, 1972, 70–71.

maritime matters, 31; agreement of October 18, 1972, 48–57, 144; agreement of Dec. 29, 1975, 144, 187–89.
medicine, agreement of May 23, 1972, 8–10; agreement of June 30, 1972 on cancer treatment, 223 (4A); agreement of Feb. 9, 1973 on heart attack studies, 224 (10A); agreement of June 28, 1974 on artificial heart studies, 122–23.
Middle East Crisis: of 1967, 115–16; of 1973, 111–12, 115–16, 131.
most-favored-nation (MFN) status, 31–32, 70–71.

naval agreements: prevention of incidents at sea (May 25, 1972), 11–12; protocol of May 22, 1973, 80.
nuclear testing. *See* nuclear weapons, peaceful nuclear explosions.
nuclear war, agreement of 1971, 1; agreement of June 22, 1973, 102, 105–6.
nuclear weapons: treaty of 1963, 1; treaty of non-proliferation (1968), 1; treaty of 1971, 1; treaty on underground tests (July 3, 1974), 126–27; *See also* peaceful nuclear explosions, Strategic Arms Limitation Talks.

ocean, agreement of June 19, 1973, 87–88.
oil, Soviet, 186.

peaceful nuclear explosions (PNE), 117–18; treaty on (May 28, 1976), 144, 191–202. *See also* nuclear weapons.
petroleum. *See* oil, Soviet.

Quadripartite agreement on Berlin (1971), 1; Final Protocol to (June 3, 1972), 223 (3A).

science (and technology), agreement of May 24, 1972, 10–11; implementation of (July 28, 1972), 37–39; protocol on exchanges (Nov. 30, 1973), 225 (21A); of agreement of May 24, 1972 (July 8, 1977), 216–19. See also Commission on Scientific and Technical Cooperation.
Scientific and Technical Commission. See Commission on Scientific and Technical Cooperation.
Shanghai Communique, 4.
space, treaty of January 1967, 1; agreement of May 24, 1972 on joint exploration, 9–10.
Standing Consultative Commission on Arms Limitation: created, Dec. 21, 1972, 19, 25, 73–75; regulations, 81–82; status, privileges and immunities for members in Switzerland, 224 (16A).
Stevenson Amendment (to the Trade Act of 1974), 143, 149.
Strategic Arms Limitation Talks (SALT), 3–4; Interim Agreement of May 26, 1972, 22–28, 205; resumption of, Nov. 21, 1972, 223 (5A); Basic Principles of Negotiations (June 21, 1973), 97–98, 105–6; 118, 129–30, 135–36; Vladivostok agreement (Nov. 24, 1974), 140–42, 145; talks to resume May 11, 1977, 214; Working Groups meet in May 1977, 214, 215; expiration of the Interim Agreement and U.S.-USSR statements of intent (September 1977), 220–21.

taxation, convention on (June 20, 1973), 93–97.
technology. See science.
Temporary Purchasing Commission, 66–69, 205, 225 (27A), 227 (44A and 47A).
Threshold Test Ban Treaty (TTBT). See nuclear weapons.
trade: agreement of Oct. 18, 1972, 58–66; agreement of June 29, 1974, 124; See also Commercial Commission, commercial facilities, Commercial Office of the U.S.A. in the USSR, grains, lend-lease, maritime matters, Trade and Economic Council, Trade Reform Act.
Trade and Economic Council, 137–39.
Trade Reform Act (or Bill) of 1973, 32, 84, 117, 224 (17A); of 1974, 143–44, 147–49; Jackson-Vanik Amendment to, 143–44, 147–48; Stevenson Amendment to, 149; Soviet rejection of, 150.
Trade Representation of the USSR (in the U.S.A.), 62–63.
transportation, agreement of June 19, 1973, 88–89.

Viet Nam, 75–77.
Vladivostok Agreement (Nov. 24, 1974), 135–36, 140–42, 143–44. See also Strategic Arms Limitation Talks.

Watergate, 118.
"Wheat deal." See grains, agreement of July 18, 1972.

Yom Kippur War (October 1973), 111.

ABOUT THE AUTHOR

CHARLES E. TIMBERLAKE is Associate Professor of Russian History at the University of Missouri–Columbia, where he has taught since 1967.

Previous publications include numerous articles in scholarly journals, chapters of books, and *Essays on Russian Liberalism* (University of Missouri, 1972), which he edited and to which he contributed two essays.

He received the B.A. degree in history and political science from Berea College in Kentucky, the M.A. degree in history from Claremont Graduate School, and the Ph.D. in history from the University of Washington.

RELATED TITLES
Published by
Praeger Special Studies

CURRENT ISSUES IN U.S. DEFENSE POLICY

Center for Defense Information
edited by
David T. Johnson
Barry R. Schneider

ARMS CONTROL AND EUROPEAN SECURITY:
A Guide to East-West Negotiations

Joseph I. Coffey

FROM THE COLD WAR TO DETENTE

edited by
Peter J. Potichnyj
Jane P. Shapiro

DIMENSIONS OF DETENTE

edited by
Della W. Sheldon